D1093558

Madame Benoit Cooks at Home

Published Expressly for
Premium Readers Club
Division Maclean Hunter Ltd.

ÉDITIONS HÉRITAGE
MONTRÉAL

Front cover and inside photography: René Delbuguet

© Les Éditions Héritage Inc. 1987
All rights reserved

Legal Deposit: 2nd quarter 1987
Bibliothèque nationale du Québec
National Library of Canada

ISBN: 2-7625-5897-2 Printed in Canada

LES ÉDITIONS HÉRITAGE INC.
300, Arran, Saint-Lambert, Quebec J4R 1K5
(514) 672-6710

Contents

This book is dedicated, with a grateful heart and warm affection,
to my family who gave me a food heritage,
to my husband Bernard, who has enjoyed his food for so many years,
and to my daughter Monique and her family.
They are so much a part of what this book is all about.

Introduction

This book is for me the culmination of a life-long involvement with food. I have looked back into the past — a nostalgic look, because much of it *is* past, yet all of it was so happy and pleasurable. I have seen many food habit changes in the last fifty years, and the most exciting may be yet to come. Looking back on it all I clearly see how the past enhances the present and the broader view of the present shows me the possibilities of tomorrow. There comes a time when one feels it is necessary to take a breathing spell, to measure all we owe to the people that have been a part of our life, and for me now is the time.

One day, when I was 6 or 7 years old, my paternal grandfather, *grand-père* Patenaude, made me climb on a chair under a beautiful apple tree, laden with fruit that looked to me a delight to be picked any old way. But no, *grand-père* made me hold an apple in my hands, without pulling it off the tree but feeling its heaviness, which indicated it was ripe and very juicy and ready to be picked. Then I had to compare it with other apples on the tree, and I had to smell a few to know which ones to pick. That day I discovered that even on the same tree, the fragrance of apples is not all the same. *Grand-père* explained to me that the more exposed to the sun the apples were, the more fragrance they had. Then he showed me how to pick an apple off the tree so it would not be bruised. You may have gathered from all this that my *grand-père* was a perfectionist, that he was not always easy to live with. The advantage I had over the grown-ups was being a very exuberant granddaughter, which I suppose gave *grand-père* the hope that he could teach me to live as a perfectionist. My sister Jacqueline is a perfectionist, though she never knew her grandfather. And me? I am still an exuberant person — in love with food. What I learned that day has followed me through my life: to always look for the perfect food at the perfect moment.

Then there was my other grandfather who taught me all about bread. *Grand-père* Cardinal was typical of the French Quebec intellectual of the 1900s, he read in French only, mostly French classics. He was a fervent

Above, me as a moon-faced five year-old,
my mother Louise, who loved fashion,
and my father Alfred, who loved food.

admirer of Voltaire, which horrified my very devout grandmother. She kept hiding the Voltaire books for fear that the visiting children would read this wicked writer. Needless to say, we all did — the usual temptation of the forbidden fruit. As I was raised in a Catholic convent, I thought that Voltaire man somewhat silly, and was far more interested in Sully Prudhomme's love poems (also forbidden fruit) and my grandmother's cook book. *Grand-père* Patenaude was a teetotaler; his favorite drink was maple syrup stirred into a glass of cold, clear well water. Never, at any time or occasion, was wine or alcohol served. At *Grand-père* Cardinal's a celebration of any kind was a time to eat good food, and to dance and sing with a little help from wines, Dutch gin and beer. In the winter the gin was served as a hot grog with a spoonful of sugar mixed with hot water. The children could have a spoonful of gin in a great big glass of hot water — to keep us warm they said. Little did they know that it made us feel very grown-up, even if we had so little we could barely taste it.

My mother was never fascinated by food and found it hard to understand my love for it. On the other hand, my father was a true gourmand (rather than a gourmet). His life seemed to be centred around my mother and food, and I am not sure which came first. Breakfast had to be an elaborate production, and during it he would discuss what would be served at lunch, and at lunch the subject would be dinner. As might be imagined, my mother was not as enthusiastic as my father, though she was an excellent cook.

In those days, women took great pride in preserving the traditions of the past. The eldest daughter (which I was) was the one who had the almost sacred duty of carrying them to the next generation. I remember how I followed handwritten recipes on yellowed pages of an old notebook written by my grandmother, aunts I had never known, and friends of our family. Many years ago I wrote a book called *Les Secrets du Cahier de ma Grand'mère*. It was filled with the treasured recipes I found in that little black book, worn out and dog-eared at the corners because *grand'mère* usually kept it in the big flour bin, in a wax paper bag. Why there? Because she was an excellent baker and her favorite bread recipes were in that little book. It also contained the recipes for her justly famous baked beans, which my mother used to prepare the same way. I can never forget those hot baked beans. They had spent the whole night in the big brick oven of our local baker, two blocks away, and were enjoyed at Friday's breakfast, which was served at 8 a.m., an hour later than usual, because someone had to fetch the big brown pot (wrapped in a double layer of hand-woven wool blanket to keep it piping hot). The pot was set on the table on a lovely hand-carved pine board, and served with a big loaf of hot brown bread, also brought back from the baker's, and homemade chili sauce — no such thing as bottled ketchup was ever on the table. The leftover beans were served with thin slices of cold ham for our Sunday breakfast.

Oh, those winter breakfasts of my youth: creamy porridge, simmered all night at the back of the wood stove and eaten with freshly-shaved maple sugar and thick cream; the stacks of piping hot homemade bread, sliced and toasted on the wood stove, a taste I have never lost; freshly churned, unsalted butter; and buckwheat honey that was cut in slices like the dark brown cheese that we always bought from our neighborhood Scottish cheeseman, since those who specialized in cheese also had a good choice of excellent honey. (To this day I still crave the delightful flavor and creamy softness of this buckwheat honey.) The whole breakfast was finished off with a big wedge of mild cheddar cheese and pots of steamy hot green tea. It is almost unbelievable that we could have eaten such huge breakfasts back then, between 1910 and 1920, and it was even more extraordinary that all members of the family were at the table by 7 o'clock, dressed and ready to go. Two habits I have never lost is an early breakfast and cheese with my toast, made with homemade bread, though now, *hélas*, I make it in the toaster.

When I was 15 years old, I met the Basil brothers. They had a fantastic shop in Montreal with foods from all over the world: grains of all types, exotic fruits, fresh and dried, nuts shelled and unshelled, and all kinds of vegetables I had never seen before. The Basils were Greek, very attractive, quiet-spoken men, with a wealth of knowledge that they always had the time and patience to impart to me and others. I used to spend hours in their shop. I remember my father, at times, giving me two dollars so I could go to the Basil brothers' shop and buy what I liked — oh how far you could go on two dollars in those days! It was then that I realized how vast the world of food really was — as a matter of fact I saw it as being as vast as our planet. I realized that people all around the world were cooking the same grains of rice or wheat, each following their traditions and culture, so that each was producing a totally different dish while using the same basic foods. I was fascinated by this concept, and decided then and there that food would be my world and my life's work.

Then came the time and the person that had the deepest influence on my cooking life, Dr. Edouard de Pomiane-Pozerski, better known simply as "de Pomiane." Born in Paris of a Polish father and a Russian mother, he was a man of many talents. He played the violin and painted, and he wrote his first cook book during World War I. Titled *Bien Manger pour Bien Vivre* (Eat Well to Live Well), the book itself has aged well. Often I open it and I am always surprised to read things that could have been written today.

In 1901 de Pomiane began his studies in medicine at the Institut Pasteur in Paris. It is at that time that he became fascinated with the "physiology of the digestive system," as he called it, and started to study the composition of foods and their chemical and physical changes during the cooking process. This led him to teaching the fruits of his research. Between the two World Wars, he gave courses in *Cuisine Raisonnée*, applying the principles of the chemical changes that occur in foods under heat and cold, in fat, in water, and so on, and finally as they reach the stomach. For all his pupils, de Pomiane was science personified, an attractive man with white hair and a deep black mustache, always dressed in his long white smock, with a little round white hat at the back of his head, both always neat and crisp. His colleagues were somewhat taken aback that a doctor of science — and a doctor of medicine at that — was giving cooking lessons. But de Pomiane used to say: "Cooking is a specific technique, invented by man to flatter some of his senses, such as taste, smell and sight. I will never stress enough the importance of being thoroughly qualified in the chemistry of food if we ever wish to understand the mysteries of food transformation and what it does to our bodies."

De Pomiane wrote 27 books altogether, giving food chemistry information as well as recipes, and he left quite a few original dishes of his own. He often said during his lectures that one day there would be so little distance from a to b on our planet that we would easily become aware of all the cuisines of the world. At that time there was no plane travel. Of course such statements were fascinating to me and I became more and more excited and intrigued with the foods of the world. Dr. de Pomiane had an extraordinary influence on me and much of his teachings I applied in one of my first cook books, *The New and Complete Encyclopedia of Cooking*.

My many years in Paris at the Institut d'Hygiène and traveling through France taught me how to use my curiosity about food and how to enjoy it all to the fullest. It was at that period that my philosophy about cooking became clear and I realized that I truly loved to cook. As de Pomiane said, "If you like to cook you can be a good cook." I cannot paint or sew, and I have little talent for music or other arts, although I enjoy them. But give me a refrigerator full of goodies, my pots and pans and my comfortable kitchen, and I am as happy as a painter with his *tableau*.

After returning to Canada from France in the early 1930s I had a cooking school in Montreal that lasted until World War II. I began writing monthly columns for *La Revue Moderne*, a French-language home magazine in Quebec, and wrote the first two popular pocketbooks to appear in Canada. At that point I met Kay Bailly, who was publishing *Home Magazine* in Toronto; and she persuaded me to start writing in English, though I was shy, and afraid that it would never work. In 1956 I was asked to write a monthly article for *Canadian Homes and Gardens*, and when I picked up my courage and did it, it was the beginning of a long and busy career. From there in 1961 I went to *Canadian Homes*, and then in 1963 began writing weekly for *The Canadian*.

And through it all was television. I had done French radio for twenty years with Radio-Canada, but television brought me to the C.B.C.'s English network, first through their program *Living*. The whole adventure lasted for a period of twenty years where I cooked and met interesting people, and made many friends. My last years on television were with Paul Soles and

Adrienne Clarkson on *Take Thirty*. It was always very pleasant work, but the moments I enjoyed the most were after the sign-off when everyone rushed to my table to enjoy the food. Wonderful memories for me!

As I carried on the food traditions of my family, so does my daughter Monique, who in many ways has been a big part of my cooking life. I would rather cook with my daughter than anyone else, since we cook very much alike. She does the "chop-chop," as we say, because I have little patience for fine chopping, and Monique does it to perfection. Monique is my best friend and a wonderful companion. She has *des doigts de fée* (the fingers of a fairy), and she can design and make the most wonderful things in needlepoint, cover a table with beautiful tiles, and make fabulous knitted scarves overnight. This year at Christmas she knitted a collection of tuques, each one more exciting than the last, all of her own design. But, you may ask, does she cook? She surely does. Very early in her life I taught her how to shop and she became an A-1 shopper. What I buy for $5.00, she gets for $3.00. She is also a very good cook. But, unlike me, she is usually looking for short cuts and the easy way to make things, and she is very humorous about the names she gives her dishes. To Monique, creative cooking is a joy. Her meals are without doubt the heart of her family life. As she says, "They're always hungry." For a few years Monique had a T.V. program in Sherbrooke, Quebec, called *La Bonne Cuisine,* where she showed the way to all her shortcuts in the kitchen. Though she decided that T.V. was not for her, I can tell you that she was extremely popular and received hundreds of letters every week. I think that neither of us is afraid to be old-fashioned in our cooking though we are open to new and better ways of preparing food in our kitchens. I hope you will enjoy the recipes from Monique's kitchen that are included in this book.

The next generation that will carry on the tradition of good food are my grandchildren, Susan, who is 25, and Ian, who is 20. Susan was recently married and according to her husband Kenneth, she is "a three-star cook." She goes from her stove to her microwave oven to her handbeater to her food processor as if they had always been there. She is part of the young generation that has been so affected by modern technology which has made most of the tedious part of cooking easy, fast and efficient. (Of course you must still give your cooking your own personal touch, since creativity and taste will always remain something special.) Susan and one of her friends just opened a charming tea room and handicraft shop in Sutton, Quebec, called *La Causerie.* I know *grand'maman* Benoit will often go and have a little *causerie* (chat) with her Susan—and a good cup of tea, too.

My grandson Ian has a natural flair for cooking, and at one time I felt sure he would follow in my footsteps. But the sheep farm won out. Since he's a Virgo, shepherding, music and poetry should bring him happiness. And he's still a pretty good cook.

I am convinced that my love of country life and the renewed pleasure I have each spring when I see the sheep back in the field are part of my heritage that comes from my grandfather Patenaude who, by the way, imported the first Hampshire lambs to Canada from Scotland. He wanted none of his six sons to be farmers, but he often said he would never leave his farm. He was never a working farmer, but rather a gentleman farmer, since men at that time who had the means retired when they were in their forties — how life has changed.

A visitor to our house on the farm will be greeted by my husband's dogs — if it's a black avalanche roaring out or roaring in, wanting to be there before you, it is only the usual boisterous welcome of Bernard's black sheepdogs, Malin the mischievous, and friendly Pogo, or silky black and white Patouche. Once inside the house, there is a more sedate greeting from my cats: the Siamese, Mademoiselle Frou-Frou II, independant, intelligent, willful and indispensible. And Tinkerbell, who runs after birds and thus got the "bell." And finally there's Bosse-Mère, who constantly fights with her son Petit Bonhomme, who thinks my husband is the "cat's meow." Of course I agree!

There were so many wonderful foods that filled the beginning of my life that I would like to try and recapture for you in this book the variety and flavor of those I have never forgotten. For me, some of that food will never be *quite* the same. That freshly churned butter; the thick cream carefully lifted from the milk terrine with a large silver spoon (which I still have in my kitchen); the homemade salted pork and smoked ham; the eggs that were gathered every morning from the nest; and the homegrown vegetables. Although I was raised in the city, my grandfather Patenaude always brought us fresh produce and eggs from the farm. I hope I may succeed in bringing to you these beautiful flavors of the past. One of the first things my husband and I did when we bought the farm was to have chickens and a garden. After 20 years we still gather the eggs from the nest and enjoy their flavor and texture, and spend the summer and autumn extolling the virtues and pleasures of gardening and living with nature.

I hope that in this book you will see what my curiosity and enthusiasm about food, a love that began so long ago, has brought to my life. I assure you there is far more to food than simply mastering techniques. I hope you will find it an exciting world and that it will bring you many pleasurable moments.

Amicalement,

Jehane Benoit

At left is the famous Dr. Edouard de Pomiane, the man who had such a great influence on my cooking life. And below is the happy picture of the last show I did on CBC-TV's Take-Thirty. *Here I am enjoying the food with Paul Soles on my right, and Ed Reed and Adrienne Clarkson on my left. What wonderful memories for me.*

1. *Herbs and Spices*

Spices and herbs are the romance of cooking.

What is a spice? What is an herb? Figuratively speaking, a spice is that which enriches the quality of a food to a small degree, as too much of a spice would alter the taste of food — it should be used in such a quantity as to give zest and pungency or a piquant and pleasant flavor.

An herb is a seed plant which does not develop woody long-life tissue such as that of a shrub or tree, but it is more or less softly and agreeably perfumed. Herbs are annual, biennial or perennial, whereas spice trees can live as long as 200 years. An herb can be used for medicinal purposes or for its sweet scent and for the delicate perfume it gives to food.

I have found it has taken a lifetime to determine just where a spice ends and an herb begins and that, through my cooking life, both are always exciting to experiment with. So never be a slave to the quantity or type of spice or herb required in a recipe. Follow it or try your taste and touch with some of your favorites.

Today, we think of spices and herbs primarily as a flavoring agent to use in cooking, but their history goes much deeper and very far back into man's past. In ancient times they were used as the basic ingredients of incense, ointments, perfumes, antidotes, and even cosmetics (these are now being revived); and were used in the kitchen only in limited quantities. It was not until the First Century A.D. in Rome that we heard for the first time of a notable increase in the use of spices and herbs in the kitchen. Maybe that explains why the Italians are still the masters in mixing and using both of these in their cooking.

After the introduction of spices into cooking in ancient Rome, we hear about them in Medieval Europe, where man fought and tried in many ways to obtain these then highly valued spices. As a matter of fact, the quest for tropical spices played a very large part in world history. Wars were once fought over those spices we take for granted nowadays. Only kings and their courts had access to them. The great Byzantine Emperor, the "Paleologue," came to visit "Medici the Magnificient," bearing tons of gifts, among them the precious bark of cinnamon, still more precious threads of saffron and fragrant cloves. Perhaps you remember being told in school that Columbus was jailed after discovering America because he failed to find spices. Ironically, five centuries later, North America is the most important user, buyer and seller of spices; in other words, they control the spice market.

It is good to know that most of the important tropical spices had their original homes in the Orient. The Asians have given us pepper, cinnamon, cloves, ginger, cardamom, turmeric, nutmeg and mace. The major spices native to the tropical countries are allspice, vanilla and chilies (capsicum peppers).

It is the Mediterranean area, including North Africa and the Middle East, which first supplied us with most of our culinary herbs, such as bay leaves, coriander, cumin, dill, fennel, fenugreek, mustard seed, rosemary (growing so beautifully out of stone walls all over Italy), and sage. And it is interesting to note that pepper alone now accounts for over one quarter of the total world trade in spices.

When we look at the little bottles of spices and herbs on our kitchen shelves, we seldom remember that no history is richer in trickery and intrigue, prestige, greed, wealth, danger, suffering and death, than the history of spices. The Orientals, the Spaniards and the Dutch were all involved in spice "trouble" at one time or another. In fact, at one time, the chief spice islands, known today as the Moluccas, belonged exclusively to the Dutch, who maintained the strictest monopoly on spices. However, the birds carried the seeds to nearby islands, and in time Holland's exclusive control broke down. What a great lesson this should be for humanity, a little bird enjoying the flavor of the spice seeds and the freedom of its wings, carried the trade where he pleased and *no man* could do anything about it!

How do we learn to season foods with herbs and spices? My answer, after long years of experience, is to keep a "light touch," but also to keep an adventurous attitude towards food and cooking. Keep trying unusual blends and proportions. Changing the quantity of an herb or spice never changes the texture of the finished recipe, only its flavor.

For instance, have you ever thought of using ginger with roast chicken, especially grated fresh ginger root rather than the dry powdered type? Try a sprinkling of turmeric on fried onions, while they are cooking, as turmeric should be cooked. Nowadays, we think that spices and herbs are an intriguing subject that cannot be ignored; we think of them in low-sodium diets; and research is now being done to determine their importance as a substitute for salt. What is sure is that many herbs and spices can safely be used in low-sodium diets, so a patient can flavor his food, helping to compensate for the loss of salt. However, no blend of seasoned salt or spices should be used — only pure herbs and spices.

Herbs Make the Difference

Herbs transform the dull into the elegant, and there is no secret about how to use them. All you need is a dollop of curiosity, a dash of interest and a pinch of common sense.

Culinary herbs have fragrance and flavor — they are a way of transforming an ordinary dish into an intriguing one. Learn to cook with herbs and you will soon understand why they deserve more attention. Too often we read about the "secrets" of seasoning with herbs, when just a little common sense and enough interest to become familiar with the basic few, to begin with, is truly all it takes. And they are easy to purchase; you can find them on the shelves of supermarkets right across the country.

How much should you use? Your common sense will soon point out the fact that more can always be added, but that none can be removed. So, when in doubt, start with a pinch or ¼ tsp. (1 mL); taste during the cooking period; and add more if you wish.

Which herb should be used with what? It's a matter of personal taste. I have used all herbs with all types of foods — letting my fancy and personal taste dictate the choice — and I've kept notes on my preferences. First, here's what you need for your herb shelf.

Using all the available herbs would only confuse, and perhaps discourage, the beginner; so first try to become thoroughly acquainted with the nine basic ones — bay leaves, thyme, basil, marjoram, mint, sage, summer savory, parsley and chives.

Bay Leaves are sold dried and should be judged by their color — the greener the better. A bay leaf or two, combined with a few thin slices of unpeeled lemon to flavor a cut-up chicken while it slowly cooks in butter, or is baked in the oven, helps make a superb dinner. When in doubt as to which herb to use, feel safe in adding a bay leaf — the flavor pleases everyone.

Thyme is one of the oldest herbs in use. It has a sweet, penetrating and sharply attractive scent but, because of this, it must be used with discretion. A small pinch will give a nice flavor to all types of meats, vegetables and soups. Some of its uses: with parsley, to flavor a bread stuffing for chicken or fish; in the flour used to roll fish fillets before frying; and for veal dishes of all kinds. A touch of thyme makes for superb clam chowder, homemade or canned; and a good combination for flavoring cooked greens, a salad or a sauce is ¼ tsp. (1 mL) of thyme to each ¼ tsp. (1 mL) of grated lemon peel.

Basil is a pleasantly scented and lively herb with a good many uses. It is popular in Italian cuisine and can always be used with pasta and all types of sauces. It is equally successful with tomato dishes, potatoes, cucumbers, sea food, and especially lamb. A pinch of basil added to eggs when they're being prepared makes for fine scrambled eggs. A good salad to serve with steak is sliced tomatoes simply sprinkled with a bit of sugar, a good bit of freshly-ground pepper and basil to taste. Try frying mushrooms with a chopped green onion, then adding salt, pepper and basil to taste.

Marjoram is an herb of the mint family, and the very popular oregano is frequently called wild marjoram. Their similarity in flavor makes them interchangeable. Marjoram is very versatile and will enhance the flavor of meats, soups, stuffings, stews, and many vegetables. For instance, make little pockets in a roast of pork and stuff them with some marjoram (and a bit of garlic if you're so inclined). Brown pork chops on one side; turn, and sprinkle with pepper and a generous amount of marjoram. Add 1 tsp. (5 mL) of marjoram to your favorite meat loaf mixture; and also add it to your favorite spaghetti sauce, combined with an equal quantity of basil. If you use canned spaghetti sauce, add a pinch of basil and marjoram and a bit of lemon peel, and simmer.

Mint and cucumber have a great affinity; and fresh, frozen or canned green peas enjoy being flavored with it, too. In India, they make a fresh mint chutney to eat with curry. Simply combine 2 cups (500 mL) chopped mint leaves, 2 chopped green onions, 3 tbsp. (50 mL) fresh lemon juice, ½ tsp. (2 mL) salt, 1 tbsp. (15 mL) sugar, and ⅛ – ¼ tsp. (0.5 – 1 mL) cayenne. This chutney will keep for several days if it is stored covered in the refrigerator. Cantaloupe, blueberries and raspberries are very fond of mint. For each 1 quart (1 L) of freshly washed fruit, mix ½ cup (125 mL) of sugar with finely chopped fresh mint to taste. Chopped fresh mint is also good sprinkled on lemon or lime sherbet. To make mint tea, simply place the fresh or dried mint in a spoon, hold carefully over a glass, and pour boiling water on top. Let it stand for 5 minutes, sweeten to taste and serve hot or cold. If you have made it too strong, dilute with boiling water.

Sage has an affinity for all game birds, as well as for pork and veal but, since it's a powerful, assertive herb, some tact is needed in its use — just a little will give a racy tang to braised meat, croquettes and stews. There is a great deal of difference in the flavor of fresh and dried sage. Both are good, but the fresh is less powerful — so experiment with it yourself. For a very nice stuffing for wild or domestic duck, combine 2 cups (500 mL) fresh breadcrumbs, 1 cup (250 mL) sausage meat, 1 cup (250 mL) grated unpeeled apples, a bit of chopped onion, ½ tsp. (2 mL) sage, and salt to taste. Triple the recipe if it's to be used for a goose. Try adding ½ – 1 tsp. (2 – 5 mL) sage to your next meat and tomato macaroni loaf, and sprinkle a bit on your sausages when they are almost cooked.

Sprinkle sage over fried onions; it also goes well with lima beans. Combine equal amounts of sage, thyme and marjoram. Keep in an airtight jar and use some when making hot biscuits or homemade bread or cornbread.

Savory is often a confusing term. Winter savory, a perennial, has a more pungent smell; but most dried savory on sale in our markets is the summer type, an annual, much milder in flavor. Savory is distinctly aromatic, but it's not as powerful as sage. If you have to be limited, savory and bay leaf could be the only two seasonings in your kitchen because, combined or alone, they can flavor almost any type of food you cook. In Germany and Holland, savory is always used with fresh green or wax beans, or with dried beans. With fresh beans, sprinkle a pinch on top before boiling. Add ½ tsp. (2 mL) savory to 1 – 2 cups (250 – 500 mL) white sauce for creamed cabbage. To coat fish and veal scallops, mix fine bread crumbs, lemon peel and savory. Add a pinch to the horseradish sauce to be served with boiled beef, and use savory to flavor corned beef hash and split pea soup.

Parsley is surely the most familiar herb of all those in present use. But it's regrettable that so many people use it only as a food garnish — and so few eat it. Parsley is most frequently chopped, to flavor and color sauces or to sprinkle on potatoes, yet it can also be very good when used in large quantities. My favorite hamburger mix is ½ lb. (250 mg) ground beef combined with ½ lb. (250 mg) ground pork; salt and pepper to taste; 1 egg; and 1 cup (250 mL) — yes, a whole cup — of chopped fresh parsley. Shape and broil. Try rolling boiled beets in butter and lots of chopped parsley; ¼ cup (60 mL) of chopped parsley added to ½ cup (125 mL) of butter, with fresh chives to taste, is perfect for hot bread. To me, the crowning glory of parsley is the way the Scandinavians use it to stuff a chicken. Brush the inside of the bird with 1 tsp. (5 mL) of salt mixed with 2 tsp. (10 mL) of cider vinegar or fresh lemon juice. Then stuff as much fresh parsley as you can use into the cavity. Tie up and roast the chicken as usual. Make a sauce by adding ½ cup (125 mL) of chopped parsley to the pan juices.

Chives are not always available if you don't grow them in your garden. They are the most delicate member of the onion family and, except for desserts, can add a happy touch to any dish you prepare. Many who do not like the tang and flavor of onion will enjoy the mild, pleasant taste of fresh chives. They are delicious blended into creamed cheese, perfect in an omelette, and are at home sprinkled on any green salad. A hard-boiled egg white sauce is especially elegant with fresh chives added, and so are deviled eggs when chives are blended into the yolks.

The Basic Three: parsley, fresh or dried; mint, fresh or dried; and bay leaf, dried. For the "Best-Known Five," add thyme and sage. For the

"Best-Known Ten," add these five: dill, seed or fresh; basil; savory; marjoram and tarragon.

Remember the rule: dried herbs are twice as potent as fresh ones, so use less of the dried.

Now, come into my kitchen and see how I use herbs.

Quick Parsley Soup: I prepare 1 cup (250 mL) of instant mashed potatoes, as directed on the package — then I add ¼ – ½ cup (60 – 125 mL) fresh-minced parsley, and cream and milk to thin it to the consistency I like. Warm up and serve.

Parsley or Mint Butter: I cream ¼ cup (60 mL) butter with 1 tsp. (5 mL) fresh-minced parsley or mint, or 1 tsp. (5 mL) of either when the dried herb is used. I store this in tightly covered jars in the refrigerator and use here and there and everywhere; for hot bread, buttering each slice; on boiled vegetables, especially carrots and green peas; on new potatoes; on roast chicken, while it is cooking; on barbecued steak, on fried fish.

Savory Hot Biscuits: To my favorite hot biscuit recipe, I add ½ cup (125 mL) of fresh minced parsley or ¼ cup (60 mL) of dried parsley, and sometimes ½ cup (125 mL) grated Cheddar cheese. A treat.

Fresh Mint Syrup: I love to keep mint syrup handy to flavor fruit cups, to sweeten drinks, and to serve with custard or sponge cake. Chop leaves and stems of a handful of fresh mint. Add to 2 cups (500 mL) sugar and 1 cup (250 mL) water. Boil 5 minutes. When it is cool, bottle to enjoy later. *Yield:* 3 cups (750 mL).

English Hamburger: To each 1 lb. (500 mg) of meat, add 2 tbsp. (30 mL) fresh mint [or 1 tbsp. (15 mL) dried mint] and a pinch of nutmeg. Then proceed as you like. *Yield:* 4 hamburger patties.

Soups: I add a pinch of herbs to canned soups, and often replace the required amount of water or milk with diluted consommé:

Tomato soups (all types)	Basil
Cream of chicken	Tarragon
Cream of mushroom	Marjoram
Cream of celery	Dill and parsley
Vegetable	Parsley (fresh) and thyme
Beef oxtail	Sage and dill
Chicken noodle	Tarragon or basil

My favorite herb blend for homemade vegetable soup is this: some savory to taste, a bit less of marjoram, and a tiny bit of dill.

My Cheese Macaroni: I add to this some marjoram and nutmeg. When tomatoes are used, replace the marjoram with basil.

My Favorite Lamb Roast: I place the leg of lamb on foil or waxed paper, sprinkle the top with 1 tbsp. (15 mL) basil or sage, wrap it well, and refrigerate for 2 days before roasting as usual.

German Potato Salad: Flavor with dill seeds or fresh minced dill to taste; blend with half French dressing, half mayonnaise.

Delicious Pickled Beets: Boil gently, for 15 minutes, 1 cup (250 mL) cider vinegar, ½ cup (125 mL) water, 1 tsp. (5 mL) basil, and 2 whole cloves. Pour while hot over 6–10 cooked, sliced beets. Pack in jars and pour 1 tsp. (5 mL) sugar over the contents of each jar. Cover and let ripen for flavor 2–3 weeks before serving. *Yield:* 1–1½ pints (500–750 mL).

Blended Herb Mixture: Some may prefer to prepare this mixture and keep it handy to add a pinch or a spoonful to foods here and there.

1 tbsp. (15 mL) thyme
1 tbsp. (15 mL) savory
1 tbsp. (15 mL) marjoram
3 tbsp. (50 mL) dried parsley
1 tbsp. (15 mL) lemon peel, grated
6 bay leaves, crushed

Blend all ingredients in a wooden bowl, crushing them with a spoon. Pack into a small, tightly-covered bottle. Will keep 8 to 12 months in a cool dark cupboard. *Yield:* 8 tbsp. (120 mL).

Make Your Own Bouquet Garni

We find many combinations of herbs and pot vegetables; some are the classic type, others chefs' creations or even your own. Whichever they are, their purpose is the same; they give a special flavor and perfume to meat, poultry, game or soup recipes. They are either tied together with a string or wrapped in a piece of cheesecloth. The true meaning of "fines herbes," which make up 90 per cent of a bouquet garni, is finely chopped herbs. Do not buy ready-mixed bouquet garni, as it is costly and can never be as good as the one you make.

A String of Bouquet Garni

Escoffier's Classic Type (very gentle)

8/10 fresh parsley with heavy thick stems, when possible
1/10 bay leaf
1/10 thyme

Tie together or break up and tie in cheesecloth.

Today's Classic (use with any meat or chicken)

2 bay leaves
2 sprigs of dried thyme
8 – 10 fresh parsley stalks, with stems
1 stalk of celery with leaves

Tie together with a string.

When using chopped herbs place the whole mixture in a cheesecloth bag.

Variations: For Beef Stew: Add 3 strips of orange peel.

For Stewed or Braised Chicken: Add a blade of mace and the green part of a small leek.

For Steamed or Simmered Fish: Add 2 fennel stalks, 3 strips of lemon peel, and 3 bay leaves (instead of 2).

When the bouquet is made from dried crushed herbs, thyme can be replaced by 1 tsp. (5 mL) of basil or marjoram or savory, or a combination of half the thyme called for in the basic recipe and half one of the chosen herbs.

A Chef's Way: Leave a piece of string on the little bunch or bag long enough so that it can be tied to the side of the pan, and easily removed from the cooked food, when ready to serve.

Sesame Seeds: An erect annual herb that may be the oldest condiment or seed grown for its edible oil, this originated in the valley of the Euphrates River. It dates back to 1600 B.C. Traditionally, the leaves and seeds have been eaten as food in Africa and India, while in most countries, sesame is grown for the oil. (We all remember Ali Baba and the forty thieves, in *A Thousand and One Nights*, who said, to open the door, "Open Sesame.") Sesame seeds are sometimes referred to by their old name "Benneseeds," especially in candy. The first pure extract of the benne seeds, which gives sesame oil, is used a lot in America in the production of margarine and good quality salad oil.

It is also used a great deal with bread, on cakes and on other baked goods, such as crackers. When the seeds are toasted while cooking, they acquire a very good nutty flavor. The famous sweet, halva, is made only of crushed sesame seeds. I think the Arabic type from Egypt is the best but it is sometimes difficult to get. Also in the Middle East, unsweetened sesame paste, usually with oil floating on top and called Tahini, is used in cooking or as a spread on bread instead of butter. Pages could be written on the virtues and uses of sesame seeds. What is important to know is that it is a versatile seed with a mild, sweet, nutlike flavor, that keeps very well.

Anise Seed: Anise, the oldest known aromatic seed, is a graceful annual herb of the parsley family, indigenous to the Greek Islands and Egypt. If you make a Greek dish of some sort, the flavor of anise is a natural. So you can experiment. When you make a ginger cake, you can replace the ginger and other spices by about 1 tsp. (5 mL) of anise seeds. To be "Roman," do the same but line the buttered pan with 8 – 10 bay leaves, then pour the batter on top. Bake as usual. Quite a treat.

Anise seeds are the basis for the French liqueur "Anisette," and the popular Turkish alcoholic beverage named Raki. Anise seed is available in seed and powdered form.

The Star Anise: A most attractive spice to look at, and so named because it is shaped like a five-point star, and it also has a licorice flavor and odor, the same as the anise. It is one of my favorite spices — it is a native of China, hence it is often used in Chinese cooking. When the evergreen is in bloom (because this type does flower) they say from a distance the yellow flowers resemble the narcissus and are very fragrant. After the flower appears, the hard brown fruit of this tree opens in the shape of a star. For many years, I dreamed of being in the Orient during this flowering time, but life said no. Two years ago I made this discovery while in Japan. Traditionally, the Japanese have used ground star anise bark as incense; and it is most exciting as a perfume, but also most expensive. If you have a fireplace, throw in 2 – 4 star anise when the fire is at its best; it burns like wood and will perfume the whole room. All over the Orient the seeds are chewed after meals to promote digestion and sweeten the breath.

How do you cook with it? First, all the previous suggestions given for the anise seed can be used, replacing each 1 tsp. (5 mL) of anise seeds by 2 star anise. Where do you buy star anise? At specialty shops, health food shops or at any Chinese grocery store.

Simmer dry prunes in leftover cold tea or coffee with a small amount of brown sugar and 1 or 2 star anise. When boiling cabbage, add 1 star anise to the water. Add 2 star anise in roasting pan with pork or veal. Add 3 – 4 star anise to a bottle of cider vinegar. Let steep for a month, strain and use as you would ordinary vinegar. Add 1 star anise to the boiling water used to cook 1 cup (250 mL) rice.

Cardamom: A tall herbaceous plant, with branching subterranean rootstock, which immediately suggests that it belongs to the ginger family. Although it is particular to part of India and Sri Lanka (formerly Ceylon), one could think it belongs to the Scandinavian countries, as it is used so profusely in those countries. In India it is an important part of the curry mixture. The fruit of the tree is a small elongated capsule, cream or pale green in color and ½ in. (1.25 cm) long. It contains 10 to 20 hard, angular brownish seeds, with a strong aromatic odor and flavor.

Cardamom is sold in three ways: whole, hulled seeds, and powdered; it is fairly easy to buy wherever they sell bottled herbs and spices. If you think you will not use it often, it is advisable to buy the whole seeds as they will keep without altering their flavor for a long time. To use, break the top skin open, and either use the enclosed seeds as they are, or grind in a food processor or crush with mortar and pestle (my preferred way). They can be crushed quite fine, which is sufficient most of the time, but they cannot be powdered without a seed grinder. An interesting fact is that cardamom is the third most costly spice, topped only by saffron and vanilla stick. The famous "Gahwa" or cardamom coffee of Saudi Arabia is the Saudis' symbol of hospitality, as well as their habitual beverage.

Cumin: *Comino* to the Spaniards and Mexicans, *kümmel* to the Germans, *comino* to the Italians, and *kammûn* to the Arabs — cumin seed, a small annual herb of the parsley family, is used all over the world. It was known in many ancient civilizations, and you find it mentioned in the Bible, along with anise and mint. One day I heard a lecturer, talking of the exotic herbs in the gardens of the world, tell us of the following belief: "Cumin seeds keep lovers from becoming fickle and poultry from straying from home." If that were true, how much cumin would be used, and how happy lovers would be.

Since Iran is the world's major exporter of cumin it stands to reason that they use it in their cooking. They have a very interesting way of using it on their goat or other white cheese. Toast a few spoonfuls of cumin seeds [spread on a baking sheet in a 350°F. (180°C) oven] and pour on the cheese while hot, spreading them with a knife — a showpiece that always creates lots of comments. Look in your cheese shop for the Dutch cumin cheese, Kumminost, perfect to eat with beer. The

Germans have their famous Kümmel liqueur and add it to their sauerkraut along with fennel seeds and juniper berries.

Black Cumin: Super-potent and difficult to find unless you go to a shop that has Iranian or other Arabic imported foods. Some refer to it as "Baraka." The seeds are much smaller than the cumin seeds, and sweeter-smelling; super sprinkled on cheese, on hot biscuits before baking, on fried onions, on cheese or other wafers — mixed with butter, spread on wafers or crackers and warmed up to serve. A pinch in cabbage soup. I sometimes mix a few spoonfuls of grated cheese and a few pinches of black cumin, to add to bread crumbs, or simply use as is to top casseroles. The aroma of black cumin will permeate the whole room when cooking or cooling.

Fenugreek: Many years ago this seed was referred to as "Greek Hay;" the Romans who got the plant from Greece gave it the name of Fenugreek. A Greek woman who I worked with in a test kitchen for a while used to ask for "goat's horn," and I could not figure out what she meant. She wrote to her sister in Greece and got her to send some. When I saw it, I laughed at my ignorance, since I realized it was "fenugreek." An interesting fact about this seed is that it is grown as a food for humans, and also as forage for cattle. It is used, too, as a "digestive." In India and Ethiopia, fenugreek is used as a tonic for gastric troubles. Try it sometime as a seed tea; simply place a full tablespoonful (15 mL) of seed in a teapot, pour boiling water on top, and let steep 10 minutes. Strain in cups and serve with honey. I often enjoy it at night or after a heavy dinner. It is a seed rich in proteins, minerals and vitamins, so it is used in many eastern countries to supplement a meatless diet. It is therefore good to remember that fenugreek adds nutritive value to foods, as well as flavoring.

The seeds of fenugreek come in a long thin pod; they are yellowish brown, and have very little aroma, unlike anise or fennel which you can tell by smell, and they are very hard, so are easily recognized. But once you heat them in a pan, or in a liquid, the whole thing changes. One way I enjoy them was given to me by a Greek woman. Place ¼ cup (60 mL) of fenugreek seeds in 2 cups (500 mL) of boiling water and simmer 20–30 minutes. Let cool in the water. Drain (reserve water) and serve the boiled seeds with a dish of honey and crusty bread. I use the water to poach fruits or add ¾ cup (200 mL) sugar, preferably brown sugar and boil in a light syrup. Bottle and serve with pancakes. You have the feeling that you are using maple syrup. Fenugreek is used to make commercial imitation maple syrup, and of course it is an indispensable in· curry powder mixtures.

Spices:

Cinnamon: Cinnamon and cassia are two of the oldest spices known to man; they are often mentioned in the Bible, which means they were known to the ancient civilizations before the Bible.

Cassia is a bark that resembles the true cinnamon bark, but is coarser and thicker, with a more intense aroma and a greater oil content and consequently, not so delicately flavored as cinnamon. When ground, it is fairly easy to recognize, as cassia is reddish brown, while powdered cinnamon is pale tan in color. Cassia comes in thick quills and, in superior quality, in delicate, small quills, usually short and tightly rolled.

As I write this, I suddenly feel I am part of a great history, since as far back as we can go, we find that cassia was brought from distant China to be exported to the Mediterranean port of Tyre.

Cinnamon, or "sweet wood" as it is called where it is grown, has been prized for more centuries than we can imagine; it was used to burn in temples, and today all over the world, a battle of words goes on concerning the difference that exists between cassia and cinnamon. Growing cinnamon trees is an important industry in Ceylon, now known as Sri Lanka. The bark is removed and allowed to ferment under cover. Later it is sliced and dried in the sun. Cinnamon has an agreeable, warm, aromatic flavor, mildly sweet. Cassia, the Chinese cinnamon, is often substituted for true cinnamon, and many prefer its stronger flavor.

How to Use: Use a stick to stir a demitasse of black coffee. Add a stick when cooking stewed prunes, poached peaches, applesauce, baked apples, spiced pears or hot chocolate. Ground cinnamon does much for a lamb stew. Sprinkle it lightly over lamb or pork chops before broiling, as you would over a slice of ham.

Allspice: Plantations of allspice trees are often called "pimento walks" because the spice is the berry of an evergreen called the pimento tree. (Do not confuse this with "pimiento," the red fleshy pepper.) Pimento is called "allspice" because it combines the flavor of cinnamon, cloves and nutmeg.

How to Use: With red cabbage, split pea soup, barbecue sauces, plum pudding, stewed and baked apples and cookies. Superb with boiled cod or haddock. Very nice combined with coriander in pot roasts. In fact, all meat stews love allspice. Try a pinch over your next barbecued steak.

Cloves: The first references to cloves are found in literature of the Han period in China, which was in the Third Century B.C. They were then referred to as "chicken tongue spice." They became known in Europe by the Fourth Century. I found a tremendous amount of information on cloves at the Musée de l'Homme in Paris, all of it fascinating. For instance, when a child was born in the Molucca Islands, the parents would plant a clove tree by which to keep a sort of record of the child's age. If something destroyed the tree, the parents were convinced it meant doom of some sort for the child. When the Dutch came and forbade this custom, the entire population felt defeated.

The clove tree is a stately slender evergreen, every portion of which is aromatic. The cloves are its dried unopened flower buds.

How to Use: Since the flavor is strong, it is best to be conservative with its use. I like to stick a few cloves in stuffed baked fish. I always use one or two in my soups, whatever the recipe. I won't consider boiling cabbage or onion without a few cloves in the water. When boiling tongue (lamb, beef or calf) there is no better seasoning than 3 – 6 cloves, 1 tsp. (5 mL) grated fresh ginger, an unpeeled slice of lemon and a bit of coarse pickling salt.

Ginger: Ginger is obtained from whole or partially peeled rhizomes or white tuberous underground stems which are pungent and aromatic. It is considered an erect perennial herb, and grows 2 to 4 feet tall. Cultivated by the ancient Chinese and Hindus, they refer to it as "Chiang," but the Latin generic name is *zingiberi,* meaning "shaped like a horn." When I have a nice rhizome, I plant it in a rich, aerated sandy loam, and bury the pot in a sunny spot in the garden. At the end of August, I bring it inside and give it tender care. It is not better than the ones I buy already grown, but the flower is interesting and growing it is a challenge. Ginger is sold in many forms, from ground to candied, but the very best and most satisfying to use is the fresh ginger root.

How to Use: Rub chicken with freshly grated ginger before roasting. I love ginger with beets and carrots, in scrambled eggs and on all my broiled food. I never cream onions or bake beans without it. Try broiled halves of grapefruit with butter, honey and ginger. Or ginger toast: ground ginger and brown sugar sprinkled on brown or rye bread, toasted and topped with shredded candied ginger. Serve with a cup of Souchong tea.

Nutmeg: What is remarkable about nutmeg is the fact that it produces two separate spices — nutmeg and mace. It is an evergreen tree with a dark gray bark and small pale yellow flowers shaped a bit like a small garden bell. The fruit looks a bit like an apricot, lemon yellow to light brown. When it is ripe, it splits in half, showing the beautiful brilliant scarlet red, netlike membrane which is the mace, all rolled around a brittle dark brown shell, inside of which is the single brown oily seed that we know as nutmeg.

The flavor of both nutmeg and mace is sweet, warm and highly spicy, although nutmeg in general tends to be sweeter and more delicate in aroma than mace. So, nutmeg should be used for dessert and mace for meat and vegetables.

How to Use: Sweet, warm nutmeg is at its best in rice pudding, custard, and mushroom soup. It's superb combined with coriander seeds in apple pie. And speaking of pie, try sprinkling the crust of your next lemon pie with ½ tsp. (2 mL) of nutmeg. Roll it into the pastry, and sprinkle the meringue with more nutmeg. There's nothing better to flavor homemade doughnuts. In oyster soup, it's delicious. I always add a sprinkling to my fruit salads. Whenever I make hamburgers, regardless of what else I add to the meat, I always put in ¼ tsp. (1 mL) of nutmeg per 1 lb. (500 g) of meat. For a wonderful, quick supper, fry sliced salt pork. When it's browned, fry some sliced unpeeled apples in the fat. Sprinkle with nutmeg and eat with hot toast. I so enjoy the flavor of freshly grated nutmeg that I would advise those who like perfection in their food to purchase a nutmeg mill.

Turmeric: Turmeric powder is ground from the roots of an East Indian plant from the ginger family. Its taste is aromatic and more or less bitter. Turmeric is the principal ingredient in Indian curries and prepared mustard. I have long enjoyed a bit of it added to my French dressing. I use it to give a rich golden color to some of my cookies — just a pinch sifted with the flour. From the Persians I have learned to add it to the seasoned flour in which I roll pieces of chicken. I also add ¼ – ½ tsp. (1 – 2 mL) to the butter or oil I use to fry onions. An old French chef taught me to add a pinch to scrambled eggs to give them perfect color. Try it with creamed egg and rice dishes.

Learn to Make Your Own Spice Blends

They are easy to do and can be exactly as you like, since the quantity of each is up to you. Make a small mixture to begin with; keep tab of it in a special book, and note your comments of each blend. In no time, you will be almost an expert.

As to how much to put into whatever food you are using the blend with, this is quite personal; you may like a pinch or a spoonful. Measure an amount and add little by little to the dish; taste after a few seconds and decide if you want more, as it is easy to add, but more difficult to remove. Then keep note in your book of quantity used. I have been doing this for a great number of years, and through it discovered many an exciting way to flavor all foods.

Poultry Seasoning: Sage, thyme, savory, freshly ground pepper, nutmeg, mace. To this I add a bit of grated fresh ginger root when ready to use.

Barbecue Seasoning: Thyme, marjoram, nutmeg, allspice, cumin seeds or powdered, coarsely ground pepper, coarse salt.

Chinese Five-Spices: Can be purchased as such in Oriental shops — but I like to make my own, as it is simply an equal quantity or a little less of one or the other, as you prefer: cinnamon, cloves, fennel, anise and black pepper, the whole mixture ground to a powder. I always bury 3 to 4 star anise in my own "five-spices." Use, of course, in all Chinese food; try it in your own stew recipes — or spice cake.

Escoffier Famous Spice Blend

This one must be blended in the quantities given. I learned to do this blend from my master, Dr. Edouard de Pomiane, while studying at the Institut d'Hygiène in Paris in the 1920s. A scale is a must if you wish to have it as it should be.

5 oz. (140 g) bay leaves, broken into small pieces
4 oz. (112 g) tarragon
3 oz. (84 g) summer thyme
3 oz. (84 g) ground coriander
4 oz. (112 g) cinnamon
6 oz. (168 g) nutmeg
4 oz. (112 g) cloves
3 oz. (84 g) ginger
3 oz. (84 g) mace
5 oz. (140 g) each ground white and black pepper
½ oz. (14 g) cayenne

Mix all the ingredients thoroughly, then pass through a fine sieve. Keep in an air-tight container. *Yield:* 2½ lb. (1.25 kg).

To make Escoffier Herb Salt, I weigh 4 oz. (112 g) of above mixture and add to 1 lb. (450 g) of salt. We always used coarse or kosher salt, which we pounded with a pestle in a mortar bowl.

Curry Powders: There are many good imported, ready-mixed curry powders available, of course; but blending your own is really the ideal way. Don't let exotic spice names scare you away from trying your hand at it—they can all be bought, ground or whole, at specialty shops, Indian food shops, health food shops, and these days, even in supermarkets. Then all you need is a mortar, blender, spice mill or pepper mill to grind them.

Curry Powder: Formula 1

The spice quantities are given in ounces of weight (and grams) to make your measurements easy to calculate—they are generally packaged in 2 oz. (60 g) bottles.

4 oz. (112 g) whole cloves
3 oz. (84 g) black peppercorns
1 oz. (28 g) cardamom seeds
4 oz. (112 g) cumin seeds
10 bay leaves
1 oz. (28 g) ground cinnamon
1 oz. (28 g) ground mace

Place all the ingredients but the last two in a cast-iron frying pan. Cook over medium heat, stirring constantly so the mixture doesn't burn. When it gives off a rich aroma, grind and add cinnamon and mace. Curry powder keeps well in an airtight jar and improves with age in quality and aroma. *Yield:* about 14 oz. (400 g).

Curry Powder: Formula 2

Not as pungent as Formula 1, this blend is made mainly with ground spices. For an even milder variation, grind the chili peppers with the peppercorns.

8 oz. (224 g) coriander seeds
1 oz. (28 g) poppy seeds
1 oz. (28 g) black peppercorns
4 oz. (112 g) ground turmeric
2 oz. (56 g) ground cumin seeds
2 oz. (56 g) ground fenugreek
½ oz. (14 g) whole mustard seeds
1 oz. (28 g) ground ginger
1–3 tsp. (5–15 mL) dry chili peppers

Roast the coriander and poppy seeds until lightly browned, either by shaking for about 5 minutes in a frying pan over medium heat, or by placing in a 400°F. (200°C) oven for the same amount of time. Then grind with peppercorns, combine well with rest of ingredients and store as for Formula 1. *Yield:* about 1¼ lb. (625 g).

French Seasoned Salt

Keep handy, and sprinkle wherever you want the subtle flavor of herbs and spices.

1 tbsp. (15 mL) each broken bay leaves, thyme, mace and basil
1 tsp. (5 mL) each rosemary and freshly ground pepper
2 tbsp. (30 mL) cinnamon
2 tsp. (10 mL) paprika
1½ tsp. (7 mL) ground cloves
½ tsp. (2 mL) each nutmeg and allspice
1 cup (250 mL) salt

Place everything in a mortar bowl, and pound until well blended. Sift through a sieve, crush any lumps again and store in a tightly sealed container. *Yield:* 1⅓ cups (330 mL).

My Mother's Pomander Balls

I will never forget my mother's pomanders. She always set us children to making them whenever she wanted to keep us amused. She'd spread a large sheet of paper on the table, give each of us a knitting needle, some thin-skinned small oranges, a few small uninteresting-looking apples, and a bag of strongly-scented cloves. We had to stick holes in the fruit and fill them with cloves until the orange or apple was completely hidden. Then mother would roll them until heavily coated in a mixture of powdered cinnamon or orris root which father purchased at the corner drugstore. As the oldest, I was in charge of wrapping each in a double thickness of tissue paper. These were always placed in the same white enameled wooden box and stored on the top shelf of mother's bedroom cupboard to cure for six to nine weeks. I still remember the pleasure we felt when we saw her cutting lengths of narrow velvet ribbon. It was time to remove the paper, shake off the surplus powder and tie a pretty ribbon around each one. To this day I still love this scent better than any other in my linen. Try them yourself.

Bring the Flowers into Your Kitchen

To go to the garden and pick a few blossoms is pleasant, but to use these same flowers in your cooking is enchanting. Not only do you enjoy the feeling of being original, but you will be astonished to see and taste that the flowers you grew with such pleasure have enhanced both your foods and drinks, and you will start to look for more and more ideas. Here are a few I have enjoyed and always will.

To me, May and June are extra-special months. It's when wild flowers and new vegetables break out to say spring and summer, full of promise, are really here — and they become fresh and unique ingredients for the table, too. When I drive around the countryside in May, I always keep an eye out for the large leaves of the marsh marigold, and its beautiful masses of yellow flowers. And I remember my grandmother saying this plant averted evil during its new growth in the month of May. I wait with impatience for the first showing of the fragrant lily of the valley. I read in an old herbal book that it used to be called "Lady's Tears," because it was said to have grown from the tears the Virgin let fall at the foot of the Cross on Calvary. Years ago I saw another reminder of this legend — in a beautiful Fifteenth-Century German painting, titled *The Virgin and the Child*, at London's National Gallery. Where the Virgin's robe touched the ground in the painting, lilies of the valley were growing.

The romantic rose is probably the most exotic and most exciting of all flowers used in the kitchen. The Persians of old have taught us quite a few things. England has followed; even in modern days the petals of wild roses are found in jams, in cakes, in custards. The famous rose water is another delight. Every summer I must have my fresh strawberries lightly sweetened with a few drops of rose water or a spoonful of finely minced wild rose petals. (I am lucky since I have a great deal of them and you can be sure I use them.) Try to get Arabic rose water, much better than the French type. Make rose vinegar to use all year round on fruit salad. Simply add 1 cup (250 mL) wild rose petals or highly scented rose petals to 2 cups (500 mL) cider or white wine vinegar. Let stand 2 months before using. Mix 1 cup (250 mL) of petals into 2 cups (500 mL) of honey and keep in cool place in covered jar.

The basketful of vegetables I am holding here comes, of course, from our own garden, which is such a joy to bring to life each summer.

2. Beverages

I Have a Thing about Coffee and Tea

To me it will always be more than a jar of instant or a bag of black dust that I throw in a cup or a pot. The history and legend of each of these beverages are so tremendous that simply when drinking a cup of Mocha, Java or Colombian coffee, just freshly ground and brewed, or a cup of hot black Assam or China Keemun or a blended Earl Grey tea, I feel they can dispel the cares and fatigue of the moment and bring pleasant moments of friendship when enjoyed *à deux*.

First, I had hesitations about taking a few pages of this book to talk of this subject; then I changed my mind, thinking of all the pleasures that can be found in a perfect cup of tea or coffee. It is not always easy to find certain types of tea, or good, well-roasted coffee beans; but if you ask, look and try, you will succeed. Then you will be able to make your own choice, and even your own blend of tea or coffee. When I find tea or coffee that I truly enjoy, I purchase a large quantity of it and keep it in freezer bags in my freezer. It keeps for 6 to 8 months. Coffee beans remain at their best when constantly kept in a closed container and refrigerated, that is, the weekly supply; the larger quantities are in the freezer.

A Bit of History Behind Coffee: The virtues of the coffee plant were recognized by the Ethiopians around 800 A.D., found by the semi-savage tribes who wandered across the desert. Amazingly, as old records showed, the only food they carried was coffee. The beans were roasted over hot ashes, then ground with stones, mixed with grease, rolled into

---

When the leaves turn and become an enchantment of color, I look at the garden full of the bounty that only the earth can give. It's autumn, my favorite season. Then I know that the kitchen will come alive with pickling and marinating, and with the fragrance of drying herbs and flowers, some for bouquets and some for cooking.

small balls and stored in leather bags. The old records indicated that just *one coffee ball* was enough nourishment for a whole day; it kept them going under battle conditions as the coffee got their metabolism up. For a long while, coffee was considered a drug. Then the Ethiopians introduced coffee to Arabia about 1200 A.D. The Arabs had a different belief; they said the brew purified the blood, alleviated stomach aches and aroused the spirit. The Arabian countries had the first public coffee houses, and these houses soon became centers for activities and discussions that had not existed before — poetry reading and organized gossip were the most renowned activities.

From then on the word about coffee spread fast. In 1500, the governor of Cairo imposed a ban on coffee drinking which lasted 30 years. Coffee was brought to Damascus in 1530, then to Constantinople in 1554, where there was a funny law: If a man refused to supply a wife with a daily ration of coffee, it became a valid ground for divorce.

Then coffee reached Marseilles in 1660, and the first shop selling different roasted beans was opened in 1671. It is strange, when you think of it today, to think that the use of coffee in England came before that of France. Records show it was sold as early as 1640 and was spelled "Cophee." As in Arabia, we soon saw coffee houses growing in importance in England, then in France. They were the news centers where intellectuals, poets, actors and politicians met and created the movements of opinion.

If you are fascinated by the history of tea and coffee, and wish to learn more, spend a few days at the Musée de l'Homme if you have the opportunity to go to Paris. They have book upon book on the subject and it is all most interesting! That is where I obtained the above information and that relating to tea. Their files and cross files are beautifully organized, so you can look at whole periods in history or just pick up quick tid-bits, depending on the time available.

How to Buy Coffee Beans: Pick your own blend of whole roasted beans, grind them at home, in your coffee grinder and immediately make your coffee by your favorite method. Mine is the automatic filter drip method. If you buy a pre-packaged brand of commercially ground coffee, it will not taste as fresh as coffee beans you would grind the moment you are ready to make your coffee. Find out what type of roast and coffee pleases you most, by purchasing small amounts and trying them. I have blends I prefer for breakfast and others after a heavy dinner. It is easy to learn, and remember that all the coffee we buy is blended in some way, which does not prevent you from blending it again yourself.

Types of Coffee

African Arabica:
Highly flavorful and aromatic, expensive and hard to find.

Brazilian Santos:
Robust, slightly sweet, and heavy-bodied when dark roasted.

Central American:
Flavorful, with a "bouquet" (one of my favorites when I can find it).

Colombian:
Full-bodied, rich and "winy."

Jamaican Blue Mountain:
Rich, mellow blend.

Kona:
Mild Hawaiian.

Mexican:
Slightly smoky flavor.

Mocha:
Unique, sharp flavor.

Mocha Java:
Heavier than Mocha, more aromatic and smoother; one of my favorites, mixed with Arabia black, in a ratio of 2 to 1.

Types of "Roasts" You Can Buy

French roast:
Dark or "Noir," the most bitter of the blends; used in espresso. I like to use it to build up the strength of milder coffee.

French roast:
Light or "Brun," slightly over-roasted blend with an oily surface which brings out a nutty flavor.

American roast:
Very lightly roasted, with a pale brown color and a mild flavor.

Now, when you blend your own type of coffee, mixing different types of roasting, you will find there is a considerable difference among the mixtures. Keep note of what you blend; for example: 1 part of x to 3 parts of y, when you prefer to serve it, "a.m." or "p.m.," etc. Even our supermarkets carry their own coffee beans, to be ground when you buy them. Many of their coffees (mostly American roast) are very good, and often the most economical. Buy the beans and grind at home when ready to use. There is one brand I like and often buy to mix three parts to one part of dark roast Arabica — excellent for breakfast. I have long been convinced that the "ideal" cup of coffee is a myth — to me it is strictly a matter of personal taste and the time at which it is served, or the food which precedes or follows it.

How to Make Consistently Good Coffee

The Arabs were the first to prepare coffee in liquid form. They called it *Kishre.* They pounded the beans with stones, placed them in boiling water and added ground cardamom, cinnamon and ginger, then simmered it. I was so intrigued with this when I first read about it around 1930, that I have been making it ever since. Nice to serve in the afternoon or after a heavy dinner, as it is almost a digestive, and the flavor is very pleasant. Try it!

4 tbsp. (60 mL) ground black coffee
1 tsp. (5 mL) ground cardamom
1 – 2 in. (2.5 – 5 cm) stick cinnamon
1 tsp. (5 mL) grated fresh ginger
4 cups (1 L) boiling water

Grind the coffee fine, place in a saucepan, add the spices, and pour the boiling water over all. Stir well, cover, and simmer over very low heat for 25 minutes. Pass through a fine strainer as you serve into small cups; top each, whenever possible, with a rose petal and serve with a jar of honey. *Yield:* 4 cups (1 L).

Some Things to Know about Making Coffee

The Water: Only cold, freshly-drawn water should be used to make coffee because hot water pipes accumulate mineral deposits that can affect the taste. When you can, pour the water over the coffee grounds when it is just under the boiling point. When the water is boiling too hard, some chemicals in the water tend to break down and affect the flavor of the coffee.

How Much Coffee Should Be Used? The coffee/water ratio remains the same, regardless of the method used to make it. For each 8 oz. (250 mL) cup of water, use a standard coffee measure of 3 tbsp. (50 mL) of ground coffee. For a strong coffee, use 3 tbsp. (50 mL) for each ¾ cup (200 mL) of water. Never let the coffee boil, as it will ruin its flavor. To me the most important rule is, serve immediately after brewing — or let sit for 1 hour at the very most, over very low heat, the coffee pot set over a wire rack so it does not come in direct contact with the heat.

Continental Café au Lait

1½ cups (400 mL) strong hot freshly brewed coffee
1½ cups (400 mL) hot milk

To make a truly perfect café au lait, it is important to have very fresh coffee and to heat and blend the milk in the following manner. Place over medium heat until the milk starts to foam, but do not let it boil. Then pour the coffee over the milk and combine the two by pouring them from one pot to another 5 or 6 times, or until foam forms on top. This is the reason the coffee must be so hot. Serve without delay, with hot croissants and sweet butter. It's a delight to carry you *au coeur de Paris*. *Yield:* 3 cups (750 mL).

How to Make Good Iced Coffee

Make your coffee double-strength, simply by using half the amount of water for the usual amount of coffee. Pour boiling hot over lots of ice cubes in a tall glass (a silver spoon placed in the glass prevents breakage, if you pour the coffee first over the spoon). This simple little rule of extra strong coffee, always makes a perfect "Café Glacé" because it allows for the dilution caused by the ice.

To save ice, make a medium-strength coffee, cool, cover, and place in refrigerator, in a non-metallic container. Don't leave it more than 3 hours. Then pour over a few ice cubes.

For a perfect café glacé, brew extra breakfast coffee and freeze into ice cubes. Then make ice coffee any time during the day by simply pouring regular-strength hot coffee over the iced coffee cubes.

For a truly delicious coffee, make it with instant coffee — for here "instant" really comes into its own. Place 1 tbsp. (15 mL) of instant coffee, more or less, in a glass. Add ¼ cup (60 mL) of cold water from the tap, and mix until well blended with the coffee. Fill glass with plain or coffee ice cubes. Slowly fill glass with cold water, stirring all the time. Made this way, it is delicious. Just how much instant coffee you use depends on the size of the glass, the type of ice cubes you use, and the strength you prefer.

Frosty Coffee

2¼ cups (560 mL) strong cold coffee
1 tbsp. (15 mL) angostura bitters
1 pint (500 mL) coffee ice cream

Make the coffee with instant coffee. To make the coffee ice cream, simply add 1 – 2 tbsp. (15 – 30 mL) of undissolved instant coffee to a pint of vanilla ice cream.

Place all ingredients in a bowl or in the glass jar of an electric blender. Beat until smooth and creamy. Serve on a chocolate sponge cake, instead of icing. *Serves 6.*

After-Dinner Coffee

Make after-dinner coffee an occasion rather than a habit or an afterthought, by adding a few other liquids to it. I assure you, half a jigger of Grand Marnier added to a cup of hot coffee makes quite a difference. A twist of lime peel and a bit of Drambuie brings you into the heart of Scotland. A bit of lemon rind and Cointreau, and you are in Paris in the spring. A bit of crème de cacao to each demi-tasse, topped with whipped cream, and you are waltzing in Vienna. Ever try to stir your coffee with a stick of bright pink rock candy? Or savored the difference when you add ½ in. (1.25 cm) of vanilla stick to the ground coffee before brewing? Vanilla extract will not do!

The Mysterious Teas

"Strangely enough, humanity has so far met in the tea-cup."

Okakura Kakuzo (*The Book of Tea*)

I read this in the Fifties, on a beautiful spring day I had decided to spend at the Mrs. Gardner Museum in Boston. Right then and there I bought the book, and only then did I fully realize the involvement of humanity with tea, not only as a beverage, but in religion, family life, the whole history of man — and even in profound philosophy. Maybe you smile at such statements. Read *The Book of Tea*, published in 1959 by the Charles E. Tuttle Co., of Rutland, Vermont. What had such instant influence on me was the following quote in the first chapter, "The Cup of Humanity:" "The subtle charm in the taste of tea makes it irresistible and capable of idealization. Western humorists were not slow to mingle the fragrance of their thought with its aroma. It has not the arrogance of wine, the self-consciousness of coffee, nor the simpering innocence of cocoa."

A fascinating book. How can anyone, after reading it, just pour boiling water over a tea bag! Why is tea such a remarkable beverage? Drinking it is always a fresh, stimulating experience, yet it has been in use longer than we shall ever know — since the Chinese knew about tea plants and used the leaves for medicinal purposes, as food, as a stimulant, and as a beverage long before the beginning of written history. A Chinese legend holds that tea was first discovered under the Emperor Shen Hung, called "The Divine Healer," around 2737 B.C. The first time we know tea plants were used to make a beverage was in the Fourth Century A.D., when it is said that the leaves were picked and made into cakes, which were roasted, then pounded into tiny pieces and placed in a pot. Boiling water was poured over them and *onion, ginger* and dried *orange rind* were added. I accept a slice of fresh ginger and a piece of Chinese dry orange rind — but refuse the onion.

At the New York City Public Library on Fifth Avenue you will find translated excerpts of the famous encyclopedia of tea, the *Ch'a Ching*, written by the poet Lu Yu in 780 A.D. This amazing book has never ceased to be consulted since it covers all aspects of tea cultivation and preparation. (Human knowledge never ceases to amaze me.)

When the Chinese civilization made its entrance into Japan in 593 A.D., it imported along with it its art and religion, its knowledge of tea, and amazingly the Japanese made the Chinese Taoism into a religion, and named their tea ceremony "Chanoyu." Tea first reached Europe around 1609, when it was called by its oriental name "Ch'a," and was brought back by the Dutch East India Trading Company. It didn't reach England until around 1650.

When it first appeared in North America, it cost $30 to $50 per lb. At that period, an elegant (and rich!) hostess would brew three to four types of tea in different pots, each offered with its proper name, not just as "a cup of tea." When flavoring was added to the tea, it used to be with a lower cost type; in the winter, saffron was added; in the late spring and summer, peach leaves replaced saffron.

What are the Tea Varieties?

In 1930 I had the good luck to visit a tea auction at Plantation House in London. It was a fascinating experience — poring over the tea brokers' catalogues and sampling all the different varieties before the auction took place. But the main thing I learned was how many teas there are and how much the flavor of each differs. Ever since then, I have always chosen tea carefully — I never go out and buy just "a pound of tea."

Tea is grown in Sri Lanka, China, India, Japan, Java, Sumatra and Taiwan. There are over 3,000 varieties, and like wines they take their names from the districts in which they are grown. These varieties can be classified in three ways.

Black Tea: The leaves are prepared following a special process of oxidation (fermentation) that turns them black and produces a strong brew. This is the type that is used the most in our part of the world.

Oolong Tea: The leaves are only semi-oxidized, which as a result gives half brown, half green leaves. It makes a light tea.

Green Tea: The leaves do not undergo the oxidation process, they remain green and have a special flavor. For centuries only green tea was known and used as a beverage. (The oxidation process really took place out of necessity; in a way it is a natural. It happened when tea was first subjected to the elements in long sea voyages.)

From the three basic classifications come the following (just like one type of grapes ferment in different ways to produce different wines).

These are the best known, and possible to purchase at good tea houses (sadly, rare and few on our continent). When you purchase your tea, read the label — it is exciting to experiment.

Black Teas

Assam (India): High-grade tea grown in Northeast India, full-bodied, rich flavor. Brews in 6 minutes.
Darjeeling (India): The finest and most delicately flavored of the Indian teas. Grown at the foot of Mount Everest. A golden liqueur, should be sipped and tasted like wine. Takes about 7 minutes to brew.
Ceylon: There are many, but the best quality Ceylon are called "high grown." Appealing flavor, aroma and strength in this tea. Fast to brew, perfect with milk or lemon.
Keemun (China): A fine grade of tea, especially the one from Taiwan.
Lapsang Souchong (China): A highly "smoked" taste, nice with game and spicy food.
Earl Grey: One of the most famous blends, originally prepared by a specialty house (Jackson of Piccadilly in London) for a particular customer and eventually the blend took his name. A black tea blend well scented with orange fragrance, but delicate in flavor. Brews in 6 minutes.
English Breakfast: Also a blend, used for blends of black teas in which the China types of tea dominate. It has the strength of Indian tea with the flavor of Ceylon tea.
Irish Breakfast: A medium strong blend of Ceylon and India black. Choose when you look for a pungent brew.

Green Teas

Basket-fired (Japan): A light and gentle brew, which I thoroughly enjoyed at all hours of the day when in Japan. Known as the white wine of teas.
Gunpowder (Ceylon): A type of Ceylonese green tea in which each leaf is rolled into a small pellet. A very interesting tea, especially after roast beef. Also I often use it as a flavoring with black tea.

Those are but the basic types; they are then divided into all types of blends; and the withering, rolling, fermenting and drying or firing can produce hundreds of varieties.

I would like here to pay homage and offer my thanks to a great tea-taster, Mr. Porter, who is still a master taster with the Red Rose firm in Montreal. Through the years he has taught me more about tea than I can write here. To watch him go through a session of blended tea-tasting, in absolute quiet and silence, was a great experience. It is to Mr. Porter, and to Okakura Kakuzo of *The Book of Tea*, that I owe my knowledge of the human poetry of tea.

What's the Best Way to Choose Tea?

With so many varieties, one of the problems is to find out which ones you like and which you don't. How can you really taste a tea? The best way is to follow the method of professional tea tasters. First examine the dry leaf — you will then discover how different the leaves of each type are. Smell its aroma. Again, each tea has a distinctive fragrance. Now place ½ tsp. (2 mL) in a small, hot, dry teapot and pour in ½ cup (125 mL) of vigorously boiling water. Cover and steep for six minutes. Pour the tea into a small cup, place the leaves on a saucer and set it on top of the teacup. While the tea is cooling, examine the leaves, noting their color (which should now be bright) and their aroma. These will give you an indication of the tea's character. When the tea is cool enough, taste but don't swallow it. This way you'll discover how each type varies in flavor, perfume, strength, richness and body. Some you will reject and some you will like.

A second test is the one for milk. If you like milk in your tea, try this after you have first tasted the tea plain. Add a small spoonful of milk to the tea in the cup. If the tea comes through the milk with a rich color, then you can drink it that way. If it doesn't, it's better to drink that particular tea plain.

When you buy tea, remember that it loses its flavor after long storage. So unless you serve a great deal of tea, it's best to buy only ¼ lb. (113 g) at a time. This amount should make between 40 and 50 cups. Always keep tea in a tight-lidded tin, in a cool, dry place. The leaves possess volatile oils that give the tea much of its flavor, and these can evaporate very easily.

A Few Words about the Cultivation of Teas

After gathering and curing, the tea leaves are divided into two main types, the green and the red (we know the red as black tea). I have sometimes heard people say that tea, unlike coffee, has no fragrance. But whoever says that has never smelt the perfume of tea leaves being fired. This process produces an aroma so fragrant that it permeates everything for miles around. I know one tea buyer who gets a yearly nostalgia for this delicious smell and yearns to return to the tea country at firing time. Once you have savored this wonderful perfume, you can never forget it.

There are several ways of firing, but the usual one is to set the leaves out on flat trays in rooms of graduated temperatures to wither or steam. After sufficient steaming, the leaves are then curled and twisted by hand. It's astonishing to think that each little tea leaf that we treat so casually has been picked and rolled by hand. After rolling, the leaves are then dried and packed loosely. The tea leaf dust is made into small bricks, used especially by the Chinese for medicinal purposes.

How to Make Tea of all Types

These are the six main pitfalls to avoid when you make tea:

1. Don't use water that has boiled too long, or that has boiled several times. In both cases it will be flat.

2. Don't make tea with water that isn't boiling vigorously.

3. Don't forget to *warm* and *dry* the teapot before you put in the leaves.

4. Don't "steep" the leaves any longer than six minutes. If you aren't going to drink the tea immediately, pour it off the leaves into another warm teapot and keep it in a warm place.

5. Don't put fresh leaves into the pot without first throwing out the old ones and rinsing and drying the teapot.

6. Don't keep the teapot standing for a long time, adding more and more fresh water until the leaves are exhausted. This is bad for you because each successive brewing brings more tannin out of the leaves. If you run out of tea, always brew a fresh pot.

If you follow these six rules carefully, you will always make a delicious and invigorating cup of tea.

How to Make a Perfect Cup of Chinese Tea

Place a generous ½ tsp. (2 mL) of leaves in each cup; pour in boiling water; put the lid on the cup and allow 4 – 6 minutes to steep. To drink the tea, hold the cup in one hand and push the lid back with your forefinger, allowing you enough space for the tea to flow freely. This is a little tricky to do the first time, but it's a wonderful way to enjoy fine tea. The Chinese porcelain cups are so pretty — my favorite is a high-glazed black one with a beautiful pink butterfly in the bottom and a tiny red one on the lid.

With Chinese tea — but none of the others — you don't have to throw away the saturated leaves. Instead you can pour more boiling water over them to make a second cup. In many cases this second steeping brings out still more of the tea's pure, delicate flavor.

Cool Drinks

As a child, during the hot summer days, I saw a great many trays of lemonade, punches and red fruit vinegar go back and forth — and each time they passed me by as "they were not for the young." Then came the day I reached my 10th birthday and I felt I should be allowed to enjoy any of them. They were always served in large glasses with "pretty colors," and no ice. The drinks were kept cold in the "icebox," but ice in the summer had to be economized. Many of the following recipes are either from my maternal grandmother or my mother. For some reason (the advent of "pop" I suppose!) the good homemade delights have all but disappeared. Do pass them on to your own — let's keep them alive!

Perfect Lemonade

At my grandparents' home, this was the traditional *Punch de Noël* for the children. Sometimes it was colored a beautiful pink or green by the addition of maraschino cherry juice — and each glass had a cherry; the girls had the red cherries, the boys the green. I have made this lemonade through all the years of my life and never found a better one.

6 lemons
1–1½ cups (250–375 mL) sugar
8 cups (2 L) cold water

Wash lemons thoroughly. Do not peel. Slice as thinly as possible. Place in large bowl with the sugar. Mash and stir together until sugar softens and partly dissolves. Add the cold water. Stir until sugar is all melted. Pour into covered container. Refrigerate. After two days, remove lemon slices. To serve, fill glass a quarter to a half full with the lemonade base. Add ice cubes to taste and fill with soda or water. *Serves 8.*

Victorian Lemonade

I use a can of frozen lemonade concentrate to make this instead of a very involved procedure following the Victorian method.

1 small can frozen lemonade concentrate
1 tsp. (5 mL) anise seed
Grated rind of 1 lemon
1 8 oz. (227 g) can crushed pineapple

Prepare lemonade following directions on can. Drain pineapple, reserving liquid. Place in saucepan the anise seed and pineapple juice. Bring to boil, then simmer 5 minutes. Add to lemonade. Cool.

Divide pineapple into 4–6 tall glasses. Pour in lemonade. Add ice to taste and serve. You do not have to strain — I don't because I like to chew on the anise seeds, but they can be strained after they have cooled in the lemonade for 15 minutes. *Serves 6.*

Ginger Limeade

In the early 1900s we easily found lime and fresh ginger, as they came from the West Indies by boat, and they were "in fashion" during the Victorian period. Today, I still use the fresh ginger, as no other type will do, but often replace the limes by lemons because of their cost and availability.

Juice of 6 limes *or* 4 lemons
2 tbsp. (30 mL) cold water
5 cups (1–1.25 L) boiling water
5–8 slices unpeeled fresh ginger root
5 whole cloves
1 tsp. (5 mL) whole allspice
1–1½ cups (250–400 mL) white sugar

Mix the lime or lemon juice with the cold water and let stand overnight. In the morning bring to a boil the remaining water and the spices, then simmer over low heat 20 minutes. Add the sugar, remove from heat, and stir until sugar is dissolved. The amount of sugar can vary with your taste. Then add the lime or lemon mixture. Bring back just to boiling point, but do not let it boil. Cover, cool and bottle. This limeade will keep 2 weeks, refrigerated. Serve as is over cracked ice or without ice. *Serves 6–8.*

Summer Garden Bowl

So called because it was made as needed, with basil or marjoram or mint freshly cut in the garden, and it was served in a punch bowl set on a tray in a bed of herbs or wild flowers.

8–10 sprigs of basil, marjoram or mint
2 tbsp. (30 mL) sugar
1 bottle dry white wine
2 bottles rosé wine of your choice
1 large bottle soda water
3 limes or 2 lemons, thinly sliced

Place the herbs and sugar in punch bowl. Work the two together, by crushing them with your fingers. This is done to release the natural oil of the herbs. Pour over 1 cup (250 mL) white wine. Let stand 1 hour. Add the remaining white wine and the rosé. Refrigerate at least 4 to 5 hours.

To serve, add the soda water, remove the herbs, and add the lime or lemon slices. Fill glasses (not punch bowl) with ice, and pour punch on top. *Serves 18–24.*

Lemon Balm Syrup

In the Thirties almost every icebox had a bottle of this pale green cool delight. Simply pour some in a glass with ice to taste (we had no ice) and cold water or soda water. The amount of lemon balm and water or soda is up to your own taste.

- 2 cups (500 mL) fresh lemon juice
- Grated rind of 2 lemons
- ½–¾ cup (125–200 mL) fresh mint leaves, chopped fine
- 1–1¼ cups (250–325 mL) fine granulated sugar

Mix all the ingredients together and stir until the sugar is all dissolved. (An easy, modern way is to blend it in the blender at fast speed for 1 minute.) The balm will then have a beautiful color and a perfect flavor. Bottle and refrigerate. To serve, pour a quantity to taste in a tall glass, add ice cubes and soda or water. *Yield:* 2½ cups (625 mL) syrup.

Haytime Freshener

When the men on the farm are in the fields, they get very thirsty; so I send them all kinds of cool drinks. This one is in great demand.

- 1 cup (250 mL) fresh raspberries
- 1 tbsp. (15 mL) honey
- 4 cups (1 L) cold ginger ale
- 1 unpeeled lemon, sliced

Mash freshly washed berries with honey and blend 30 seconds at high speed. Divide among 6 glasses. Almost fill each glass with ginger ale, add a slice of lemon and a few cubes of ice. *Yield:* 5 cups.

Apple Water

Slice 4 medium unpeeled and uncored apples into an earthenware jug. Add strips of lemon rind and 2 tbsp. (30 mL) sugar. Pour 1 pint (500 mL) of boiling water on top. Cover the jug and leave until cold, preferably in the refrigerator. This drink was served in the early 1900s to children and to the men working in the fields. It was brought to Canada by Scottish settlers. *Serves 2–4.*

Peach Punch

How good, cool and colorful this one is. I still enjoy it, especially when we have the fresh juicy tasty peaches from the Niagara Valley. Like mother, I use Earl Grey Tea and serve each punch cup topped with a pale pink rose petal.

½–1 cup (125–250 mL) honey
1 cup (250 mL) fresh orange juice
Grated rind of 1 orange
½ cup (125 mL) fresh lemon juice
2 cups (500 mL) peeled and mashed peaches
2 cups (500 mL) strong tea
Pinch of salt
2 cups (500 mL) dry cider or ginger ale

Place all the ingredients, except the cider or ginger ale, in a punch bowl. Stir well and let stand in refrigerator 1 hour. [I prefer ½ cup (125 mL) of honey, but it is up to you to put more or less, as you like.] I peel and stone the peaches, and put them in the blender for 40 seconds. My mother crushed the fruit with a fork, a long process that did not produce the fine peach purée that results from the blender. Mother and I, and now my daughter, always prefer to use the Earl Grey tea because of its light, elusive flower flavor, but any other tea can be used. Dry cider is better than ginger ale, but it *must* be dry and somewhat sparkling. Just before serving, add a good sized piece of ice. Stir well, and add cider or ginger ale. *Serves 12–14.*

Do-It-Yourself Liqueurs

I do not write this as a treatise on liqueurs. It's meant to be a practical guide for anyone wanting to make liqueurs at home — and then enjoy the pleasure of a perfect creation. The art of making any liqueur lies in choosing fresh, good quality ingredients, blending them with care and waiting patiently for just the right moment of maturity. A properly-made liqueur goes on changing — getting better — and maturing indefinitely, providing the measuring, blending and storing have been done with gentle care.

Blue Plum Liqueur

Use Ontario blue plums, or B.C. cherries. Each fruit will give a different color and flavor to the liqueur. With the plums it will be a deep rich purple, with the cherries, a ruby red.

1 lb. (500 g) blue plums (or cherries)
25 oz. (750 mL) dry gin or vodka
1½ cups (400 mL) brown sugar
6 whole cloves

Wash the plums or cherries. Prick plums 5 or 6 times with a sharp needle so they won't burst when cut. Cut fruit into small pieces. Break 5 or 6 of the plum or cherry stones and remove the kernels.

Place in glass container the cut-up plums, the kernels and the remaining ingredients. Stir until the sugar is dissolved. Cover with a double thickness of white cotton. Let ferment 4–8 weeks, the longer the better. Filter through a paper coffee filter, bottle and cork. *Yield:* 3–4 cups (750–1000 mL).

Black Currant Liqueur

My favorite! It keeps without refrigeration of any kind from one black currant season to another. I make one recipe with dry gin, one with brandy. The two are equally good — it's a matter of personal choice.

Black currants
Sugar
25 oz. (750 mL) dry gin or brandy

Fill a 40 oz. (1200 mL) glass container with washed and stemmed currants. Add enough sugar, about 1 cup (250 mL), to cover the fruit. Cover and shake the bottle. Add ½ cup (125 mL) sugar, shake again. Repeat once more. Shake and pour the gin or brandy on top. When available, top jar with 5 or 6 well-washed fresh currant leaves. Cover and let mature 3–4 months in the dark, at any temperature. Shake a few times during this period. Then filter through a paper coffee filter, bottle and cork. *Yield:* 28 oz. (850 mL).

Coffee Cordial

"Once tried, forever used" should be the name of this liqueur. Another perfect keeper, it can be stored at room temperature for months.

2½ cups (625 mL) sugar
3 tbsp. (50 mL) instant coffee
1½ cups (400 mL) cold water
1 tbsp. (15 mL) vanilla
12 oz. (360 mL) Five-Star Canadian brandy

Place the sugar in a saucepan. Dissolve coffee granules in water, add to sugar. Bring to a rolling boil and boil for 2 minutes. Turn heat as low as possible and simmer 3 minutes, stirring most of the time. Let cool. Stir in vanilla and brandy until well mixed. Pour into bottles (no filtering is needed); cork and set aside. *Yield:* 2 cups (500 mL).

Instant Maple Liqueur

I was served this liqueur at a friend's home one evening and I've been using it ever since. When prepared with good quality scotch whisky, the flavor is very near to that of Drambuie.

Maple syrup
Scotch whisky

Refrigerate the syrup, whisky and glasses a few hours before using. This is important, as no ice should be used, yet the drink should be served "with a cool feeling." Pour 1 tsp. (5 mL) maple syrup into each glass; top with 3 tbsp. (50 mL) of whisky. Stir or not, according to taste, and serve.

Raspberry Syrup

We call it *sirop de vinaigre* (vinegar syrup). Every summer for about 65 years I have made this syrup. Bottled in a sterilized container, it may be kept anywhere you wish. (For many years, I have kept some in my bar.) The flavor is truly at its best when 3 years old, although it can be used as soon as it is ready. You may wish to try it sometime on maple or raspberry ice cream, or on custard or rice pudding, or use it to perfume a dish of strawberries, about 2 tbsp. (30 mL) of syrup per 1 pint (500 mL) of very lightly sweetened strawberries.

5–6 quart (litre) baskets of raspberries
4 cups (1 L) cider vinegar
Sugar

Clean 2 baskets of the raspberries, place in a bowl. Pour the vinegar on top. Cover and let stand overnight in a cool place.

Wet a jelly bag. Place over a bowl, and pour in the soaked raspberries, hang the bag over the bowl, and pour into it 2 more boxes of washed and cleaned raspberries. Cover and let stand 24 hours. Repeat process the next day over the 1 or 2 remaining baskets of raspberries. Cover and let stand overnight only. The next day, pour the remaining juice and raspberries in the bag and strain again until *all* the juice is extracted. This may take 4 to 6 hours. Then measure the juice per cup and add an equal amount of sugar. Bring to a fast rolling boil, while stirring; then boil 3–4 minutes. Pour into sterilized bottles or jam pots. Seal and store in a dark place. [Most people use ¼ cup (80 mL) of the syrup to 1 cup (250 mL) of ice-cold water or soda.] *Yield:* 6 cups (1.5 L).

Blackberry Cordial

How often in my youth the children were sent to the woods to gather wild blackberries. Of course, we ate half of what we could have brought back. In the winter, when we had a glass of Blackberry Cordial, we remembered those good moments. It will keep many months, even a few years, the same as the *Raspberry Syrup*. At times, it is possible to find blackberries on the market.

12 cups (6 L) "picked-over" blackberries
3 tbsp. (50 mL) cream of tartar
Sugar

Place the cleaned fruits in a large bowl with the cream of tartar. Stir well and let stand at room temperature, covered, for 48 hours.

Force the mixture through a fine sieve or food mill. Measure the juice and add 1 cup (250 mL) of sugar for each cup of juice. Bring to a boil, over medium heat, stirring often, until sugar is dissolved, then bring to a rolling boil. Boil 5 minutes. Pour into a sterilized jar. To serve, place 2–3 tbsp. (30–50 mL) of syrup in a glass. Add 2–3 ice cubes. Fill with water or soda. *Yield:* will differ, according to the ripeness of the fruit.

3. Soups

I often think of my mother ladling steaming hot soup from the blue China tureen, and each time I do I have a warm contented feeling about it.

To me, on the first cold autumn nights, when the sky changes from geranium pink to deep violet, I have a strong desire for the fireplace with the fire burning with a clear flame, and in the kitchen the soup kettle sending forth a rich savory smell. I can almost smell the crisp cold weather that will soon follow.

To me, soup must be ladled out generously into large *hot* soup plates or bowls. There should be hot bread with a soup meal. Add a bowl of grated cheese, one of crisp greens or carrot sticks or celery or even slivers of raw turnips. For dessert, a bowl of buckwheat honey (hard to find nowadays) or wild rose strawberry jam or wild raspberry jam — homemade of course. A big pot of steaming hot tea to finish it off. Oh, what a meal — one of my favorites.

Scotch Broth

My mother was taught how to make this by a dear Scottish friend who came to settle in Canada in the 1920s.

8 cups (2 L) cold water
1 bay leaf
½ tsp. (2 mL) pepper
2 lb. (1 kg) lamb's neck or shank, or both
2 tsp. (10 mL) salt
4 tbsp. (60 mL) pot barley
2 carrots, sliced
2 onions, diced
1 large leek, diced
1 cup (250 mL) diced turnip
2 celery stalks, diced

2 cups (500 mL) finely chopped green cabbage
¼ cup (60 mL) fresh parsley, minced
3 tbsp. (50 mL) butter
½ cup (125 mL) rolled oats

Add bay leaf, pepper and meat to water in a large saucepan. Slowly bring to a boil. Empty into colander. Rinse meat under running cold water, cover again with same quantity of cold water, and bring back to boil. (This part is important — it improves the soup's color and flavor.) Add salt, boil a few seconds and skim again. Add remaining ingredients, except butter and oats. Slowly bring to a boil, then cover and simmer 2 hours. Melt butter in a frying pan, add oats and stir over medium heat until nutty brown. Add to soup and cook 10–15 minutes more. *Serves 8–10.*

Mother's Creamed Tomato Soup

In the winter, when I was young, it was impossible to buy fresh tomatoes — so we used canned tomatoes. A 25-oz. can of big tasty tomatoes with very little juice cost fifteen cents! It was our Friday night special, served with homemade crackers (that really crunched), cheddar cheese and homemade bitter orange marmalade. Yummy!

1 19 oz. (540 mL) can tomatoes
1 large onion, finely chopped
A few celery leaves, minced
1 tbsp. (15 mL) sugar
½ tsp. (2 mL) savory
1 tbsp. (15 mL) cornstarch
2½ cups (625 mL) milk

Simmer the first 5 ingredients together 20 minutes.

Mix the cornstarch with ½ cup (125 mL) of the milk. Add the remaining milk, simmer over medium heat, stirring often, until it comes to the boil. When ready to serve, pour this hot milk over the hot tomatoes. Stir quickly. Do not let it boil. (When cooked rice was available, mother added ½-1 cup (125-250 mL) of the rice, at the same time as she added the milk.) *Serves 6.*

Green Tomato Soup

In the Twenties, only Canadian seasonal foods were on our tables, so autumn had its big share of green tomatoes. Much of it was simmered into *ketchup vert* (green ketchup), but at home we also had our grandmother's *soupe aux tomates vertes*. I never saw this recipe anywhere, so I do not know how *grand-mère* came by it. What I do know is that today I still make it and enjoy it. Now I even make the base of the soup in autumn, and freeze it to use in the winter. I then thaw it out and add the white sauce.

3 full cups (750 mL) unpeeled and chopped green tomatoes
1 large onion, chopped fine
Generous pinch of cloves
¼ tsp. (1 mL) cinnamon
¼ tsp. (1 mL) pepper
1 tbsp. (15 mL) sugar
4 cups (1 L) water
¼ tsp. (1 mL) baking soda
3 tbsp. (50 mL) butter
3 tbsp. (50 mL) flour
4 cups (1 L) milk

Place the first seven ingredients in a saucepan. Bring to boil, lower the heat, and simmer 20 minutes. Add the soda and stir well. Make a light white sauce with the butter, flour and milk. When bubbling and creamy, add to the green tomatoes. Stir well, and season to taste. *Serves 8.*

Tomato Vermicelli Soup

Unlike ***Mother's Creamed Tomato Soup***, this was made when fresh tomatoes were available. It could also be made a day or so ahead and warmed up. At home, the liquid used was potato or vegetable water.

2 tbsp. (30 mL) butter
2 onions, chopped fine
3 large ripe tomatoes, peeled and sliced
½ tsp. (2 mL) thyme
1 bay leaf
1 tsp. (5 mL) sugar
5 cups (1.25 L) vegetable water or consommé
¼–½ cup (76–125 mL) vermicelli
Fresh parsley or chives to taste

Melt the butter in the soup pot, add the onions, and let brown lightly over medium heat, stirring often. Add the tomatoes, thyme, bay leaf and sugar. Simmer over medium heat 15 minutes, stirring often. Add the liquid of your choice, and bring to boil. Add the vermicelli, salt and pepper to taste. Boil 8–10 minutes. Sprinkle parsley or chives over each bowl of soup. *Serves 4–6.*

Cold Asparagus Soup

It is not necessary to use any asparagus tips in this blender soup, although you may want to keep a few to use as a garnish.

2 cups (500 mL) asparagus, cut in 1 in. (2.5 cm) pieces
2 stalks celery
1 sprig parsley
Pinch of tarragon or thyme
1 tsp. (5 mL) salt
2 cups (500 mL) hot consommé
1 cup (250 mL) light cream or milk
1 chicken bouillon cube
Minced chives (optional)

Place all the ingredients in a blender jar in the order given. Blend 1 minute, then pour into a saucepan, and just heat (don't let this boil). Taste for seasoning, and garnish with minced chives or cooked asparagus tips. *Serves 4.*

Monique's Blender Vegetable Soup

Ten minutes to prepare everything, 10 seconds to blend, 5 minutes to simmer — and a tasty fresh vegetable soup is ready to be served to six hungry people. See the variation if you prefer to serve a cream of vegetable soup.

2 10-oz. (284 mL) cans undiluted consommé
1 7½-oz. (213 mL) can tomato sauce
1 cup (250 mL) water
1 cup (250 mL) potatoes, peeled and diced
½ cup (125 mL) sliced carrots
½ cup (125 mL) celery ends, with leaves
1 onion, peeled and cut in four
1 clove garlic, peeled
½ tsp. (2 mL) salt
1 tsp. (5 mL) basil or savory
½ tsp. (2 mL) sugar

Place the consommé and tomato sauce in a saucepan, over medium heat. Place the water and all the remaining ingredients in the glass jar of a blender. Cover and blend off and on for 10 seconds or just enough to chop the vegetables; too long a time will purée the mixture. Pour chopped vegetables into hot liquid, bring to boil, then simmer for 5 minutes. Taste for seasoning and serve. *Serves 6.*

Variations: Add to soup any leftover cooked rice or noodles or macaroni.

In the summer, replace the tomato sauce with 3 fresh medium-size tomatoes, cut in four and blended with the other vegetables.

To make a cream of vegetable soup, replace the cup of water with 1 cup (250 mL) of light or heavy cream and 3 tbsp. (50 mL) flour, poured over the cream. Cook same time, stirring more often, because of the flour.

Fish Broth

As mother used to do, I still buy a bag of cods' heads and tails for pennies, then use them to make a delicious fish broth that can serve as a bouillon.

8 cups (2 L) water
3 stalks celery
1 bay leaf
1 onion, sliced
1 carrot, sliced
8 peppercorns
½ tsp. (2 mL) thyme
2 lb. (1 kg) cods' heads and tails
2 tbsp. (30 mL) vinegar
2 tbsp. (30 mL) butter
Salt and pepper to taste

In a saucepan bring first 7 ingredients to a rolling boil and add fish. Cover and simmer 40 minutes, then strain through a fine sieve or a coarser one lined with cheesecloth. Pour fish stock back into pot, and add vinegar, butter, salt, and pepper just before serving.

To serve as a soup, add 1 cup (250 mL) fine noodles, 1 finely chopped, unpeeled tomato, and simmer until noodles are soft. Or serve the Italian way by placing 1 tbsp. (15 mL) of grated Parmesan cheese in each soup bowl and pouring hot fish stock on top. Sprinkle with parsley. This fish stock freezes well and will keep 3–4 months. *Serves 6.*

Cream of Scallop Soup

One of my Christmas specials, this is also good for an elegant after-ski party around the fireplace. It is a meal in itself. Serve with toasted French bread and a glass of dry Muscadet wine.

¼ cup (125 mL) butter
1 cup (250 mL) celery, diced
1 cup (250 mL) carrot, grated fine
1 medium onion, minced

1 leek, thinly sliced
¼ cup (60 mL) butter
½ cup (125 mL) flour
2 cups (500 mL) light cream
1 lb. (500 g) scallops, cut in four
1 cup (250 mL) bottled clam juice
½ cup (125 mL) dry white wine or dry sherry
Salt and pepper to taste.

Melt the ½ cup (125 mL) butter in a sauce pan. Add the celery, carrots, onion and leek, stir over medium heat until well coated with the butter. Cover and simmer over low heat for 20 minutes, stirring once or twice. Make a white sauce with the butter, the flour, the milk and the cream. Cook, stirring constantly, until thick and creamy. Add to the vegetables, salt and pepper to taste. Mix well. Cover and let stand until ready to serve. (Or make the day before and refrigerate.) When ready to serve, bring the clam juice to boil, add the scallops, the white wine or sherry. Simmer over low heat for 10 minutes, but do not boil, as this would harden the scallops. When very hot, pour into the hot creamed vegetable mixture. Taste for seasoning and serve. *Serves 6–8.*

Lentil Soup

Five minutes of preparation and you have one of the very best winter soups. It is my own creation, and I always keep some ready in the freezer, as it is my husband's favorite soup. A bowl of lentil soup, a thick wedge of apple pie with cheese, and a large cup of hot tea make a perfect winter lunch.

2 cups (500 mL) brown lentils
4 cups (1 L) cold water
2 tbsp. (30 mL) salt
¼ tsp. (1 mL) pepper
½ cup (125 mL) butter
1 19 oz. can (540 mL) tomatoes
1 onion, diced
2 tbsp. (30 mL) fresh dill or
1 tbsp. (15 mL) dill seeds
2 garlic cloves, crushed
2 bay leaves

Place the ingredients in a saucepan and slowly bring to a boil. Cover and simmer over low heat for 2–2½ hours. *Serves 10–12.*

Cream of Split Pea

A delightful soup and a nice nourishing way to use a ham bone. When possible, flavor the soup with fresh mint, although dried mint may be used.

1½ cups (400 mL) green split peas
6 cups (1.5 L) hot water
1 ham bone
1 onion, finely chopped
½ cup (125 mL) celery, diced
2 cups (500 mL) milk
1 tbsp. (15 mL) butter
1 tsp. (5 mL) fresh mint
Salt and pepper to taste

Rinse the split peas and soak them overnight in enough cold water to cover. The next day, drain and place peas in large saucepan and add hot water, ham bone, onion and celery. Cover and simmer over low heat for 2 hours, stirring occasionally.

Remove the ham bone and pass soup through sieve or a food mill. Put the purée back into the saucepan and add the milk, butter, mint, salt and pepper to taste. Simmer together for a few minutes and serve with buttered croutons. *Serves 6.*

Cream of Pumpkin Soup

Delicate, yes; and elegant, light and easy to make. If you have a blender or a food processor, do use it.

4 cups (1 L) pumpkin, peeled and diced
3 tbsp. (50 mL) butter
¼ tsp. (1 mL) nutmeg
Salt and pepper to taste
1 cup (250 mL) milk
½ cup (125 mL) heavy cream
½ cup (125 mL) small bread croutons (optional)

Melt the butter in saucepan, add the diced pumpkin and the nutmeg. Cover and simmer over low heat for 20 minutes. Add water and milk. Continue to simmer for another 10–15 minutes. Force through a sieve or a food mill, or blend in the blender or food processor. Add the cream, and warm up. Serve with croutons to taste, sprinkled on top of the soup. *Serves 4.*

Cream of Noodle Soup

In the Thirties, this soup was cooked in the double boiler because of its delicate texture — and it was served as an elegant soup at dinner time. When I have no homemade consommé, I used diluted canned consommé.

4 cups consommé, beef or chicken
1 cup (250 mL) *fine* noodles
2 tbsp. (30 mL) butter
1 tbsp. (15 mL) flour
2 tbsp. (30 mL) strong Cheddar cheese, grated
2 egg yolks
1 cup (250 mL) light cream
Salt and pepper to taste
Minced chives (fresh when available)

Bring the consommé to a boil, add the noodles and simmer 10 minutes over direct heat. Melt the butter on top of double boiler, add the flour, and stir over boiling water until well mixed. Add the grated cheese and stir well. Add the boiling consommé with the noodles. Cook 15 minutes, stirring often.

Beat the egg yolks with the cream. Add a bit of hot consommé. Stir well and pour into the soup, stirring for a minute. Do not let it boil. Serve garnished with chives or a sprig of watercress. *Serves 4.*

Nanny's Creamed Cheese Soup

When our "Nanny," Clara (who hated cooking), decided to cook, this was one of her favorite recipes that young and old of the family enjoyed. The quantity of cheese may seem a lot, but try it, and you will be pleasantly surprised.

3 tbsp. (50 mL) butter
2 medium carrots, grated
1 large onion, chopped fine
½ cup (125 mL) diced celery
¼ cup (75 mL) flour
4 cups (1 L) chicken consommé
1 full cup (250 mL) strong Cheddar cheese, grated
2 cups (500 mL) hot milk
2 tbsp. (30 mL) minced parsley

Melt the butter in a saucepan, add the carrots, onion and celery. Simmer over medium heat, until vegetables are softened and start to brown lightly; this will take about 15 minutes.

Add the flour and mix thoroughly with the vegetables. Add the consommé. [You may also use 4 cups (1 L) hot water with chicken bouillon cubes added.] Stir over medium heat until the mixture is boiling gently. Add the cheese and milk. Stir a few seconds, and remove from heat. Add parsley and serve. (To prepare ahead of time, follow directions, adding the hot milk and cheese only when ready to serve.) *Serves 4.*

4. Salads and Dressings

Nasturtium Salad

When I was about 15, I attended a lecture on summer garden flowers. The speaker told us, and I quote, "Nasturtiums should be grown every year, because they are prolific, colorful, can be used to cook and pickle, and their early morning perfume is very piquant. They have an extraordinary quality. Each blossom of your summer nasturtiums will have 8 males and 1 female." I rebelled — how could the poor female fight the 8 males? Then and there, I decided I would cook the males! But the problem was that I never knew how many of the males I had cooked and whether the female was in it too! It's funny, but I have never forgotten this.

1 head Boston or garden lettuce
6–10 fresh nasturtium leaves
French dressing to taste
3 green nasturtium seeds
A few flowers

Wash lettuce a few hours before needed. Place a folded piece of absorbent paper in the bottom of a plastic bag. Add washed lettuce. Close bag loosely. Refrigerate. (This can be done even 12 hours before needed.) Place the lettuce in a salad bowl. Add the nasturtium leaves, chopped up with scissors. Then toss the whole thing with French dressing to your taste. Chop the seeds coarsely and sprinkle on the salad. Make a ring of single flowers around the bowl or in a bouquet in the middle. Serve a flower or two with each salad. *Serves 4.*

Dandelion Salad

May is dandelion time. Did you ever go, early in the month, into the fields, armed with a basket and sharp knife to gather the foliage of the *dent de lion*

(lion's tooth), small and green and tender? It can be such a devil in your lawn later during the summer, but in May the dandelion can make such a delicious salad. Wash the greens thoroughly and separate the "branches." Wrap these in a clean cloth and refrigerate for a few hours to make them fresh and cool. To serve, place the cleaned dandelion greens in a salad bowl and top them with 5-7 slices of crisp, crumbled bacon, or small squares of fried salt pork (the salt pork is the traditional way in Quebec). Fry a minced onion in hot bacon or pork fat until it is golden brown, then add 2–3 tbsp. (30–45 mL) of cider or malt vinegar. Pour this over the dandelions, then add salt and pepper to taste. Toss and serve the dandelion greens without delay — spring is truly with us when we can eat this delicious *dent de lion* salad with plenty of hot homemade bread and fresh cream cheese. *Serves 4.*

Health Salad

In this salad, the standard oil dressing is replaced with a mixture of cottage cheese and commercial sour cream. In combination with summer vegetables, it makes a cool, healthy treat.

1 head Boston lettuce
½ cucumber, peeled and thinly sliced
8 radishes, thinly sliced
1 tomato, cut in wedges
3 green onions (including tops), chopped
¾ cup (200 mL) commercial sour cream
1 cup (250 mL) cottage cheese
¼ tsp. (1 mL) salt
1 tsp. (5 mL) minced chives (optional)
Pepper to taste
Garlic powder, to taste

Tear the cleaned lettuce into small pieces and put it in a mound in a serving bowl. Surround with cucumber, radishes, tomato and onions. Mix remaining ingredients, beat thoroughly and pour over lettuce. Toss together when ready to serve. *Serves 4–6.*

Whipped Cream Green Salad

This salad and the old-fashioned Wilted Salad have all but disappeared from our tables. This one is still the best of salads to serve with thinly sliced cold chicken or veal or cold poached salmon. As it was a spring salad, we used to make it with a combination of long leaf lettuce and a soft, round ball Boston type lettuce.

1 or 2 heads of leaf lettuce
1 head of Boston lettuce
1 cup (250 mL) heavy cream
1 tbsp. (15 mL) sugar
1 tsp. (5 mL) salt
1 tbsp. (15 mL) cider or white wine vinegar
2–3 green onions, chopped fine
2 tbsp. (30 mL) parsley, finely chopped
A sprig or two of fresh mint (optional)

Core, break up and wash lettuce in *ice cold* water. Drain well, in a lettuce basket, if available. Pour into a large plastic bag, with a folded piece of kitchen paper in the bottom. (This absorbs the excess water that otherwise will remain in the lettuce.) Refrigerate until ready to serve.

To serve, whip the cream, add all the remaining ingredients, except the mint, one by one, beating at each addition, just enough to mix. Place the lettuce in a salad bowl. Spoon the dressing on top and toss lightly with 2 forks. Garnish with the sprigs of mint and serve. *Serves 6.*

Onion-Cottage Cheese Salad

Colorful, appetizing and tasty, this is a pleasant change from the usual cottage cheese–fruit salad combination.

Boston or Iceberg lettuce
A small carton of cottage cheese
4 small cooked beets
3 tbsp. (50 mL) lemon French Dressing
Grated rind of ½ lemon
1 small white or yellow onion, sliced
¼ cup (50 mL) minced parsley

Make cups of lettuce leaves, and set on plates. Into each lettuce cup, place a mound of cottage cheese. Toss the beets in the dressing and lemon rind, cut in wedges, and place as a crown around the bottom of the cottage cheese. Slice the onion thinly and break into rings. Roll each ring in the parsley. Place on top of cottage cheese, and pour over it 1 tsp. (5 mL) of the dressing. *Serves 2-4.*

Monique's Crisp Cole Slaw

What follows seems to be so simple, you may wonder why bother with the ice treatment? I can assure you that it makes the real difference between a good and a mushy cole slaw.

3 cups (750 mL) finely chopped cabbage
3 tbsp. (50 mL) vegetable or olive oil
Juice and grated rind of ½ lemon
Salt and pepper to taste
2 green onions, chopped fine

Place the chopped cabbage in a bowl of cold water. Cover with a layer of ice cubes. Refrigerate 3–5 hours. Drain and dry by rolling in a cloth or absorbent paper. Add the remaining ingredients to the cabbage. Toss and refrigerate until ready to serve. *Serves 4.*

Cabbage Salad in Mustard Cream

If you care about good food, this will please you — it has nothing to do with restaurant cole slaw. Keep it in mind for your next buffet supper, especially if you serve baked ham.

2–4 cups (500–1000 mL) cabbage, finely shredded
4 eggs
1/4 cup (60 mL) sugar
1 tbsp. (15 mL) dry mustard
1/2 tsp. (2 mL) salt
1/2 tsp. (2 mL) white vinegar
1 tbsp. (15 mL) unflavored gelatine
1/2 cup (125 mL) cold water
1/2 pint (250 mL) rich cream, whipped
1/2 cup (125 mL) parsley, chopped
3–5 green onions, finely chopped
1 tbsp. (15 mL) sugar
3 tbsp. (50 mL) cider vinegar
2 tbsp. (30 mL) vegetable oil
1 tsp. (5 mL) salt

The day before serving, shred the cabbage for the cole slaw. Place it in a bowl, top with ice cubes and refrigerate. The next day, beat the eggs until light, then add the sugar, mustard and salt. Mix well and beat in the vinegar. Soak the gelatine 5 minutes in 2 tbsp. of the cold water and add to the egg mixture. Then add the rest of the water.

My husband Bernard with some of his sheep. To him this spells happiness. We both enjoy the warm clothes knitted from the wool from our sheep, which keeps us snugly warm in the winter's deep freeze.

Cook over low heat, stirring constantly, until as thick as a custard. Do not boil — the mixture will curdle. Refrigerate about 1 hour, or until the mixture is the consistency of egg whites, then fold in the whipped cream. Oil a ring mold, pour in the cream mixture and refrigerate until set.

Drain the cabbage and squeeze it dry in a tea towel. Put it in a bowl and add the parsley, green onions, sugar, vinegar, oil and salt. Toss together thoroughly. To serve, unmold the cream mixture onto a platter. Fill the hole with the cole slaw and surround the ring with it. *Serves 6-8.*

The Best of Potato Salads

The secret of this salad is the cup of hot consommé poured over the hot cooked potatoes. It is all absorbed by the potatoes, so the salad is a good 24-hour keeper, and the texture is light and pleasant.

6 – 8 medium unpeeled potatoes
1 cup (250 mL) hot consommé
3 tbsp. (50 mL) vegetable oil
2 tbsp. (30 mL) fresh lemon juice
2 tbsp. (30 mL) table cream
2 French shallots, chopped fine
Salt and pepper to taste
Pinch of nutmeg
1 tsp. (5 mL) capers (optional)

Scrub, and boil or steam (I prefer steaming) the potatoes, without overcooking. When done, drain, dry and peel while still hot. Slice potatoes to desired thickness, place in a bowl and pour the hot consommé on top. [It can be home-made chicken or beef consommé, canned consommé, as is, or diluted to taste; or use a spoonful of chicken or beef base in 1 cup (250 mL) of hot water or vegetable water.] Stir gently, with a rubber spatula. Cover bowl with paper. Let stand 20 minutes.

Blend together the remaining ingredients. Add to the potatoes, stir gently. Taste for seasoning. Keep at room temperature until ready to serve. *Serves 6.*

One way to enjoy this salad is to place in a bowl, surround with crisp, green watercress or leaves of Boston lettuce, and serve with thinly sliced cold chicken or roast beef — and a pot of good Dijon mustard.

The braided bread for prosperity, the two doves for love, the silver cups for the champagne, the wedding cake covered with daisies, the petitpoint cushion for the rings – to me these are reminders of a happy day, my granddaughter Susan's wedding.

Sour Cream Cucumber Salad

Serve this in a glass dish if possible, and decorate it with fresh dill sprigs.

4 medium cucumbers
1 tbsp. (15 mL) salt
1 cup (250 mL) commercial sour cream
2 tbsp. (30 mL) white vinegar
1/4 cup (60 mL) vegetable oil
1 tsp. (5 mL) sugar
3 tbsp. (50 mL) chopped dill
Salt and pepper to taste

Scrub the cucumbers, but don't peel them. Cut off ends, score lengthwise with the tines of a fork, then slice as thinly as possible. Place slices in a bowl, sprinkle with the salt, and let stand 1 hour at room temperature. Drain and rinse under running cold water to remove salt; then squeeze dry.

Combine sour cream, vinegar, oil, sugar, dill and pour over cucumbers. Add salt and pepper, then refrigerate, and toss just before serving. *Serves 4.*

Cucumber Mizeria

In 1954 I did a 30-minute T.V. show with some Ukrainian ladies, each of them teaching me one of her specialties. This one has been my favorite since that day.

3 medium cucumbers
1 tsp. (5 mL) salt
4 – 5 chopped green onions
1 tbsp. (15 mL) minced fresh dill
3 tbsp. (50 mL) white vinegar
1/2 tsp. (2 mL) salt
1/2 tsp. (2 mL) sugar
1/4 tsp. (1 mL) pepper
1/4 cup (60 mL) commercial sour cream

Peel the cucumbers; but if they are young and freshly gathered, just wash them. Peeled or unpeeled, run a fork down their length to make parallel grooves and an attractive scalloped edge. Then slice them as thinly as possible. Place them on a dish, sprinkle on the salt and let stand for 15 minutes. Drain, press out the water that has accumulated, and place the slices in a bowl.

Add the onions, dill, vinegar, salt, sugar and pepper. Toss well and refrigerate for 1 hour, or just let stand for 5 minutes. Spread the sour cream on top just before serving. A sprig of dill placed on top of the sour cream looks very nice. *Serves 4 – 6.*

Fresh Mushroom Salad

Serve this gourmand's choice for a luncheon with toasted unbuttered French bread. It is a truly delicate, delectable salad.

1 head Boston or Iceberg lettuce
¾ cup (200 mL) commercial sour cream
Juice and grated peel of 1/2 a lemon
1 tsp. (5 mL) salt
1 tsp. (5 mL) sugar
1/4 tsp. (1 mL) pepper
2 green onions (including tops), chopped
½ lb. (250 g) mushrooms, thinly sliced
3 hard-boiled eggs

Core, wash and cut the lettuce into 4 wedges, then refrigerate so it will be cool and crisp. Mix remaining ingredients, except eggs, and taste for salt.

To serve, set lettuce wedges on a plate and top each with one quarter of the mushroom cream. Slice eggs and place around lettuce, or grate on top. *Serves 4.*

Mixed Vegetable Salad

The simple and tasty dressing on this salad can be used with many vegetables, varied to suit your taste.

1 cup (250 mL) grated raw carrots
1 cup (250 mL) grated unpeeled apples
1 tsp. (5 mL) fresh lemon juice
1 cup (250 mL) finely shredded cabbage
4 tbsp. (60 mL) water
1 tbsp. (15 mL) sugar
2 tbsp. (30 mL) fresh lemon juice

Place the carrots in a bowl. Toss apples with 1 tsp. (5 mL) of the lemon juice to prevent discoloration, add to carrots, then add cabbage. Blend remaining ingredients, add to salad, and toss. Refrigerate in a bowl until ready to serve. *Serves 4.*

Classic Vegetables à la Grecque

This classic is one of the very best ways to serve a cold cooked vegetable salad. The choice is varied — try it with celery, asparagus, cauliflower, cucumbers, mushrooms, zucchini, green beans, pickling onions or leeks, about 1 cup (250 mL) per person.

1 tsp. (5 mL) fennel seeds
1/2 tsp. (2 mL) thyme
12 coriander seeds
2 bay leaves
10 peppercorns
2 cups (500 mL) water
1/2 cup (125 mL) dry white wine
1/3 cup (80 mL) olive oil
1/2 tsp. (2 mL) salt
Juice of 1 lemon

Cut the vegetables of your choice into bite-sized pieces, but not too small. Cauliflower and broccoli should be cut into flowerets and small onions left whole; mushrooms can be sliced, quartered or, if small, left whole. Cook only one kind of vegetable at a time, as cooking times differ. You can, however, re-use the same liquid.

Make a small bag from a double layer of cheesecloth and fill with the first 5 ingredients. Tie bag and place it with a mixture of remaining ingredients in a saucepan. Bring slowly to a broil, then cover and simmer over low heat for 30 minutes.

Bring back to a full rolling boil. Add the prepared vegetables gradually, so the boiling isn't stopped. Lower heat to simmer and cook vegetables until just tender but still a bit crunchy. Repeat procedure for vegetables with different cooking times, removing vegetables from liquid to a non-metal bowl. When all vegetables are prepared, pour liquid over them, and let cool. Cover and refrigerate overnight. Drain vegetables from marinade before serving. (All vegetables prepared *à la Grecque* may be served "as is," combined in a mixed salad, or used as a salad garnish.) *Serves 6.*

Monique's Romanian Ratatouille

The Romanians call it *Ghivetch;* the French say *Ratatouille;* for the Italians, it is a *Caponata:* My daughter says, "It goes with the seasons and what's in the frig." What is important is to keep it crisp, tender, colorful and light. The Romanian way is the very best, and at the same time the easiest. It will keep two weeks refrigerated.

1½ cups (400 mL) carrots thinly, sliced or cut into sticks
1 cup (250 mL) celery, slivered on the bias
2 – 3 small to medium unpeeled zucchini, sliced thickly
1 green and 1 red pepper (or 2 of one type), cleaned
and cut into ½ in. (1.25 cm) strips
1 small head cauliflower, broken into flowerets
1/2 cup (125 mL) vegetable or olive oil

2 tsp. (10 mL) salt
2 large cloves garlic, crushed
1 tsp. (5 mL) dried tarragon
1 tsp. (5 mL) dried marjoram or savory
1/2 tsp. (2 mL) fennel or dill seeds
1/4 cup (60 mL) chopped parsley
1 cup (250 mL) undiluted canned consommé

Wash, cut and mix all the vegetables in a large bowl. You can vary the vegetables but keep to quantity. Pour 2 tbsp. (30 mL) of the oil over the mixture and mix gently with your hands until the vegetables are coated and shiny. This is important, as it allows the vegetables to retain all their vivid color even after cooking. Heat the remaining oil with the remaining ingredients.

Place vegetables on a large cooky sheet or in a roasting pan. Pour the hot mixture on top. Cover tightly with foil, and bake in a 350°F. (180°C) oven 45 minutes. (Do not peek or worry — it always turns out perfect.) Cool in a *covered* dish. Then, when cold, uncover, taste for salt and pepper. Pour into a serving dish. (Monique uses a large clear glass bowl.) Cover and chill overnight. Surround with lemon wedges or serve with a cruet of wine or cider vinegar. *Serves 6-8.*

Raw Beet Salad

Serve in a lettuce cup as a garnish to a fruit salad. Different, colorful and tasty. Rub your hands with a piece of lemon to prevent your hands from being stained by the beet juice.

2 cups (500 mL) shredded peeled raw beets
1 cup (250 mL) chopped salted peanuts
2 tbsp. (30 mL) mayonnaise
4 tbsp. (60 mL) French dressing
1 tsp. (5 mL) lemon juice
Salt and pepper to taste

Mix the beets and peanuts. Blend in the remaining ingredients. To serve as a salad, set in lettuce cup or over finely shredded cabbage and top with more mayonnaise. *Serves 4.*

French Dressing

A classic French dressing consists of 4 ingredients: vegetable or olive oil, wine or cider vinegar, salt and *freshly* ground pepper. Of course, there is no emulsifier, as there is in mayonnaise, so be sure to shake the dressing well. Each type, even each brand of oil and vinegar, you use will vary the flavor of the dressing.

Basic French Dressing

Enough for 3 cups of greens or other vegetables.
Mix in the bowl:

1 tbsp. (15 mL) of vinegar
1/4 tsp. (1 mL) salt
1/8 tsp. (0.5 mL) freshly ground pepper
3 tbsp. (50 mL) vegetable or olive oil

The French way is to mix the dressing in the bottom of the salad bowl. If a salad must wait, prepare the sauce in the bottom of the bowl, and cover with a square of wax paper and place greens or any other ingredients you wish to use on that paper. This can be done even 2 hours before tossing, providing it is kept refrigerated. To serve, gently pull the paper, rub oily side on top of lettuce, throw paper away, and toss salad — a trick used by many a chef.

How to Vary Your Basic French Dressing:

Lemon Dressing: Replace the vinegar by the juice and grated rind of 1/2 lemon to 3 tbsp. (50 mL) of oil dressing.

Garlic: Do not add to dressing, but take a large clove of garlic, cut off a small slice at one end, and rub salad bowl all over until the garlic starts to "melt" by the constant rubbing, then you have a well *aillé* (garlicked) salad bowl. Make a simple dressing in the bowl, and toss your salad.

Mustard Dressing: Stir into the vinegar of the basic French dressing, 1 tsp. (5 mL) of prepared mustard (or half prepared, half dried mustard). Try any of the mustards recommended for basic mayonnaise. Each type will change the flavor of the salad.

Lemon French Dressing

Keep on hand, as it may well become your favorite on all salads.

1/4 cup (60 mL) fresh lemon juice
1 tsp. (5 mL) Dijon-type mustard
1/2 tsp. (2 mL) sugar
1/2 tsp. (2 mL) salt
1/4 tsp. (2 mL) pepper
1/2 – 3/4 cup (125 – 200 mL) vegetable or olive oil

Mix together with a small whisk, the lemon juice, mustard, sugar, salt and pepper. Add the oil and mix again for 2 minutes. Pour into glass container. Keep well covered. Shake thoroughly before using. *Yield:* 1 1/4 cups (325 mL).

Thousand Island Dressing

Another elegant salad dressing of the Thirties that has survived. It was especially popular served on wedges of head lettuce or with crab or shrimp salads. (A large one with all the coffee you wish and hot popover cost $1.35! I found an old receipt in my file. What it was doing there I do not know.) We once had such a crab salad in Prince Edward Island. I still remember the beauty of that salad. They presented the freshly picked crab in a porcelain dish and said crab should never touch metal – but the Thousand Island Dressing was in a silver bowl.

1 cup (250 mL) mayonnaise of your choice
1/3 cup (80 mL) chili sauce
1 tbsp. (15 mL) French dressing of your choice
1/4 cup (60 mL) commercial sour cream
1/4 cup (60 mL) chopped olives
1/4 cup (60 mL) chopped dill or sour pickles
2 tbsp. (30 mL) diced green peppers (optional)
1 tbsp. (15 mL) green onions, diced
2 tsp. (10 mL) chopped parsley
1 tbsp. (15 mL) red or white wine vinegar

Combine all the ingredients together and mix thoroughly. Keep refrigerated. *Yield:* 1 cup (250 mL).

Oil and Yogurt Salad Dressing

4 tbsp. (60 mL) unflavored yogurt
2 tbsp. (30 mL) peanut oil
1/4 tsp. (1 mL) salt
Pepper to taste
2 green onions, chopped fine
Chopped parsley to taste

Blend together the yogurt and oil. Add remaining ingredients. Mix well. Bottle and keep refrigerated. *Yield:* 6 tbsp. (90 mL).

Honey-Yogurt Salad Dressing

Anyone trying to reduce will appreciate this dressing, although I like it whether I'm dieting or not. Try it over a wedge of lettuce, sprinkled with chopped green onions.

- 1/2 cup (125 mL) plain yogurt
- 1/4 tsp. (1 mL) honey
- 1/4 tsp. (1 mL) plain salt
- ½ tsp. (2 mL) fresh lemon juice
- Grated peel of ¼ lemon

Beat all the ingredients together with a whisk or rotary beater. Keep refrigerated in a covered jar and shake before using. Keeps 3 – 4 months. *Yield:* 1/2 cup (125 mL).

Mayonnaise: Mayonnaise made in the classic manner is a non-cooked cold emulsion. A cold emulsion is a combination of two liquids which are basically incompatible, such as oil and vinegar or another type of acid. In order to combine them, an emulsifying agent is needed; in the case of mayonnaise, an egg yolk is used. This emulsified mixture will separate without such an agent. For instance, French dressing will separate as soon as one stops stirring the mixture; there is nothing in it to bind the ingredients together.

You will find that the best mayonnaise will be the one made by you in your kitchen; and once tried and mastered, you will want to make it and serve it often. From the basic recipe you can make many variations with simply with the addition of a few ingredients.

The choice of oil for mayonnaise depends on what you are going to use the mayonnaise for and also your personal taste in flavor. A pure olive oil makes a very pungent mayonnaise; half olive oil and half peanut oil makes a very pleasant mayonnaise; all other types of vegetable oils make a mild flavored mayonnaise. The vinegar is also very important since each type — malt, cider, red or white vinegar; Oriental, especially Japanese; or herb — will give its particular flavor to the mayonnaise. Even the types of mustard — Dijon, Gering, dry, homemade, Finnish — will give another dimension to the flavor.

As to the time involved, the whole process of emulsifying a mayonnaise will take 20 – 25 minutes once you have your ingredients and utensils assembled.

Basic Mayonnaise

Master this recipe and you will soon have learned all the tricks.

- 2 egg yolks
- 1/2 tsp. (2 mL) dry mustard, or other type of your choice
- 2 – 4 tbsp. (30 – 60 mL) cider vinegar, white wine or fresh lemon juice
- 1 cup (250 mL) vegetable or olive oil
- 1 tsp. (5 mL) salt

Place the egg yolks in the bowl. Add the dry mustard and 2 tbsp. (30 mL) of the vinegar, wine or lemon juice. Mix well with a wire whisk. When well mixed, add the oil; the way the oil is added is the secret of making mayonnaise successfully. Add it almost drop by drop, and beat vigorously and constantly with the wire whisk until the mixture is emulsified. You will know when this takes place because the texture will become smooth and creamy. Once this happens the oil may be added a little more quickly, but never add too much at one time. Make sure the oil added has been completely beaten in before adding more. The more slowly the oil is added in the beginning, the firmer the mayonnaise will be. A perfect mayonnaise should have the consistency of thick whipped cream. Add the salt toward the end and taste to be sure the seasoning is just right.

If the oil is added too quickly, the mayonnaise will separate and no amount of beating will bind it together again. If this should happen, make a fresh start with a clean bowl. Place in the bowl 1 tsp. (5 mL) dry mustard and mix it into a thin cream with a few drops of water or beat an egg yolk until smooth; then, beating vigorously, start adding to this the separated mayonnaise, drop by drop, as with the oil when you began. As it re-emulsifies you may speed up the process of adding oil.

If you want a mayonnaise with a tart flavor, add 1 – 2 tsp. (5 – 10 mL) of cider vinegar or fresh lemon juice once the mixture has thickened, but while you are still beating.

Remember, the secret of a perfect mayonnaise lies in the slow addition of the oil and the use of a wire whisk with which to beat it, an electric hand beater at medium speed, a food processor (the easiest of all), or a blender jar.

Mayonnaise may be stored in a well-covered glass jar and kept in a cool place. Do not refrigerate, because the oil will solidify at too cold a temperature, and in all probability the emulsion will break down. *Yield:* 1 1/2 cups (400 mL).

Cornstarch Mayonnaise

Somewhat similar in texture and flavor to the commercial type of mayonnaise. Quicker and less costly to make than the basic type.

- 1 egg, unbeaten
- 1 – 2 tbsp. (15 – 30 mL) sugar

1 tsp. (5 mL) salt
1 tsp. (5 mL) dry mustard
1/8 tsp. (0.5 mL) paprika
1/4 cup (60 mL) lemon juice or vinegar
3/4 cup (200 mL) vegetable oil
4 tbsp. (60 mL) cornstarch
1 cup (250 mL) water

Place in a bowl the unbeaten egg, sugar, salt, dry mustard, paprika, lemon juice or vinegar and vegetable oil. Prepare the mayonnaise base by blending together the cornstarch and water in a saucepan and cooking over low heat, stirring constantly until boiling. Boil for 1 minute, stirring constantly. It will be very thick.

Remove from heat and pour this cream over the egg mixture. Beat with an electric beater until smooth and creamy. Keep refrigerated in a closed jar. *Yield:* 2 cups (500 mL).

Boiled Salad Dressing

Many prefer this light, less oily type of salad dressing, as it is usually referred to, although it is a sort of cooked mayonnaise.

3 eggs
1 tsp. (5 mL) dry mustard
1/4 cup (60 mL) sugar
1/2 cup (125 mL) vinegar of your choice
1/4 cup (60 mL) water
1 tsp. (5 mL) salt
1 tbsp. (15 mL) flour
2 tbsp. (30 mL) butter
3/4 cup (200 mL) milk

Beat the eggs in a saucepan until well mixed. Add the mustard, sugar, vinegar and water. Blend well. Add the salt. Then beat in the flour, the butter and the milk. Place over medium heat and stir constantly until smooth and thick. Lower the heat and simmer another 5 minutes, stirring often. Remove from heat. Cover with paper. Cool, then pour in glass jar and keep refrigerated. *Yield:* 1¾ cups (350 mL).

French Shallot Salad Dressing

If you have a blender or a processor, by all means use it as you will produce the creamiest and tastiest dressing. An excellent "keeper," when kept in a cool place in a covered glass jar. Shake before each use. Type of oil and vinegar can be varied, but each one will give a different flavor to your dressing. Experiment and keep note of your favorite brands and types.

½ tsp. (2 mL) sugar
1 tsp. (5 mL) salt
¼ tsp. (1 mL) pepper
¼ tsp. (1 mL) paprika
1 tsp. (5 mL) dry mustard
1 cup (250 mL) olive oil
¼ cup (60 mL) red wine vinegar
1 French shallot, peeled and cut in half

Place all ingredients in blender or processor, and blend 40 – 50 seconds. Pour into a glass jar. Cover and let stand at room temperature 1 – 2 hours before using. *Yield:* 1⅓ cups (330 mL).

Variations:

To Use with Meat Salad: Add to ingredients 2 tbsp. (30 mL) chutney of your choice. Blend.

To Use with Fish or Boiled Meat: Add 2 tsp. (10 mL) capers to dressing after it has been blended.

Creamy French Dressing

It has the consistency of light cream, very nice with chicken salad, endives and toasted almonds salad, summer garden leaf lettuce, thinly sliced cucumbers, cubed Swiss cheese and toasted croutons on lettuce, chives and slivers of cooked ham on a bed of chopped hard cooked eggs. This dressing is almost a mayonnaise — but it is not emulsified.

2 tbsp. (30 mL) Dijon mustard
1 egg
½ tsp. (2 mL) salt
1 drop Tabasco sauce
3 tbsp. (50 mL) cider or white wine vinegar
1 crushed clove garlic
1 cup (250 mL) salad or olive oil
½ tsp. (2 mL) fresh tarragon or basil or chives or parsley

Measure into a bowl the mustard and egg. Beat with a rotary beater until foamy and pale. Then, beat in the salt, Tabasco sauce, and vinegar. Next, gradually beat in the oil, 1 tbsp. (15 mL) at a time. Add the garlic, crushed but left whole; pour in a jar. Cover and refrigerate. Shake hard before using. *Yield:* 1¼ cups (330 mL).

5. *Breads, Buns and Biscuits*

My *grand-père* Cardinal very often told me that the food aroma that I would remember best would be the smell of homemade bread just coming out of the oven. I could not quite understand what he meant then, but now I do — I have for a long time — and I know he was right. Of all the memories of food in my early youth, the smell and crunchiness of homemade bread is my most cherished childhood memory. Maybe I come by it naturally, since my grandfather was a master baker, specializing in *le pain sur la sol,* home-style bread baked on the stone floor of a brick oven. Out of it would come big round loaves, with a deep cut in an X shape on top, with a special texture that has never been equalled by other modern methods.

Grand-père Cardinal also made his own flour blend of soft wheat from Quebec, two types of hard wheat from the West, and some freshly-milled wheat germ. He used raw sugar or western honey and always added to the yeast some freshly-ground ginger root, which an elderly Chinaman brought to the bakery once a week, so I learned very early to appreciate the flavor of fresh ginger. *Grand-père* used to tell his Chinese friend that the ginger warmed up the yeast, and filled it with "dancing pep," so the bread rose better and the flavor was enhanced. *Grand-père* showed me all about bread. The men who worked for him used to knead 75 to 100 pounds of dough at a time, place it in large wooden boxes attached to the floor, then cover it with a large linen cloth, handwoven by women who grew the flax themselves. On top of that went a heavy wooden cover. A young man stayed all night in the bakery, warming up the huge oven with large maple logs and keeping it at just the right temperature for the bread to rise like a big, puffy round-top cushion. To me the "fireboy," as he was referred to, was a wizard, building the fire to maintain a constant 400°F. (200°C) temperature all over inside those big ovens. Then, almost at dawn, came the big strong men who punched down the dough, pulled off pieces of dough and placed them on the scale — each one had to be a two-pound loaf, or *miche de pain* as they were called. When there was enough to fill the oven, they placed 6 or 8 of these on long flat paddles after they had risen, and slipped them onto the oven floor. (I've always found that difficult to do even with one loaf and often wondered how they managed eight of them.) They knew by instinct or smell, I never knew which, when the bread was done, and that is when the aroma of freshly-baked bread would permeate the whole place. It's no wonder I never forgot.

My Hundred-Year-Old Bread

I have adapted the method and some of the ingredients from a recipe left to my mother by her father. Packed full with flavor, very nutritious, easily mixed in an electric mixer, providing you have a dough hook. No need to leaven, punch down, mold, rise again; simply knead, place in greased bread pan, let it rise and bake. Toasted, it has a nutty flavor and a crunchy texture.

1 tsp. (5 mL) sugar
1/2 tsp. (2 mL) dry ginger
3–4 cups (750–1000 mL) hot water
1 envelope active dry yeast
2 tbsp. (30 mL) molasses
1 cup (250 mL) wheat germ
2 tsp. (10 mL) salt
4–7 cups (1–1.75 L) whole wheat flour
Egg white or milk
2 tsp. (10 mL) sesame seeds

In mixing bowl, stir in sugar, ginger and hot water. Sprinkle the yeast over it and let it stand 8–10 minutes. Stir well.

Add molasses, wheat germ and salt, and stir at low speed for 1 minute. Add half the flour, and stir again until well mixed. Add another cup of flour; beat at medium speed 3 minutes. Spread last cup of flour on table, turn dough on top, roll in flour to remove stickiness. Knead 5 minutes. Divide dough in half, shape and place in two buttered 9 × 5 × 3-in. (22.5 × 12.5 × 7.5 cm) loaf pans. Cover with a cloth and allow to rise in a warm place until double in bulk. This can take 1–2 hours, depending on the weather.

Gently brush tops with lightly-beaten egg white or milk, and sprinkle with sesame seeds. Bake in preheated 350°F. (180°C) oven 45–55 minutes, or until golden brown and well cooked. Remove from pans immediately, and let cool on cake rack.

Wheat Germ Bread

Tasty toasted, and excellent for sandwiches. The wheat germ gives this bread added nutrition plus an interesting nutty flavor.

3 cups (750 mL) boiling water
2 cups (500 mL) wheat germ
1/4 cup (60 mL) shortening or margarine
2 tsp. (10 mL) sugar
1 tsp. (5 mL) sugar
1 cup (250 mL) lukewarm water
2 envelopes active dry yeast
3/4 cup (200 mL) molasses
4 tsp. (20 mL) salt
Approximately 8 cups (2 L) all-purpose flour
2 tbsp. (30 mL) sesame seeds

Pour the boiling water over the wheat germ and the shortening. Stir until fat melts, and let stand about 20 minutes, stirring once or twice. Meanwhile dissolve the sugar and ginger in the lukewarm water. Sprinkle yeast on top. Let stand 10 minutes. Stir well and add to partially-cooled wheat germ mixture, stir, and add the molasses and salt. Mix thoroughly, then start adding the flour — first add 3 cups (750 mL) — and beat vigorously by hand or, when possible, with electric mixer. I like to beat the dough about 4 – 5 minutes at this stage. Then gradually beat in with a spoon the remaining flour, using just enough to make a smooth soft dough. I always use my hands for the last cups added as I get a better feeling for the texture of the dough. Turn dough onto floured surface and knead 8 – 10 minutes. Shape into a large ball, and place in a greased bowl. Cover and let rise in warm place until double in size. Punch down and shape into 3 loaves, and let rise again until double. Brush top of risen bread with milk and sprinkle with the sesame seeds. Bake in a preheated 400°F. (200°C) oven, 30 – 35 minutes, or until golden brown. Unmold on cooling rack as soon as cooked. *Yield:* three 9 × 5-in. (22 × 12.5 cm) loaves.

Farmer's Bread

A family favorite at Noirmouton! Cornmeal and oatmeal were often used in olden days because many farmers grew, dried and ground their own corn; and oats were readily available.

1 cup (250 mL) rolled oats
1/3 cup (80 mL) cornmeal
2 tsp. (10 mL) salt
3 tbsp. (50 mL) molasses
½ cup (125 mL) brown sugar
3 tbsp. (50 mL) margarine or shortening
2½ cups (625 mL) cups boiling water
1 tsp. (5 mL) sugar
1 tsp. (5 mL) ground ginger
½ cup (125 mL) lukewarm water
1 envelope active dry yeast
6 – 8 cups (1.5 – 2 L) all-purpose flour

Place in a bowl the rolled oats, cornmeal, salt, molasses, brown sugar and margarine or shortening. Pour boiling water on top. Stir and let stand 15 minutes. Meanwhile dissolve the 1 tsp. (5 mL) of sugar and the ginger in the lukewarm water. Add the active dry yeast. Let stand 10 minutes. Stir briskly with a fork, add to the oat mixture, and stir well. Start adding the flour, 3 cups (750 mL) to start with, beat vigorously by hand or electric mixer for 5 minutes, then gradually add flour until dough can be handled in a soft ball. Knead 8 – 10 minutes. Cover and let rise in warm place until doubled in size. Punch down and shape into loaves. Place in greased pan. Let rise until double in bulk. Bake in a preheated 400°F. (200°C) oven, 30 – 40 minutes, or until golden brown. *Yield:* three 9 × 5-in. (22.5 × 12.5 cm) loaves.

Halifax Bread

A young lady from Halifax sent me this recipe that had won her quite a few prizes at farm fairs — and rightly so — because it is a delicious and nourishing bread.

1 cup (250 mL) Grapenut cereal (whole oat flakes)
2 Shredded Wheat biscuits, crushed
2 tbsp. (30 mL) shortening
2 tsp. (10 mL) salt
3 cups (750 mL) boiling water
1 cup (250 mL) instant dry milk
1/3 cup (80 mL) molasses
¼ cup (60 mL) brown sugar
1 cup (250 mL) lukewarm water
1 tsp. (5 mL) sugar
1 tsp. (5 mL) ground ginger
2 envelopes active dry yeast
6 – 8 cups (1.5 – 2 L) all-purpose flour

Place in a large bowl the oat flakes, Shredded Wheat, shortening and salt. Pour the boiling water on top, and stir until shortening is melted. Let stand 20 minutes. Meanwhile pour on top the dry milk, molasses and brown sugar. Stir until well mixed just before adding the prepared yeast.

To the cup of lukewarm water, add the sugar and ginger. Mix well and add the active dry yeast. Let stand 10 minutes. Stir well and add to the cereal mixture. Mix thoroughly.

Add 3 cups (750 mL) of the flour, stir with wooden spoon or electric mixer until well mixed. Add more flour gradually until you have a soft ball of dough. [This dough is a bit unpredictable. Sometimes it may take 6 cups (1.5 L) of flour but at other times, as much as 9 cups (2.25 L) will be needed.]

Beat vigorously, and knead in the bowl with your hands. Cover and let rise in warm place until double in bulk. Shape, and place in greased pans. Bake in pre-heated 400°F. (200°C) oven, 40–60 minutes. *Yield:* three 9 × 5-in. (22.5 × 12.5 cm) loaves.

Potato Bread

An old-fashioned farm bread. Up to my generation all the Quebec farm women knew how to make this bread. It is very white with a creamy flavor. Do not use instant potatoes, as the texture, color and flavor are different — so make it if you have the patience to cook and use fresh potatoes.

2 medium potatoes, unpeeled
2 cups (500 mL) hot water
1¼ cup (325 mL) lukewarm potato water
1 tsp. (5 mL) sugar
1 tsp. (5 mL) ground ginger
1 envelope active dry yeast
2 cups (500 mL) rye or 3 cups (750 mL) whole-wheat flour
1 tsp. (5 mL) salt
¼ cup (60 mL) molasses
1 tsp. (5 mL) caraway seeds (optional)
2 cups (1.5–2 L) all-purpose flour

Cut the potatoes in four, put in a saucepan with the hot water, and bring to boil, and boil until tender. Measure out 1¼ cups (325 mL) of the potato water and let stand until lukewarm. Peel and mash the potatoes, and set aside. To the lukewarm water add the sugar and ground ginger and the yeast. Stir, and let stand 10 minutes. In a large bowl place the mashed potatoes, salt, molasses, caraway seeds and the yeast. Stir until well mixed. If there is any potato water remaining, add it to the mixture when all is thoroughly mixed. Add enough of the all-purpose flour, gradually, to have a soft dough.

Turn onto a floured board. Knead 10 minutes, adding flour if necessary, and place in a large bowl. Butter top of dough lightly. Let rise in a warm place until double in bulk, about 1½ hours. Punch down. Shape into 1 large or 2 medium round loaves; or if you prefer a less crusty bread, bake in a bread pan; the round one will go in a 9 × 9-in. (22.5 × 22.5 cm) casserole. Let rise again until double in bulk, about 35–40 minutes.

Bake in a preheated 375°F. (190°C) oven 40–45 minutes. In the last 10 minutes of the baking, brush top of bread with the following glaze: Bring to boil ¼ cup (60 mL) water. Mix 1 tsp. (5 mL) cornstarch with 1 tbsp. (15 mL) cold water. Add to boiling water, and stir over medium heat until thickened and clear. Unmold and cool bread on cake cooler. *Yield:* three 9 × 5 in. (22.5 × 12.5 cm) loaves.

Pumpkin Bread

Make into a beautiful twist, or bake in bread pans. A golden bread with a golden taste, perfect enjoyed with whipped butter and honey.

½ cup (125 mL) warm water
1 tsp. (5 mL) sugar
¼ tsp. (1 mL) ground ginger
2 packages active dry yeast
¾ cup (200 mL) warm water
½ cup (125 mL) brown sugar
1 cup (250 mL) all-purpose flour
½ cup (125 mL) powdered skim milk
½ cup (125 mL) soft butter
1 tsp. (5 mL) salt
1 tsp. (5 mL) cinnamon
1 cup (250 mL) cooked mashed pumpkin
3 cups (750 mL) all-purpose flour

Stir the 1 tsp. (5 mL) sugar and the ground ginger in the ½ cup (125 mL) warm water until dissolved. Add the yeast. Let stand 10 minutes. Stir well.

Place in a large bowl the ¾ cup (200 mL) warm water, brown sugar, the 1 cup (250 mL) flour, the powdered milk and the well-stirred yeast. Beat until well blended.

Add the butter, salt, cinnamon, mashed pumpkin and the 3 cups (750 mL) of flour. Beat until the dough comes away from the bowl. Turn onto a floured board, knead until smooth and elastic. Place in a greased bowl, oil the top of the dough, cover and let rise in a warm place until double in bulk. Punch down; knead for a few minutes. Divide the dough in half. Cover and let stand 10 minutes.

Roll the dough 1/3 in. (0.85 cm) thick and 6 in. (15 cm) wide. Fold in two lengthwise. Twist as tightly as possible. Place the twists in a round 8 in. (20 cm) mold. Brush the top with melted butter, generously enough for the butter to penetrate into the folds of the twist. Cover and let rise in a warm place until double in bulk. Twist the other half in the same manner.

Bake in a 350°F. (180°C) oven 45 minutes. Ten minutes before the end of the cooking, brush the top with evaporated milk or cream. It will give the bread a deep brown color. *Yield:* 2 loaves.

Tea Biscuit Master Mix

On the farm, we save time and money by making our own ready mixes. A quantity is prepared ahead of time, and stored in an airtight plastic container, ready to use in minutes with a minimum of dishes, in the same way you would do with a commercial mix. The advantage is the extra quality and much lower cost.

8 cups (2 L) sifted all-purpose flour
4 tbsp. (60 mL) baking powder
1½ tsp. (7 mL) salt
1 cup (250 mL) powdered skim milk
2 cups (500 mL) shortening

In a large bowl, combine the flour, baking powder, salt and skim milk powder. Using a pastry blender or two knives, cut in the shortening until the mixture is of fine cornmeal consistency. Store in an airtight container. *Yield:* 11 cups (2.75 L).

Family-Size Master Mix

This will give you 23 – 25 cups (about 6 L) of Master Mix. It will be easy for you to check the cost of your homemade mix with that of the commercial type.

5 lb. (2.5 kg) all-purpose flour
2 cups (500 mL) instant powdered milk
2/3 cup (160 mL) baking powder
3 tbsp. (50 mL) salt
2½ – 3 cups (625 – 750 mL) shortening

Place flour, powdered milk, baking powder and salt in a large bowl. Mix thoroughly and divide mixture equally into two large mixing bowls. Divide shortening in half and cut into each bowl, working with fingertips until mixture resembles cornmeal. Then mix the two together. Store in airtight container.

Note: The mix will not be as rich with 2½ cups (625 mL) of shortening, but if you are on a low-fat diet, the ½ cup (125 mL) less will be significant. Another factor is the milk required to make the different types of baking: whole milk or reconstituted dry milk can be used; or just plain water can be substituted for milk in all the recipes given for the basic mix, in order to lower the fat content. So, let it be your choice.

Hot Tea Biscuits (Master Mix)

2 cups (500 mL) Master Biscuit Mix
2/3 cup (160 mL) milk (liquid)

Stir the milk slowly into the Master Mix. Form dough into a ball and knead gently about 10 times on a floured board. Handle gently. Roll or press dough to ¾ in. (2 cm) thickness. Cut into rounds. Bake on an ungreased cookie sheet in a preheated 450°F. (230°C) oven, for 15 – 18 minutes or until golden brown. *Yield:* 6 – 8 biscuits.

Cheese Biscuits (Master Mix)

I sometimes make them with ½ cup (125 mL) of grated strong Cheddar, as the strong cheese gives much more flavor to the biscuits than the mild Cheddar, and I add ¼ cup (60 mL) Swiss cheese or mild Cheddar, cut into small cubes.

2 cups (500 mL) Master Mix
2/3 cup (160 mL) milk (liquid)
½ cup (125 mL) strong Cheddar, grated
¼ cup (60 mL) finely diced Swiss cheese or mild Cheddar
2 tbsp. (30 mL) parsley, chopped fine.

Stir the milk slowly into the Master Mix. Add the grated and cubed cheese and the parsley. Form dough into a ball; knead gently, about 10 times, on floured board. Roll or press dough to a ¾ in. (2 cm) thickness. Cut in rounds or squares. Sprinkle with paprika. Bake on ungreased baking sheet in a preheated 450°F. (230°C) oven 10 – 15 minutes, or until golden brown. *Yield:* 6 – 8 biscuits.

Dumplings (Master Mix)

There is an additional amount of baking powder in this one, to obtain light and airy dumplings.

2 cups (500 mL) Master Mix
½ tsp. (2 mL) baking powder
⅔ cup (160 mL) water

Mix baking powder in dry Master Mix. Then add water and mix together with a fork. Just enough to blend. It does not have to be extra smooth.

Moisten spoon in cold water, drop a spoonful of batter into hot stew, wet spoon again, and repeat until all the dumplings are dropped. Cook uncovered 10 minutes. Cover and cook 10 minutes more, and serve. *Yield:* 6 – 8 dumplings.

Caramel Nut Rolls

More breakfast or tea-time tasty buns that can be prepared with the Master Mix.

2 cups (500 mL) Master Mix
2 tsp. (10 mL) granulated dry yeast
2 tbsp. (30 mL) hot water
½ cup (125 mL) warm milk
2 tbsp. (30 mL) sugar
1 egg, lightly beaten
½ tsp. (2 mL) vanilla
2 tbsp. (30 mL) melted butter
1 tbsp. (15 mL) water
½ cup (125 mL) brown sugar
Walnuts, chopped

Soften the yeast in the water, and let stand 5 minutes. Heat milk, add sugar, 1 cup (250 mL) of the Master Mix, and beat thoroughly. Add well-stirred yeast, the egg and vanilla, and beat well. Add remaining Master Mix, gradually, until you have a stiff batter; then beat thoroughly until smooth. Cover and let rise in a warm place until risen and bubbly, about 1 – 1½ hours. When batter is light, stir down. Grease 12 muffin pans. Heat together the melted butter, water and brown sugar. Put a good spoonful of the syrup into each muffin pan. Place a few chopped walnuts in the syrup. Drop risen dough by spoonful into each of the pans. Let rise again, in a warm place, until double in size, about 30 – 45 minutes. Bake in a preheated 375°F. (190°C) oven, about 20 minutes or until golden brown.

To remove, place a piece of wax paper on the table, and top with a wire cake rack. Then invert pan on rack, and let cool. Any of the syrup that falls through can be picked up with a spatula and placed on rolls. *Yield:* about 12 rolls.

Homemade Biscuit Mix

Ready to be mixed and baked in minutes — and with no mess to clean up afterwards. You simply store it in a tightly covered container and keep it in a cool place.

8 cups (2 L) all-purpose flour
¼ cup (60 mL) baking powder
1 tbsp. (15 mL) salt
2 cups (500 mL) shortening
⅔ cup (160 mL) milk

Sift together into a large mixing bowl the flour, baking powder and salt. Cut in the shortening with a pastry blender or two knives until mixture resembles coarse meal. Pour into a container, cover and store.

To make the biscuits, lightly stir mix with a fork and measure 3 cups (750 mL) of it into a bowl. Make a well in the middle and add the milk all at once. Stir with a fork until dough follows fork. Gently knead into a ball and pat to ½ in. (1.25 cm) thickness, then cut with a 2 in. (5 cm) cutter. Place on an ungreased baking sheet and bake in a 450°F. (230°C) oven 10 – 16 minutes, or until browned. *Yield:* about 18 small biscuits.

Note: For a dropped biscuit, increase milk to 1 cup (250 mL), and drop by spoonfuls onto a baking sheet.

Old-Fashioned Biscuits

Soda, lard and sour milk make the difference between the old-fashioned biscuit and today's baking powder variety. I particularly like these for their distinctive flavor, lightness and texture.

2 cups (500 mL) all-purpose flour
½ tsp. (2 mL) baking soda
1 tsp. (5 mL) cream of tarter
½ tsp. (2 mL) salt
¼ cup (60 mL) lard
⅔ – 1 cup (160 – 250 mL) buttermilk or sour milk

Preheat the oven to 450°F. (230°C). Sift together the flour, soda, cream of tartar and salt. Cut in the lard lightly and quickly. Add the buttermilk or sour milk gradually, reserving 2 – 3 tbsp. (30 – 50 mL) until a soft dough is formed.

Turn onto a lightly-floured board and knead as gently as possible with the tips of your fingers, mixing in the remaining milk if needed. Pat into a shape

½ in. (1.25 cm) thick, then cut into 1½-in. (3.75 cm) rounds. Bake on an ungreased baking sheet 10–12 minutes. *Yield:* about 18 small biscuits.

Note: The amount of milk required depends on the brand of flour used.

Whipped Cream Biscuits

These rich, light, creamy-flavored biscuits are well suited to buffet suppers or dinners. The whipped cream replaces both the shortening and the moistening ingredients, so the cost is the same as for ordinary biscuits.

1½ cups (400 mL) all-purpose flour
3/4 tsp. (3 mL) salt
4 tsp. (15 mL) baking powder
1 cup (250 mL) rich cream, whipped

Preheat the oven to 400°F. (200°C). Mix the flour, salt and baking powder. Whip the cream and fold in the dry ingredients with a fork until a soft dough is formed. Turn onto a lightly-floured board and knead slightly. Roll out the dough to about a ½ in. (12.5 cm) thickness. Cut into 2 in. (5 cm) rounds, and place on an ungreased baking sheet. Bake for 10–12 minutes. Serve hot with unsalted butter, currant jelly, or honey. *Yield:* About 16 biscuits.

Yogurt Whole Wheat Hot Biscuits

This health food recipe makes delicious biscuits. Serve them hot with equal amounts of soft butter and honey mixed together.

1 3/4 cups (450 mL) whole wheat flour
4 tsp. (20 mL) baking powder
¼ cup (60 mL) instant milk powder
½ tsp. (2 mL) salt
1/3 cup (80 mL) peanut or safflower oil
¾ cup (200 mL) plain yogurt

Stir the flour, baking powder, milk and powder and salt in a bowl; add oil and cut in with two knives to bind it. Stir until it resembles coarse meal.

Make a hollow in the middle, pour in yogurt and mix quickly. Knead lightly 10–15 times, pat out to a 1 in. (2.5 cm) thickness, and cut with a biscuit cutter. Bake in a 450°F. (230°C) oven, 12–15 minutes. *Yield:* 8–12 biscuits.

Home-on-the-Range Hot Biscuits

This recipe was given to me in Winnipeg in 1968 by a 13-year-old who told me her mother made the "very best biscuits on the range." She sure was right. The honey butter was her favorite topping. At holiday time, they preferred the Cranberry Applesauce. Both are very good.

2 cups (500 mL) all-purpose flour
½ tsp. (2 mL) salt
3 tsp. (15 mL) baking powder
1 tsp. (5 mL) soda
½ tsp. (2 mL) cream of tartar
½ cup (125 mL) shortening
⅔ cup (160 mL) buttermilk

Sift together in a bowl the flour, salt, baking powder, soda and cream of tartar. Cut in the shortening. Stir the buttermilk in with a fork. Stir just enough to blend. Do not overmix.

Turn on lightly floured board and knead gently ½ minute. Pat to desired thickness. Cut with floured biscuit cutter.

Bake at 425°F. (225°C) for 10–12 minutes. *Yield:* 8–12 biscuits.

Honey Butter

Mix an equal quantity of soft butter and honey until creamy and smooth. (I have a weakness for Manitoba honey, she said; and how right she was!) Add the grated rind of 1 lemon. Pour into an attractive dish; keep refrigerated, covered. Will keep 4–6 weeks. Serve cold with the hot biscuits.

Cranberry Applesauce

Wash and cut in four 6–8 apples (do not core nor peel). Place in a saucepan with ½ cup (125 mL) water and 1½–2 cups (375–500 mL) cranberry jelly. Cover and simmer until tender. Pass through food mill or sieve. Serve cold with the hot biscuits.

Instant Muffins

They are known by many names: "Six-week Muffins," "Perpetual Muffins," "Ready-mix Muffins." Whatever the name, they are very good to eat, can be varied in many ways, and are constantly ready to pop into the oven. And who doesn't like a hot muffin with their coffee? These muffins are really light and tender.

6 cups (1.5 L) pure bran flakes
2 cups (500 mL) boiling water
1 cup (250 mL) shortening, melted
2 – 3 cups (500 mL – 750 mL) sugar
4 eggs, beaten
4 cups (1 L) buttermilk
5 cups (1.25 kg) flour
2 tbsp. (30 mL) baking soda
2 tsp. (10 mL) salt

Pour the boiling water over 2 cups (500 mL) of the bran. Let stand 10 minutes, then mix in the melted shortening. Stir together the rest of the bran, the sugar, the eggs and buttermilk.

Sift together the flour, soda and salt, and combine all the ingredients together. Pour into plastic containers. Cover and refrigerate until needed.

To bake, fill greased muffin pans and bake in a 400°F. (200°C) oven, 20 – 25 minutes. The mixture will keep 6 weeks refrigerated, and it will yield 6 dozen muffins.

Note: Do not use bran breakfast cereal, but use the unprocessed type of bran. Easy to find at health food or specialty shops.

Oatmeal Muffins

A 10-year-old girl made these for me when I was judging a honey contest in Winnipeg. They were so good that I asked her for the recipe. Serve them hot with whipped butter and Manitoba honey.

1½ cups (400 mL) sour milk or buttermilk
1 cup (250 mL) old-fashioned rolled oats
4 tbsp. (60 mL) melted butter
½ cup (125 mL) honey or light brown sugar
Pinch of mace
1 egg, beaten
1 cup (250 mL) all-purpose flour
1 tsp. (5 mL) baking powder
½ tsp. (2 mL) soda
¼ tsp. (1 mL) salt

Pour the milk over the oats and let stand 30 minutes (don't use instant or quick cooking oats — they make a tasteless muffin). Mix butter, honey or sugar, mace and egg in a bowl; then add oatmeal and mix again. Sift remaining ingredients together, add and stir just enough to blend — the less stirring, the better the muffins. Grease 1½ – 2 in. (3.75 – 5 cm) muffin cups, fill 2/3 full with batter and bake in a 400°F. (200°C) oven 12 – 15 minutes. *Yield:* 8 – 12 muffins.

Corn Bread

Corn bread has been a tradition in Canada ever since the Indians first turned their hand-pounded corn into cakes baked on hot stones. The early settlers refined the tradition and set up water mills to grind their corn into meal. The women turned the cornmeal into a variety of breads: hot bread, raised bread, quick bread, corn cake and — best of all — Johnny Cake. They were served hot with either butter and molasses or a mass of sausages and salted pickles. Today, in our modern kitchens, we can still bake corn bread with pleasure and serve it the old-fashioned way. And when the budget is tight, corn bread, plain or fancy, can provide good food and nourishment at low cost.

Sugaring June Corn Bread

This is a must after maple sugaring has started and there is plenty of fresh maple syrup available. It is wonderful served hot with freshly-boiled syrup poured on top. The bread toasts beautifully and keeps moist and fresh for 5 – 6 days.

½ cup (125 mL) cornmeal
2 cups (500 mL) Graham or whole wheat flour
1 tsp. (5 mL) soda
1 tsp. (5 mL) salt
3 tbsp. (50 mL) melted butter
½ cup (125 mL) maple syrup
2 cups (500 mL) buttermilk

Preheat the oven to 350°F. (180°C). Combine the cornmeal, flour, soda and salt. In another bowl, beat together the melted butter, maple syrup and buttermilk. Pour all at once over the dry ingredients and stir just enough to blend. Pour into a generously-buttered loaf pan, then bake 45 – 50 minutes. Cool 15 minutes on a cake rack before unmolding. *Serves 6 – 8.*

Golden Cornbread

Although this is at its best when steaming hot, it is also tasty and tender when cold. Serve it with marmalade into which a few spoonfuls of fresh orange juice and some grated orange peel have been beaten, with a few spoonfuls of butter.

- 3/4 cup (200 mL) sugar
- ½ cup (125 mL) vegetable oil
- 2 eggs, beaten
- 1 cup (250 mL) all-purpose flour
- 3 tsp. (15 mL) baking powder
- ¼ tsp. (1 mL) salt
- 1½ cups (400 mL) cornmeal
- 1 cup (250 mL) milk

Preheat the oven to 400°F. (200°C). Blend together the sugar and oil, then beat in the eggs. In another bowl, combine the flour, baking powder, salt and cornmeal. Add this gradually to the creamed mixture, alternately with the milk, stirring just enough to blend after each addition. Pour into a well-greased, floured 9 × 9-in. (22.5 × 22.5 cm) baking pan and bake 30–40 minutes. *Serves 6.*

Orange Bread

This requires a little more work than most quick breads, but it is well worth the effort.

- 3 oranges
- 1 cup (250 mL) fresh orange juice
- ½ cup (125 mL) sugar
- ¼ cup (60 mL) water
- 1 tbsp. (15 mL) butter
- 1 egg
- 2½ cups (625 mL) all-purpose flour
- 2 tsp. (10 mL) baking powder
- ½ tsp. (2 mL) soda
- ½ tsp. (2 mL) salt
- Grated peel of one orange
- 3 tbsp. (50 mL) sugar

Wash oranges, pare off orange peel with a sharp knife, then cut it into thin slivers with scissors. Squeeze juice to use later. Place sugar and water in a saucepan, add orange peel and simmer while stirring until sugar is dissolved. Continue to simmer 3 minutes without stirring, then measure. If there is not 2/3 cup (160 mL) of liquid, add more water. Pour into a bowl, add butter and orange juice. Beat until well mixed and add egg.

Sift together the flour, baking powder, soda and salt, then pour orange juice mixture on top. Stir just enough to moisten ingredients — the batter should be somewhat lumpy.

Pour into a greased and floured 9 × 5-in. (22.5 × 12.5 cm) loaf pan. Thoroughly blend orange peel and sugar, and sprinkle on top. Bake at 325°F. (160°C) for 1½ hours. *Yield:* 1 loaf.

Banana Bran Bread

Use those black, hopeless-looking bananas for this — the riper the better. The walnuts may be replaced by raisins and you can also substitute rum for the orange juice.

3/4 cup (200 mL) soft butter or margarine
1½ cups (400 mL) light brown sugar
3 eggs
2 cups (500 mL) whole or flaked bran
3 cups (750 mL) mashed ripe bananas
¼ cup (60 mL) fresh orange juice or dark rum
3 cups (750 mL) all-purpose flour
4 tsp. (20 mL) baking powder
1 tsp. (5 mL) salt
1 tsp. (5 mL) baking soda
1 cup (250 mL) chopped walnuts or raisins

Cream soft butter or margarine with sugar and eggs until light and fluffy, then stir in bran. Mix bananas with fruit juice or rum.

Sift together flour, baking powder, salt and soda. Add to creamed mixture, beating thoroughly by hand at each addition.

Fold in walnuts or raisins and pour into 3 greased and floured 9 × 5-in. (22.5 × 12.5 cm) pans. Bake at 350°F. (180°C) for 1 hour. *Yield:* 3 loaves.

Country Raisin Bread

The first year we bought the farm, I was asked to judge the Bread Contest at the nearby Brome Fair. This recipe was one of the winners and the woman offered me her recipe. It is surely good enough to be passed on.

1 cup (250 mL) firmly packed brown sugar
1 cup (250 mL) raisins
1 cup (250 mL) hot water
½ cup (125 mL) lard
2 eggs, lightly beaten
1 tsp. (5 mL) baking soda
1 tbsp. (15 mL) cold water
1½ cups (400 mL) flour
2 tsp. (10 mL) ground allspice
1 tsp. (5 mL) cinnamon
1 tsp. (5 mL) ground cardamom
¼ tsp. (1 mL) ground ginger
1 tsp. (5 mL) baking powder
½ tsp. (2 mL) salt

Place in a saucepan the brown sugar, raisins, hot water and lard. Bring to a boil over medium heat, stirring often; then boil gently for 5 minutes. Pour into a large mixing bowl and cool.

When mixture is cool, stir in the soda mixed with the cold water and the eggs. Sift together the remaining ingredients, and add to eggs and raisins mixture. Mix well.

Pour into a well-buttered and floured 9 × 5-in. (22.5 × 12.5 cm) loaf pan and bake in a preheated 325°F. (160°C) oven 1 hour, or until cake tester comes out clean. Let it cool in its pan, set on a cake rack. Unmold, cool completely, then wrap in foil and let stand 12 – 24 hours before serving. *Yield:* 1 loaf.

Tipsy Date Bread

Leftover coffee, a touch of rum, plus a bit of work equal a very special date bread that will remain fresh for 2 – 3 weeks. Freezes well too. Served hot, it has the flavor and feeling of plum pudding.

½ cup (125 mL) chopped walnuts
1 cup (250 mL) chopped dates
1½ tsp. (4 mL) baking soda
½ tsp. (2 mL) salt
1 tsp. (5 mL) coriander seeds (optional)
3 tbsp. (50 mL) butter
½ cup (125 mL) boiling coffee
¼ cup (60 mL) rum
2 eggs, lightly beaten
1 tsp. (5 mL) vanilla

½ cup (125 mL) brown sugar
½ cup (125 mL) white sugar
1½ cups (400 mL) all-purpose flour
Grated rind of 1 orange

Place nuts, dates, soda, salt, coriander seeds and butter in large bowl and pour boiling coffee and rum over the mixture. Mix thoroughly and let stand 20 minutes.

In a separate bowl, combine eggs, vanilla, and brown and white sugars. Then stir mixture into the dates, alternately with the flour and orange rind. Mix just enough to blend, being careful not to overmix. Pour into a well greased 9 × 5 × 2-inch. (22.5 × 12.5 × 5 cm) bread pan or two small pans. Bake in a preheated 350°F. (180°C) oven 1 hour, or until well done. Cool on rack. For a very special treat, pour 2 tbsp. of orange liqueur on top of bread as soon as out of the oven. *Yield:* 1 loaf.

Apple-Cheese Bread

Apple and sharp Cheddar combine to give a tangy-sweet flavor to this quick bread. I always keep a few loaves frozen for emergencies — 30 minutes in a 325°F. (160°C) oven will thaw them out.

½ cup (125 mL) shortening
⅔ cup (160 mL) sugar
2 eggs, beaten
1½ cups (400 mL) grated unpeeled apples
½ cup (125 mL) grated sharp Cheddar
¼ cup (60 mL) chopped walnuts
2 cups (500 mL) all-purpose flour
1½ tsp. (7 mL) baking powder
½ tsp. (2 mL) each soda and salt

Cream shortening with sugar, add eggs, and mix well. Blend in apples, cheese and nuts. Add sifted dry ingredients and mix lightly. Pour into a well-greased 9 × 5 in. (22.5 × 12.5 cm) loaf pan, and bake in a 350°F. (180°C) oven 50–60 minutes. *Yield:* 1 loaf.

Homemade Pancake Mix

Prepare this dry mix ahead of time and store it in a clean, well covered glass jar in your pantry. It will keep 2–3 months.

6 cups (1.5 L) all-purpose flour
4 tbsp. (60 mL) sugar
1 tbsp. (15 mL) salt
3 tbsp. (50 mL) baking powder
½ lb. (250 g) vegetable shortening

Sift the flour with the sugar, salt and baking powder. With 2 knives or a pastry blender, cut in shortening until mixture has the consistency of coarse cornmeal. Pour into a glass jar and cover.

To use, measure 1 cup (250 mL) of mix, beat in 1 egg and ⅔ cup (160 mL) — or a little more — of milk or water. Blend and cook per instructions. *Yield:* 6 – 8 small pancakes.

For Buckwheat Pancakes: Use the same recipe, replacing the all-purpose flour with 3 cups (750 mL) of all-purpose and 3 cups (750 mL) of buckwheat flour.

For Buttermilk Pancakes: Use same recipe and, when ready to cook, add ½ tsp. (2 mL) of soda to 1 cup (250 mL) of mix. Add 1 egg and replace milk with ⅔ cup (160 mL) of buttermilk.

Quebec Pancakes

These traditional Quebec pancakes have little in common with ordinary pancakes. They are crisp and crunchy, with a sort of lacy appearance. They cook fast in a thick layer of hot fat and should be served as soon as ready, which to us means someone has to stand at the stove while the others enjoy. They are served with maple syrup or molasses as they are unsweetened.

2 eggs
1 cup (250 mL) flour
½ tsp. (5 mL) baking powder
Pinch of salt
½ – ¾ cup (125 – 180 mL) water

Beat the eggs until foamy. Sift together the flour, baking powder and salt. Add gradually to the eggs while stirring. Then add the water gradually while stirring constantly until mixture is smooth and running.

Melt fat in a frying pan to cover bottom ¼ in. (0.625 cm) deep; pour in a few spoonfuls of the batter and cook until crisp and brown. Serve immediately. *Yield:* 6 – 9 pancakes.

Note: The fat used for cooking pancakes should be either lard or vegetable shortening.

Bacon and Egg Pancake

In Quebec French cuisine, the bacon is replaced by thin slices of fat salt pork fried golden brown. We call it *Crêpe au lard.* The secret of success in this pancake is to remove none of the fat, even if it seems a lot.

6 eggs
½ lb. (250 mL) bacon
1 cup (250 mL) milk or light cream
3 tbsp. (50 mL) flour
½ tsp. (2 mL) salt
3 tbsp. (50 mL) chives or parsley, minced

Fry the bacon in a heavy metal frying pan until crisp and brown. Remove bacon, set aside in a warm place. Keep all fat in the pan. Beat the eggs with the milk or cream, flour, salt and chives. Pour into the hot bacon fat and cook same as a large pancake, about 8 minutes on each side over medium heat, turning only once. Place on a warm platter and top with the bacon left whole or crumbled into coarse pieces. *Yield:* 6 – 8 pancakes.

Blueberry Pancakes

A light, fluffy pancake with an interesting flavor. Any small berries can replace the blueberries; but if using frozen berries, thaw them out, and drain thoroughly. The juice, slightly thickened, can be used as a sauce.

1 cup (250 mL) all-purpose flour
1 tbsp. (15 mL) baking powder
¼ tsp. (1 mL) salt
1 tbsp. (15 mL) sugar
1 egg
1 cup (250 mL) milk
¼ cup (60 mL) commercial sour cream
2 tbsp. (30 mL) melted butter
½ cup (125 mL) blueberries

Sift the flour with baking powder, salt and sugar. Beat egg with milk and sour cream. Pour milk mixture over dry ingredients and blend with a rotary beater until batter is just smooth. Stir in butter and fold in blueberries.

The double loaf baked in an earthenware mold, the sweet braided bread, the knotted brioche to be served at tea time with whipped butter, dainty rolls for dinner. How can you resist homemade breads?

CBC
Japanese One-pot Cookery

Use 2 tbsp. (30 mL) of batter for each pancake and cook as directed. *Yield:* about 12 pancakes.

Pumpkin Pancakes

In Jamaica, where the allspice trees grow in profusion, they serve these allspice-flavored pancakes with a thick syrup of currants and raspberries.

1 cup (250 mL) **Pumpkin Purée**
½ cup (125 mL) all-purpose flour
½ tsp. (2 mL) baking powder
½ tsp. (2 mL) allspice
1 egg, beaten

Beat all ingredients together until smooth. Heat a griddle or frying pan until hot, grease well and drop pancake batter on to it by spoonfuls. Cook on one side, until it bubbles, turn, cook on the other, then sprinkle with icing sugar and serve — or omit sugar and serve with syrup. *Yield:* 8 – 10 pancakes.

Water Pizza Dough

It seems to me that in the Sixties, the pizza became as much part of Canadian lives as the Chinese food we'd already learned to love. You often wonder, why the fuss? Well, to master your pizza crust, use either this one, which is the favorite in the south of Italy; or the Brioche type favored in northern Italy; or make it the Canadian way with a milk base dough. The three are all well worth the effort, but the Brioche type is the "super" one.

As the topping is the triumph of a pizza, don't stick to a recipe, but use your imagination — and don't be stingy with the olive oil or the herbs.

I sometimes make little pizzas, each of them no bigger than a cooky — brush them with olive oil, sprinkle generously with Parmesan, top with a slice of Swiss cheese or mild Cheddar and a sprinkling of fresh dill or a sprig of fresh basil — to be served hot with a cool green salad or ***Vegetables à la Grecque.***

Simple, easy, and economical; just make sure that the water you use is the right temperature, and that you're lighthanded with the flour.

A Victoria Day brunch I sometimes serve: Cheese Petits Pots, Capitaine à la Campagne, and Bacon Ragoût Omelette. How very Victorian!

1 tsp. (5 mL) sugar
½ cup (125 mL) tepid water
1 envelope active dry yeast
¾ cup (200 mL) lukewarm water
5 tbsp. (75 mL) vegetable oil
1 tsp. (5 mL) salt
3 – 4 cups (750 – 1000 mL) all-purpose flour
1 egg
2 tbsp. (30 mL) cold water

Stir the sugar into the tepid water until it's dissolved. Add the yeast, and let stand 10 minutes, or until foamy. Warm a bowl with hot tap water and in it mix the lukewarm water, 2 tbsp. (30 mL) of the oil and the salt.

Stir yeast and add to mixture. Stir well, then start adding flour by the ½ cup (125 mL), beating hard at each addition, until you have a soft dough that can be kneaded. Turn on to a well-floured board and knead 5 minutes, or until it hardly sticks to the hands. Cover with a cloth and let rise in a warm place until double in bulk, about 1½ – 2 hours.

Punch down with your fists and divide into 2 or 4 balls. Place on lightly floured board, cover with a cloth and let stand 15 minutes. Using your fingers, flatten the 4 balls so each will cover an 8 – 9 in. (20 – 22.5 cm) pizza pie plate, or the 2 balls so they'll each cover a 12 in. (30 cm) plate. Cover again and let rest 15 minutes.

Flatten the centers, pushing toward the rims so they'll be raised to contain the filling. Beat egg with cold water, brush over each pizza, then brush with remaining oil. They're now ready for your choice of filling. When garnished, bake in a 400°F. (200°C) oven about 25 minutes, or until pizza is golden. *Yield:* two 12-in. (30 cm) or 2 8 – 9 in. (20 – 22.5 cm) pizzas.

Brioche Pizza Dough

This is a rich, light pizza dough for special occasions. It's especially good for piccolina, the very mini pizza made for cocktail parties or served as a luncheon entrée.

1 tsp. (5 mL) sugar
½ cup (125 mL) lukewarm water
2 envelopes active dry yeast
1 cup (250 mL) scalded milk, cooled to lukewarm
1 tsp. (5 mL) salt
¼ cup (60 mL) sugar
5 eggs
4 – 5 cups (1 – 1.25 L) all-purpose flour

½ cup (125 mL) melted butter
2 tbsp. (30 mL) cold water
3 tbsp. (50 mL) vegetable oil

Stir the 1 tsp. (5 mL) of sugar into the lukewarm water until it's dissolved. Add yeast and let rest 10 minutes, or until foamy. Stir together lukewarm scalded milk, salt and the ¼ cup (60 mL) of sugar. Beat 4 of the eggs and add while stirring. Stir yeast and add to mixture.

Add 2 cups (500 mL) of the flour and beat until mixture is smooth (a wire whisk or mixer's dough hook are perfect for this). Beat in melted butter until the mixture is very smooth. Add remaining flour gradually until dough is smooth and thick, then cover with a cloth and let rise 15 minutes.

Turn dough onto a floured board. Flour your hands and keep them floured all the time you're working the dough. Knead until dough is satiny, elastic and smooth, about 15 – 20 minutes. Cover, set in a warm place and let rise until double in bulk, about 1 – 2 hours.

Punch down, then proceed as for **Pizza Water Dough**, or as follows for "piccolina" pizza: pinch off small balls of dough about 2 in. (5 cm) in diameter and place 4 in. (10 cm) from each other on a greased baking sheet. (The smaller the balls, the smaller the pizza. What is important is to give them plenty of room to expand during the baking.)

Cover baking sheet and let dough rise 15 minutes. Then, using your fingers, flatten balls to a ¼ in. (0.625 cm) thickness. Cover and let rise another 15 minutes. Follow Water Dough instructions for flattening and brushing with egg, water and oil; and for baking. *Yield:* four 8 – 9 in. (20 – 22.5 cm) or two 12 in. (30 cm) pizzas.

Canadian Pizza Dough

Using shortening instead of oil gives a quite different texture to this dough.

¾ cup (200 mL) scalded milk
¼ cup (60 mL) sugar
2 tsp. (30 mL) salt
5 tbsp. (75 mL) shortening
1 tsp. (5 mL) sugar
½ cup (125 mL) lukewarm water
1 envelope active dry yeast
3 – 4 cups (750 mL – 1 L) all-purpose flour

Pour the scalded milk into a large bowl and add the ¼ cup (60 mL) of sugar, the salt and the shortening. Stir until shortening is soft and sugar almost dissolved. Stir the 1 tsp. (5 mL) of sugar in lukewarm water until dissolved, add yeast and let stand 10 minutes, or until foamy. Stir well, then stir into milk until mixed.

Add 2 cups (500 mL) of the flour, beating hard until smooth and creamy. Gradually add remaining flour, beating and mixing until you have a soft dough. Turn onto a floured board and knead 5 minutes, or until smooth and elastic.

Place dough in an oiled bowl, cover with a cloth and let rise in a warm place until doubled. Punch down; then prepare, shape, fill and bake as for the Pizza Water Dough. *Yield:* four 8 – 9 in. (20 – 22.5 cm) or two 12 in. (30 cm) pizzas.

Freezing Pizza Dough

When you divide the risen dough, roll it into 8 or 12 in. (20 – 30 cm) circles. Place one on a well-oiled plate; then add others, placing a double thickness of wax paper between each. Wrap the whole bundle and freeze for up to freeze for up to 2 months at 32°F. (0°C).

To use one or a few at a time, just remove the paper between each one, and they'll lift right up. Let stand in a warm place until dough is soft — about 30 minutes — then fill and bake.

6. Cereals, Rice, Pasta and Legumes

Granola

So many requests for recipes for "granola" have come to me, by mail and telephone — around 600 of them — that I felt I must write about a few of my favorites, so you can have your choice.

Honey Granola

Whenever possible, I like to prepare this one with fresh grated coconut.

- 1 cup (250 mL) chopped almonds or walnuts
- 1 cup (250 mL) unsweetened grated coconut
- ½ cup (125 mL) wheat germ
- 3 cups (750 mL) rolled oats
- ½ cup (125 mL) honey

Mix together nuts, coconut and wheat germ. Spread on a baking sheet and toast 6–9 minutes in a 350°F. (180°C) oven, stirring three to four times. (It must toast but not burn.) On another baking sheet, toast the rolled oats, 10–12 minutes.

Heat the honey by setting its container in a pan of hot water. Mix all the toasted ingredients in a large bowl, add the honey and mix thoroughly. Spread on a baking sheet and place in the 350°F. (180°C) oven 10–12 minutes or until light golden brown, again stirring 3 or 4 times. Let cool, break apart and store in a tightly closed container in a cool place. *Yield:* about 5 cups (1.25 L).

Flaked Granola

If you don't like chewy cereal, this one, made entirely with flakes, is much softer. Eat it like ordinary cereal with milk and cream or, as my husband and I often do, raw as snack food, along with a cool apple. This is also a good natural laxative.

5 cups (1.25 L) oat flakes
1 cup (250 mL) hulled sunflower seeds, chopped
½ cup (125 mL) sesame seeds
½ cup (125 mL) corn or safflower oil
½ cup (125 mL) honey
5 cups (1.25 L) wheat flakes
2 cups (500 mL) raisins

Mix together the oat flakes, seeds, oil and honey. Spread thinly on a baking sheet and toast in a 375°F. (190°C) oven 3 – 5 minutes, or until light brown. Watch carefully as the flakes brown very quickly.

Remove from oven, pour over wheat flakes and raisins in a large bowl and mix thoroughly. Let cool and keep in covered container in a cool place. *Yield:* about 14 cups (3.5 L).

Maple Syrup Granola

An equal quantity of honey can replace the maple syrup, but this version remains my favorite.

2 cups (500 mL) rolled oats or wheat flakes
  or 1 cup (250 mL) of each
1 cup (250 mL) coarsely chopped almonds or walnuts
⅓ cup (80 mL) peanut oil
¼ cup (60 mL) maple syrup
½ tsp. (2 mL) vanilla
¼ tsp. (1 mL) salt

Mix all ingredients together. Spread thinly on a baking sheet and toast in a 325°F. (160°C) oven 20 – 25 minutes, or until a light golden color. Let cool, break up, then store in a tightly closed container in a cool place. *Yield:* 3 cups (750 mL).

Whole Grain Mix

All the ingredients can be purchased at health food or "ethnic" food shops, or even in some supermarkets. I keep a large container of this mixture handy to serve whenever I wish.

4 cups (1 L) whole grain wheat
4 cups (1 L) whole grain buckwheat
4 cups (1 L) whole grain rye
4 cups (1 L) whole grain oats
2 cups (500 mL) whole grain barley

Mix thoroughly, and store in a tightly covered container and keep in a cool place.

In some parts of Russia, they dry roast this mix for a nuttier flavor. Spread mix on baking sheet, place in a 350°F. (180°C) oven and toast until nutty brown — about 15 minutes — stirring once or twice. Cool and store. Do just enough at a time to cover the bottom of the baking sheet. *Yield:* 18 cups (4.25 L).

Kruska

This is fantastic, both in taste and nutrition — and so easy to prepare.

2 cups (500 mL) Whole Grain Mix
1 cup (250 mL) raisins or prunes

Bring 6 cups (1.5 L) of water to a fast rolling boil, add the grain mix and raisins; then bring back to a rolling boil, stirring constantly. Remove from heat, cover and let stand overnight on the kitchen counter. In the morning, it is ready to eat, reheated and sprinkled with raw sugar or honey to taste. Once cooked, keep leftovers refrigerated. *Serves 6.*

My Favorite Cereal

This one isn't economical, but it's worth the money.

2 cups (500 mL) rolled oats
2 cups (500 mL) wheat germ
1 cup (250 mL) unblanched almonds
1 cup (250 mL) unsalted cashews
1 cup (250 mL) hulled sunflower seeds
½ tsp. (2 mL) sea salt
1 cup (250 mL) buckwheat or unpasteurized honey
⅔ cup (160 mL) water
1 tsp. (5 mL) vanilla extract
⅔ cup (160 mL) peanut or safflower oil

Combine oats, wheat germ, nuts, seeds and salt. Thoroughly combine remaining ingredients in a separate bowl, then pour over dry ingredients and mix well. Spread on a baking sheet and place in a 350°F. (180°C) oven 15 minutes. Stir thoroughly and bake 15 minutes longer. Let cool, store in a tightly covered container and refrigerate. *Yield:* 9 cups (1.75 L).

Toasted Oatmeal

An old-fashioned Scottish trick to help those who don't like oatmeal enjoy it.

- 1 tbsp. (15 mL) peanut oil or butter
- 2 cups (500 mL) rolled oats or oat flakes
- 4 cups (1 L) boiling water
- ¼ tsp. (1 mL) salt

Heat the oil in a cast-iron frying pan over medium heat. Add oats and stir until they're lightly browned all over. Pour into a saucepan, add the boiling water and the salt, and simmer 30 minutes, stirring often. Top each serving with a large spoonful of raisins if you wish. *Serves 4 – 6.*

Wild Rice

In my youth, wild rice could not be bought anywhere. If we had some, it had to be a "gift" from our Indian friends. My paternal grandfather lived near Caughnawaga and loved fishing. He used to go to the rapids of the Lachine Canal where all the Indians used to fish, standing up in their canoes. That was one feat my grandfather could never accomplish — he caught his fish sitting down. I witnessed many an exciting moment, sitting on the shore, thinking of how good the fish would be. Before we left, our Indian friends always gave us a bag of wild rice. It is also known as Indian rice or "Water Oats," but it is not a rice despite its name. Ordinary rice is cultivated, but wild rice is a grass-like perennial. It grows along the edges of lakes and ponds in many spots through the north central portion of North America, and also in similar habitats in Northern Asia. It is very attractive with stems up to nine feet tall. As they go though their seasonal growth, they produce large terminal panicles (loose clusters) resembling hairy candelabra, hung with the seeds, which are what we know as wild rice.

The harvesting is done mostly by Indians in the ancestral way, by paddling through the marshes in a canoe, bending the grass over the boat, and beating the kernels into it.

All of this explains partly why the price is always a bit of a shock, as is all food that is hand picked. Its redeeming feature is that it swells to twice its quantity when cooked, and it is a terrific mixer. As a matter of fact, there is such a prepared mix on the market, which of course, reduces the price of the true wild rice, but a still more economical way is to mix a cup of wild rice with an equal amount of, for example, a double quantity of brown rice which has a somewhat wild flavor and a chewy consistency that resembles wild rice. Or you can use converted or long grain rice for a lighter mixture.

Because wild rice is quite special, serve it as a main dish for lunch or as a vegetable for an elegant dinner. A friend of mine has tremendous success serving it "popped" with drinks before dinner. The first time I tasted the crunchy, crispy little bits, I did not know what they were, but we all found them so terrific that everyone wanted to know. So, now she does it in front of guests in one of those attractive electric fryers — half filled with peanut oil — setting the pan at 375°F. (190°C). The fryer is placed on a large wooden tray — the wild rice in a lovely colorful straw basket with a silver soup spoon in it. On the other side, a long dark brown ceramic plate lined with attractive paper napkins. Guests have only to follow suit, by gently putting a couple of spoonfuls into the hot fat — and cooking it until it pops, about 1 – 2 minutes. Then, drain it on paper towels. My friend has small copper Japanese strainers to draw the rice out of the fat. And her guests are treated to quite elegant "popped wild rice" before dinner.

Basic Boiled Wild Rice

Use approximately 1 cup (250 mL) for 4 servings. For more servings, combine the cooked wild rice with the **Basic Boiled Brown Rice.**

¾ – 1 cup (200 – 250 mL) wild rice
3 cups (750 mL) cold water
1 tsp. (5 mL) coarse salt

Combine the wild rice, water and salt in a large saucepan, bring to a fast rolling boil over high heat, stirring once or twice. Then cover and simmer over medium low heat 45 minutes or until rice is tender. Drain, if necessary, but reserve the water to add to gravy of any type. *Serves 4.*

Steamed Wild Rice

I learned this method of cooking wild rice from a Western friend many years ago. She contended that it was the only proper way. I wondered then, but I agree now that it is surely one of the best.

Place 1 cup (250 mL) wild rice in a strainer, let cold water from the tap run over it until water is clear.

Then set the strainer into a deep saucepan. Pour rapidly boiling water on top, enough to completely cover the rice. Leave on kitchen counter. Cover the pan, and let stand 20 minutes. Lift out the strainer, and pour out the water. Put the strainer back in the saucepan and cover again with rapidly boiling water, and let stand until steam ceases to rise from the rice, about 10 – 15 minutes. Repeat this twice, which makes 4 times altogether.

If you do not find the rice tender to your taste, repeat once more. When wild rice is to be used in a salad, this is the only way to cook it.

My Own Wild Rice Chasseur

A take-off on my Mother's way, quicker and also very nice, served with all birds, game or smoked turkey.

1½ – 2 cups (400 – 500 mL) wild rice, cooked
2 tbsp. (30 mL) brandy
1 tbsp. (15 mL) curry
3 – 5 tbsp. (50 – 75 mL) chutney
¼ cup (60 mL) butter
Salt and pepper to taste

Mix together the brandy and curry in a cup, and add the chutney.

Warm the rice in a double boiler, if necessary; and 5 – 10 minutes before serving, add the brandy mixture. Add salt and pepper to taste, stir in the butter with a fork until melted, and serve. *Serves 4 – 6.*

Basic Boiled Brown Rice

There are many ways to cook brown rice. This way is perfect when it is to be mixed with wild rice, as the browning gives it the nutty taste of wild rice. When possible use sesame oil.

1 cup (250 mL) brown rice
2 tbsp. (30 mL) sesame or peanut oil
4 cups (1 L) cold water
1 tsp. (5 mL) coarse salt

Heat the oil in a saucepan, add the rice and stir over low heat until the rice is light brown and makes a popping sound. Slowly add the water, add the salt, and bring to a fast rolling boil. Cover, simmer over low heat 40–45 minutes, or until all the water is absorbed. Mix with the cooked wild rice and use in the recipe of your choice calling for wild rice. *Serves 4.*

Armenian Rice and Noodle Pilaf

This Armenian staple is made with rice and fine noodles, and is simple and different.

4 tbsp. (60 mL) butter or margarine
½ cup (125 mL) fine noodles
1 cup (250 mL) long grain or parboiled rice
2 cups (500 mL) hot water or chicken broth
1 tsp. (5 mL) salt

Melt the butter or margarine in a heavy metal saucepan, add the noodles, and stir over medium heat until they're golden brown. Add rice and stir constantly for 2 minutes; then add hot water or broth, and salt. Bring to a fast, rolling boil, cover and cook 10–14 minutes over low heat, or until rice is cooked and liquid evaporated. Serve immediately. *Serves 4.*

Barley Pilaf

Whenever I cook game, such as venison or Cornish hens, I make sure to serve it with a pilaf of barley. I have yet to meet the person who does not like it.

1¾ cups (450 mL) pot barley
4 tbsp. (60 mL) butter
2 onions, minced
½ lb. (125 mL) mushrooms, chopped
4 cups (1 L) consommé
½ tsp. (2 mL) salt

Melt 2 tbsp. (30 mL) of the butter in a large frying pan. Add the onions and mushrooms, and stir over high heat until lightly browned, stirring most of the time.

Remove from the fat and drain them as much as possible. Melt the other 2 tbsp. (30 mL) butter in the same pan. Add the barley and stir over medium heat, until a nutty brown color. Add the onions and mushrooms. Pour the mixture into a casserole and add the consommé and the salt. Cover and bake 45 – 55 minutes in a 350°F. (180°C) oven. If necessary, add a little hot water during the cooking period.

For a main dish, brown chicken wings or legs in butter and then bury them in the barley. Add an extra cup (250 mL) of consommé or water. Bake in the same manner. *Serves 6 – 8.*

Monique's Fifteen-Year-Old Pasta

She gives all kinds of funny names to her creations. It is true she has made this one for many years, and I still enjoy it whenever she serves it to me.

8 oz. (227 g) elbow or other macaroni
1 tbsp. (15 mL) vegetable oil
2 cups (500 mL) canned tomatoes
1 tsp. (5 mL) basil
1 cup (250 mL) milk
2 eggs, beaten
2 cups (500 mL) *strong* Cheddar cheese, diced
Salt, pepper to taste
Paprika

Cook the macaroni following directions on the package. Drain and toss with the vegetable oil. Place macaroni in a baking dish. Pour the tomatoes and basil on top, and add salt and pepper to taste; mix well. Stir in the cheese.

Beat together the eggs and the milk, and pour over the macaroni, but do not mix. Bake, uncovered in a 350°F. (180°C) oven, 40 – 50 minutes. You will then have a cheesy tomato macaroni in a custard. Yummy! *Serves 4 – 6.*

Monique's Meatless Lasagne

My daughter's large recipe to serve 10 people can be made in two casseroles if you wish to freeze one for emergency use — and it also can have meat in it if you like.

20 cups (5 L) water
1 tbsp. (15 mL) each salt and vegetable oil
1 lb. (500 mL) lasagne noodles
2 lb. (1000 mL) cottage cheese
1 cup (250 mL) commercial sour cream
2 eggs

½ tsp. (2 mL) each pepper and oregano
1 lb. (500 mL) Mozzarella cheese, thinly sliced
3 tbsp. (50 mL) vegetable oil
2 large onions, finely chopped
¼ cup (60 mL) finely chopped celery
28 oz. (796 mL) can tomatoes
2 cans tomato paste, 6 oz. (160 mL) each
¼ tsp. (1 mL) pepper
1 tsp. (5 mL) basil
2 tsp. (10 mL) sugar
2 cans chopped mushrooms, and/or
1½ lb. (750 g) ground beef

Bring water to a boil in a soup kettle, add salt and tbsp. of the oil. Put lasagne noodles in one by one, and boil 10 – 15 minutes, or until tender. When done, pour cold water into pot until noodles are cold enough to be handled, but don't drain them. While lasagne cooks and cools, prepare the following: Mix cottage cheese, sour cream, eggs, pepper and oregano with salt to taste. Butter a large oblong baking dish, or two 8 × 8 in. (20 cm × 20 cm) dishes. Set out sliced Mozzarella.

Heat 2 tbsp. (30 mL) of oil in a large frying pan and stir-fry onions and celery until lightly browned. Strain tomatoes to remove seeds, pressing down the pulp. Add to onions with tomato paste and seasonings, and boil 10 minutes.

If using mushrooms, heat remaining 1 tbsp. (15 mL) of oil, add drained mushrooms and stir until hot. If using ground beef, brown and add to sauce, with mushrooms or without; then taste for seasoning. Place a layer of noodles in long strips to cover the bottom of casserole(s). Next, place a layer of creamed cheese mixture, then slices of Mozzarella, then sauce. Repeat layers until dish is filled, ending up with noodles, sauce and a topping of sliced cheese.

Whatever the size of the dish, bake uncovered in a 325°F. (160°C) oven for 1½ hours. (Or, if you wish, cover and refrigerate, or freeze without baking. To serve, bake at 350°F. (180°C) for 1½ hours. *Serves 10.*

My Favorite Tomato Sauce

Not only the very best, but the simplest, of all tomato sauces. Try it for a surprise, especially when made with fresh summer tomatoes.

2 – 3 large, ripe unpeeled tomatoes, cut into chunks
1 tbsp. (15 mL) butter or olive oil
1 tsp. (5 mL) sugar

Place the tomatoes in an enamelled cast-iron casserole and cook uncovered (without any fat or liquid) over high heat, stirring occasionally, until they have the texture of a thick pulp, about 15 – 20 minutes. When thick, remove from heat and stir in butter or olive oil and sugar until smooth and sort of creamy. Serve over pasta of your choice. *Serves 2.*

Elbow Macaroni in Eggplant Sauce

The time to make this sauce is from June to September, when eggplant and green peppers are readily available.

1 medium eggplant, peeled and diced
2 tbsp. (30 mL) bacon fat
1 garlic clove, chopped
1 green pepper, chopped
½ tsp. (2 mL) basil
1 19 oz. (540 mL) can tomatoes
1 tsp. (5 mL) salt
¼ tsp. (1 mL) pepper
2 cups (500 mL) elbow macaroni, cooked

Soak the eggplant in cold water for 10 minutes and drain well. Heat fat, add garlic, green pepper and basil, and cook over low heat until vegetables are tender. Add tomatoes, salt, pepper and eggplant, and simmer uncovered over medium heat 1 hour.

Mix with hot pasta and serve with a bowl of grated cheese of your choice. *Serves 4 – 5.*

Succeeding with Dried Beans

It's odd, but for years many people have considered the bean too heavy a food, and one to be served only if you could afford nothing else. Suddenly dried beans are starting to occupy an honored place in the world's food basket. There is much to be said for these succulent little beans, be they kidney, Garbanzo, chick-pea, lima, chili, lentils — to mention only a few. Most of us usually limit our bean cookery to baked beans or pea bean soup and, at that, use mostly the warmed-up canned type. But there is much more than that to beans. They can run the gamut from good sturdy economical family fare to elegant soups, salads and casseroles.

Water: All beans should be soaked before cooking to make up part of the water that has been lost in drying. The proportion is 3 cups (750 mL) of water for each 1 cup (250 mL) of beans. Never throw away the soaking water — use it for cooking the beans. I use my grandmother's way to reduce soaking time: Add the beans to the water, bring to a full rolling boil, and boil 2 – 3 minutes (no more). Remove pan from heat, cover and let them soak 1 – 2 hours. The beans are then ready to cook.

(Split green or yellow peas, lentils, and black-eyed peas are the exception to the rule; they should *not* be soaked.)

Salt: 1 tsp. (5 ml) of salt for each 1 cup (250 mL) of uncooked beans is about right — but when salt pork, bacon or ham is to be added, reduce salt by 1 tsp. (5 mL) per 1 lb. (500 g) of meat. Never stir in the salt before the beans are a third or half cooked, because salt prevents the beans from softening. Often I salt them just before serving them.

Cooking: For any type of beans, the rule is to cook them *slowly*. Keep them simmering; after the first half of the cooking, stir them as little as possible and very gently. Tomatoes — fresh, canned or paste — should be added only at the halfway point because, like salt, they delay the softening of the beans. To prevent heavy foaming, add 1 tbsp. (15 mL) of butter or oil for each cup (250 mL) of beans.

Serving: 1 lb. (500 g) of beans gives 8 – 9 servings of about ¾ cup (200 mL) each.

Storing: Dry beans of any type are best kept in a well-covered glass jar or plastic container, stored in a cool place. When cooked, keep covered in the refrigerator. Beans freeze very successfully, but thaw them out for a few hours before reheating.

If a bean dish looks a bit dry when cooked, add some liquid of your choice — water will do. Always use a hot liquid, even if the beans are cold, and add only ¼ – ½ a cup (60 – 125 mL) at a time.

Lentils as a Vegetable Sidedish

Lentils originated in Central Asia, and, like all legumes, they are rich in thiamin and riboflavin, two very valuable Vitamin Bs. Never soak the split or small lentils.

2 cups (500 mL) green lentils
1 onion, left whole
2 whole cloves

1 carrot, cut in four
1 garlic clove, minced
½ tsp. (2 mL) each savory and basil
Salt and pepper to taste

Place the lentils in a sauce pan, cover with cold water, and bring slowly to a boil. When boiling, remove scum. Add remaining ingredients, cover and simmer until tender, about 1 – 1½ hours. Drain if necessary. To serve, add butter and lemon juice to taste. *Serves 8.*

Moors and Christians

A classic of South American kitchens. The "Christians" are the white rice and the "Moors," the black beans. I have often served this as a luncheon dish or with roasted wild birds for dinner.

1½ cups (400 mL) black beans
1 cup (250 mL) long grain rice
4 slices side bacon, finely chopped then fried
1 garlic clove, crushed
1 large onion, finely chopped
½ – 1 tsp. (2 – 5 mL) chili powder
Salt and pepper, to taste
1 cup (250 mL) beef consommé
2 tbsp. (30 mL) chutney

Soak beans overnight in 6 cups (1.5 L) cold water. In the morning, bring to a boil, then cover and simmer 1 – 1½ hours, or until just tender. Drain. Cook the rice and set aside.

Add remaining ingredients to beans, stir until well mixed, then simmer uncovered until beans start to "break up" a little, to make a thick sauce. A few can be mashed if necessary, to obtain a creamy texture.

When ready to serve, heat the rice, salt to taste, and stir in 1 tbsp. (15 mL) of butter. Make a nest of it in a serving dish, and pour the black bean sauce in the middle. *Serves 8.*

Maple Syrup Beans

A very, very old recipe that came from my great-grandmother. When my granddaughter Susan makes them, it becomes a sixth generation recipe. And "yummy" they still are!

I have never seen a recipe for beans with apples in any book, nor heard about it from anyone. At my parents' home, and in my home, we used the big yellow beans, twice the size of the navy beans, and pale yellow in color. They are not easy to find. When you do, buy lots. But navy beans can also be used.

- 4 cups (1 L) dried navy beans, precooked
- 1 lb. (500 g) lean and fat salt pork
- 1 large onion, peeled, left whole
- 1 tsp. (5 mL) dry mustard
- 1 cup (250 mL) maple syrup
- 1 tbsp. (15 mL) coarse salt
- 4 unpeeled apples, cored
- 1 cup (250 mL) brown sugar
- ½ cup (125 mL) butter
- ½ cup (125 mL) rum

Note: How to Precook the Beans:

In our family we never soaked beans overnight — here is the quick method we always used.

Pick over 1 lb. (500 mL) beans, and wash thoroughly in cold water. Place in a saucepan and add 8 cups (2 L) rapidly boiling water and 1 tbsp. (15 mL) molasses. Cover and let stand 1 hour. Uncover, then bring to a rapid boil in the same water. Cover, and lower the heat and simmer for about 1½ hours, until the beans are just starting to become tender. Time varies according to the age and dryness of the beans. The beans are baked in the same water. Again, *never salt* the soaking and parboiling water, as it hardens the beans.

To Bake: Slice the salt pork and use to line the bottom of the pot, place remaining slices here and there in the beans. Then pour in the beans and their water. Roll the onion into the dry mustard, until all of the mustard sticks to it. Then bury it in the middle of the beans. Pour the maple syrup and the coarse salt on top, and cover.

Slow-bake 4 – 5 hours, in a preheated 325°F. (160°C) oven. After 3 – 4 hours, stir, and add hot water slowly (only if top is dry). Return to oven.

In the last hour of the cooking, remove the bean pot cover and place the apples on top of beans, as close together as possible.

Cream together the brown sugar and the butter. Spread on top of the apples. As the beans finish baking, the apple cover forms a delicious topping.

Pour the rum slowly on top of apples just before serving.

Serve a portion of apples with each serving of beans. *Serves 10 – 12.*

7. Eggs and Cheese

A Chef's Glossary of Eggs

A la Bonne Femme: 1 tsp. (5 mL) of cider vinegar added to a large onion chopped and fried in butter. Top with a poached or fried egg.

A la Bourgeoise: Thin slices of buttered toast, topped with a thin slice of Swiss cheese, topped with a fried egg.

A la Colette: A few sliced mushrooms, a couple of lamb kidneys cut in four, quickly fried in butter, flavored to taste with tarragon. Serve around a platter of fried eggs.

A la Duchesse: Mashed potatoes with chives, shaped in an individual nest into which is placed a fried egg.

A L'Indienne: Make a light white sauce; flavor with curry and lemon juice to taste and use to poach egg. Serve with the egg.

A la Marie: A salad of hard-boiled eggs and sliced cooked beets, blended with oil, vinegar, salt, pepper and topped with capers, in a nest of watercress or endives.

A la Mornay: Poached egg on toast topped with a cheese sauce and fried mushrooms.

A la Portugaise: Poached eggs served on toasted, buttered rolls garnished with fried tomato halves.

Au Gratin: Slices of hard-boiled eggs in layers with white sauce and grated cheese, sprinkled with bread crumbs, dotted with butter and baked in a 400°F. (200°C) oven.

How to Make an Omelet

1. Take the frying pan and set it over low heat to warm it up. You must be able to touch the bottom of the pan quickly with the tips of your fingers.

2. Place in a hot pan a well-rounded 1 tbsp. (15 mL) of butter. Unsalted butter gives a perfect creamy flavor, but salted butter can be used. Let the butter melt.

3. While the butter is melting over low heat, break 3 eggs into a bowl, add salt and pepper to taste and 1 tbsp. (15 mL) cold water. Now beat the eggs briskly for 30 – 40 seconds. For 6 eggs, add 2 tbsp. (30 mL) water.

4. Turn the heat high under the frying pan and when, after a few seconds, the butter has a deep gold color, pour the eggs into it. Wait 10 seconds.

5. Take the handle of the pan in your left hand and a fork in your right hand. With the fork gently push the eggs from the side to the middle, going around and around the pan. While doing this as quickly as experience will permit, shake the pan gently so the eggs will not stick to the bottom of the pan. Keep on pushing eggs from the outside edge to the middle, lifting with your fork the part which has set and allowing the liquid to run under it. This operation should not take more than 1 – 1½ minutes, once you understand the work.

6. Now quickly transfer the omelet to a warm plate or dish, because on no account can an omelet be allowed to wait in the pan after being cooked. Lift the edge of the omelet that is nearer to you and fold the omelet in half, tilting the pan as the folding proceeds. Tilting the pan still further, let the omelet slide onto the plate. Use a large spatula at the beginning. With experience, this folding and slipping will take only 10 seconds to accomplish. If the omelet does not slide freely onto the plate, don't give up. You can free it with the spatula and also slip a little piece of butter under it, which will act as lubrication.

   Remember that only practice will make you an omelet expert.

Scrambled Eggs Bombay

Curry, bacon and onion combine very well. Serve with hot rice for lunch.

6 eggs, well beaten
¼ tsp. (1 mL) salt

4 tbsp. (60 mL) cream
4 – 6 slices bacon, diced
1 onion, thinly sliced
3 tbsp. (50 mL) butter
1 tsp. (5 mL) curry powder

Add the salt and cream to the beaten eggs. Fry the diced bacon until crisp, add the onions and fry until light brown. Discard excess fat and pour egg mixture over the bacon and onions. Scramble over low heat, stirring constantly while the eggs cook.

Melt the butter to a light brown color, add the curry and stir together until thoroughly blended. Place the cooked eggs on the service platter and pour the curry butter over all. *Serves 6.*

Boston Scrambled Eggs

The nicest way I know to eat cottage cheese. Use this for breakfast or lunch.

4 eggs
1 cup (250 mL) cottage cheese
3 tbsp. (50 mL) fresh parsley or chives
½ tsp. (2 mL) salt
Freshly ground pepper to taste
Hot, buttered toast

Melt the butter in a frying pan until it is the color of walnuts. Remove from the heat and break the 4 eggs into the pan; beat them with a fork just enough to mix the yolks and the whites. Add the cottage cheese (a dry type is better than a creamed one), and the parsley or chives. Return to low heat and cook, stirring constantly until set. Beware of overcooking. As soon as it is done, place on hot serving platter. Sprinkle with pepper and serve with the toast. *Serves 4.*

Golden Eggs Mayonnaise

This is the English version of French Egg Mimosa. It makes an elegant, tasty luncheon served with garlic bread sticks or homemade melba toast.

4 tbsp. (60 mL) butter
1 tbsp. (15 mL) oil
2 tbsp. (30 mL) curry powder
8 hard-cooked eggs

1 cup (250 mL) mayonnaise
3 tbsp. (50 mL) chopped chutney
1 head of lettuce
¼ cup (60 mL) chopped green olives (optional)

Heat the butter and oil in a saucepan over medium heat. Stir in curry powder until well blended. Add peeled whole eggs and turn constantly over low heat 10 minutes to coat them thoroughly. Remove to a plate with a slotted spoon, cover and cool. (Do not refrigerate.)

To serve, mix the mayonnaise with the chutney; cut eggs in half. Make a nest of lettuce in a salad bowl, add eggs, then pour mayonnaise over to coat them. Sprinkle chopped olives around the mayonnaise. *Serves 4 – 6.*

Swiss Egg Casserole

A simple dish with class. The texture, the flavor, the appearance — all of them are good.

6 hard-boiled eggs
2 large onions, thickly sliced
4 tbsp. (60 mL) butter
¼ tsp. (1 mL) thyme
4 tbsp. (60 mL) flour
2 cups (500 mL) table cream or milk
2 tbsp. (30 mL) lemon juice
3 tbsp. (50 mL) chopped chives or parsley
⅔ cup (160 mL) grated cheese
1 cup (250 mL) diced bread

Shell and slice the eggs. Sauté the onions in the butter, flavored with thyme, until soft but not browned. Remove from the butter with a slotted spoon. Butter a casserole and arrange in it alternate layers of eggs and onions. To the fat remaining in the pan, add the flour, mix well and add the cream. Cook, while stirring, until smooth and creamy. Salt and pepper to taste, add the lemon juice and parsley. Pour over the eggs and onions.

Mix together the grated cheese and croutons, and sprinkle on top of casserole. Bake 20 minutes in a 375°F. (190°C) oven. *Serves 4 – 6.*

Egg Cheese

This recipe was given to me in 1963 by a Mennonite woman at the Kitchener market. All her breads, cakes and cheese were perfect. She told me she fed this to her family often because it was nutritious as well as economical — and very good, she should have added.

4 cups (1 L) milk
2 eggs
1 cup (250 mL) sour milk or buttermilk
½ tsp. (2 mL) each salt and sugar

Bring fresh milk to boiling point and remove from heat. Beat eggs lightly with sour milk, salt and sugar. Pour slowly into hot milk without stirring. Cover and let stand 10 minutes, then stir slowly until the curds separate from the whey.

Remove cheese with a small sieve or a perforated spoon. Place in a mold with holes, so the cheese will drain through the holes — or use a cloth-lined sieve. Set over a bowl, let drain 6 – 8 hours. Unmold and serve with molasses or maple syrup and thick slices of homemade bread. *Yield:* 1 – 1½ cups (250 – 400 mL).

A Few Pointers on Cheese

All cheeses should be served at room temperature. Keep them refrigerated, individually wrapped in their own wrapper or in a clear plastic paper, and take them out at least 2 hours before serving. No cheese can stand a series of abrupt temperature changes; its true flavor must have enough time to come into its own. My own rule is at least 3 hours at room temperature.

How many cheeses should be served depends on the number of guests. Six, one of each type, are sufficient for 8 – 10 people. If there are large amounts left over, they can be wrapped individually in plastic wrap and should keep a month refrigerated.

Choose your cheeses wisely — better to have only a few that are of the best quality. If your knowledge is limited, a good cheese man can be your best friend. But why not read the following short list, take the plunge and be your own judge? These are the best known cheeses, and they're available at supermarkets and specialty cheese shops.

The Fresh Milk Cheeses: These are variations of cream and cottage cheese, and are very mild. Because they have similarities in flavor, one or two of them is sufficient for a party. They will be appreciated by those who don't care for a strong cheese flavor.

Italian Mozzarella is a soft cheese that's delicate and mild in flavor.

French Petit-Suisse is mild, creamy, and very nice with French bread topped with coarse salt or freshly ground pepper.

Imported double cream cheese is rich and creamy. Though popular, it's not as readily available as the first two. The best are the French St-Florentin and Boursault.

The Bland Buttery Cheeses: There are many of these, and they're always popular because of their lightness.

Italian Bel Paese is creamy and delicate, with a well-rounded and pleasing flavor. The Galbani type is the very best.

Danish Esrom, Samsoe, Fynbo and Danbo are most pleasing, and loved by almost everyone. Esrom is creamy and mild; Samsoe is semi-hard and semi-strong; Fynbo is semi-hard and fairly strong. Danbo can be thought of as the Danish equivalent of Swiss cheese.

Dutch Edam and Gouda are smooth and mellow, Gouda having the more pronounced flavor. Edam — the one with the red rind — is made from partly skimmed milk, Gouda from whole. As a rule, the higher the butter-fat content, the softer the cheese. Of all the bland, buttery cheeses, these two are the most readily available throughout Canada.

Swiss Emmenthal and Gruyère are high-quality cheeses for the sophisticated taste, and always welcome. They're a must for a wine and cheese party. Emmenthal is the most delicate of Swiss cheeses, Gruyère is more salted, less refined in flavor, and higher in fat content.

The Cheddar Family: The most versatile cheese family. Its texture ranges from semi-hard to hard, its flavor from mild to really strong, and its color from pale cream to deep yellow.

Canadian Cheddar is a famous cheese that very closely resembles the English Farmhouse Cheddar. The best quality is that cut from a well-aged 5 lb. (2.25 kg) wheel. Its color ranges from that of pale butter to orange pumpkin, and its taste from mild, to medium, to very sharp.

English Cheshire, closely related to Cheddar, is England's oldest cheese. A good one is delectable and should have a place of prominence on the cheese table. It's moist and crumbly, with a salty, buttermilk flavor.

English Double Gloucester is another type of Cheddar, but it's hard to get at its best here.

Welsh Caerphilly is a superb cheese, and my favorite type of medium Cheddar. Firm and lean, with a slightly granular texture, it's delicious with freshly ground pepper on water biscuits.

Scottish Dunlop, when it's mature, has a sweet, buttery flavor with just a little "bite," but no bitterness. One has the sensation of going straight through the cheese into the fresh rich milk when biting into a Dunlop.

English Derby isn't a spectacular cheese like Dunlop, but it's mild and has a very good taste.

Greek Kasseri, a sheep's milk cheese, is white, with a strong flavor that falls between Cheddar and Parmesan. It's easily found in cheese specialty shops and Greek or Polish neighborhood stores.

Camembert and Brie: These creamy, classic cheeses are the best known foreign ones, and you may eat the rind or not, as you prefer. There are decided differences between brands of Camembert, and there is also no comparison between domestic and imported Camembert. Both are difficult to buy, because you require some knowledge of their texture and appearance in order to find the perfect one.

A few general rules: Imported Camembert is at its best from October to June; at its very best from January to April; in the summer months, the domestic brands are more dependable. But whether domestic or imported, Camembert should be passed up if it's not plump and somewhat yielding to the touch. If it looks too small for its round box, beware — it has lost needed moisture and the crust is dry.

As to Brie, which has less salt than Camembert, no cheese has been more celebrated, and with good reason. Easily recognized by its distinctive shape — large, round, flat and rather thin — it is the ultimate cheese, even among connoisseurs. The only good Brie is a French Brie, the very best being the Brie de Meaux.

The Monastery Cheeses: These include a large selection of local and imported cheeses with a semi-hard texture and a somewhat creamy flavor. Some are mild, some strong, but all will keep up to three months refrigerated in plastic wrap.

French Port-Salut is made by Trappist monasteries. It is pale yellow and creamy, with a soft texture and a robust taste. St-Paulin is somewhat like it, but not quite as delicate.

Canadian Oka is one of the most delicious of all cheeses of the Port-Salut type. It's made by the Quebec Oka Trappist monks and known the world over.

French Munster is a rich, creamy cheese often coated with caraway seeds, which give it an unusual flavor.

French Tome de Savoie has a flavor somewhere between a Munster and a Port-Salut. There are two types, the plain type, and the one covered with black grape seeds.

The Blue Cheeses: Almost as well known as Cheddar, their creamy-white color is always veined with blue streaks. All have a piquant, snappy flavor.

French Bleu de Bresse is the king of all blue-veined cheeses, and from it came the rich Roquefort.

English Stilton, made from top quality Cheddar, is superb and the most sophisticated of all blue cheeses.

Cheshire, another English blue, is also of high quality.

Italian Gorgonzola, forms along with the Roquefort and Stilton, the famous triumvirate of blue cheeses. Serve only one of them at a time.

Danish Blue, the mildest blue of all, is very creamy. The fact that it's made from very rich cream accounts for its buttery consistency.

A Wine and Cheese Party

There's nothing new about the combination of wine and cheese—references to it are found in the Bible—but the simple fare of old has been transformed into the elegant ingredients of a successful party.

The resemblances between cheese and wine may account for their affinity: Cheese preserves milk just as wine preserves grapes. Both wine and cheese masters have their secrets that can never be copied. And the varieties of wine are as countless as those of cheese.

For these reasons and many more, a wine and cheese party is a melding of two substances truly made for each other. A certain amount of knowledge is necessary if it's to be a good party, and the only way to acquire it is by tasting both ingredients—in small amounts, deliberately and leisurely, taking notes of your preference in cheese and wine, alone and together.

Appreciating them to their full value is important, because both are personal foods. No one can say, "You must eat this Camembert with this Bordeaux," because you may prefer a Brie with a rosé.

On the long-debated question of whether butter should be eaten with cheese, I can only give you my own feelings. I find that unsalted butter has a most agreeable effect on a very strong, salty cheese such as Roquefort, whereas I feel that rich, soft, ripening cheeses don't need butter.

Don't distract the taste of a cheese with breads that have dominating flavors: anise seed or onion rye, or sweet breads, for instance. The very best ones to use are the crusty French bread and the Italian water bread, both of which are easily made at home. Also good are the dry Scandinavian-type hard breads or biscuits; plain, unsalted crackers, or the perfect English water biscuits.

Along with bread and butter, juicy fruits such as apples and pears are delicious with all types of cheese. Crisp food is also nice—watercress, celery, cucumber, carrot sticks, even small gherkins and special pickles. And any cheese is excellent eaten with a dash of mustard, particularly the French Dijon or strong English type.

All that's needed to complete the cheese table is some of the above, baskets of assorted breads or biscuits, a dish of sweet butter and another of salted butter. Good sharp knives are a necessity. For dessert, which should be light and fresh, nothing could be better than a beautiful basket of assorted fruits and one of nuts and raisins.

The Wines: The cheese itself will often suggest the type of wine. Swiss cheese, for example, is nice with a light white wine; Roquefort and other blues call for a full-bodied Burgundy or a full-bodied red like St-Emilion.

When you have many types of cheeses, the light, creamy, mild ones, should be eaten first with a light, dry, white wine that's been well chilled Follow with the strong, definite cheeses and a heavier wine such as Burgundy. Cheeses in the middle range, such as the Trappist ones, are best with a light red wine, Bordeaux or Claret.

It's not necessary, though, to have three types of wine — the French Alsatian, German Rhine, Italian Chianti or Valpolicella can be served with all types of cheeses (make sure the first two are well chilled).

But, when you make your selection, remember that you can be as flexible as you wish. Despite the "rules and regulations," any wine you prefer still remains the best one to serve.

Wine is, of course, the classic accompaniment to cheese, but beer is traditional with some. It isn't, however, as appropriate with as many cheeses — Cheddar and the strong cheeses such as Limburger are the best accompaniment for beer.

Yogurt

Despite its antiquity and widespread use throughout the world, yogurt is relatively new to Canada. First known here as a health food, one you had to search for, it's now regarded as a glamorous ingredient in almost any kind of cooking and is within easy reach at any supermarket.

Yogurt is simply fermented milk with a flavor that stimulates the palate. It's good for people of all ages because it's digested so easily, and the type made with skim milk is especially helpful to the dieters among us. I prefer the more natural Swiss-style, but the wide range of flavors, textures and colors will give you plenty of choice. If you're completely unfamiliar with yogurt, check the labels on each brand. Every additive is listed and they'll help you choose the type that suits you best.

All these recipes call for plain yogurt; the beautifully flavored ones can stand alone as a snack or dessert. And even frozen yogurt with half the calories of ice cream is readily available.

Ways to Serve Unflavored Yogurt

Try eating yogurt when you're tired (or drinking it — it liquifies when you stir it). If you like it sweet, stir in a spoonful of brown sugar, maple syrup, honey, jam or crushed fresh fruits.

Bake potatoes, or boil them in their jackets, and cut in half. Top with yogurt stirred with lots of parsley or a few chopped green onions.

Beat the contents of a small container of yogurt into a large glass of tomato juice with 1 tsp. (5 mL) of lemon juice and a pinch of salt. You now have a "white and red Mary."

Fill the core space of apples with raisins, sugar and spice to taste, top with yogurt and bake.

Use an equivalent amount of yogurt in place of sour cream or buttermilk in pancakes, cookies and cakes.

Place in a blender 2 cups (500 mL) of yogurt, 1 cup (250 mL) of fresh orange juice, and 1 tbsp. (15 mL) of honey. Blend 2 seconds and use as a pick-me-up, or serve before a light lunch.

For a quick dessert, pour on top of each plain yogurt a spoonful or two of undiluted fruit juice — concentrated orange, pineapple, grape, lemonade, for instance.

Homemade Yogurt

Making your own yogurt is easy, but sometimes tricky. Temperature plays an important role and you may make it perfectly ten times, then miss four. But if you want to try, here's the way I've made mine for years. Yogurt culture can also be bought at health food stores.

4 cups (1 L) milk (whole, skim, reconstituted powder, or diluted evaporated)
2 tbsp. (30 mL) commercial yogurt

Heat the milk to lukewarm (but not to the boiling point), then mix in yogurt with a wooden spoon. (For coffee yogurt, add a few grains of instant coffee when you warm milk.)

Divide into custard cups, or pour into a wide-mouthed bottle and set in a warm place — over a pilot light, near a radiator, in a bowl of hot water or, if using a bottle, wrapped in a piece of old wool blanket and kept in a warm place. The point is to keep the yogurt warm without cooking it.

Let stand 6 – 8 hours, or overnight (the milk will curdle and look like a soft jelly). Then refrigerate 12 – 24 hours before using, by which time it will have solidified. *Yield:* 4 cups (1 L).

To make a second batch, use 2 tbsp. (30 mL) of yogurt from the first one. After the third batch, start again with a fresh commercial yogurt. And once you're successful with a brand, keep using it.

Skimmed Milk Farm Cheese

This fresh, creamy country cheese was made every week at my grandparents', to be served at the Friday night supper with baked potatoes and rich cream. (I still enjoy it today.) Only skimmed milk was used in the old days, and it was pasteurized just before using. Today, I use instant powdered skim milk and save myself a lot of work.

The Starter:

1 cup (250 mL) instant dry milk
1½ cups (400 mL) water
½ cup (125 mL) yogurt or sour cream

The Cheese:

16 cups (4 L) skim milk
1 cup (250 mL) prepared starter
1 tsp. (5 mL) salt

Mix the starter ingredients in a bowl. Stir well, cover with paper and let stand at room temperature for 24 hours to sour. The smell will be strong enough to tell you when this has happened. When cheese is going to be made regularly, set aside 1 cup (250 mL) of the starter for future use. Keep covered in a cool place, or refrigerate. Will keep 8 – 10 days.

Make the 16 cups (4 L) of instant milk according to package directions. Heat milk to 75°F. (25°C) in a stainless steel pan. (A thermometer must be used for good results). Add 1 cup (250 mL) of the starter, bring back to 75°F. (25°C), then remove from heat.

Let stand overnight at room temperature, lightly covered. In the morning, there'll be a firm clot (the curd) formed with a little whey (the watery residue) on the surface. (It may take 12 – 18 hours to clot, so just let it be if it doesn't seem to be clotting fast enough). When ready, cut curd into ½ in. (1.25 cm) squares by passing a long knife through lengthwise and crosswise. Then set pan of clotted milk in a larger pan containing hot water (double-boiler style).

Cook over gentle heat to separate the whey and make small firm curds. Stir gently so the curds cook evenly but avoid breaking them into small pieces. Keep cooking until temperature reaches 110°F. (44°C) (Do not overheat.) Then test curd by gently rubbing between fingers. It should feel slightly granular.

Pour mixture into a colander that has been lined with cheesecloth. Let it drain 2 minutes. Shift curd once or twice by gently lifting one corner of cheesecloth.

When drained, pick up four corners of cloth and dip curds 5 or 6 times into ice water, to cool and to remove all the whey. Remove to a bowl and stir in the salt. Cover and refrigerate until ready to use. To make it even smoother, add rich cream to taste when ready to serve. *Yield:* 3 – 4 cups (0.75 – 2 L).

8. *Meat*

Ground Meat:

Did you know that from Russia to the Côte d'Azur ground meat is king and can be turned into soups, loaves, casseroles, hors-d'oeuvres and even sophisticated dishes? Ground meat offers a great range of prices and a choice of quality. When cost is important in menu-planning, minced beef, lamb, veal or pork can be an interesting answer. So, let's learn a few things about ground meat.

Purchasing: The meat most commonly used in recipes calling for ground meat is beef chuck, round or flank. Packages labelled "hamburger" are all right, but this meat usually has a lot of fat, and will be better when used with an extender, such as bread, eggs or cracked crumbs.

Meat labelled "ground beef" or "minced beef" has a lower percentage of fat; consequently, it is more economical to use when prepared as plain hamburgers. Sometimes you'll find beef labelled "very lean." It is usually ground round, and rather expensive. Use it for low-fat diets or dishes requiring lean meat. If ground beef must be refrigerated for longer than two days, it should be frozen quickly. Cook it as soon as it has partially or completely thawed, according to the recipe; otherwise there will be a marked loss of juice and flavor. You'll need 1 lb. (500 g) of ground meat for 4 servings.

Preparation: Adding liquid — water, consommé, apple juice, wine, milk or cream — to ground meat gives it juiciness, especially when making meat balls or a meat loaf. About 2 tbsp. (30 mL) for each 1 lb. (500 g) of meat is a good ratio. Eggs are sometimes added as a binding agent, and they also help to make the meat tender. Use 1 egg for each 1 lb. (500 g) of ground meat.

Many flavoring ingredients are suitable. For each 1 lb. (500 g) of meat, use ½ – 1 tsp. (2 – 5 mL) of salt, and one or two of the following to taste: a chopped onion; a crushed garlic clove; ¼ – ½ cup (60 – 125 mL) of parsley;

¼ cup (600 mL) of minced chives; ¼ – 1 tsp. (1 – 5 mL) of dried thyme, oregano, marjoram or savory; ¼ – ½ tsp. (1 – 2 mL) of peppercorns, coriander, cumin or caraway seeds, crushed or left whole; 1 tsp. (5 mL) of curry powder, or any table sauce such as Worcestershire or Tabasco.

Ground beef with a high fat content can be extended so that most of the fat is absorbed, or so that a pound can be stretched to make 6 servings. Use any one of the following for each 1 lb. (500 g) of meat: A slice of stale bread, diced and soaked in 2 tbsp. (30 mL) of milk or water for 10 minutes. (Squeeze with your fingertips until creamy). Or use ½ cup (125 mL) of fine dry bread crumbs soaked for 20 minutes in 1 cup (250 mL) of milk or light cream. Or you can add 1 cup (250 mL) of cooked rice, or use 3 tbsp. (50 mL) of milk and ½ cup (125 mL) of instant mashed potato mixture. The best way to blend ground meat is to place all the ingredients in a bowl and use a kneading motion with your fingers held apart. When the mixture holds together, it is ready to use. Pack loosely, rather than tightly.

Cooking: When baking a meat loaf, never fill the pan more than ⅔ full. If you prefer meat loaf with a brown, all-over crustiness, place the shaped mixture in a shallow dripping pan. The cooking period remains the same as for one baked in a loaf pan.

To cook frozen hamburgers, which should be stored with wax paper between each patty, thaw them out just enough so that you can get the paper off, then season each patty with salt, freshly-ground pepper and paprika. Spread the seasonings on with a knife. Place butter in a cast-iron frying pan and brown the patties on each side over medium – high heat; the whole process takes 8 – 10 minutes.

To pan-brown regular hamburgers, use a cast-iron pan. Heat, then add 1 – 2 tsp. (5 – 10 mL) of butter, or other fat of your choice, for each lb. (500 g) of meat. Melt the fat and move the frying pan back and forth to grease the entire bottom of the pan. When the fat sizzles, place the meat patties in the pan and cook for about 2 – 3 minutes over high heat, until browned on one side. Turn the heat down to medium, and brown the other side for about 4 – 6 minutes, depending on the thickness of the meat patties. Serve immediately — never let them stand in the pan or over low heat.

To broil hamburger, preheat the broiler at least 10 minutes. Place well-seasoned meat patties on a broiler pan, rub each one with a little oil, and sprinkle the top with paprika. Set the pan 2 in. (5 cm) from the source of heat, and broil 4 – 5 minutes on each side, again depending on the thickness of the meat. If you are using a barbecue, place the patties 3 in. (7.5 cm) above the coals.

If you have a wooden board and a mixer, grinder, or mortar and pestle, you can make your own tasty sausages. Veal, fresh pork, even beef, will give you perfect sausages. With different spices and seasonings, each batch can be something special.

Wild Rice Loaf

This dish is prepared at Stampede time in Calgary, by my friend Mary, a charming hostess.

4 cups (1 L) boiling water
1 1/3 (230 mL) cups wild rice
3 cups (750 mL) chicken broth
1 ½ tsp. (7 mL) salt
1 bay leaf, crumbled
1 tsp. (5 mL) Japanese soy sauce
½ tsp. (2 mL) curry powder
½ cup (125 mL) butter
1 large onion, chopped fine
1 lb. (500 g) fresh mushrooms, thinly sliced
1 lb. (500 g) ground beef
½ cup (125 mL) grated sharp Cheddar cheese

Pour the boiling water over the rice and let stand 15 minutes. Drain, add the chicken broth, salt, bay leaf, soy sauce and curry powder. Mix well. Melt the butter in a large frying pan, brown the onion lightly, add the mushrooms and stir together over high heat for 1 minute. Add the beef and cook, stirring all the time, until meat loses its red color. Add the rice mixture, and place in a 13 × 9 in. (32.5 cm × 22.5 cm) casserole or loaf pan. Top with the grated cheese.

Bake 1 hour in a preheated 350°F. (180°C) oven. Serve hot or at room temperature. *Serves 6.*

Russian Kotlety

Kotlety literally means "chops," but they're made with ground beef. The milk-soaked bread added to the beef is a creation of Russian cuisine, which is now used in so many parts of the world.

1 cup (250 mL) stale bread, diced
1 ½ cups (400 mL) milk
1 lb. (500 g) ground beef
½ tsp. (2 mL) salt
¼ tsp. (1 mL) pepper
2 eggs

For many people, pumpkins mean Halloween and pumpkin pie, and that's all. But there are many delicious dishes you can prepare with this versatile vegetable. I hope you will enjoy some of the ones I have chosen for this book.

Pinch of caraway seeds
2 tbsp. (30 mL) butter
2 tbsp. (30 mL) vegetable oil
3 tbsp. (50 mL) commercial sour cream

It is important to use very stale bread. Place it in a bowl, pour the milk on top, and cover. Let it soak for 30 minutes, then squeeze it hard to remove the excess liquid.

Place the bread in another bowl and add the ground beef, salt, pepper, eggs and caraway seeds. Knead with your fingers until the mixture is well-blended. Wet your hands and shape the meat into 4 oval patties.

Heat the butter and vegetable oil in a heavy frying pan. When very hot, put the "chops" in, and immediately reduce the heat to low. Fry on both sides, turning a few times to prevent the meat from forming a crust or browning too much.

Remove the chops to a warm serving platter and take the frying pan off the heat. Add the sour cream to the pan and stir while scraping the bottom of the pan. When the cream is hot, pour over the meat and serve. This is very good surrounded with thinly-sliced mushrooms that have been quickly fried in butter. Around both, try a crown of mashed potatoes, sprinkled with paprika. *Serves 4.*

Mexican Tamale

Not to be confused with **Italian Polenta** — both are quite different; only the cornmeal base is similar. Both are good examples of the type of casserole one can make with a pound of ground beef, and even serve 8 to 10 people.

Polenta Base:

3 cups (750 mL) chicken broth or consommé
1½ cups (400 mL) uncooked cornmeal
1 cup (250 mL) white wine
2 tsp. (10 mL) salt
2 eggs, beaten
¾ cup (200 mL) grated Parmesan cheese

Heat the broth or consommé. Stir together the cornmeal and white wine, then add to the hot consommé. Cook over medium heat, stirring constantly, until mixture is thick. Stir in the salt. Set over boiling water, cover and cook 20 minutes. Then stir a couple of tablespoons of the hot polenta into the beaten eggs, mix well, and add to remaining polenta with the Parmesan cheese. Mix well and use as directed for the Tamale or Polenta.

Tamale Meat Mixture:

1 lb. (500 g) ground lean beef
2 tbsp. (30 mL) vegetable oil
1 large onion, chopped
1 small green pepper, diced
1 large clove garlic, minced
3 medium tomatoes, peeled and diced
1 can whole corn kernel
2 tsp. (30 mL) salt
⅛ tsp. (0.5 mL) pepper
1 tbsp. (15 mL) chili powder
⅓ cup (80 mL) cornmeal
⅓ cup (80 mL) water
½ cup (125 mL) sliced black olives

Brown the beef in the hot oil over high heat. Add the onion and stir into the meat until well mixed. Add the green pepper, garlic, tomatoes, corn, salt, pepper and chili powder. Stir well, cover and simmer 10 minutes over medium heat. Blend the cornmeal with the water and stir into the meat mixture. Cook over medium heat, stirring until mixture boils and thickens. Remove from heat and stir in the olives. Taste for seasoning.

Butter a 9 x 13-in. (22.5 x 32.5 cm) casserole and line bottom and sides with a thick layer (about half) of the prepared Polenta Base. Fill center with meat mixture and spoon remaining polenta over top of dish in mounds. Then sprinkle with grated cheese.

Bake in a preheated 350°F. (180°C) oven, about 30 minutes or until thoroughly heated. *Serves 8 – 10.*

Italian Polenta

The cornmeal base is the same as for the **Mexican Tamale,** but the sauce is quite different, and, I would add, more delicate.

2 tbsp. (30 mL) vegetable oil
½ lb (250 g) ground beef
1 large onion, chopped
½ lb (250 g) thinly sliced mushrooms
1 large clove garlic, chopped fine
1 19 oz. (540 mL) can tomatoes
1 7½ oz. (213 mL) can tomato sauce
1 tsp. (5 mL) salt

1 bay leaf
½ tsp. (2 mL) basil
1 tsp. (5 mL) oregano
½ tsp. (2 mL) sugar
1 cup (250 mL) mild Cheddar cheese, grated
¼ cup (60 mL) grated Parmesan cheese
1 basic recipe of **Polenta Base**

Prepare the basic polenta, and turn into a buttered ring mold. Bake in a preheated 350°F. (180°C) oven about 5 minutes. To serve, unmold on hot platter, pour polenta sauce in middle and around the ring.

To Make the Sauce: Heat the oil in a large frying pan, add the ground beef, onion and mushrooms. Stir well and add the garlic; cook a minute, stirring all the time. Add the tomatoes, tomato sauce, salt, bay leaf, basil, oregano and sugar.

Simmer, uncovered, over low heat for 35 to 45 minutes, or until sauce is slightly thickened. Taste for seasoning.

Sprinkle the grated mild cheddar over the polenta ring and fill ring with sauce. Sprinkle sauce with the grated Parmesan. *Serves 8 – 10.*

Beef Colbert in Chafing Dish

At the turn of the century, nothing was more elegant than meat or seafood in a tasty sauce served in a silver chafing dish — even when the meat was minced, usually shaped into an apricot-sized meatball. Of course, minced beef was never sold as such, but only on request, or else it was prepared at home. This was an early autumn dish when we had fresh peaches. I have changed the recipe somewhat by using my own peach preserves and cutting the sugar out of the sauce.

2 lb. (1 kg) minced round of beef
¾ cup (200 mL) milk
½ cup (125 mL) crustless bread crumbs
1 clove garlic, crushed and chopped
1½ tsp. (7 mL) salt
¼ tsp. (1 mL) each of nutmeg and ginger
¼ tsp. (1 mL) freshly ground pepper
Juice and grated rind of 1 orange
2 tbsp. (30 mL) vegetable oil

Place in a bowl, all the ingredients except the oil. Mix thoroughly, then shape into 2-in. (5 cm) balls.

Heat oil in a large frying pan, and fry meatballs, just enough to brown, shaking the pan rather than turning the meatballs. Remove with a slotted spoon to a dish.

To Prepare the Peach Sauce: Combine in a bowl:

1 cup (250 mL) peach jam or preserves
½ cup (125 mL) light brown sugar
½ cup (125 mL) brandy
¼ cup (60 mL) orange liqueur
¼ tsp. (1 mL) nutmeg

Remove excess fat from frying pan. Add peach sauce, and stir, scraping the pan, until the mixture comes to boil. Lower heat and simmer 10 minutes, stirring a few times.

Add meatballs to sauce and stir well coated.

Cover and simmer over low heat 30 to 40 minutes.

To serve, pour into hot chafing dish. Serve with plain boiled rice. *Serves 6 – 8.*

Cantor Meat Loaf

A recipe my daughter Monique found in a magazine years ago, but she can't remember which or when. I make it often myself and I can assure you that no one can tell how it is made. Try it!

2 lb. (1 kg) minced beef or a mixture
  of beef, pork and veal
1 10 oz. (284 mL) can undiluted vegetable soup
1 egg
Salt and pepper to taste
½ tsp. (2 mL) powdered garlic
2 tbsp. (30 mL) grated strong Cheddar cheese

Place all the ingredients in a bowl. Mix well. Pack into a 9 × 5 in. (22.5 cm × 12.5 cm) loaf pan.

Cook in a preheated 350°F. oven (180°C) for 40 – 50 minutes. *Serves 6.*

Greek Youbarlakia

These are the world-famous meat balls served with a sharp, tasty lemon sauce, referred to as *Avgolemono.* I often use it as a sauce for a simmered lamb or chicken.

1½ lb. (750 g) ground beef
1 medium onion, chopped fine
½ cup (125 mL) uncooked rice
Salt and pepper to taste
1 beaten egg
Parsley, chopped fine
2 tbsp. (30 mL) butter
Consommé or water

Avgolemono Sauce:

3 egg yolks
1 whole egg
4 tbsp. (60 mL) fresh lemon juice
½ – 1 cup (125 – 250 mL) hot bouillon

Beat yolks and whole egg until pale yellow. Add lemon juice gradually beating constantly. Gradually add the hot bouillon, beating constantly. Then use as indicated after the meat balls are cooked.

Mix together the meat, onion, rice and seasoning to taste. Add the egg, and mix again. Form into small balls, and roll into the parsley. Melt the butter in a large, deep frying pan (a *sautese*), remove from fire and place meat balls side by side in hot butter.

Pour in enough boiling consommé (diluted canned consommé is fine) or water to completely cover the meat balls.

Simmer over low heat, uncovered, until meat balls are cooked, about 20 minutes. Use some of the cooking bouillon for the sauce.

Remove meat balls from heat, drain and reserve the excess consommé. Pour Avgolemono Sauce on top. Put pan back over very low heat, until it comes just to the boil, shaking the pan often. Serve as soon as ready or keep in warm place. If the sauce boils, it will curdle. *Serves* 6.

Greek Keftedes

The combination of fresh mint and lemon makes these quite special.

1 lb. (500 g) ground beef or lamb
1 beaten egg
1 medium onion, chopped fine
2 slices dry toasted bread
½ cup (125 mL) water
Grated rind of 1 lemon
1 tbsp. (15 mL) vegetable oil
1 tbsp. (15 mL) fresh lemon juice
2 tbsp. (30 mL) chopped parsley

1 tbsp. (15 mL) chopped fresh mint
¼ tsp. (1 mL) cinnamon
Salt and pepper to taste

Beat the egg, add the meat and the onion. Pour mixture of water and lemon rind over the bread. Stir well, and squeeze bread dry, with your hands. Add to meat, stir together and add the remaining ingredients. Cover and let stand 1 hour.

Shape mixture into balls; you should have 5 or 6 depending on size. (In Greece, where they make them the size of a large unshelled walnut, you would then have 10 – 12.) Roll in flour. Fry in half butter, half oil, medium heat. *Serves 4 – 6.*

Deutsches Hamburger

The father of all hamburgers was born in Hamburg, Germany. Many a tourist has been confused when, after ordering *Deutsches Beefsteak*, and he's received what he knows as hamburger. The following recipe is the original.

1 lb. (500 g) ground beef
1 lb. (500 g) lean pork, ground
1 medium onion, quartered
2 tbsp. (30 mL) parsley, minced
2 eggs,
2 tsp. (10 mL) salt
½ tsp. (2 mL) pepper
Pinch of caraway seeds or
grated peel of half a lemon
2 tbsp. (30 mL) butter, melted
3 tbsp. (50 mL) all-purpose flour
2 tbsp. (30 mL) butter or fat
2 medium onions, thinly sliced

Pass the ground beef and ground pork through a food grinder along with the onion and the parsley. Add the eggs, salt, pepper, caraway seeds or grated lemon peel, melted butter and flour. Knead with your fingers until the ingredients are thoroughly mixed. Shape the meat into 8 patties, then cover and refrigerate 1 – 4 hours.

Heat the butter or fat of your choice in a heavy cast-iron frying pan. When the fat is quite hot, add the meat patties and fry on both sides according to the instructions in the cooking section at the beginning of this chapter. Remove to a hot platter. Separate the onion slices into rings and add them to the fat remaining in the pan. Sauté a few minutes over high heat, stirring constantly until the onions are soft and golden brown. Spoon over the hamburgers. *Serves 6 – 8.*

My Father's Favorite Roast Beef

The cut was a choice 6 – 8 lb. (3 – 3.5 kg) prime rib, grass-fed beef from the east, of course, with bone-in — or a 10 lb. (4.5 kg) fat western beef rump roast. Today, these would be sheer extravagance. In my family, we sometimes do one or the other for the Christmas dinner. Whatever the weight or the cut of beef, the roast is still super when you make it this way.

Grass-fed beef is now very difficult to find, and people are not attracted to its dark, almost mahogany, red color. It was a favorite winter Sunday dinner.

My sister still makes this beautifully, but she uses chutney instead of chili sauce, and she sears the roast in butter in a large cast-iron frying pan over high heat.

4 – 6 lb. (2 – 4 kg) roast beef of your choice
3 tbsp. (50 mL) soft butter
2 tbsp. (30 mL) Dijon-type mustard
1 tbsp. (15 mL) dry mustard
2 tbsp. (30 mL) homemade chili sauce
½ cup (125 mL) Bordeaux red wine, dry sherry or dry Madeira
10-oz. (300 mL) undiluted consommé

Blend the butter, Dijon mustard, dry mustard and chili sauce.

Place meat in a shallow roasting pan and cover red part of the meat generously with the butter mixture.

Roast in a preheated 350°F. (180°C) oven 15 – 25 minutes per lb. (500 g) according to your taste, depending on whether you like it rare or well done.

When meat is cooked, remove from the pan to a hot platter. Cover lightly with foil. (My grandmother and mother covered the roast with a thick hand woven linen cloth kept for that very purpose.)

Lift all the visible fat from the gravy (a tasty fat that can be used in many ways such as for browning potatoes and adding to stew.) To the remaining pan juices add the wine of your choice and the consomme. Bring to boil over direct heat, while scraping the bottom and sides of roaster. Boil 3 – 4 minutes. Pour into hot sauceboat.

Variation: In the fall and spring, mother used to make this roast on the Saturday and serve it cold on Sunday. It was sliced quite thin, and set on a large blue platter (which I now proudly own). The gravy was made into a jelly, and refrigerated overnight, then chopped, rolled in parsley or chives and placed around the meat.

To Make the Jelly: Cool the gravy until the fat has congealed on top. Remove all fat, add the consommé, and bring to boil. Dissolve 1 envelope of unflavored gelatine for each 2 cups (500 mL) of gravy in the sherry, dry

Madeira, or red wine. Let stand 10 minutes, then add to the boiling gravy. Stir for a few minutes or until gelatine dissolves. Pour into an oiled 8 × 8 in. (20 cm × 20 cm) square pan. Refrigerate overnight. *Serves 8.*

Beef Vinaigrette

If you think there is nothing glamorous about brisket, chuck, shank cuts or oxtail, take a step back into the past, into my mother's kitchen and see how wrong you are. Even in the Twenties, meat was considered the most costly item in the food budget. Mother lowered the cost by using the above cuts; the choice was dictated by the cost, as they could easily be interchanged when making "beef vinaigrette," which was boiled beef served piping hot surrounded by colorful vegetables and a sauce-boat of cold herb vinaigrette. I still make this at least once a month, and now my married granddaughter has discovered how easy it is to make, and how perfect to lower the cost of her food budget. May she pass it on to *her* daughter.

3 – 4 lb. (1½ – 2 kg) rolled brisket or chuck roast
4 – 5 celery stalked with leaves
6 medium onions, whole
1 parsnip, peeled, and cut in 4
1 small turnip, peeled and cut in ½ in. (1.25 cm) slices
2 tsp. (10 mL) salt
½ tsp. (2 mL) pepper
3 whole cloves
2 bay leaves

Place the meat in a large saucepan, add enough cold water to cover completely, and bring to boil uncovered. Boil 10 minutes, remove from heat and skim the fat off the top of the water. Cut the celery into 1-in. (2.5 cm) pieces, chop the leaves, add to the water, and stir. Then add the carrots, onions, parsnip and turnip. Bring the water back to a boil and add the remaining ingredients. Then cover and simmer over medium-low heat 2½ – 3 hours, or until meat is tender.

It is important to keep the water at simmer only, as this will make for tender, tasty meat and vegetables that will not get mushy or lose their color and shape, as happens when the water is allowed to boil.

While the meat is cooking, prepare the herb vinaigrette, to be served in a bowl. To serve, slice meat, set on a plate with some of the vegetables and let each one pour some of the Vinaigrette over the meat.

We used to serve this with a big bowl of steamed unpeeled potatoes, that were rolled in melted butter to make them shiny and in minced parsley to make them attractive.

Vinaigrette Sauce

4 tbsp. (60 mL) cider, wine or malt vinegar
¾ cup (200 mL) vegetable or olive oil
½ cup (125 mL) chopped fresh parsley
3 green onions, chopped
½ tsp. (2 mL) dry mustard
1 tsp. (5 mL) Dijon-type mustard
1 hard-cooked egg, chopped
Salt and pepper to taste

In the summer, we added ½ cup (125 mL) minced chives; in the winter, capers to taste. Beat all ingredients together and serve. Keep leftover sauce refrigerated. To use, leave 1 hour or more on kitchen counter and shake well before using. *Serves 6.*

Barbecues: The word "barbecue" derives from the tropical practice of *barbacoa,* where beef or lamb carcasses were roasted on great spits. The three Fs — Fire, Fuel and Food — then as now, are the essentials of a barbecue; so it is important to understand them.

Always stand with your back to the wind. Never cook over the flame or in a thick smoke — success will be achieved only when the fuel has burned down to a mass of radiant embers, topped with gray ashes. Far too often, people cook over an open flaming fire, with the mistaken idea that the charcoal forming on the meat will smoke it.

It will take 30 minutes to build a fire to embers or to a temperature of 375° – 400°F. (190° – 200°), using kindling and a double layer of briquets. The fire then slowly decreases to 300°F (150°C), giving about 1½ hours of good heat from the time it reaches 375°F. (190°C).

I like to line my firebox with foil, because it increases the radiant heat and eliminates the messy business of cleaning the barbecue.

In dealing with steaks — and most of you are steakmen — remember that any cut can be done to your preference.

Round steak, cut 1½ – 2 in. (3.75 – 5 cm), thick, almost fat-free makes a very good steak for a family meal, but it must be marinated — it is too lean to be tender unless some oil or fat is added. The simplest way to marinate is to pour ¼ – ⅓ cup (60 – 80 mL) of vegetable oil per lb. (500 g) of steak and the juice of 1 lemon into a platter. Roll the steak in it and let it marinate a few hours or overnight, turning it a few times. After cooking, slice the steak in very thin slices at a 45-degree angle.

Porterhouse steak with its big fat tenderloin is the best of all, but the price is the biggest too, and there is quite a bit of bone adding to the weight. Save this for special occasions.

Sirloin steak must be thick for good results. It is also an expensive cut, but like round steak, there is no waste.

Charcoal Broiled Steak

For this method the best steak is a thick one weighing about 4 lb. (2 kg). I often baste it during cooking with a sauce of equal parts sweet or dry vermouth and olive oil. Served with potatoes baked on the grill, and sliced tomatoes topped with lemon tartar sauce, it is quite a meal.

4 lb. (2 kg) steak, 2½ in. (6.25 cm) thick
Melted butter or vegetable oil
Paprika
Salt and freshly ground pepper to taste

Trim most of the excess fat from the steak to prevent the dripping from catching fire in the coals. Gash the edges of the fat so steak won't curl, and keep at room temperature until ready to cook.

When your fire is a lively bed of coals covered with gray film — but there is no active fire — rub grill (or broiling rack, if you prefer) with melted butter or oil, or with a piece of steak fat. This is important so that meat will not stick when you are ready to turn it.

Paint steak on both sides with butter or oil and sprinkle one side generously with paprika. Place steak 5 – 6 in. (12.5 – 15 cm) from hot coals. A thinner steak should be placed 2 – 3 in. (5 – 7.5 cm) away. Grill first side for about 12 minutes, until it is dark crusty brown, wafts of delicious aroma filling the air. Flip steak with a turner, as poking it with a fork causes the precious meat juices to drip into the firebed. Salt and pepper the browned side and cook second side 10 – 12 minutes.

The result will be a medium-rare steak, so for rare or well-done, adjust cooking time accordingly. When ready, salt and pepper second side, place on a hot platter and top with a generous hunk of butter. Serve by slicing slightly on the bias. *Serves 8 – 9.*

Minnesota Six-Pounder

If you hold a big cook-out for 8 – 12 friends, the six-pounder is the steak to serve. Tender, luscious and as easy to carve as it is to cook. The rubbing with whisky and herbs puts it in a class by itself.

6 lb. (2.7 kg) sirloin steak, 2 in. (5 cm) thick
Scotch whisky or rye (be generous)
1 tsp. (5 mL) salt
½ tsp. (2 mL) freshly ground pepper
½ tsp. (2 mL) thyme or tarragon
2 tbsp. (30 mL) melted butter or salad oil
2 tbsp. (30 mL) sherry
2 tsp. (10 mL) Worcestershire sauce

Make gashes in fat around edges of the steak; brush both sides with whisky or rye and cover and let stand 3 hours at room temperature. Mix salt, pepper, thyme or tarragon and rub all over steak just before cooking. Combine remaining ingredients and set aside to use as a basting mixture.

When fire is ready, brush grill with oil. Brush one side of steak with basting mixture and set it on grill, 5 – 6 in. (12.5 – 15 cm) from the heat. Broil 15 minutes on one side, basting every 5 minutes; turn and broil for another 15 minutes, basting top every 5 minutes. Do not turn more than once. This timing is for a rare steak; cook 25 minutes per side for medium-rare, and 35 minutes per side for well-done.

To serve, place steak on a board and cut into thin slices, slightly on the bias. *Serves 8 – 12.*

Braised Beef A la Française

This thick round steak with its intriguing flavor becomes a company dish when served with "pommes vertes": equal quantities of mashed potatoes and cooked spinach beaten together until pale green, then seasoned to taste.

2 – 3 lb. (1 – 2 kg) piece bottom round of beef
2 tbsp. (30 mL) vegetable oil
6 thin slices side bacon or fat salt pork, diced
Paprika to taste
4 carrots, cut in 1 in. (2.5 cm) pieces
4 onions, thinly sliced
2 whole cloves
1 garlic clove, finely chopped
½ tsp. (2 mL) thyme
¼ tsp. (1 mL) sage
Peel of 1 orange, cut in slivers

Remove and dice all visible fat from the beef. Heat fat, oil, and bacon or salt pork in pan and, when suet is brown, sprinkle one side of meat with paprika and place that side down in the fat. Brown until golden, then sprinkle with paprika, and again place that side down in fat. Brown until golden; then sprinkle with paprika, turn and brown other side — 20–25 minutes in all.

Add carrots, onions separated into rings, and herbs and orange peel, being careful to see that there's no white on the orange skin. Add salt and pepper to taste, stir together a bit, and cook covered in a 300°F. (150°C) oven for 1½ hours, or until meat is tender.

Remove meat to a hot serving platter. To thicken sauce: either mash vegetables in the pan juices, or pass them through a sieve and return to pan with ½ cup (125 mL) of sour cream. Warm up, but don't let mixture boil; then pour over meat. *Serves 8.*

Basting Sauce

Meat cooked outdoors is always something special, but brush on a basting sauce as it cooks and it will be heavenly. Use with broiled or barbecued meat.

1 garlic clove, halved
½ cup (125 mL) each fresh lemon juice and vegetable oil
2 tbsp. (30 mL) marjoram or basil
½ tsp. (2 mL) pepper
2 tsp. (10 mL) salt
1/3 cup (80 mL) Worcestershire sauce

Place all ingredients in a glass jar with a tight-fitting cover. Shake well and keep refrigerated. If you prefer a very mild flavor, remove garlic after 24 hours. Will keep 2–3 weeks. *Yield:* 1 1/3 cups (350 mL).

Tenderizing Marinade

Chuck or blade roast, or other less tender cuts of meat can be excellent when marinated with this mixture. It will keep refrigerated 10–12 days in a glass jar with a tight-fitting cover.

2/3 cup (160 mL) chopped onion
¾ cup (200 mL) chopped celery, with leaves
1/3 cup (80 mL) cider vinegar
½ cup (125 mL) vegetable oil

1 cup (250 mL) grape juice
1 tbsp. (15 mL) Worcestershire sauce
½ tsp. (2 mL) salt
⅛ tsp. (0.5 mL) garlic powder

Combine all ingredients, pour into a glass jar, cover and refrigerate. To use: shake mixture, pour over meat, cover and refrigerate 12 – 18 hours, turning meat a few times. To cook: drain marinade from roast, brown roast lightly on all sides over medium heat. Cook over medium-low heat or in a 350°F. (180°C) oven until tender. Baste with marinade occasionally while cooking. *Yield:* enough to marinate 12 lb. (5.5 kg) of meat.

Chef's Baked Steak

Cut on the bias into luscious slices, this is a gastronomic masterpiece. Use a 2½-in. (6.25 cm) thick T-bone, club or rib steak to serve 2 – 4 people; a 2½-in. (6.25 cm) porterhouse for 4 – 6; a 2½ – 3 in. (6.25 – 7.5 cm) sirloin for 6 – 8 (or more — it depends on how large the steer was). This is my favorite way to make roast beef for 2, all of it superb, with very little leftovers, easy to use.

2½ – 3 in. (6.25 – 7.5 cm) thick steak
Sugar and freshly ground pepper
Soft butter *or* good quality olive oil

Remove the steak from the refrigerator 2 – 3 hours before cooking. To prevent curling, trim excess fat from edges and slash remainder in several places, being careful not to cut into the lean part. Oil the rack of your broiler pan so steak won't stick to it.

Place meat on rack and sprinkle top generously with pepper (but no salt). Sprinkle with sugar, using about 1 tsp. (5 mL) for a 5 lb. (2.5 kg) steak. Blend pepper and sugar on top with a knife — the pepper flavors, the sugar caramelizes to give the top a rich brown color (it doesn't sweeten the steak). Rub with butter or olive oil.

Preheat broiler for 20 minutes, then place steak 2 in. (5 cm) from source of heat and leave oven door open slightly. Broil 10 minutes; turn and broil 4 minutes.

Place pan on lower rack and set oven to bake at 400°F. (200°C). Close door and leave steak about 10 minutes for rare, 15 for medium. (This is approximate — one man's medium is another's rare).

When steak is done to taste, remove from rack and place in pan gravy. Move the steak back and forth for a few seconds on each side. Then slice on the bias and serve on heated plates. If you prefer, place on a hot platter and slice at the table, making sure your serving plates are heated.

Monique's Pepper Steak

My daughter makes a delicious 10-minute green pepper steak, using a 1 – 1½ lb. (500 – 750 g) round steak. Very nice served with plain boiled rice.

1 – 1½ lb. (500 – 750 g) round steak
⅓ cup (80 mL) Japanese soy sauce or Teriyaki sauce
¼ tsp. (1 mL) crushed peppercorns
¼ cup (60 mL) vegetable oil
2 onions, peeled and quartered
2 – 3 green peppers
1 tsp. (5 mL) salt
1 tsp. (5 mL) fresh ginger root, grated (optional)
Juice of ½ a lemon *or*
  2 tbsp. (30 mL) cider vinegar
3 tbsp. (50 mL) cold water
3 tbsp. (15 mL) cornstarch

Cut the steak on the bias into very thin slices. Place in a bowl with the soy or Teriyaki sauce and the peppercorns. Let stand while preparing the rest of the ingredients.

Cut the green pepper in half lengthwise. Clean out seeds and cut peppers into long shreds [when green peppers are expensive, or you have none on hand, replace by 2 cups (500 mL) slivered celery].

Heat half the oil in a large frying pan or a wok. When hot, sprinkle with the salt, and add the onions; stir for a minute, or until onions break up, then add the green pepper or celery and stir well until they are coated with oil. All of this takes about 2 minutes. Remove vegetables from pan with a perforated spoon.

Heat the rest of the oil. Then add the meat and stir continuously for 1 minute. Add the green peppers and onions. Stir again until all is mixed.

Have ready in a separate bowl, the lemon juice or cider vinegar, water and the cornstarch, mixed together and add to meat. Stir until it turns into a creamy sauce, and serve immediately. *Serves 4 – 6.*

Onion Butter for Steak

Keep in refrigerator in a closed container, to have on hand for broiled steak or sausages or chicken. The heat of the meat will melt the butter.

4 tbsp. (60 mL) grated raw onions
4 tbsp. (60 mL) minced parsley
4 tbsp. (60 mL) soft butter
1 tsp. (5 mL) Worcestershire or A1 sauce or chutney

½ tsp. (2 mL) salt
¼ tsp. (1 mL) dry mustard
½ tsp. (2 mL) freshly ground pepper

Mix all the ingredients into a smooth paste. Place in glass jar, covered. Keep refrigerated. *Yield:* ½ cup (125 mL).

My All-Purpose Sauce

I always have 3 – 4 cups (750 – 1000 mL) of this in my freezer or refrigerator to be used in emergencies. It's extremely versatile.

1 cup (250 mL) diced onion
⅓ cup (80 mL) olive or vegetable oil
1½ cups (400 L) ketchup or chili sauce
½ cup (125 mL) each water and fresh lemon juice
¼ cup (60 mL) sugar
2½ tsp. (15 mL) salt
1 tsp. (5 mL) thyme
½ tsp. (2 mL) each pepper and garlic powder
2 bay leaves

Cook onion in hot oil until soft and light golden. Add remaining ingredients, stir well and simmer 15 minutes. Let cool, then bottle and refrigerate or freeze. *Yield:* about 4 cups (1 L).

To Use with Minced Beef or Veal: If meat is uncooked, brown over high heat in 1 tbsp. (15 mL) of fat, add sauce to taste, and simmer 20 minutes. With cooked meat, stir it in melted fat until coated, add sauce and simmer 10 minutes. Taste for seasoning; serve on toasted buns or spaghetti.

To Use with Chicken: Brown chicken pieces in fat, put a spoonful of sauce on top of each piece and simmer until done.

To Use as Dressing: Combine 2 – 3 tbsp. (30 – 50 mL) of sauce with ½ cup (125 mL) of mayonnaise and 1 finely chopped hard-cooked egg. Refrigerate until needed, then pour on salad, or use in sandwiches. Or use a spoonful over hot hamburgers. And try a spoonful stirred into cooked vegetables, too.

To Use in Sandwiches: Cream 8 oz. (227 g) of cream cheese or 1 cup (250 mL) of grated cheese with ¼ cup (60 mL) of sauce.

Oxtail with a Dash: What dash can you give to an oxtail? I promise you that, from buying to preparation the work is as little as the cost, and the result — magnificent.

Even to my guests, I serve oxtail. To those keenly interested in the French Riviera — who talk of Nice and Cannes with delight and rave about the taste of food in the South of France — I like to serve Oxtail Menton, which in itself has all the charm and flavor of the South.

To please my husband and family, I make a thick oxtail soup and serve it as a meal. We like to eat it as they do in Ireland, placing a large, mealy, boiled potato, cut in four, in the bottom of an old-fashioned soup plate and sprinkling it generously with minced parsley or chives. A piece or two of tasty, tender oxtail go on each side, then the meat and potato are completely covered with the thick soup and all its little bits of shredded vegetables.

To my family, this means autumn is all around with its bright colors and nippy air. Our big plate of hot oxtail soup makes us feel the quiet pleasure of eating good food in the warmth of our home. Happiness, after all, is made of these little things.

Braised Oxtail

Start the meal with grapefruit halves that have been sprinkled with a mixture of sugar and a few crushed cardamom seeds. Baked potatoes are a good accompaniment.

2 oxtails, cut into 2 in. (5 cm) lengths
2 tsp. (10 mL) salt
½ tsp. (2 mL) pepper
1 tbsp. (15 mL) sugar
3 tbsp. (50 mL) flour
4 tbsp. (60 mL) brandy
2 carrots, thinly sliced
1 onion, stuck with 2 cloves
½ tsp. (2 mL) thyme
2 bay leaves
2 cups (500 mL) red wine or beef consommé

Place oxtails on a baking sheet. Mix salt, pepper, sugar and flour, sprinkle over oxtails, then toss until the meat is coated. Roast 30 minutes in a 450°F. (230°C) oven, shaking pan from time to time to baste the meat with its own juices.

Pour off excess fat. Pour brandy over meat, set alight and let flames die. Transfer oxtail to a deep 2-quart (2 L) casserole and add remaining ingredients. Cover and bake in a 325°F. (160°C) oven 3 hours or until oxtail is tender. This is even better if it's made the day before, cooled, and refrigerated. Skim the fat off the rich broth and reheat at 325°F. (160°C) until hot. *Serves 6.*

Oxtail Menton

In the long, slow-cooking process, the flavor of the many ingredients blends into one delectable sauce. The ripe olives acquire a soft, rich texture that is very interesting. Don't hesitate to use this as a hot buffet dish for a party.

1 or 2 oxtails, cut in pieces
3 tbsp (50 mL) vegetable oil
1 thick slice salt pork
1 large onion, minced
4 fresh tomatoes
¼ tsp. (1 mL) thyme
2 bay leaves
1 tbsp (15 mL) sugar
1 garlic clove, crushed
½ cup (125 mL) ripe olives
2 cups (500 mL) water

Heat the oil, add the salt pork cut into small squares, and cook over medium heat until pork is crisp and brown. Add the onion and stir until slightly browned. Add the pieces of oxtail and stir until they are well coated with the onions and fat. Salt and pepper to taste. Add the tomatoes, thyme, bay leaves and sugar. Stir together until well blended.

Add the garlic, ripe olives and water. Bring to a boil, cover and simmer over low heat 3 – 4 hours, or until the oxtail is tender. The secret of a good oxtail dish is the long, slow cooking. There is no need to stir more than once or twice. It reheats beautifully, and freezes very well. Serve with a bowl of parsleyed rice. *Serves 4.*

Marinated Leg of Pork

Good fresh pork is somewhat difficult to find nowadays, first because most of it is turned into ham, and secondly because the know-how of roasting it is somewhat lost. Know what weight you require (it is the same as ham). It is also equally good served hot or cold.

What is important to make a perfect roasted leg of fresh pork is to marinate it 24 – 48 hours before cooking, then to baste it with the marinating mixture, and to keep the meat covered with foil or a cover at least 15 minutes before carving, or for the whole cooling period, if served cold.

The best roasting temperature for all types of fresh pork roast is a 325° – 350°F. (160 – 180°C), roasting 22 – 24 minutes to the pound.

A full fresh leg of pork (sometimes referred to as Fresh Ham) usually weighs 8 lb. (4 kg) boned and rolled. Keep the bones when the butcher has them, to place under the roast during the roasting period. A roast of that size should serve 12 – 16 people.

1 cup (250 mL) consommé or water or cider
½ cup (125 mL) fresh lemon juice
Grated rind of 2 lemons
½ tsp. (2 mL) fennel seeds
⅛ tsp. (0.5 mL) nutmeg
1 tsp. (5 mL) savory or sage
3 cloves garlic, crushed
Half or whole leg of fresh ham or
(any other cut of fresh pork)

Mix all the ingredients in a large bowl. (Do not use metal.) To crush the garlic, place the unpeeled clove on a wooden board, place a large knife flat on top, and give a bang on the blade of the knife — the clove will be crushed and the paper thin peel will be very easy to pull off. Place as is in the marinating mixture. Marinate 2 – 3 days, covered and refrigerated.

Place the uncooked roast in a roasting pan — on a rack or on flat bones. Pour the marinating mixture on top. Roast in a preheated 325°F. (160°C) oven, 20 – 22 minutes to the pound. (Marinating tenderizes the meat which explains why it may take only 20 minutes per lb.) Baste roast every 30 minutes with pan juices. Remove to a hot platter, and cover while making gravy.

Simple Gravy: Place roasting pan on direct heat. Add 1 cup (250 mL) *cold* water or *cold* tea, stir with a wooden spoon, scraping bottom and all around the roasting pan, over medium heat. The cold water melts the browning residue that sticks to the pan. Then add 2 tbsp. (30 mL) dry Madeira. Strain in hot sauceboat.

To Thicken Gravy: Add 2 tbsp. (30 mL) flour to fat in pan, before adding water. Mix thoroughly. Add the cold water or cold tea. Stir and scrape over medium heat until creamy. Adjust thickness of sauce to your taste by adding first the Madeira then, little by little, cold tea or water. Stir well. Strain in sauceboat.

Southern Orange Sauce: Combine in a saucepan, 2 tbsp. (30 mL) each of brown sugar and cornstarch. Stir in 1 cup (250 mL) fresh orange juice, 1 cup (250 mL) diluted consommé or 1 cup (250 mL) of ham gravy done as "simple gravy," ¼ cup (60 mL) dry sherry. Bring slowly to a boil, stirring most of the time. When transparent and creamy, pour into roasting residue. Scrape and stir, add a little cold water if necessary. Strain in sauceboat.

Braised Loin of Pork

This was not only a year-round family favorite, it also was an authentic Quebec roast. At home the justly famous *graisse de rôti* was served cold on homemade bread toasted on the big shiny wood stove. It is made with the meat dripping. The roast was served cold and the *graisse de rôti* was for another meal.

3 – 4 lb. (1½ – 2 kg) loin of pork
2 garlic cloves
1 tsp. (5 mL) dry mustard
1 tsp. (5 mL) savory
Salt and pepper to taste
1 pork rind or 1 pig's foot
1 cup water

Make 4 incisions in the loin and place ½ clove garlic in each. Rub the meat all over with the dry mustard, letting most of it adhere to the fat. Then sprinkle with the savory again with most of it on the fat.

Place in a Dutch oven, fat side down. Salt and pepper to taste.

Cut the pork rind or pig's foot in several pieces and place them around the meat. Add the water.

Now there are two ways to roast the meat:

1) Place the Dutch oven over high heat and bring the whole to a boil. Then cover and simmer over low heat for 2 hours. Then uncover and cook over high heat until the liquid evaporates, and the fat part of the meat starts to sizzle and brown. Then set the meat on a platter.

2) Roast uncovered, in the Dutch oven at 300°F. (150°C) for 45 minutes per lb. (500 g). When done, remove the meat to a platter and place pan over direct heat to make the gravy or *graisse de rôti*.

To make a gravy in both cases, add to juice in pan, 1 cup of cold water, then simmer 10 minutes, stirring often and scraping the bottom and sides of pan.

To make the *graisse de rôti* instead of gravy — add only ½ cup (125 mL) cold water, stir and scrape pan over high heat for 2 – 3 minutes, then pass through a fine sieve in a bowl. Refrigerate overnight.

With the pig's foot or pork rind, make a cold crackling in the following manner. Turn what is in the sieve into a bowl. Remove all the bones (pig's feet have many) and cut up the meat into small pieces. Place in a small mold — pour on top 2 – 3 spoonfuls of *graisse de rôti*. Cover and refrigerate until set. To serve, unmold, slice and serve with pickles and toast. *Serves 6.*

Aunt Antoinette's Pork Chops

Apples with meat were used a great deal apart from pies and *fruits couteaux*. In the Twenties there was no problems for farmers to sell their apples, since it was almost the only easily available fruit, along with the bananas which came from the British Possessions. Apples were bought by the 50–100 lb. barrel, and the bananas by the cluster. Oranges, grapefruits, lemons and pears were strictly a Christmas pleasure.

6 pork chops
Salt, pepper to taste
½ tsp. (2 mL) sage or savory
1 tsp. (5 mL) butter
3 unpeeled apples, cored and sliced into thick round slices
1 tsp. (5 mL) brown sugar
¼ tsp. (1 mL) cloves or cinnamon

Remove some of the fat from the pork chops. Dice, melt until brown and crisp in a heavy metal frying pan. Add the chops and brown on both sides over medium low heat. Season to taste, sprinkle with the sage or savory. Remove to a platter.

Melt the butter, in the frying pan, add the sugar, cloves or cinnamon. Stir gently until the apples are well coated with the butter, sugar and spices. Cook over medium heat, about 10 minutes, stirring once or twice.

Place pork chops in the pan, set the apples on top. Cover pan and cook over very low heat another 10 minutes.

Serve each chop with a portion of apples on top. *Serves 4–6.*

Manitoba Special

This recipe is a combination of Scandinavian and Mennonite cooking.

6 rib or blade pork chops
2 tbsp. (30 mL) flour
1 tsp. (5 mL) salt
½ tsp. (2 mL) pepper
1 tsp. (5 mL) paprika
2 tbsp. (30 mL) diced pork fat
2 cups (500 mL) dry breadcrumbs
1 onion, finely chopped
1 apple, diced
¼ cup (60 mL) raisins
½ tsp. (2 mL) salt
¼ tsp. (1 mL) pepper

1 tbsp. (15 mL) sage
1 egg, beaten
2 tbsp. (30 mL) butter, melted

Roll the chops in a mixture of the flour, salt, pepper and paprika. Brown lightly in melted pork fat in a cast-iron frying pan.

Combine remaining ingredients in a bowl and mix thoroughly.

Place in an 8 × 8-in. (20 × 20 cm) buttered casserole, top with chops, and bake uncovered in a 350°F. (180°C) oven 40 – 50 minutes, or until tender. *Serves 4 – 6.*

Devilled Pork Chops

This flavorful dish is very nice served with spinach and mashed potatoes.

6 rib or blade pork chops
1 onion, finely chopped
3 tbsp. (50 mL) lemon juice
1 tsp. (5 mL) dry mustard
1 tbsp. (15 mL) brown sugar
4 tbsp. (60 mL) chili sauce or catsup
2 tsp. (10 mL) Worcestershire sauce

Remove most of the fat from chops and set aside. Soak chops 1 hour in a marinating mixture made of remaining ingredients.

Melt and brown reserved fat in a frying pan. Drain chops, brown on both sides in fat, then add marinating mixture. Cover and simmer over low heat — 1 hour for rib chops. *Serves 4 – 6.*

Barbecued Spareribs

I have used this recipe for years with success. It is especially useful because it freezes perfectly for 4 – 6 months and keeps refrigerated for 8 – 10 days. In any case, it reheats without losing any of its flavor.

3 lb. (1.5 kg) pork spareribs
1 garlic clove, minced
3 tbsp. (50 mL) bacon fat
3 onions
1 cup (250 mL) ketchup
½ cup (125 mL) cider vinegar
1 tsp. (5 mL) curry
1 tsp. (5 mL) paprika

¼ tsp. (1 mL) chili powder
1 tbsp. (15 mL) brown sugar
1 cup (250 mL) consommé
½ tsp. (2 mL) salt
Pinch of pepper
½ tsp. (2 mL) dry mustard

Brown the garlic in the bacon fat and cut the spareribs into individual serving-size portions. Remove the garlic from the fat and brown the spareribs quickly. Place both the garlic and the meat in a baking dish. Slice the onions over the meat.

Mix together the remaining ingredients. Pour over the meat and onions. Cover and bake at 350°F. (180°C) for 1½ hours. *Serves 6.*

Homemade Sausages: Sausages (*saucisses*) derive from the Latin *salsus*. The Romans are in fact the first recorded sausage-makers, because they found it a way of preserving the smaller parts and scraps of the pig for winter eating. The Italians are still supreme producers of dried and smoked sausages. But when it comes to fresh sausage, France is the country. The art of sausage-making is an easy one to acquire, since recipes are simple and pork is readily available. A freshly homemade sausage, well flavored and properly cooked is almost a forgotten pleasure.

Making a good sausage is a simple affair since it is only ground meat and seasoning, the same as a meat loaf, even if you do not have an electric mixer with a sausage-making attachment or a square of caul or *crépinette* — although most of the time your butcher could supply you with it. Or you may want to follow the European style — making a tube of clean cotton (an old dishcloth is good) about 1½ – 2 in. (3.65 – 5 cm) in diameter. Cut the width you need and machine-stitch the length you need. Wet the cloth and fill tightly with sausage meat, then wrap in foil. Refrigerate 24 hours. To use, cut a slice the thickness you prefer, remove cotton and cook same as sausage.

Feel free to adjust any of the recommended seasonings and flavorings to suit your personal taste — only the proportions of meat and fat should remain the same.

Basic Formula for Sausage Meat

Prepare in double or triple quantity — as homemade sausages will freeze well for 3 – 4 months, properly wrapped. 1 cup (250 mL) of meat or fat, minced, is about ½ lb. (250 g).

1 lb. (500 g) *lean* pork from neck or shoulder
½ lb. (250 g) all fat (taken from back)
1 tbsp. (15 mL) salt
½ tsp. (2 mL) allspice
½ tsp. (2 mL) freshly ground pepper
¼ tsp. (1 mL) sage or thyme

Put the lean and the fat pork through the mincer once or twice, according to the texture desired. (Twice gives a fine minced sausage.) Add seasonings. Blend with hands, until thoroughly mixed. *Serves 6.*

Variations: Replace ½ lb. (250 g) back fat by 1 lb. (500 g), add ½ tsp. (2 mL) cinnamon or replace allspice by 1 tsp. (5 mL) cinnamon.

Veal-Pork Sausage: Use ½ lb. (250 g) pork, ½ lb. (250 g) veal from shoulder, ½ lb. (250 g) fat, back or top of bacon fat, omit spices and reduce salt to 2 tsps. (10 mL). Thyme or sage remains the same.

Hunter's Sausage: ½ lb. (250 g) raw chicken (preferably the thigh, legs and wings), turkey, duck or game meat; ¼ lb. (125 g) lean pork, ¼ lb. (125 g) veal, ½ lb. (250 g) fat back. Same seasonings as basic type, add ¼ cup (60 mL) fine breadcrumbs, ¼ cup (60 mL) brandy or dry port wine. Hunter's sausage was the world famous breakfast in the early Twenties at the St. Regis Hotel in New York.

Traditional English Sausage Meat

Unlike the French type of sausage, the English type usually has a binder, mostly dried fine breadcrumbs or oatmeal.

2¼ lb. (1.25 kg) lean pork
1½ lb. (750 g) back fat or top fat of loin
4 cups (1 L) fine breadcrumbs
2 tbsp. (30 mL) salt
1 tsp. (5 mL) white pepper
¼ tsp. (1 mL) mace
½ tsp. (2 mL) ground ginger
¼ tsp. (1 mL) sage

Grind meat and fat twice, together when possible. Add remaining ingredients. Blend thoroughly. Form into any type of sausage. Always cook these over medium low heat, with 2 tsp. (10 mL) of fat per 1 lb. (500 g), as the filler makes them drier. *Yield:* 4 lb. (2 kg).

Oxford Sausages

Homemade sausages are so good that once you start, you will always want to make them yourself. To pan fry them, no fat is better than bacon fat. If you have a food processor, grind the meat yourself, this way you are in perfect control of your ingredients. Homemade sausages will keep 4 – 5 days refrigerated, and 2 – 3 months frozen.

1 lb. (500 g) ground pork or lean pork shoulder
¾ lb. (200 g) beef suet, ground
2 cups (500 mL) fine bread or cracker crumbs
Grated rind of 1 lemon
¼ tsp. (1 mL) nutmeg
1 tsp. (5 mL) pepper
1 tsp. (5 mL) dried sage leaves
1 tsp. (5 mL) salt
1 tsp. (5 mL) marjoram

If you are using a food processor, first grind the pork shoulder very fine; this takes about 40 seconds. Remove and do the same for the beef suet. (I like to use beef kidney suet, as I was taught to do in England; it is more delicate in flavor than other fat. I also use veal kidney fat, when beef is not available.) Or else, ask butcher to grind pork and suet together twice.

Place in a bowl and add the remaining ingredients. Then mix and knead with your hands until very smooth. Shape into sausages — the size depends on your preference. Roll into fine breadcrumbs mixed with enough paprika to give it a tinge of color. Place in plastic box in a single layer, to make two rows, and separate with a sheet of wax paper. Broil or pan fry as you would regular sausages. *Serves 6 – 8*

Note: Flavor and texture are a bit different, depending on whether bread or crackers are used, although both are nice.

Cornell Sausages

A quick easy formula created by the Food Science Education Department at Cornell University, quickly prepared from sausage meat sold for stuffing at your butchers.

1 lb. (500 g) pork sausage meat
1 tsp. (5 mL) salt
½ tsp. (2 mL) freshly ground pepper
½ tsp. (2 mL) sage

Blend ingredients thoroughly. Form into sausage patties or long sausages. Cook according to basic rule. This mixture will freeze for 3 – 5 weeks. *Serves 4 – 6.*

Cooking Sausages

Sausages are usually thrown in a pan and cooked any old way until browned. I would like to give you three easy perfect methods to cook them.

Broiled Sausages: For each 1 lb. (500 g) of sausages, mix in a plate ½ tsp. (2 mL) paprika, ¼ tsp. (1 mL) sugar, ½ tsp. (2 mL) sage, savory or curry powder and 1 tsp. (5 mL) flour. Roll separated sausages in this mixture. Set on broiler rack or a grill pan. Preheat broiler for 10 minutes. Place sausage pan, 3 in. (7.5 cm) from source of heat. Broil 3 – 4 minutes, turn sausages, and broil 2 minutes or until browned. *Serves 4.*

Pan Fried Sausages: Place sausage links in a single layer in a cold cast-iron frying pan. *Cover* and cook over low heat, about 8 minutes, shaking pan once, without uncovering pan. Then uncover and increase heat to medium. Cook until golden brown all over, shaking pan once or twice during cooking period. Drain fat. Salt, pepper and serve.

Sweet Sour Sausages: Pan-fry 1 lb. (1 kg) sausages. Mix over low heat in small saucepan, ¼ cup (60 mL) prepared mustard, ½ cup (125 mL) red currant jelly, 1 tbsp. (15 mL) brandy, 1 tsp. (5 mL) soy sauce, stir until hot and well mixed. Pour over the sausages. Simmer 5 minutes. Serve with mashed potatoes. *Serves 4.*

Apple and Sausage Patties

½ lb. (250 g) sausage meat or fresh pork minced twice
¾ cup (200 mL) bread crumbs
1 cup (250 mL) grated apples, unpeeled
2 tbsp. (30 mL) all-purpose flour
1 egg
Salt and pepper to taste

Mix together sausage meat (or minced pork), bread crumbs, grated apples and flour. Blend with egg and season to taste. Form into small flat cakes, similar to fish cakes. Roll in fine bread crumbs, and fry in shortening over medium heat, 10 minutes on both sides. Serve hot with a dish of homemade chili sauce, large slices of homemade bread toasted on the coal stove, and a large cup of steaming green tea. This is still the traditional breakfast on many a French-Canadian farm, especially *dans le bas de Québec*, (between Quebec City and Sept-Isles). And, of course, I often enjoy it myself. *Serves 4.*

Monique's Bacon and Sausage Grill

Prepare meat on grill pan and keep refrigerated until ready to serve. Place under heat before starting the eggs.

½ lb. (250 mL) bacon
1 lb. (500 mL) sausages
Paprika to taste
Port wine

Spread bacon on grill, then the sausages. Sprinkle with paprika. Broil 3 in. (7.5 cm) from source of heat for 5 minutes. Turn sausages and remove the pieces that are cooked, to a warm platter. Finish cooking 3 – 4 minutes. Set on platter. Spoon a little port wine over each sausage (not on the bacon). *Serves 3 – 4.*

Easy Chop Suey

For a practical, economical pork dish, there are few recipes better than this. Once you have everything ready, the cooking is not complicated.

3 tbsp. (50 mL) vegetable oil
2 tsp. (10 mL) salt
½ tsp. (2 mL) pepper
1 lb. (500 g) cubed pork shoulder
3 tbsp. (50 mL) soy sauce
3 cups (750 mL) celery, in 1-in. (2.5 cm) pieces
2 large onions, each in 6 pieces
1 tbsp. (15 mL) molasses
2 cups (500 mL) boiling water
2 cups (500 mL) bean sprouts
3 tbsp. (50 mL) cornstarch
¼ cup (60 mL) cold water
3 cups (750 mL) cooked rice

Heat the oil, salt and pepper in a large frying pan. Sear the pork over high heat for 2 – 3 minutes. Turn the heat down to low, and cook uncovered for 5 – 8 minutes.

Add the soy sauce, mix well, then add the celery and onions. Cook for 3 minutes, then mix the molasses and boiling water and pour over the mixture. Cover and cook over low heat for 10 – 20 minutes, then add the bean sprouts and cook for another 3 minutes.

Blend the cornstarch with the cold water. Add to the chop suey and continue cooking for 3 – 4 minutes, stirring constantly, until the sauce thickens and becomes transparent. Serve with the rice. *Serves 6.*

A Few Notes on Lamb

For some people, lamb has never been in style. For many years it was almost unpopular, mainly because it was too often cooked until it was grey and stringy and had lost its flavor. But Canadians seem to have finally learned what the Europeans have always known — lamb is superb when done to just a pink succulent degree.

When roasting lamb, the shape of the particular cut must be taken into consideration. The leg, crown and saddle are roasted at 325°F. (160°C), to a meat thermometer reading of 135 – 140°F. (55 – 60°C) for medium-rare. Young spring or baby lamb is best roasted at 425°F. (225°C) to 160°F. (70°C) on the thermometer.

A meat thermometer, incidentally, is almost mandatory for success in roasting any cut of lamb. And remember, lamb should be served on hot plates.

French Glazed Leg of Lamb

This is equally good served hot or cold with potato salad. When serving cold lamb, remove it from the refrigerator and leave it at least 4 hours at room temperature, or roast it in the morning and leave it out until dinner time.

4 – 4½ lb. (2 – 2.5 kg) leg of lamb
¼ cup (60 mL) prepared mustard (Dijon preferably)
½ cup (125 mL) honey
½ tsp. (2 mL) rosemary
1 tsp. (5 mL) salt
¼ tsp. (1 mL) pepper

Place lamb on a rack in a shallow roasting pan and cook at 325°F. (160°C) for 1 hour. Combine remaining ingredients, pour over meat and roast at same temperature for another 2 hours or until thermometer registers 160°F. (70°C) for well done. Baste 4 – 5 times during roasting. *Serves 6 – 8.*

Steamed Lamb

When I'm busy, I prepare this after breakfast, slip the pots into a 200°F. (95°C) oven and go away until mealtime. It is a complete dinner by itself.

3 – 4 peeled potatoes, thickly sliced
4 carrots, cut into thick sticks
3 unpeeled tomatoes, cut into eighths

2 onions, thickly sliced
3 – 4 whole garlic cloves, peeled
2 – 3 lb. (1 – 1.5 kg) stewing lamb, sliced or cubed
2 tbsp. (30 mL) butter
1 green pepper, cut into sticks
½ cup (125 mL) minced parsley
1 tsp. (5 mL) salt
½ tsp. (2 mL) crushed peppercorns

Two pots are needed for this stew — one, uncovered, to be filled with the ingredients and another large enough, tightly covered, to take the first.

In the smaller pot, make layers of all the ingredients in order given, breaking onions into rings, dabbing butter over meat, and sprinkling salt and pepper here and there. Repeat layers until all ingredients are used.

Place the smaller pot in larger saucepan, and add hot water to the larger pot until it comes halfway up the outside of the smaller pot. Cover the larger one, and simmer for 2 – 3 hours or until meat is tender.

There will be a lot of clear, tasty gravy; so, to serve, place a large slice of dry bread in a soup plate for each person, cover with some gravy and top with meat and vegetables. *Serves 6.*

Pan Fried Lamb Kidneys

This is my husband's favorite breakfast.

4 – 6 lamb kidneys
Wine vinegar
Prepared mustard (Dijon Style) or Chutney
1 tbsp. (15 mL) bacon fat or butter
Salt and pepper to taste
1 tsp. (5 mL) water

Remove outer membrane from the kidneys. Leave whole, or halve lengthwise. Rub the kidneys with vinegar, then brush with prepared mustard or chutney. Melt the fat in a frying pan; when lightly colored, add the kidneys and brown. Cook over medium-high heat, 3 minutes for each side. Salt and pepper to taste. Stir, add the water, stir for a few more seconds and serve. *Serves 2 – 3.*

Dorchester English Grill

Lamb chops for a brunch are the height of extravagance and delight to me. Serve this with a large bottle of good chutney and split English muffins toasted and buttered; you may even use homemade muffins.

4 sausages
4 small rib lamb chops
Paprika, to taste
8 slices bacon
4 lamb kidneys, split
Chutney juice
4 medium tomatoes, halved
1 tsp. (5 mL) sugar
1 tbsp. (15 mL) chopped parsley
2 tbsp. (30 mL) fine breadcrumbs
Salt and pepper, to taste
Soft butter
Juice of ½ a lemon

Preheat broiler for 15 minutes. Set sausages on a broiler rack. Set lamb chops beside them and sprinkle with paprika. Arrange bacon alongside, and next to it the lamb kidneys, with cut side down. Brush top of kidneys with a little bit of chutney juice.

Sprinkle tomato halves with sugar, then parsley, then breadcrumbs. Place on rack, salt and pepper to taste, and place tiny lumps of soft butter on each kidney.

Set pan in preheated broiler, at least 4 in. (10 cm) from source of heat, and broil 4 – 5 minutes. Turn chops, sausages and broil 2 – 4 minutes more. Place on a hot platter and sprinkle fresh lemon juice over all. *Serves 4.*

Mint and Onion Dressing

The perfect sauce to serve with thinly sliced cold cooked lamb — or with a vegetable plate or green salad.

¼ cup (60 mL) fresh mint, chopped fine
1 small mild white onion
1 small green pepper, chopped fine
¼ cup (60 mL) lemon French dressing
Salt to taste

Place all the ingredients in a jar, cover and shake until well blended. Shake well before using. It is not necessary to keep it refrigerated; simply keep in a cool place. *Yield:* 2/3 cup (160 mL).

Braised Roast of Veal

This way of cooking veal has mostly disappeared even in Quebec, where it was such a traditional spring Sunday roast. Of course, good milk-fed veal is more and more difficult to find. It is my husband's favorite and surely one of mine.

In my youth, if we had the big roast of beef in the winter, it was *veau braise* in the spring. I prefer to make this with a 4 – 6 lb. (2 – 3 kg) roast because it is just as good cold as it is hot. As the vegetables lose some of their goodness when reheated, I add just the amount I need for the first meal. The rolled shoulder roast was served on week days. For an elegant Sunday dinner, we used a whole loin of veal with the kidney attached.

4 – 6 lb. (2 – 3 kg) rolled shoulder of veal
2 crushed cloves of garlic
3 tbsp. (50 mL) bacon fat or olive oil
6 – 8 even medium potatoes, peeled, left whole
6 – 8 medium onions, peeled, left whole
½ tsp. (2 mL) each thyme and savory
2 tsp. (10 mL) salt
¼ tsp. (1 mL) pepper

Crush the garlic with the flat of a heavy knife — it will then be easy to remove the paper-thin skin. Break up the pieces as they come and stuff bits here and there into incisions made in the meat with the point of a knife.

Melt the fat of your choice (we always used bacon fat) in a heavy metal Dutch oven, then brown the meat until golden all around, over medium heat. As this must be done slowly for the meat to retain its golden color once cooked, it should take about 30 minutes. Then place the part of the roast you wish to have on top when serving, touching the bottom of the pan.

Place the potatoes and onions around the meat and sprinkle with the thyme, savory, salt and pepper. (No liquid is added — veal makes its own gravy.) Cover and braise over medium low heat 1½ – 2 hours or until the meat is tender. As it cooks slowly the vegetables are never overcooked or broken up.

A lot of creamy, nicely-flavored gravy will accumulate in the bottom of the pan. Remove the meat to a hot platter. To give a nice glaze to the vegetables, boil the gravy over medium heat for 5 minutes, turning the vegetables gently with a rubber spatula, until they are well coated with the gravy. With a perforated spoon, place the vegetables on a hot service dish and the gravy in a sauceboat. *Serves 6 – 8.*

Veal Forestière

A stew to grace your dinner table. It's just as good made with lamb, too. When made with veal, I like to use a 1-in. (2.5 cm) thick steak which makes nice cubes. When using lamb I recommend boned shoulder. Both reheat very well.

2 tbsp. (30 mL) each butter and vegetable oil
12 small onions, left whole
1 tsp. (5 mL) sugar
½ lb. (250 g) thinly sliced mushrooms
2 lb. (1 kg) veal steak or boneless shoulder
2 tbsp. (30 mL) brandy
2 tbsp. (30 mL) flour
1 tbsp. (15 mL) tomato paste
½ cup (125 mL) each water and white vermouth
1½ cups (375 mL) undiluted canned consommé
½ tsp. (2 mL) each salt, pepper and thyme
¼ cup (60 mL) heavy cream
Chopped parsley
Grated rind of ½ a lemon

Heat the butter and oil in a frying pan. Add the onions. Sprinkle with the sugar and stir over medium heat until there is a touch of brown here and there. Add the mushrooms. Stir over medium heat 3 minutes. Then remove with a perforated spoon to a 2-quart (2 L) casserole. To fat remaining in the pan, add the veal, cut in 1 in. (2.5 cm) cubes. Stir over high heat until brown here and there. Pour the brandy on top, and put a match to it. When the flame dies down, pour over the onions. Again, in the same pan, stir together the flour and tomato paste. Then add the water, vermouth and consommé. Stir until boiling, salt, pepper and add thyme. Stir again over medium heat. When boiling, pour over meat and onions. Cover and cook in a preheated 350°F. (180°C) oven, 1 hour or until meat is tender. Just before serving, stir in the cream, until well blended in the sauce, sprinkle with parsley and serve.

I use an elegant earthenware casserole that can go on the table — it saves time and dishes. *Serves 6.*

Lièvre Tshiti-Shine

Another Indian delight (pronounced tee-chee-shine) I learned from grand-mère who lived on a farm near Caughnawaga. The mountain Indians used to bring her beautiful hares in January. This dish is so named because it means "January, month of the Great Moon," and it was the perfect time to hunt this delicious mountain hare. I now have six of them in my freezer, which I surely will cook Tshiti-Shine.

1 wild hare, 2 – 3 lb. (1 – 1.5 kg)
½ cup (125 mL) flour
½ tsp. each (2 mL) salt and pepper

1 tsp. (5 mL) savory or sage
3 slices salt pork *or*
 6 slices bacon
2 large onions, thinly sliced
2 cloves garlic, chopped fine
¾ cup (200 mL) water or Dutch gin

Cut the hare in individual pieces — 2 front legs, 2 back legs or shoulder; cut the back in 2 or 3 pieces — the back is the choice piece.

Mix the flour, salt, pepper, and savory or sage. Roll the meat in this until well coated. Reserve any leftover flour. Cut each slice of salt pork or bacon into 3 or 4 pieces. Melt over medium heat until well browned in a Dutch oven. Then, add the pieces of hare and brown on all sides, setting them on a plate when they are done.

Add to the fat in the pan, the onion and garlic, stir until all of it is well coated with the fat. Put the meat back in the pan, and mix in with the onions. Add the water or Dutch gin. If the hunter has given you the liver and kidneys of the hare, both of which are very small, cut them up and add to the meat.

Cover and simmer over low heat, 1 – 1½ hours, or until tender. If you like, the sauce can be thickened by mixing leftover flour with cold water, and simmering until creamy. Pour over the hare and serve. At home, we serve it with buckwheat pancakes instead of the usual potatoes. *Serves 4.*

Rendering Fat

There is little need to buy so much extra fat for cooking if you learn the old and well-proven method of making use of all the fats you usually throw away. The following sterilized fat will keep 2 – 3 months refrigerated, 12 months in the freezer.

Gras Normand: Keep refrigerated in a covered bowl, all types of fat pieces of steak suet, diced and melted, fat dripping from bacon, leftovers, flour-free gravy, etc. Simply add one on top of the other. When you have about 2 cups (500 mL), empty into a saucepan, add 2 cups (500 mL) water, 1 potato, scrubbed, unpeeled and cut in half. Bring to boil. Cover and simmer 25 minutes over low heat. Remove the potato. Pour into a bowl. Cover and refrigerate 12 – 24 hours. Then carefully lift the solid, hard, block of fat from the water. Wrap the fat and keep refrigerated. In the water you will find all the bits and pieces that would sour the fat. They should be thrown out.

Variation: Add 1 small onion cut in half or 2 cloves garlic along with the potato.

Bacon Fat for Baking: Use for gingerbread, spice cake and pudding, oatmeal cookies, to fry onions, etc. Accumulate same as for Gras Normand, without mixing any other fat in the bacon fat. Proceed to sterilize it using 1 cup (250 mL) bacon fat, 1 cup (250 mL) water, 1 small potato. Cook, strain, cool, and refrigerate. Remove block of fat, and proceed same as above.

Nya Fat or Kosher Fat: One of the best things of the kosher table is the intelligent lavish use they make of rendered chicken fat. I have been making it and using it for at least 30 years.

Cut off all the visible yellow fat from a roasting or boiling chicken, or from a turkey. Place in a saucepan. (I like to use an enamelled cast-iron pan.) Pour enough cold water on top to just cover the fat, and simmer uncovered until the water has evaporated. Then, add 1 small onion, chopped, for each cup of fat used.

Note: Sometimes I add a clove of garlic left whole and a bay leaf (although I admit, it is not kosher).

Then, add a thick slice of unpeeled potato and keep cooking over low heat, stirring often, until the yellow fat has turned into brown crackling; the potato will also brown. Strain through a fine sieve. Cover and refrigerate. The next day, unmold and clean the under part of the fat with the blade of a knife. Wrap and keep refrigerated.

9. Fish

Simmered Fresh Cod

When I was young, every Friday noon saw a fish dish of some sort on the luncheon table. When mother could get cod from the Grand Banks of Newfoundland, everyone looked forward to the lunch.

Fresh cod is misunderstood; it is a lean, flaky fish available in many forms, salted, smoked, pickled, flaked, and dried, but to me a 2 – 3 lb. piece of fresh cod is the best.

Mother's simmered cod *garni* was not only colorful and attractive, but delicious to eat. She served it with or without her parsley sauce.

3 – 5 lb. (1.5 – 2.5 kg) fresh cod, in one piece
1 tbsp. (15 mL) coarse salt
8 cups (1½ L) cold water
10 peppercorns
Cut peel of 1 lemon

Rinse cod in cold water and brush all over with salt. Cover and let stand 1 hour in refrigerator, then place in the cold water with peppercorns and lemon peel.

Heat until water is warm, then simmer, uncovered, for 10 minutes per inch of thickness of fish, or until it flakes. When ready, remove fish from water with a perforated ladle. Set on a hot platter. Top with a few sprigs of parsley and serve with bowls of the following garnishes: potatoes boiled in their jackets; melted butter with grated lemon peel to taste; finely-chopped raw onions mixed with parsley; chopped hard-boiled eggs; or grated raw apples (stir in a little lemon juice so they won't darken). Let each person take his choice of garnishes. *Serves: 6 – 8.*

Boiled Cod

In this recipe the cod is truly boiled. As far as flavor and texture are concerned, it is completely different from the Simmered Fresh Cod recipe. At home, we never could say which one we liked best.

Women of the 1900s had many culinary tricks that got lost unless they were passed from one generation to the other. For instance, I have never seen cod cooked in the following manner, but I can assure you that if you try it, you will find it gives the cod a firm, interesting texture. The parsley sauce is the perfect mate, but melted butter with parsley or dill and a chopped hard-cooked egg is also pleasant.

6 – 9 thick slices (fillets or steaks) of fresh cod
8 cups (2 L) water
½ tsp. (2 mL) ground ginger
2 bay leaves
2 thick slices of unpeeled lemon
½ cup (125 mL) melted butter
¼ cup (60 mL) chopped parsley or dill
Grated rind of 1 lemon

Put the fish fillets (or steaks) in a bowl and set under running cold water for one hour. Then rub each fillet all over with salt. This cold water bath gives the cod a firm, interesting texture.

Bring to boil the water, ginger, bay leaves, lemon slices. Gently lower each steak into the boiling mixture and *boil* 5 – 7 minutes.

Lift cod from water, with a perforated spoon to a hot platter.

Melt the butter with the parsley or dill and lemon rind and pour over the fish steaks, or omit this step and serve with Mother's Parsley Sauce. *Serves 6 – 8.*

Mother's Parsley Sauce for Boiled Cod

2 tbsp. (30 mL) butter
3 tbsp. (50 mL) chopped parsley
1 tsp. (5 mL) salt
Pepper to taste
¼ tsp. (1 mL) sugar
1½ cups (400 mL) milk
3 tbsp. (50 mL) flour
¼ cup (60 mL) reserved fish cooking stock
1 tbsp. (15 mL) cider vinegar

Melt the butter until it has a nutty color. Remove from heat, add the parsley, salt, pepper and sugar. Stir well. Cover pan and simmer over *very low heat* for 5 minutes. Add milk, and increase heat. Blend the flour and the cooled fish stock. Add to milk and stir until mixture thickens. Keep hot in top of double boiler. Stir in the vinegar when ready to serve. *Yield:* 2 cups (500 mL).

Haddock à la Royale

A la Royale originally meant cooked wrapped in parchment paper or bag. Today, we have the transparent coating bag which makes it easy. The advantage is that the delicate, elusive flavor, which can be so easily lost, and the light flakiness so easily destroyed with other cooking methods, are saved with this method.

4 medium haddock fillets, fresh or frozen
2 tbsp. (30 mL) butter
4 tbsp. (60 mL) flour
1 tsp. (5 mL) salt
½ tsp. (2 mL) pepper
½ tsp. (2 mL) paprika
½ cup (125 mL) grated mild Cheddar cheese
½ cup (125 mL) milk

When using frozen fillets, thaw out just enough to separate. Cut fresh or frozen fillets into individual portions.

Brush each piece lightly with butter. Blend together in a bowl the flour, salt, pepper and paprika. Roll each piece of fish in this mixture, then into the grated cheese.

Set the plastic bag on a baking sheet. Place fillets in the bag, one next to the other, and gently pour in the milk. Tie loosely, and make two small incisions in top of bag.

Place in a preheated 400°F. (200°C) oven, and bake 20 – 25 minutes.

Open bag, and place fish on hot platter. Sprinkle lavishly with chopped parsley and pour natural gravy remaining in the bag around the fish. *Serves 4 – 5.*

Sole Amandine Grenobloise

Too often this delectable *sole au beurre* is drowned in an overcooked oily butter sauce; beware of that.

1 tbsp. (15 mL) olive or salad oil
1 tbsp. (15 mL) unsalted butter
1 French shallot, chopped fine
1 – 2 lb. (500 – 1000 g) sole fillets
Salt and pepper to taste
1 tbsp. (15 mL) flour
¼ cup (60 mL) blanched almonds, coarsely chopped
1 tbsp. (15 mL) brandy or sherry (optional)

Place the oil and butter in a frying pan large enough to hold the fish comfortably. Set over medium heat. Add the chopped shallots.

Meanwhile dry the fish with absorbent paper, salt and pepper to taste, then sprinkle each piece of fish lightly with the flour. Place fillet in the hot fat. Let cook, 3 minutes on each side, over medium heat. Turn fish with a wide spatula, so it won't break. When ready, the fish should have a golden color, and what fat remains in the pan should still be pale brown. (When too quickly cooked or over too high a heat, the fish dries up and loses its fine delicate flavor. Remove cooked fish to a hot platter. Add the almonds to frying pan. Stir a few seconds over medium heat. Add the brandy or sherry, and stir and pour over fish. If you wish, another spoonful of butter can be added at the same time as the brandy. *Serves 3 – 5.*

Sole Fillets En Cocote

This is equally good served hot or cold. For a very elegant table setting, use those English egg cups with a silver cover. It is then a lovely surprise when the covers are removed by your guests. Individual French ceramic *cocotes* are also attractive.

6 small pieces fresh sole fillets
3 tbsp. (50 mL) butter
Juice of 1 lemon
¼ tsp. (1 mL) curry powder
½ cup (125 mL) finely chopped mushrooms
Salt and pepper to taste
2 – 3 tbsp. (30 – 45 mL) minced parsley

Salt and pepper the fillets, and roll into individual portions. Place each portion in an English egg cup or a ceramic *cocote.* Melt the butter, and add the lemon juice, curry, mushrooms and parsley. Pour a few spoonfuls of this mixture over each cup of fish. Cover, place cup or *cocote* in 2 in. (5 cm) of boiling water, and boil 6 – 8 minutes. Serve with a bunch of watercress on the side, or a green salad. *Serves 6.*

Sage and Onion Bread Sauce

A perfect sauce for fish — in the summer use fresh sage. Super!

1 large onion
1 tbsp. (15 mL) butter
Salt and pepper to taste
½ tsp. (2 mL) sage

½ cup (125 mL) light cream
½ cup (125 mL) consommé
2 tbsp. (30 mL) fresh, coarse dry breadcrumbs

Peel and chop the onion fine, and add the butter, over medium heat, until soft. Add the salt and pepper to taste, then the sage. Mix well and add the cream, consommé and breadcrumbs. Cook, uncovered, over low heat, stirring often, until mixture is creamy-looking and slightly thickened. *Yield:* 1⅓ cups (330 mL).

Fish Fumet

Fumet, used in haute cuisine as part of the liquid in fish sauces, or to poach fillets or small whole fish, is almost a must for the French touch. A very concentrated court bouillon, it always contains fish bones, heads or tails, or all three. It will keep a few weeks refrigerated or three months frozen. It is a luxurious delicate fish bouillon.

1½ – 2 lb. (625 – 1000 g) fish trimmings
(bones, heads, tails, fins)
2 cups (500 mL) water
1 bay leaf
1 onion, sliced
2 cups (500 mL) white wine
1 carrot, scrubbed and sliced
2 celery stalks, in 1-in. (2.5 cm) pieces
2 tbsp. (30 mL) chopped parsley
¼ tsp. (1 mL) each salt and pepper

Bring all the ingredients to a boil in a heavy saucepan, cover and simmer 1 hour, or until liquid is reduced by half. Pour into a sieve lined with cheesecloth, letting it drip through untouched for about 30 minutes. *Yield:* about 3 cups (620 mL).

Spring Salmon with Chive Sauce

I have always found that seasonal foods make the best companions. Try a poached Gaspé salmon caught in the cold spring water of the St. Lawrence, served cold with this simple — but superb — sauce.

4 tbsp. (60 mL) fresh chopped chives
Juice of ½ lemon

3 hard-cooked eggs
4 – 6 tbsp. (60 – 90 mL) vegetable or olive oil
Salt to taste
Pinch of sugar

Stir the chives into the lemon juice.

Mash the yolks and chop the egg whites fine.

Add the oil slowly to the yolks, while stirring with a whisk until it becomes a sort of paste. Add salt and sugar. Mix well and add the chives and lemon juice. Stir thoroughly. Add the chopped egg whites, and stir until well mixed.

Keep in refrigerator until ready to use. Stir well before using. *Yeild:* enough sauce for 2 – 3 lb. (1 – 1.5 kg) poached salmon.

Medway Lake Spiced Salmon

I made this one day in 1959 with a gentleman guest on a T.V. show, taped in Nova Scotia. Through the years, I have received over 600 letters asking for the recipe. I can vouch for its goodness since I have been making it every spring since then with Gaspé Salmon. Young speckled trout are also very nice prepared in the same manner.

½ cup (125 mL) white or cider vinegar
1 cup (250 mL) water
3 tbsp. (50 mL) coarse salt
2 tbsp. (30 mL) honey
¾ cup (200 mL) water
2 tbsp. (30 mL) black peppercorns
2 cinnamon sticks
2 – 4 lb. (1 – 2 kg) fresh salmon or speckled trout

In a large frying pan (stainless steel if possible), mix all ingredients except fish and bring to a boil.

Cut fish into slices about 1½ in. (3.75 cm) thick and place in boiling vinegar mixture. Cover and simmer 20 minutes over low heat. Remove to a non-metal dish and pour vinegar mixture over — it must cover fish completely. Remove cinnamon sticks but leave peppercorns in.

Let cool, cover tightly and keep refrigerated. Serve cold with hot boiled potatoes or a salad. Pickled fish will keep refrigerated for three weeks. *Serves 3 – 6.*

Mayonnaise Chaud-Froid

Basically a variation on mayonnaise (blender or basic type can be used), a *chaud-froid* is often used to coat a poached salmon, or a cooked ham or chicken for presenting on a buffet table. (Also good to add to vegetables.)

1 tbsp. (15 mL) gelatine, unflavored
2 tbsp. (30 mL) cold water
2 cups (500 mL) mayonnaise of your choice

Soak the gelatine in cold water for 5 minutes. Dissolve over hot water. Pour the melted gelatine slowly over the mayonnaise, stirring vigorously. *Yield:* 2 cups (500 mL).

Jiffy Salmon Mousse

My daughter Monique has a few superlative recipes done in 1-2-3, using her blender. Her secret for this one is that she makes it with canned salmon. Make it in the a.m. to serve it p.m.

1 envelope unflavored gelatine
2 tbsp. (30 mL) fresh lemon juice
Grated rind of ½ a lemon
2 French shallots, peeled and cut in half *or*
 3 green onions, cut in four (white and green parts)
½ cup (125 mL) hot bottled clam juice or boiling water
½ cup (125 mL) mayonnaise
1 tsp. (5 mL) dried tarragon *or*
 1 tbsp. (15 mL) fresh dill
1 15½-oz. (439 g) can pink or sockeye salmon
1 cup (250 mL) whipping cream

Place first 4 ingredients in glass jar of blender. Cover and blend at high speed until onion is chopped fine. Add next 5 ingredients (make sure liquid is boiling hot), cover and blend again for 1 minute. At this point, the cream can be whipped or used just as is; the difference is that the mousse will be lighter when the cream is whipped. Whichever way it is used, add to mixture in blender 1/3 at a time, blending for 20 seconds each time. Taste for seasoning. Rinse a 1 quart (1 L) mold in water, and pour in mousse. Cover and refrigerate until set (about 4 hours).

To unmold, dip mold into hot water for a second and invert on service platter.

Decorate with crisp cool watercress or parsley or surround with devilled eggs. *Serves 4.*

Howard's Crustless Salmon Pie

Howard is my daughter's husband. He enjoys good food, and as a good Scot enjoys salmon. This "quicky" of Monique's is truly nice and an economical way of feeding four.

1 15½-oz. (439 g) can red or pink salmon
Milk
1 cup (250 mL) fresh bread cut in cubes
1 onion, minced
1 tsp. (5 mL) salt
¼ tsp. (1 mL) pepper
½ tsp. (2 mL) basil or dill
Juice and grated rind of 1 lemon
2 eggs well beaten

Preheat oven to 350°F. (180°C).

Drain the salmon juice into the 1 cup (250 mL) measure. Fill the cup with milk.

Mash the salmon with a fork, and add the remaining ingredients. Mix well.

Melt about 2 tbsp. (30 mL) of butter in a pie plate. (Monique uses a glass pie plate.) Pour the salmon mixture into the buttered plate. Bake 40 minutes or until golden brown. Serve with a green salad or a coleslaw. In the summer she serves it with delectable baked tomatoes. *Serves 4.*

A Word about Scallops: In North America scallops are sold already cleaned, without their beautiful symmetrical shells. Although this makes the job of preparing them a lot easier, it also makes it a little less romantic. (The shells are sold separately in specialty stores and used as elegant baking dishes.)

Containing high levels of well-balanced protein and very little fat, scallops are among our least expensive shellfish because most of the world's catch comes from the Atlantic coast. Most are sold frozen, and these should be thawed, still in the package, in the refrigerator — 1 lb. (500 g) takes four to six hours. Then dry them in a single layer on absorbent paper for an hour to get rid of any excess water.

Always take care not to overcook scallops, or they'll be tough and stringy instead of tender and creamy.

West Coast Scallops

This delectable way of serving scallops requires the bare minimum of cooking.

1 lb. (500 g) scallops
1 tbsp. (15 mL) lemon juice
1 cup (250 mL) white wine
2 grapefruit
¼ cup (60 mL) melted butter
Salt and paprika to taste
A bunch of watercress or fresh parsley

If frozen, thaw the scallops just enough to separate them. Bring to a boil over high heat with lemon juice and water or wine, then cover and simmer over very low heat 5 – 6 minutes. Drain and cut scallops crosswise into ¼ in. (0.625 cm) slices.

Peel grapefruit, leaving no white skin, and cut into sections, discarding membrane. Arrange sections with scallops in 6 generously buttered scallop shells, individual ovenproof ramekins, or a shallow baking dish.

Pour melted butter evenly over scallops, and sprinkle lightly with salt and paprika. Bake in a 350°F. (180°C) oven 6 minutes, or until heated through, then sprinkle generously with chopped watercress or parsley and garnish with sprigs of either. *Serves 6.*

Baked Scallops

Cooking them in the oven at a high temperature ensures crispness, uses less fat, takes less attention, and eliminates frying odors.

1 lb. (500 g) scallops
1 cup (250 mL) milk
½ tsp. (2 mL) salt
½ tsp. (2 mL) turmeric (optional)
1½ cups (400 mL) fine dry breadcrumbs
1 tsp. (5 mL) paprika
¼ cup (60 mL) melted butter or oil

If frozen, thaw and dry the scallops. Dip them into a mixture of the milk, salt and turmeric, then into breadcrumbs mixed with paprika. Place in a well-greased baking dish, and brush each with melted butter or oil. Bake in a 500°F. (260°C) oven — (make sure it has reached that temperature) — for no more than 8 minutes and serve immediately, with Remoulade Sauce or plain mayonnaise. *Serves 4.*

Scallops Cantonese

Here, the brief cooking time and perfect seasoning enhance the delicate flavor of the scallops. Serve with instant canned fried rice for a complete meal.

1 lb. (500 g) scallops
1 tbsp. (15 mL) cornstarch
4 tbsp. (60 mL) cold water
2 tbsp. (30 mL) vegetable sesame oil
1 tsp. (5 mL) salt
1 green onion, chopped
2 slices fresh ginger

If frozen, thaw and dry the scallops. Cut each across in 4 slices. Mix cornstarch with cold water, and set aside.

Heat oil in a large frying pan over high heat, add scallops and stir for 1 minute. Add salt, green onions and ginger (use nothing but fresh ginger) and stir over high heat for 2 minutes. Add cornstarch mixture and stir for 1 minute over low heat, or until pan juices become translucent and creamy (the scallop slices will be opaque). Serve immediately. *Serves 4.*

Cold Poached Lobster Tails

With the freshness of this dish all the promises of spring are fulfilled. To me this is true because I like to serve these when I get the first young fragrant mint in the garden. Serve cold with a cool bottle of Rhine wine and crunchy, cold celery, and it is perfect!

4 – 6 frozen lobster tails
1 cup (250 mL) dry white wine
1 cup (250 mL) boiling water
1 tsp. (5 mL) salt
Large bouquet of fresh mint
3 lemons, unpeeled, thinly sliced

Choose the 4 lobster tails to give you a total of 2½ lb. (1.25 kg) enough to serve 4, but you may wish to have 1 or 2 more. They can be added without changing anything else.

Thaw the lobster overnight in the refrigerator. Split each tail lengthwise with a sharp knife or scissors. Place in a saucepan with the wine, boiling water and salt. Bring to a fast rolling boil. Then immediately cover and turn off heat. Let stand 20 to 30 minutes or until shells turn pink.

Drain, let cool covered at room temperature. Line a platter with mint, top with the sliced lemons. Place lobster tails on top. Cover with plastic wrap. Let stand at least 1 hour before serving. I like to eat this with hot popovers. *Serves 4 – 6.*

Note: The best is to use the same wine for cooking as for drinking. The French Muscadet costs less than the Rhine wine and it is also very nice.

10. *Poultry*

Chicken Every Which Way

Ah, chicken . . . there is no bird more accommodating or more versatile. Chicken can be purchased fresh, frozen, ready-to-cook, in parts, as broilers, roasters, fowl or capon — even canned whole or in half or boned.

In the kitchen it can be boiled, poached, fricaseed, broiled, barbecued, roasted, deep fried, pot roasted or served in casseroles or pot pies. Even the left-overs are most obliging: they can be turned into sophisticated salads or delicious soups, served in sandwiches or in creamy sauces, or combined with rice or other ingredients. What more can one ask of any bird — except, of course, eggs?

Creating any of these delicious dishes calls for some basic knowledge, of course, but once you have mastered that, you can go on creating your own new dishes indefinitely. After all, roasting a chicken every Sunday should not be the end of your repertoire of chicken cuisine.

The Kinds and Quantities of Chicken You Can Buy: Cornish hens weight up to 1 lb. (2 kg) and you need one bird per serving. Squab broilers, up to 1½ lb. (3 kg) ½ – 1 bird per serving. Broilers and fryers, 2½ – 3½ lb. (5 – 7 kg) ¼ – ½ bird per serving. Roasters run over 4 lb. (12 – 16 kg) and capons 6 – 8 lb. (8 kg) and for both kinds allow ¾ – 1 lb. (1.25 – 2 kg) per serving.

How to Recognize a Good Bird: See that the bird has a wide body, that it is plump and round-breasted, with short legs. Look for streaks of fat down the back, sides and thighs. Make sure the skin is clean and soft, with very few pin feathers and no bruises.

How to Store Chicken: Remove it from the store wrapping. Take out the little paper bag containing the innards. Rewrap the chicken loosely in waxed paper. Store it in the coldest spot in your refrigerator, but not in the freezer. Use it within two or three days.

Frozen chicken should be kept frozen until time to thaw for cooking. After thawing it, cook within 24 hours, meanwhile keeping refrigerated.

To thaw frozen chicken, place unwrapped in the refrigerator and allow 5 hours per lb. of chicken, or place it unwrapped in cold water and allow 1 hour per lb. One important rule: all fresh or frozen chicken will taste much better and be more tender if it is brought to room temperature before cooking.

How to Tell When It's Cooked: The old-fashioned method of estimating cooking time for poultry — by minutes per lb. — was based on undrawn poultry, not on the eviscerated bird you buy today. So it is not accurate.

A meat thermometer inserted into the middle of the dressing in a stuffed bird is by far the best guide to tell you when the bird is cooked. It should register 165°F. (74°C) when done. For an unstuffed bird, place the thermometer in the middle of the thick muscle on the inside of the thigh. (Be sure it does not rest on the bone.) Temperature here will be 190°F. (90°C) when the bird is cooked.

When you don't have a meat thermometer, test for doneness by twisting a drumstick. It should move easily. (Don't stab the chicken with a fork. This allows juices to escape, and dries out the bird.) The best roasting heat is 350°F. (180°C) for a bird up to 3 lb. (1.5 kg) 325°F. (160°C) for a 3 – 6 lb. (1.5 – 3 kg) one.

How to Stew a Chicken

When Mother said "stew," she really should have said "simmer" a chicken. Done that way, we had chicken fat to cook with; broth and meat for sandwiches, and meat for salads or chicken pie or chicken à la King. This is another of my grandmother's ways that I learned from Mother, and one my daughter and granddaughter now use.

During the winter holiday season, when turkey was plentiful, the leaner or smaller type was also simmered, then the skin, bones and fat removed, the meat cut into small pieces and packed into a loaf pan. The liquid was defatted and reduced to 1½ cups (400 mL) then poured over the chicken pieces. There was just enough jelly to hold the chicken together. It was used in all sorts of ways. Sliced and served on crispy lettuce with a good homemade lemon mayonnaise was, and still is, my favorite way.

4 – 5 lb. (2 – 2.5 kg) chicken
2 tbsp. (10 mL) coarse salt
1 large onion stuck with 2 cloves
2 carrots, peeled, left whole
1 large rib of celery with leaves
6 – 10 peppercorns

2 bay leaves
1 tsp. (5 mL) thyme

Leave whole or cut chicken into four pieces. Add 3–4 cups (750–1000 mL) hot water. Add the remaining ingredients. Cover, bring to boil, then *simmer* over low heat 2–4 hours, depending on age and size of chicken. When done, remove chicken to a large bowl. Pour the hot consommé over it, cover the bowl, and let stand overnight, preferably on a kitchen counter or in a cool room.

The next day, remove bones and skin. Skim off the fat, and strain the broth. Keep the whole thing covered and refrigerated or frozen. *Serves 6.*

Fried Chicken

If there were ten, twelve or fifteen of us at our family table when I was growing up, and chicken was served, this was a favorite. I have often used it as a hot buffet dish. It can be prepared ahead of time and warmed up in about 20 minutes in a 200°F. (95°C) oven. Everyone used to agree that the success depended on using pure fat to fry the pieces, such as pure lard; but the favorite was always bacon fat. To prepare the bacon fat, a cup or two of it was placed in a saucepan with ½ cup (125 mL) of water and 1 small potato, unpeeled and left whole. The fat was simmered for 15 minutes, the potato was removed and the fat poured into a bowl and kept in the refrigerator for 2–3 hours. (This could be done anytime, as it keeps 1 month refrigerated.) When the fat had hardened, it was lifted from the water that fell into the bottom of the bowl with all the bits and pieces that were in the fat. Then you have a pure unsalted fat to work with. To this day, I do this, using all the available meat fat I have; and mix them, sterilize them, and keep them refrigerated. Not only do you save money by not having to buy expensive fat, but the flavor of the food cooked in it is greatly enhanced.

1 cut-up broiler chicken or 2 lb. (1 kg) chicken legs and wings
Sterilized bacon fat or pure lard
½ cup (125 mL) butter
1 tsp. (5 mL) tarragon or thyme or basil
1 large clove garlic, left whole
Salt and pepper to taste

Brown chicken pieces in large frying pan containing ½ in. (1.5 cm) shortening. Do not crowd the pieces; turn only once. Transfer to a shallow baking pan. (I use a large cookie sheet). Salt and pepper. While the second batch cooks, finish the first batch. Now here is the flavoring secret: melt the butter, add the herbs and the clove of garlic. Using a pastry brush, coat each piece of browned chicken with this butter. When the pan is full (with one piece next to the other), transfer to a preheated 300°F. (150°C) oven to finish frying and cooking. It will then be crisply coated, brown and buttery; and the dripping in the pan can make a very good gravy by adding flour and consommé or wine.

When all the chicken is ready, set attractively on a large warmed-up platter. Cover with foil paper. Make a few slits in the paper with the point of a knife. Turn off oven heat and put in the platter. The chicken will stay hot for about 1 hour. If it has cooled a little, set the oven at 200°F. (95°C) for 15 – 20 minutes. *Serves 4.*

Milk-Fried Chicken

This recipe was given to me by a farmer's wife in the Eastern Townships of Quebec. She remembered this way from her grandparents' time. She told me that up until 1925, no one roasted a chicken; rather, they milk-fried it. It was a Loyalist tradition. I usually serve this recipe with her light and tasty *'Buttermilk Biscuits.'*

2½ – 3 lb. (2 – 2.5 kg) frying chicken
¼ cup (60 mL) flour
2 tsp. (10 mL) salt
¼ tsp. (1 mL) pepper
¼ tsp. (1 mL) sage
Generous pinch of turmeric
2 tbsp. (30 mL) any fat
3 tbsp. (50 mL) flour
2 cups (500 mL) milk

Cut chicken into serving pieces. Mix the ¼ cup (60 mL) flour with the seasonings, then dredge chicken thoroughly. Melt fat (the cook who gave me this recipe likes to use chicken fat) and brown chicken over medium heat. Place pieces in a baking dish as done.

To fat remaining in pan, add the 3 tbsp. (50 mL) flour and stir until blended. Add milk, cook until creamy and smooth, then pour over chicken. Cover and bake at 350°F. (180°C) for 45 – 60 minutes, or until chicken is tender. *Serves 3 – 4.*

Monique's Spiced Fried Chicken

Another one of Monique's quick specialties. Very good hot — or cold. When there is any left-over chicken, place the pieces in a dish, and pour a spoonful of dry Madeira on top. Cover and place in a 300°F. (150°C) oven for 5 – 10 minutes, depending on quantity. Use a cut up chicken or chicken legs and wings.

¼ cup (60 mL) flour
1 tsp. (5 mL) cinnamon
½ tsp. (2 mL) garlic powder
½ tsp. (2 mL) curry powder
½ tsp. (2 mL) thyme
2 lb. (1000 mL) chicken
Juice of 1 lemon
2 tbsp. (30 mL) oil, margarine or butter

Mix together on a large plate the first 5 ingredients. Rub each piece of chicken with the lemon juice. Roll into spice mixture to coat.

Melt the fat in large frying pan. Brown chicken slowly on both sides. Cook, uncovered, over low heat 30 – 40 minutes, or until chicken is tender. Turn once during the cooking period. *Serves 4.*

Monique's Half-and-Half Broiler

This is done with a 3-lb. broiler, but she sometimes does the same with wings and legs. There is a devilled and a barbecued sauce on top — it is half and half — hence the name of her creation.

1 – 3 lb. (0.5 – 1.5 kg) broiler, cut in 6 or 8 pieces
1 cup (250 mL) ketchup or chili sauce
6 tbsp. (100 mL) honey
1 lemon, unpeeled, thinly sliced

Place the chicken pieces in a roasting pan about 2 in. (5 cm) high.

Mix together the ketchup or chili sauce and the honey. Spread on top of chicken pieces. Place 1 or 2 slices of lemon on top of each piece. Cook, uncovered, in a preheated 300°F. (150°C) oven, 1 hour or until chicken is tender. Place chicken on a hot platter. Place roasting pan over medium heat. Add ½ cup (125 mL) cold water or ¼ cup (60 mL) each of Port or Madeira, and cold water. Scrape the bottom and sides of pan to remove all the crunchy bits and pieces sticking to the pan. Serve separately as is or strain. *Serves 4 – 6.*

Variation: Replace chicken with 6 – 8 pork chops 1 – 1½ in. (2.5 – 3 cm) thick. Prepare and cook same time as the chicken.

Monique's Baked Chicken Legs and Hot Biscuits

On Saturday night, when there could be from three to eight people at the table, this dish is one of her favorites, because she can use more or less chicken legs and usually add hot biscuits and gravy. As the chicken legs are very good cold, she tells me it is more economical to cook a few more than you will need, to have some handy for a quick meal.

4 – 8 chicken legs
½ cup (125 mL) flour
1 tsp. (5 mL) salt
1 tsp. (5 mL) tarragon or savory
½ tsp. (2 mL) turmeric or paprika
3 tbsp. (50 mL) butter, margarine or bacon fat.

Place in a plastic bag the flour, salt, tarragon or savory, turmeric or paprika. Shake well to mix.

Melt the fat in a 15 in. × 10 in. × 2 in. dripping pan (37 cm × 25 cm × 5 cm). Place a few chicken legs in the bag of seasoned flour, and shake until well coated; then place in melted fat one next to the other. Repeat until all has been used. Bake in a preheated 400°F. (200°C) oven 30 – 45 minutes, or until tender, crusty and brown.

Meanwhile prepare a batter of hot biscuits or *if you must,* use a package type.

Then move the cooked chicken legs to one side, piling together, and place biscuits on the other side, one next to the other, right in the chicken gravy. Bake 15 minutes or until biscuits are golden brown. *Serves 4 – 8.*

Biscuits

2 cups (500 mL) all-purpose *or*
1 cup (250 mL) whole wheat flour *and*
1 cup (250 mL) white flour
3 tsp. (15 mL) baking powder
½ tsp. (2 mL) salt
¼ cup (60 mL) shortening, bacon fat or margarine
About ⅔ cup (200 mL) milk

Place together in a bowl the flour, baking powder and salt. Drop the fat into this dry mixture, and with a knife or fingertips work the mixture into coarse crumbs. Add the milk and blend with a few vigorous strokes. As flour varies in texture, you may need a little more milk, but add it only a spoonful at a time. Turn the dough on a lightly-floured board and knead gently with fingertips for 30 seconds.

Pat out or roll dough to a ½-in. (2.5 cm) thickness. Cut biscuits and bake as directed. *Serves 4 – 8.*

Bacon Chicken Wings

Monique's unusual way of cooking chicken wings, equally good hot or cold, makes it a perfect finger food in the summer, for a meal in the garden. Monique serves them with hot parsleyed noodles and a green salad.

8 – 12 chicken wings
½ – ¾ lb. (250 – 400 g) bacon

Dice the bacon. Spread in bottom of heavy metal deep frying pan. Place the wings over the diced bacon. Cover and place over low heat for 30 minutes, then turn the wings, which will be covered with the diced, crisp golden bacon. Cover again and cook another 30 minutes over low heat — and that is it. Salt and pepper to taste, and serve. *Serves 4.*

Summer Picnic Chicken

When the grass is thick and rich, the vegetable garden is spilling over with its bounty, and the winds are balmy — time has come for at least one picnic. For me, this cold chicken with marinated garden fresh tomatoes is the best of all.

When I can have fresh strawberries, I wash them, but do not remove the stems, wash the basket, line it with a pretty paper doily, and put the strawberries back in their nest. I crush 6 – 8 petals from wild rose bush in a cup of sugar, place in a glass jar. When time comes, we dip a strawberry in the rose-sugar, close our eyes and live a second of romance, even if we are old!

¼ cup (60 mL) each fresh lime and lemon juice
⅓ cup (80 ml) white wine or cider
1 crushed clove garlic
1 tsp. (5 ml) salt
½ tsp. (2 mL) tarragon
¼ tsp. (1 mL) pepper
2 – 3 lb. (6 kg) broiler chickens, quartered
3 tbsp. (50 mL) butter

Mix the lime and lemon juice with the white wine or cider, garlic, salt, tarragon and pepper. Place quarters of broiler side by side in a shallow non-metal pan. Rub each piece of chicken with the lemon – lime mixture, and pour any remaining mixture on top. Cover and refrigerate overnight.

To cook, arrange drained chicken in a baking pan, without overlapping, skin side up. Dot with the butter. Bake uncovered in a preheated 400°F. (200°C) oven, about 40 minutes, or until done and golden brown. Baste every

10 minutes with the remaining marinade, then with the pan juices. Remove to a dish. Pour drippings into a separate dish. Cover. Keep chicken in a cool place, but do not refrigerate. Refrigerate drippings. Remove the hardened fat from the top of the cold drippings. Use the golden-coloured jelly to serve with the chicken. *Serves 4.*

Lister Sinclair Chicken Special

I have admired the learning of Mr. Sinclair, author, actor, critic and mathematician, for many years. On T.V., he taught me how to make this luscious dish, which showed me another of his many talents.

4 whole chicken breasts with skin
Salt and pepper to taste
¼ – ⅓ cup (60 – 80 mL) butter
pinch of thyme
1 large unpeeled lemon, very thinly sliced

Split breasts into halves and arrange in a shallow, generously-buttered casserole, skin-side up. (Mr. Sinclair used a lovely oval casserole of white English earthenware.) Sprinkle generously with salt and pepper. Dot with butter, and sprinkle with thyme, then arrange lemon slices on top so that all chicken pieces are covered.

Cook uncovered at 350°F. (180°C) about 30 – 40 minutes, or until breasts are tender. Serve hot, at room temperature, or cold — with buttered brussels sprouts and hot chips. *Serves 4 – 6.*

Embassy Club Chicken Casserole

Planning a dinner, for me, is a serious task, since the dinner should create contentment and joy and satisfaction for all concerned. In olden days this seemed easier to do, since there were seasons for certain foods which set the rules and restricted the choice of foods; but this is surely not true anymore, with the year-round abundance of so many different foods. In spite of myself, I still have a real "thing" about serving seasonal foods. Another aspect that has changed greatly is the "help" — it has almost disappeared. That is why an unusual casserole, when we have 8 – 10 guests, can be of great help.

The following casserole created many years ago at the Embassy Club in London is one that will bring grace, elegance and food excellence to your table.

3 chicken broilers, quartered
4 cups (1000 mL) small white onions
¼ cup (60 mL) butter
1 tsp. (5 mL) basil
1 cup (250 mL) chicken broth or undiluted consommé
2 cups (500 mL) light cream
1½ cups (400 mL) uncooked long grain rice
½ cup (125 mL) finely chopped fresh parsley
¼ cup (60 mL) Scotch Whisky
Salt and pepper to taste

Place in top of double boiler, the peeled white onions, butter and basil. (Maybe you have some fresh basil in your garden — then chop up 2 sprigs.) Place over boiling water. Cover and cook for 1 hour.

Add enough water to chicken broth or undiluted canned consommé to make 3 cups (750 mL). Bring to boil. Add the broiler quarters. Salt and pepper to taste. Cover and simmer over low heat until chicken is tender. Then remove pieces to a casserole with a perforated spoon. Pour the onions on top, then the light cream. Cover and set aside.

Add the rice to the liquid mixture (consommé and water). Bring to boil, then simmer 15 – 16 minutes or until tender, but let it not get too soft. Then pour the whole thing over the chicken and gently mix the rice with the cream using a fork. Add the parsley, and stir again. Salt and pepper to taste.

At this point, you can cover the casserole and set in the refrigerator until ready to serve.

Preheat the oven to 400°F. (200°C) 40 – 50 minutes before serving, and bake covered 30 minutes or until chicken is hot. It does not have to be refrigerated if you wish to cook it immediately. Just before serving, pour the whisky evenly on top. (Irish whisky can be used instead of Scotch, but it gives a completely different "perfume" to the casserole.) *Serves 8 – 10.*

Chicken Sindhi

A guest on one of my T.V. shows was the son of an English missionary in India where he had lived as a boy and learned from the country women how to make real curry. He was a master at it, but the precious gift he left me was Akni water which gives an exciting flavor to so many foods.

The *Sindhi* is one of their many *pilau* made with rice and chicken. The flavored water used in cooking it is known as *Akni.* Ever since, I have made plain rice cooked in Akni water to serve with roast or barbecued chicken.

5 cardamom pods
5 whole cloves
10 peppercorns
2 sticks cinnamon, 2 in. (5 cm) each
1 tsp. (5 mL) coriander seeds
1 thick slice fresh ginger
3 – 4 lb. (1.5 – 2 kg) chicken
4 onions, thinly sliced
¼ – ½ cup (60 – 125 mL) butter
2 cups (500 mL) raw long grain rice
1 cup (250 mL) milk or cream
1 tsp. (5 mL) turmeric
1 garlic clove crushed
½ cup (125 mL) cold water

Place the first 5 ingredients in a cheesecloth bag, tie and place in a large saucepan with 6 cups (1.5 L) of water. Add ginger to water (do not replace by ground ginger), bring to boil, then cover and simmer over medium heat 20 minutes.

Cut chicken into individual serving pieces, add to flavored water, cover and simmer 20 minutes. Fry onions to a deep brown color in the butter, remove from fat with a slotted spoon and add to chicken.

Add rice to remaining fat and brown lightly, stirring over medium heat. Pour over chicken, add milk or cream and salt to taste.

Add turmeric and garlic mixed with ½ cup (125 mL) of cold water, cover and simmer until chicken is tender. Stir with a fork before serving. This can be kept covered and refrigerated overnight, then reheated covered in a 300°F. (150°C) oven without losing its quality. *Serves 6.*

How to Bake a Hen

This was how the elders in our family treated a chicken which had outgrown its tenderness and egg laying. Now that I live on a farm and have chickens, I do the same, and you will be surprised how good it is. Even a year-old laying hen becomes tender and is full of true tender chicken flavor that we sometimes forget because of the flatness of the commercial bird. The one important point is that you need an old-fashioned roaster with a cover, or you should use a pan large enough to hold the chicken, which goes in the oven.

Cut away the excess fat around the opening. Cut a lemon in half and rub the hen all over inside and outside, pressing the lemon as you work to get some of the juice out. Then place the two halves in the cavity, with unpeeled cloves of garlic and 1 onion. I place 1 tsp. (5 mL) tarragon or a handful of fresh parsley into the cavity, especially when I can get them fresh from the garden in the summer. (*Grand-mère* never used herbs in the cavity, but stuffed it with bread and sage stuffing. I find it too heavy.)

Rub the chicken with salt and pepper to taste. Place in roasting pan with 1 cup (250 mL) of cold water in the bottom. Cover pan tightly and bake in a 300°F. (150°C) oven for 3 – 4 hours, or until chicken is tender.

Uncover roaster last half hour to brown the skin. Baste 3 to 4 times during the cooking period, which will permit you to check the doneness. Make gravy with the liquid in the pan, removing excess fat if necessary.

To serve cold, leave overnight in the pan, with the fat and liquid remaining in the pan, in a cool place. The next day, remove hen from pan and lift out the coagulated fat. The juice will be jellied; cut up and place around the chicken.

My Know-How with Turkey

Through the years, I have seen many a change in the preparation and service of turkey. Some now-forgotten recipes I felt were not a loss to the gastronomic world, while others should still be alive among cooks who care. These are the "know-hows" I would like to talk about. They go deep into my past, recipes such as my paternal grandfather's "broiled baby turkey," his usual New Year feast, simply because he wanted to use the turkeys that did not grow fast enough — but how good they were — or the molded turkey on a bed of holly, used when there were 30 – 40 of us at the *Réveillon* after Midnight Mass. Or the yearly winter dinner at my grandfather's old Scottish friend. His wife could make a prune-stuffed turkey with a bread sauce that had no equal. And then there is the Champagne Turkey which my mother prepared for my wedding dinner. I never forgot it. Yet for all the years I have written and talked about food, I never mentioned it, nor much less gave the recipe.

A Few Turkey Basics

Advice No. 1: I was told years ago that a female (or hen bird) gives better results than a male (cock), and that the females with broad thick breasts and short legs were the best of all. You laugh? Well, next time you look for a turkey, search for the short legs and broad breast, and you too will quickly discover they are the best, as I did.

A good female or hen bird usually weighs from 8 – 12 lb. (3.6 – 5.4 kg). Above that, you are sure to have a husky male — with more fat than tenderness.

Advice No. 2: If the turkey is frozen, just remove Kraft paper, but do not remove plastic covering. Keep 3 days in the refrigerator, turning once a day. Slow defrosting keeps the meat more supple.

Advice No. 3: Unwrap the turkey — remove giblet and excess water accumulated in the cavity. Then run the inside of the turkey and the outside skin with a large lemon cut in half. (I rub and rub until I wear out the lemon.) Then grate half a nutmeg and mix with 1 tbsp. (15 mL) salt and sprinkle all over inside the turkey. Stuff or prepare according to your recipe.

Advice No. 4: A proven fact: *Slow roasting* reduces shrinkage and dryness.

Quick roasting seals the delicate fat of the turkey and gives better flavor. How do you cope with this? Like everything else in life and politics — *compromise*. Start the turkey in a preheated 425°F. (230°C) oven, cook 20 minutes. *Then* reduce heat to 375°F. (190°C) for the remaining cooking time. Baste when heat is lowered, and baste once more during last period of cooking. When bird is cooked, baste with pan juices for a full 5 minutes.

For a turkey *under* 14 lb. (7 kg) allow 15 minutes for each 1 lb. (500 g) and 15 minutes standing time (outside of oven before carving). For larger turkeys count 10 minutes for each 1 lb. (500 g) and 10 minutes standing time.

Champagne Roasted Turkey

There were always two served together on a large Old Quebec blue and white platter, which I still use in my home. Between the two turkeys were beautiful glistening green leaves, with a big bowl of bread sauce, on each side thick slices of peeled oranges. (In those days, oranges were hard to buy in September — Christmas was the orange season.) Each slice of orange was topped with a cube of tart homemade currant and port jelly. In the Twenties, a wedding dinner was quite a production. The champagne can be replaced with a good white muscadet wine or a dry sparkling rosé, but of course, a certain "finesse" given by the champagne would be missing.

A 10 – 12 lb. (5 – 6 kg) turkey
Salt and pepper to taste
1 tsp. (5 mL) tarragon
1 large bunch of fresh parsley
1 large onion, cut in half
½ cup (125 mL) butter
3 tbsp. (50 mL) flour
½ cup (125 mL) dry champagne (to baste)

1/3 cup (80 mL) dry Madeira
3 tbsp. (30 mL) flour
2 tbsp. (30 mL) flour
1½ cups (400 mL) dry champagne
¼ cup (60 mL) hot brandy

Wash, dry and blot any excess water in the cavity with absorbent paper towel. Generously salt and pepper the cavity. Place the parsley and onion in the cavity just as they are (they are removed before carving). No stuffing was ever used with this type of turkey. Close the opening. Fasten the skin of the neck down over the back, and tie the turkey in the usual way.

Cream together the ½ cup (125 mL) butter and the 3 tbsp. (50 mL) of flour. Spread all over top of turkey. Set on one side on the rack of a roasting pan. Do not cover. Roast in a preheated 425°F. (230°C) oven for 20 minutes. Then reduce heat to 375°F. (190°C) and continue to roast, 20 minutes to each lb. (500 g) in all.

When the heat is lowered, dip a large single layer of cheesecloth in champagne and 1 tbsp. (15 mL) salad oil or melted butter. Turn the turkey on its back and cover the top with the cheesecloth. Baste once or twice as needed with champagne.

When done, turn off the heat. Place turkey on platter. Let rest at least 20 minutes. (This increases the smooth texture of the white meat and makes the carving of thin slices much easier.)

Meanwhile, make the gravy. Skim as much fat as possible from the liquid remaining in the roaster. (Keep this fat, which can be used in many ways.) Pour the liquid residue left in the pan in a measure cup — you should have 2 cups, add champagne to make up the quantity if necessary.

Pour the Madeira into the roaster, scrape and stir the whole thing with a wooden spoon. Make a ball with the remaining butter and flour. Add the 1½ cups (400 mL) of champagne to the roasting pan, bring to a boil, while stirring and scraping. Gradually add the butter-flour ball, stirring with a whisk, until it has a light cream texture. Taste for seasoning. Strain and keep warm. To serve, pour hot brandy over turkey and flame. At my wedding, this was done by my brother, at the table. It is supposed to be a sign of "eternal love," mine burned bright. How romantic we were. I sometimes wonder if a little more romance is not what we now need! *Serves 9 – 12.*

Broiled Young Turkey

Of course, it can be cooked on a barbecue for a nice summer party, but I especially like the following oven method.

If you are lucky enough to have a pot of lemon thyme, forget the lemon rind, juice and thyme in the recipe — simply replace with 1 tsp. (5 mL) lemon thyme.

1 4 – 6 lb. (2 – 3 kg) young turkey
½ cup (125 mL) butter
Grated rind and juice of ½ a lemon
¼ tsp. (1 mL) thyme
Salt and pepper to taste
¼ cup (60 mL) butter
½ cup (125 mL) white vinegar or white vermouth

Line the bottom of a broiling pan with foil. (Do not use the rack.) Cut the cleaned turkey into 4 sections. Rub each section with the ½ cup (125 mL) butter mixed with the lemon rind and juice and the thyme. Spread equally over each section. Salt and pepper.

Place buttered skin side down in the pan. Broil 4 inches away from source of heat for 25 minutes or until lightly browned.

At this point, turn the turkey skin-side up, baste with the butter and white wine or vermouth heated together. Continue to broil for another 25 minutes, at which time the skin should be browned. Transfer pan to a preheated 350°F. (180°C) oven. Cover with foil and bake until fork tender, about another 25 minutes. Super! *Serves 6.*

Turkey Roll

This is steamed and served cold, thinly sliced. In texture, it is somewhat like those pâté meats you buy in small tins to make sandwiches. But there is a difference — it costs little for what you get, and it is an elegant way to serve leftovers, and makes a very nice lunch with a salad or as an appetizer at dinner time.

1½ cups (400 mL) ground cooked turkey
1 cup (250 mL) chopped cooked ham
1 onion, passed through grinder or chopped fine
¼ tsp. (1 mL) mace
1 tsp. (5 mL) salt
½ tsp. (2 mL) marjoram or tarragon
1 egg, lightly beaten
1 cup (250 mL) fine breadcrumbs
2 tbsp. (30 mL) dried green parsley

Mix the ground turkey, ham and onion. Add the mace, salt and marjoram or tarragon. Mix again, add the egg, and thoroughly mix with your hands.

Pack into a buttered mold or loaf pan. Cover tightly with foil. Place pan on rack in saucepan. Add enough water to come halfway up the mold, and bring to a boil. Cover saucepan, lower heat, and bake for 1 hour. Remove from water, cool 20 minutes, unmold and completely cover loaf with the fine breadcrumbs and dried green parsley mixed together. Cool completely and refrigerate, covered. *Serves 6.*

Turkey Bread Sauce

In the early 1900s, this rich, creamy sauce was a must. Today we tend more toward cranberry sauce or thickened gravy as an embellishment for our turkey, but this is a worthwhile replacement if you have never tried it.

1 cup (250 mL) well packed fresh bread cubes
1 thick onion slice
1 cup (250 mL) very hot chicken or turkey consommé
⅛ tsp. (0.5 mL) nutmeg
Salt and pepper, to taste
2 tbsp. (30 mL) butter
Heavy cream, as needed

Make sure no crust remains on the bread. Place with onion in a saucepan, then pour consommé on top and add seasonings. When the bread has soaked up all the consommé, simmer over low heat, stirring often, until liquid has disappeared but bread is not sticking. Remove onion, then add butter and enough cream to dilute sauce to thickness you desire. *Yield:* 1 cup (250 mL).

My Own Leftover Turkey Casserole

The quantities of the different ingredients that go into this recipe must be determined by what you have on hand. For some reason it never seems to matter much whether there is more or less of one or the other. That is the way leftovers should be.

5 – 7 bacon slices
About 2 cups (500 mL) leftover cooked turkey
About 2 cups (500 mL) leftover cooked dressing
About 1 cup (250 mL) cranberry sauce
About ½ cup (125 mL) bone stock or canned consommé

Line a pie plate or a small loaf pan with the slices of bacon. Top with a layer of coarsely chopped turkey, then a layer of cranberries and the stock over all.

Bake uncovered in a 325°F. (160°C) preheated oven for 30 minutes. Spread stuffing on top and bake for another 30 minutes. If you have a small quantity cut baking in half, 15 minutes at the beginning and 15 minutes at the end. Place on cake rack until cold (room temperature), then unmold to serve. *Serves 4 – 6.*

To Prepare a Duck for Cooking: If you have bought a 4½ – 5 lb. (2 – 2.5 kg) frozen duck, thaw it, unwrapped, in the refrigerator 24 – 48 hours. This will thaw the bird gradually without affecting its flavor.

Do not wash the duck under running water. Instead, pat the inside of the duck with absorbent paper and then rub it, inside and out, with a cloth that has been dipped in fresh lemon juice or cider vinegar or brandy.

Before roasting, if you wish, remove some of the hidden excess fat from the duck by the following method: dry and rub the duck with lemon juice or cider vinegar and then brown on all sides in an enamelled cast-iron pan, over medium heat. This will release a good amount of the fat.

Remove the duck from the pan and cook it according to the recipe. Do not, however, throw away the fat. You may cool it and store it for later use in general cooking. You'll find that it gives an interesting flavor to many foods.

How to Roast a Duck: A shallow, enamelled cast-iron baking pan is best, but any pan about 10 × 15 in. (25 cm × 37.5 cm) will serve well for roasting.

Place the duck, breast side up, on a large crust of dry bread, a flat beef bone or a rack. This will prevent drying. A crust of bread will absorb a good deal of the fat, but a beef bone will give a deep brown gravy. Roast the duck in a 325°F. (160°C) oven, 25 minutes per lb. (2.2 kg) for medium, 35 minutes for well done. Do not cover, baste or prick the duck with a fork or knife during roasting — piercing the skin of the duck will release the juices and cause drying.

When 1 hour of roasting remains, you may brush the duck with a mixture of 2 tbsp. (30 mL) of honey and 1 tsp. (5 mL) of Kitchen Bouquet or Japanese soy sauce. This will give the skin a golden brown color and a crispy texture.

How to Carve a Duck: You may carve the duck the same way you would a chicken or a turkey. Be careful, however, with the breast and more or less scrape the meat off the bone. Serve each guest half a breast, plus a drumstick or thigh section. You may, if you wish, also carve the duck as follows: place the duck breast upward, and point the legs to your right. With poultry shears or kitchen shears, cut through the top of the bird from end to end. Turn the duck over and proceed in the same manner along the center of the back. Cut each half crosswise, just in front of the thigh. You will then have 2 portions with the drumsticks and thighs and a small amount of the breast meat, and 2 portions with the wings but a major part of the breast meat. My favorite piece is the drumstick and thigh.

Wild Duck à la Cardinal

My maternal grandmother's name was Cardinal, and in the autumn she always had a Sunday feast with the Châteauguay wild ducks, brought home by the boys of the family who were very good shots.

Dutch gin was used since it was almost the only type available at the turn of the century, and the favorite of French-Canadians. Again, I have never seen this recipe written down. I learned to prepare duck in this manner from *Grand-mère* when I was 12 years old.

- 2 wild ducks, plucked and cleaned
- 2 quarts (2 L) cold water
- ¼ cup (60 mL) brandy
- 1 tbsp. (15 mL) salt
- 2 onions, peeled and quartered
- 2 apples, unpeeled and quartered
- 1 tbsp. (15 mL) brown sugar
- ½ tsp. (2 mL) cloves, cinnamon
- 1 cup (250 mL) Genever (Dutch gin)
- 1 tbsp. (15 mL) juniper berries
- 1 cup (250 mL) Seville orange marmelade

Place in a large saucepan the ducks, cold water and salt. Bring to a boil, then boil 5 minutes. Remove ducks from water, let cool 10 minutes, then rub all over, inside and out, with the brandy.

Roll the onions and apples in the sugar, cloves and cinnamon, mixed together. Stuff into the ducks, dividing equally.

Place ducks in roasting pan, breast side up. Pour the gin over the ducks, sprinkle with the juniper berries, and coat each of the duck breasts with the marmalade.

Cover and roast in a 300°F. (150°C) oven for 1½ – 2 hours, or until ducks are tender, basting 2 or 3 times during the cooking period.

Grand-mère made her gravy by adding 1 cup (250 mL) of black strong tea to the pan, and simmering it for a few minutes while scraping the pan. Then she removed the stuffing from the ducks and crushed it in the sauce. If you do it this way, strain or serve as is. *Serves: 4 – 6.*

Mother's Way with Duck à l'Orange

I have tried many new ways of cooking duck, but one I shall always find outstanding is this recipe, which my Mother learned from my grandmother. Do try it, with domestic or wild duck. The difference will be in the flavor and the cooking period, so be sure of the weight and count on about 25 minutes per lb. (2.2 kg).

1 4 – 5 lb. (2 – 2.5 kg) duck
¼ cup (60 mL) brandy
1 tsp. (5 mL) salt
2 tbsp. (30 mL) fresh mint, chopped fine
2 tsp. (10 mL) brown sugar
Grated rind of 1 orange
Juice of ½ an orange
1 orange, unpeeled and thinly sliced
2 cups (500 mL) toasted diced bread
½ tsp. (2 mL) marjoram or savory
10 juniper berries, crushed
1 medium onion, chopped

Mix the brandy and the salt. Rub the duck's skin and cavity all over with this mixture.

With the back of a wooden spoon, mix and pound together the mint, brown sugar, orange rind, gradually adding the orange juice.

To this add all the remaining ingredients. Stir well and use to stuff the duck. Place the prepared duck on the rack of a roasting pan, and roast in a preheated 325°F. (160°C) oven, 25 minutes per pound. Baste 2 or 3 times with pan juices during the cooking period. Fifteen minutes before the end of the cooking time, baste with the following mixture, which grandmother called "Duck's Devil." Mix 1 tbsp. (15 mL) chutney, 1 tsp. (5 mL) French-type mustard, ½ tsp. (2 mL) Worchestershire sauce, and 1 drop Tabasco sauce. *Serves 3 – 4.*

Grand-mère never made gravy with the pan juices, but served the dish instead with the following bread sauce:

Bread Sauce:

1 medium onion
8 whole cloves
1½ cups (400 mL) milk
1 cup (250 mL) diced fresh bread with crust removed
1 tsp. (5 mL) salt
¼ tsp. (1 mL) freshly ground pepper
¼ tsp. (1 mL) freshly grated nutmeg
Grated rind of ½ a lemon
2 – 3 tbsp. (30 – 50 mL) butter

Halve the onion and stud each half with cloves. Heat milk over low heat, add the onion and simmer over *very* low heat for 1 hour. Mix the breadcrumbs, salt, pepper, nutmeg and lemon rind. Let stand 30 – 40 minutes. Twenty minutes before serving, pour half the hot milk over the bread. *Do not stir.* Cover and keep in warm place. By then the milk will be absorbed. Then stir in the remaining hot milk just before serving if the sauce seems too dry. It is a matter of taste. Stir in the butter, which should be at room temperature.

Grandmother often sautéed a few spoonfuls of dry breadcrumbs in very hot butter. Add them sizzling hot to the bread sauce and top with finely chopped parsley.

This is an unusual bread sauce since the bread never really cooks, but is creamed by the addition of very hot flavored milk, and that makes quite a difference.

Mother's Marinade to Thaw out a Duck

In my youth, we had no freezer; but in the winter, we used to pile food that we wished to freeze in a bank of snow, in the garden, and sprinkle each layer with coarse salt which kept the ice cold. But, with the first bright sunshine, we had to cook and eat certain foods faster than others; duck was one of those. Mother prepared the following marinade, poured it over the frozen duck and let it thaw out a day or so in the "icebox" — then stuffed and roasted it as usual. But the tangy marinating mixture made quite a difference. I still use this recipe sometimes for frozen ducks, and also very often for lamb.

1 cup (250 mL) fresh orange juice
Juice of 1 lemon
3 tbsp. (50 mL) vegetable oil
2 tsp. (10 mL) honey
2 tsp. (10 mL) dry mustard
¼ cup (60 mL) fresh or dried mint leaves
2 cloves garlic, crushed
8 peppercorns, crushed

Mix the ingredients thoroughly. Pour over the duck. Cover and marinate at least 12 hours. Drain and reserve marinade before roasting duck. Marinade can be used to baste the bird and the remainder added to the gravy.

Bread and Parsley Stuffing

Simple, full of flavor, quick, and easy to make. Spread 6 – 8 slices of brown or egg bread on a baking sheet. Place in a preheated 400°F. (200°C) oven, until golden brown. Remove a slice from the top of a large clove of garlic and rub both sides of the bread with it. It may take 3 – 4 cloves of garlic. Dice the bread, place in a bowl and add 1 cup (250 mL) of coursely chopped fresh parsley, 6 green onions, chopped fine, ½ tsp. (2 mL) thyme, and the grated rind of 1 lemon. Salt and pepper inside of bird. Fill with stuffing and roast according to rule. *Yield:* enough to stuff a 4 – 5 lb. (2 – 2.5 kg) chicken. [Double quantity for a 10 – 12 lb. (4.5 – 5 kg) turkey.]

Baked Stuffing

Pack your favorite stuffing lightly into a nice shallow casserole, previously rubbed with some of the bird's gravy. Punch a few holes here and there in the stuffing with the round handle of a wooden spoon. Spoon drippings from the roasting pan into the holes and all over on top.

Then bake 35 – 45 minutes in a 375°F. (190°C) oven. I usually keep the prepared stuffing in a bowl. When the turkey has 30 – 35 minutes left to cook, I take some of the drippings to grease the casserole, and put in the stuffing, add the gravy, then place on the top shelf of the oven. It will be easy when the turkey is cooked to turn off the heat, and leave the stuffing in oven during the standing period.

Giblet Gravy

This recipe can be used for roast chicken, capon or other types of fowl.

Giblets of 1 bird (neck, tips of wings, trimmings, gizzard, heart and liver)
1 small onion, cut in half
1 stalk of celery with leaves
1 small carrot, sliced
1 bay leaf
¼ tsp. (1 mL) thyme
1 tsp. (5 mL) salt
10 peppercorns
2 cups (500 mL) water

Place all the above ingredients, except the liver, in a saucepan, bring to boil, cover, and simmer 1½ hours over low heat. Add the liver 15 minutes before the end of the cooking. Strain through a fine sieve (reserving the bouillon). Chop fine the liver, bits of meat in the wings, and set aside. To make 3 – 4 cups of "Giblet Gravy," first remove excess fat floating on top of gravy. Then add to remaining residue ⅓ cup (80 mL) of flour. Stir and scrape into the pan; when lightly browned and well mixed, add 2 cups (500 mL) of the reserved bouillon. Stir and scrape until well mixed. Add more hot water if you wish a thinner sauce. Add 2 tbsp. (30 mL) dry sherry. Strain through a fine sieve. Add the reserved chopped meat. Taste for seasoning and keep hot until ready to serve. *Yield:* 2 cups (500 mL).

11. Vegetables

Vegetables are Beautiful

We live in an age of complications, even chaos, but out of these usually emerge forgotten truths. One of them is that health is the greatest of all our possessions.

When I was young, we didn't have complicated creations from the laboratory to cure our ailments or to make us beautiful. The common cold was soothed with blossom or herb tea sweetened with unpasteurized honey, and we ate raw vegetables and fruits because we knew instinctively that they were what gave us clear skin and good eyes.

The vivid greens, oranges, reds and yellows of fresh vegetables can be so appetizing on a plate and so good to eat that it seems a pity they are often served soggy, pallid and tasteless — especially when learning a few basics can make your vegetable-eating a joy.

A vegetable is still alive after being picked. It deteriorates gradually as it stands, and as soon as it is exposed to heat — any type of heat — its cells cease all activity. Hot water or steam softens its cellulose, its pectic substances dissolve to form pectin and the starches swell and absorb moisture — you can see a vivid example of this when boiling potatoes. Learn to cook each type of vegetable properly, and all their goodness will be yours.

Like meat and fish, vegetables are cooked by moist or dry heat methods. Boiling, blanching and steam-cooking are the moist heat methods; stir-frying, steam-baking and baking are the dry heat procedures.

Season Vegetables with Imagination

One of our greatest mistakes is to take vegetables for granted. When it comes to serving them, too many cooks expect them somehow or other to look out for themselves. Even the humblest vegetable should be treated with respect and affection.

To Sweet-Tasting Vegetables: such as cabbage and greens, add a little lemon or lime juice (or grated peel). Or a pinch of rosemary. Or a few whole cloves. Or a sprinkling of curry.

To Carrots, Potatoes or Turnips: add minced chives or parsley or coarsely ground black pepper. Or a pinch of thyme or bay leaf.

To Spinach: add a little mace or nutmeg. Or a dash of tarragon vinegar. Or a bit of crushed or sauteed garlic. Or sour cream and sesame seeds.

To Beets: add 2 whole cloves while cooking. Or serve with sour cream or minced green onions. Good with a dash of malt vinegar or a pinch of fresh dill or dill seeds.

To Green Peas or String Beans: add the classic touch of finely chopped mint while cooking. Or a pinch of summer savory or crisp bacon when ready to serve. Or add a dash of curry. Any vegetable can be the highlight of a meal with the addition of a little lemon juice, chutney, vinaigrette sauce, or salad dressing. Whichever one you use, add it just before serving.

Uncooked Vegetables

The very best way to eat them! Serve as is, put through a juicer; or process in a blender with ½ cup (125 mL) of water. And don't stick with these combinations — go on to create your own. For maximum nutrient value, wash, scrub and prepare fresh vegetables just before serving. (Simply thaw if frozen.)

Flavor grated raw carrots with chives, parsley, fresh lemon juice and a bit of grated lemon rind, plus safflower or peanut oil. Mix grated beets with oil, fresh lemon juice and honey. Grate a small squash, mix with green peas, season with salt, chives and, if you wish, a little oil. With scissors, cut tender green beans into small slivers, mix with a little chopped green onion, and flavor with a dash of soy sauce. Dice unpeeled tomatoes finely, mix with minced broccoli flowerets, chives or green onions, and flavor with salt, basil and lemon rind.

Crudités: What are *crudités?* A friend of mine says they are "life in the raw." For some unexplained reason, there are times when they are the very fashionable to serve.

They are raw "fresh" vegetables — like small garden carrots, scraped and left whole; half a cucumber, skin on, all crisp and icy cool; wet round red-red radishes, big wedges of tomatoes; bowls of crisp lettuce leaves; a basket of fresh herbs and green onions, to name but a few. Serve them with little bowls of salt mixed with herbs and minced onion to your taste to dip your crunchy cool finger foods in.

Of course, a vegetable to be served as a *crudité* must be absolutely fresh, beautifully trimmed and in perfect condition and texture, otherwise the whole point of *crudités* is lost—and just think, they are good for the complexion and not a bit fattening.

Preserving Nutrients and Flavor: Never let vegetables stand in water before cooking. (The only exceptions are members of the cabbage family — they should be soaked for several minutes in cold salted water to dislodge insects.)

Do your peeling, slicing or dicing just before cooking. Vegetables lose much of their vitamin content and flavor when exposed to air or soaked in water for any length of time.

Never add baking soda when cooking green vegetables. It keeps them green but also destroys their vitamin content. A far better method, both for appearance and nutrition, is to cook the vegetables by blanching.

Do not add salt to vegetables (except potatoes) while they're cooking. But do add ½ tsp. (2 mL) of sugar for each lb. (500 g) of vegetables. This will improve the flavor, and in some cases even the color. It will not make the vegetables taste sweet; it will simply restore their natural sweetness. Add salt only when ready to serve, or let people add their own.

Cook vegetables whole or in large pieces whenever you can. For example, nutrients are present next to the skin of potatoes. When they are peeled and cut into pieces, their surfaces become exposed to air, the greatest enemy of vitamins.

Use herbs to liven up a vegetable without destroying their natural flavor. A few combinations I like are savory with green beans, mint with peas, sage with lima beans and thyme with carrots.

Some experts think all vegetables should be covered while they cook. Others say never cover green vegetables because they lose their color. Obviously, baked or braised vegetables are covered to prevent loss of moisture, and spinach steamed in the water that clings to its leaves must be covered too.

Cook vegetables only until fork-tender; they must retain a bit of their original crispness. To give your vegetables a meaty flavor when served with a roast or chops, add half a bouillon cube to the cooking water.

Warmed Vegetables

For those who want all the goodness of uncooked vegetables, but aren't partial to completely raw vegetables, the warm-up method is best. Pack vegetables (plain, or use any of the uncooked combinations) into small custard cups, cover and place in a saucepan. Pour hot water into pan to halfway up sides of cups, cover pan and place over low heat for 10 minutes. Remove vegetables from cups, and top with a bit of butter if you wish.

Another method is to oil a stainless steel pan as you would a cake mold, using safflower, sesame seed or peanut oil. Add vegetables, cover and leave 10 – 20 minutes over very low heat — just long enough to warm them up. Dot with butter, stir and serve.

With frozen vegetables, just put as is into a pan (with no water) and cook over low heat about 10 minutes.

Here are a few more combinations to serve warmed: grated Jerusalem artichokes, green onions and chopped tomatoes; grated peeled turnip and chopped celery flavored with dill; grated parsnips, carrots and fresh coconut moistened with a little cream or yogurt; grated carrots with currants or seedless raisins, and walnuts or pecans that have been crushed with a rolling pin.

Cooked Vegetables

Vegetarians know that no fruit or vegetable has ever been improved by long or improper cooking. Vegetables should be cooked for the shortest possible time in the least possible amount of liquid — and the liquid saved for soups, stocks and drinks. This goes for frozen vegetables, too. You don't have to follow the package directions; you can usually get away with adding less liquid — or none at all — and a shorter cooking time.

Blanching and Refreshing: To serve a deep green vegetable so that it's even greener than when it was fresh, blanch it. This is not complicated and it has the added advantage of enabling you to cook vegetables hours ahead of time. When ready to serve, dip them into hot water for a few minutes to reheat, or sauté briefly in butter or oil, or heat in an appropriate sauce. The vegetables will lose none of their flavor, texture or colour.

Fill a large saucepan with water and bring it to a rolling boil. Gradually add the cleaned vegetables. If you have lots of water, it will quickly return to a boil. This is important because the more quickly it does, the greener the vegetable will be.

The cooking period varies with different vegetables, their degree of freshness, and the way they are cut. On the average, count 8 – 12 minutes for a whole vegetable and only 3 – 4 minutes for a sliced one. To test, just taste — you'll be surprised how quickly most vegetables cook. Once you have experimented, make notes for yourself, stating exactly how long you prefer to cook each particular vegetable.

If the vegetables are to be served immediately, drain and butter them. If they are to be eaten cold, or hot later in the day, then they must be refreshed.

Drain the blanched vegetables and toss them into a bowl of ice-cold water as soon as they are cooked. This cold bath stops the cooking, sets the color, and preserves both the texture and the flavor. Skim the vegetables out of the cold water and place them on an absorbent cloth in a dish. Refrigerate until ready to serve. To reheat, place in a saucepan and pour enough boiling water over them to cover. Boil for 30 seconds, drain and serve. Or sauté or heat briefly in a sauce.

Pan-Steaming: All vegetables — whole, pared or cut-up — can be cooked by pan-steaming. However, steamed green vegetables will not have the beautiful color blanching gives them.

For steaming, use a heavy stainless steel or enameled cast-iron saucepan. Add just enough liquid — water, bouillon, consommé, homemade stock, vegetable water or milk — to cover the bottom of the pan. Add herbs or spices to the liquid, but no salt or pepper. Bring to a rolling boil, add the prepared vegetables and return to a boil. Cover, reduce heat and cook over medium-low heat until tender. The degree of heat is important because there must be enough steam produced to cook the vegetables — but if the liquid boils too fast, it will not steam properly; also it may boil away.

The cooking time ranges from 5 – 25 minutes; make notes of your preferences for each vegetable. Uncover the pan as little as possible.

Drain in a colander as soon as the vegetable is done to taste. Place in a hot dish, add salt, pepper and butter — or any other seasonings you like — and serve. Do not put the vegetable back into the saucepan before serving because the hot pan will continue to cook it.

A vegetable can be steamed ahead of time and refreshed, as described for blanching, then reheated in water or in a sauce at serving time.

Chinese Stir-frying (Pan-Cooking): To many vegetable lovers, the Oriental way of cooking and serving vegetables is the height of perfection. Crisp, flavorful and bright — nothing is cooked out of them. Once you have learned this dry heat technique, you can use it for any vegetable. The timing is almost the same for all; if there is any difference, it is only a matter of a minute or two.

Cut the vegetable into thin slices on the bias. For each lb. (500 g) — approximately 3½ – 4 cups (1 L) of prepared vegetable — measure ½ cup (125 mL) of water or bouillon, add ½ tsp. (2 mL) of sugar, and set aside. (As a variation, add 1 tbsp. (15 mL) of soy sauce, fresh lemon juice or cider vinegar.)

Next, for each lb. (500 g) of vegetables, heat 2 tbsp. (30 mL) of vegetable oil in a large frying pan or Chinese wok. Add ½ tsp. (2 mL) of salt, stirring for a few seconds. (At this point, you can also add 3 thin slices of ginger root if you like.)

Put the prepared vegetable into the hot, salted oil and stir over high heat until well coated — just a few seconds. This seals the pores so that the vegetable retains its flavor and color.

Add the prepared liquid. Stir quickly for a few seconds over high heat. Cover, lower heat and simmer until tender but not mushy, about 3 – 5 minutes.

Whole vegetables or large pieces must be blanched first for 3 – 5 minutes, then refreshed as previously explained. When drained and patted dry, they are stirred into the hot oil and cooked just as you would cook the thin slices.

When a stir-fried vegetable cannot be served immediately, do not cover it. The heat retained will create a moist steam that will soften the crisp texture, fade the color and make the pieces limp.

When several vegetables are being cooked together, those needing a longer cooking period, such as onions, celery, green peppers and carrots, go into the pan with the hot oil first; they are stirred for a few seconds longer than usual. Then the more tender vegetables, such as tomatoes, spinach and green onions are added. You can vary the liquid and flavoring in many ways, and you may decide this method is the easiest and most creative way of cooking vegetables.

Steam-baking: We seldom consider that any vegetable other than the potato can be baked, yet many vegetables — especially the winter root ones — gain by it. Some may be steam-baked, while others should be baked with dry heat.

To steam-bake, simply scrub the vegetable — carrots, beets, or parsnips — and remove any imperfections. Then rub all over with vegetable oil, bacon fat or soft margarine. An easy way to do this is to place a small piece of fat in your hand, or pour a little oil into your palm, then roll the vegetable round. Place the oiled vegetables in a casserole without crowding them. Add just enough boiling water to cover the bottom of the dish. Cover tightly and steam-bake in a preheated 350 – 375°F. (180 – 190°C) oven for 40 – 50 minutes, or until tender. (Time varies according to the size of the vegetable and the oven temperature.)

When the vegetable is half done, turn the pieces over. Leave uncovered for rest of the cooking period if you prefer to have the liquid completely evaporated and the vegetable browned on top.

Dry Baking: Beets, onions, potatoes, pumpkin and squash can be baked this way. If you've never tasted a baked onion, you're in for a pleasant surprise. There is a world of difference between onions that have been boiled and those that have been baked.

Scrub but do not peel the vegetable — just remove imperfections as for steam-baked vegetables. Rub with oil or fat, then roll in coarse salt until a few grains stick to the vegetable.

Place a sheet of foil on the oven rack to protect the stove from drippings and put the oiled vegetables on it. Bake in a preheated 375 – 400°F. (190 – 200°C) oven until the vegetable is tender — about 1 hour.

Pumpkins and squash are often cut into halves before baking. The seeds and strings are scooped out, a small pat of butter placed in the bottom and a pinch of salt or a few spoonfuls of honey or maple syrup added. This improves the bland flavor without making it too sweet.

The Ecstasy of New Vegetables

Suddenly it's mid-summer. The vegetable plot has reached its peak now, every row, every vine spilling over with goodness. To me this is a glorious time, a time to eat all garden-fresh vegetables with ecstasy, to cook them in such a way that their fine flavor is not destroyed but brought out to its fullest. Believe me, a truly fresh vegetable, properly cooked, is really something to experience.

Have you ever tasted corn rushed straight from the field to the boiling pot and cooked in two minutes? Have you ever delighted in a tomato, full of the warmth of the sun, ready to drop from its vine in full red ripeness? Have you ever cooked yellow or green beans, so crisp, and so fresh from the garden that they snap in your fingers as you gather them? Have you ever delighted in young carrots, pulled from the good earth when they are still slim and only three or four inches long, gently scrubbed, sliced in two, and gently cooked with a few sprigs of fresh basil or pineapple sage? If you do, you will see that the good earth will give you the *very best* she can offer.

Vegetables take on new personalities when you gather them in your own garden. This is especially so when you, yourself, with a hoe and lots of work, have brought out all this plentiful taste. But, of course, fresh vegetables can be found in cities; all towns have markets where farmers bring their summer bounty, and we also have many country roadside stands. Even at the supermarket, careful shopping will reward you with almost-garden-fresh vegetables at this time of mid-summer fullness.

Peas — The Pearls of the Pod

One morning each year, when I was a child, we were sent to the garden to pick the first green peas of the season. We gathered on the porch to take part in the shucking; then mother cooked the crop for lunch. They were served with freshly baked bread, fresh mint and homemade strawberry jam. How much I enjoyed that day each year.

If you have to shop for your peas, be sure you get young, tender, sweet ones. Choose pods that are light green, well-filled, uniform in size and velvety to the touch. Avoid any flat, dark green ones that look wilted.

Wash the pods and shell just before cooking. If the shelling must be done a few hours earlier, wrap the peas in a wet cloth or place them in a plastic bag (don't wash them), and refrigerate — if you don't, they'll dry out and be hard when cooked.

Green peas can be cooked in many ways, but one basic method is to place them in a saucepan (stainless steel or enamelled cast-iron if possible), pour boiling water over them to a depth of 1 in. (2.5 cm) and sprinkle with ⅛ tsp. (0.5 mL) of sugar for up to 2 lb. (1 kg) of peas. Cover, boil over medium heat for 8–10 minutes, then have yourself a feast.

Fresh June Green Peas

This is so good that I usually double the recipe and serve it as a main course for lunch, with crispy French bread and thin slices of Gouda cheese.

3 tbsp. (50 mL) butter
2 white onions, finely chopped
1 medium head of lettuce
2–3 lb. (1.5 kg) unshelled green peas
½ tsp. (2 mL) sugar
4 sprigs parsley

Melt the butter in a frying pan. Add onions, cover and simmer until soft and transparent, but not brown. Reserve outer leaves of lettuce; shred the rest and place on onions. Shell peas, and place over lettuce and sprinkle with sugar.

Top with reserved lettuce leaves, cover and simmer. When done, remove large lettuce leaves. Season to taste, adding a piece of butter and a bit of lemon juice, mix and garnish with parsley. *Serves 4.*

Snow Peas

To me, snow peas are the utmost in refined flavor and texture — a joy to eat, but hard to find. They can be purchased in season at good Japanese and Chinese grocery stores, or you could grow them from seeds in your own garden. They are at their best when about 2 in. (5 cm) long, quite flat, with a waxy appearance. Both the pod and the small peas are eaten. Prepare them as you would string beans, breaking off tips of pods and removing any strings. Do not cut the pods. Steam-cook or pan-fry them for 5 – 10 minutes, season lightly, and add butter to taste.

Glazed Carrots

Delicious with ham, roasted pork and all types of wild game.

6 medium carrots
1 cup (250 mL) boiling water
½ tsp. (2 mL) sugar
¼ tsp. (1 mL) thyme
2 tbsp. (30 mL) butter
2 tbsp. (30 mL) honey
2 tbsp. (30 mL) fresh mint, chopped
Grated rind of ½ a lemon *or*
  3 tbsp. (50 mL) dry Madeira

Peel carrots and cut in sticks ½ in. (1.25 cm) wide. Place in a saucepan, add the sugar and thyme, pour boiling water on top, cover and boil over medium heat about 15 – 20 minutes. Do not overcook. If preferred, place prepared carrots in a steamer, add sugar and thyme and steam until tender, about 20 – 25 minutes.

Melt the butter in a casserole or saucepan. Pour in the carrots, dribble honey on top, and sprinkle with the mint and lemon rind or Madeira. Mix lightly with a fork. Cover and simmer over very low heat, stirring once, until very hot, or place the covered casserole in a 300°F. (150°C) oven, and cook until piping hot, about 15 minutes.

It can be prepared ahead of time, and heated up again when ready to serve. *Serves 4 – 5.*

Minted Carrots

There is an interesting affinity between carrots and mint. Serve these with lamb, veal, cold cuts or omelets.

5 – 6 medium carrots
½ cup (125 mL) chicken stock
2 tbsp. (30 mL) chopped fresh mint
Salt and pepper to taste

Peel carrots and cut into thin slivers or small sticks. Bring the chicken stock to boil, add the carrots, and bring back to boil. Cover and boil over medium heat until tender, but beware of overcooking. Depending on the way the carrots are cut, it should take from 10 to 20 minutes. Remove cover in the last 5 minutes, and boil somewhat faster, so all the liquid evaporates.

Add the mint and a small piece of butter. Salt and pepper and stir well. *Serves 4 – 5.*

Beans

Are they snap beans, wax beans, string beans or green beans? Well, there are two types of snap beans: the bush and the pole; within these types there are green and yellow (commonly called wax) varieties. Some pods are round, some oval, and some flat. That's it — except that there are really no such things as "string" beans. That expression comes from the stringy beans sold during the Depression.

When buying beans, find a market where they're in large bins instead of in packages. Then you can choose the most tender and youngest beans — 3 lb. (1.35 kg) will serve 6 – 8 generously.

To cook green or wax beans the basic way, cut both ends off the beans, then slice or cut them up if you wish. Place them in a saucepan, preferably one of stainless steel, and sprinkle with ¼ tsp. (1 mL) of sugar for each 3 lb. (1.35 kg) of beans. Don't add salt. Pour boiling water on top and cook uncovered over high heat for 10 minutes. Then take a bite of one — it should be tender, yet still somewhat crisp (but you can cook them 3 – 8 minutes longer if you prefer them softer).

Drain water off immediately and, if the beans are to be served hot, dry them by shaking the pan over high heat for 1 – 2 minutes. Season with salt and pepper or summer savory and add butter.

If the beans are to be served cold, drain, then run cold water over them for 2 – 3 minutes, shaking them a few times to cool them more quickly. This stops the cooking and keeps the color. Drain again and turn onto a cloth or paper towels. When cool, cover and refrigerate.

When beans are prepared ahead of time, cook and proceed as if they were to be served cold. To reheat, put the cold cooked beans in a saucepan and toss with 1 tbsp. (15 mL) of hot melted butter per lb. (500 g). Season, cover and let warm up over very low heat. Don't flavor green beans with lemon juice; it gives them a bleached look.

Shaker Green Beans

The onion-sour cream sauce makes this a quite special casserole.

2 tbsp. (30 mL) each butter and flour
¼ tsp. (1 mL) pepper
1 tsp. (5 mL) each sugar and salt
1 medium onion, grated
1 cup (250 mL) commercial sour cream
1½ lb. (750 g) green beans
½ lb. Cheddar, grated
½ cup (125 mL) bread crumbs tossed with
  1 tbsp. (15 mL) melted butter or margarine

Over medium heat, melt butter and mix in flour. Remove from heat and stir in seasonings, onion and cream until well blended. Set aside.

Cook the beans according to basic directions above. Drain, place in a shallow 2-quart (2 L) casserole, pour over sour cream sauce and mix gently. Sprinkle with cheese (it will make a thick layer), then top with crumbs. Bake uncovered in a 350°F. (180°C) oven 30 minutes. *Serves 4 – 5.*

Harvard Green or Wax Beans

In the 1920s all the vegetables seemed to be called "Harvard" and it all started with an ad for "Harvard Beets." This recipe for green or wax beans is rather unusual.

Buy crisp pods that snap when broken in two. Remove both ends and string if necessary, although very few fresh beans have them nowadays. Cut crosswise or lengthwise.

3 cups (750 mL) green beans, sliced thin
2 tbsp. (30 mL) brown sugar
1 tbsp. (15 mL) cornstarch
½ tsp. (2 mL) salt
¼ tsp. (1 mL) curry powder or savory
½ tsp. (2 mL) Dijon-type mustard
¼ cup (75 mL) cold water
¼ cup (75 mL) cider vinegar
1 tbsp. (15 mL) butter

Place green beans in saucepan, pour enough boiling water on top to cover them, and bring back to boil; boil, uncovered, 6 – 8 minutes. Drain in colander. Measure all remaining ingredients, except the butter. Cook and stir over medium heat, until creamy, smooth and transparent. Add well-drained, cooked green beans. Mix well. Cover and let stand over very low heat for 15 minutes. Add butter, stir and taste for seasoning. *Serves 4.*

Asparagus

Asparagus was a delicacy to the Ancient Greeks, and it has been prized by gourmets the world over for some two thousand years. It is still considered the aristocrat of vegetables, in a class with artichokes and hearts of palm, but popularity has done a lot to lower its price and bring it within the range of the average homemaker, even if only as an occasional treat.

Spring is the time to enjoy them with the rest of the world, because it's the peak of the short asparagus season, when both price and quality are at their best.

Here are some tips on how to buy, prepare and cook these tender young shoots of the lily plant.

Buying:

Look for fresh, green stalks that are firm, straight and somewhat brittle. They may be anywhere from 6–10 in. (15–25 cm) long, but each bundle should contain stalks of about the same size. Never buy asparagus with loose tips; 1 lb. (500 g) is enough to serve two people.

Storing:

There are three ways to keep asparagus crisp and fresh:

Break off the woody ends, then stand the stems in water to about half their length, and place in the refrigerator.

Break off the woody ends, wash the asparagus thoroughly in cold water, wrap in moisture-proof paper, and store in the vegetable drawer of your refrigerator.

Wrap the asparagus in aluminum foil and place flat on the refrigerator shelf.

Preparing:

Break off the woody end of the stalk by holding the asparagus at both ends and bending it until it snaps naturally at the point where the tough portion begins. (The ends can be used in a casserole, soup or sauce.)

Wash the tips well to remove any sand which may have lodged in the scales. Some people like to peel the stem, but I think it loses too much of the flavor this way.

Cooking:

There are three very good ways of cooking asparagus:

1. Tie together, at the top and bottom, bundles of 3–10 cleaned asparagus stalks. Use stalks of the same size in each bundle. Stand upright in the bottom of a deep but narrow double-boiler, and pour over 1½ cups (400 mL) water. Do not add salt. Cover with the inverted top of the double

boiler and cook about 15 minutes, or until the tops are tender. They will be dark green and slightly crisp when done to the peak of perfection. If you prefer to have them more tender, cook an extra 5 – 8 minutes.

2. Split each stem lengthwise, stopping at least 1 in. (2 cm) below the tip, and place in a large frying pan. Sprinkle with a pinch of sugar, then pour over boiling water to cover on top. Cover the pan and boil over medium heat for 5 minutes. Uncover and boil 8 – 10 minutes more, then drain. Remove them from the pan with tongs and set on absorbent paper on a hot platter. Transfer to another dish or just pull out the paper, then season and serve.

3. The most extravagant way to serve asparagus is to just serve the tips, no longer than 3 in. (8 cm), and use the stems for soup. Scrub the tips with a soft vegetable brush under cold running water. Leave the tips to soak in cold water for 10 minutes, then drain and place in a perforated pan. Set over boiling water, cover and steam for 15 minutes. Season with butter and serve.

Asparagus Amandine

Sauté ¼ cup (60 mL) slivered, blanched almonds in 3 tbsp. (50 mL) butter until light brown. Salt and pepper 1 – 2 lb. (500 – 1000 g) freshly-cooked asparagus to taste and top with the sautéed nuts.

Asparagus au Jus

Cook asparagus by method 1 or 2 above, using chicken consommé instead of water. Remove the cooked vegetable to a hot platter and keep warm. Beat an egg yolk with the juice of ½ a lemon. Add a little of the cooking juice and beat briskly. While beating, add the remaining juice and season to taste. Pour over the asparagus and serve.

Oriental Asparagus

This fast stir-fry method of cooking asparagus retains its nutritional value, delicate taste and crunchy texture. If you have a wok, use it.

2 lb. (1 kg) fresh asparagus
3 tbsp. (50 mL) peanut oil
1 tsp. (5 mL) coarse salt
½ tsp. (2 mL) sugar
3 tbsp. (50 mL) cold water
Fresh unsalted butter to taste

Clean the asparagus and cut on an extreme diagonal into pieces about 2 in. (5 cm) long. Heat oil in a large frying pan, add asparagus, and stir well with a wooden spoon until pieces are well oiled.

Sprinkle with salt and sugar, stir again, then add water. Cover and steam over medium heat 3 – 4 minutes. Uncover, add butter and serve immediately. *Serves 4.*

Marinated Summer Tomatoes

5 large firm tomatoes
3 tbsp. (50 mL) chopped green onions *or*
  3 tbsp. (50 mL) chopped fresh chives
½ cup (125 mL) vegetable oil
¼ cup (60 mL) cider vinegar
1 crushed cloved garlic
2 tbsp. (30 mL) chopped parsley
1 tsp. (5 mL) each sugar and curry powder
½ tsp. (2 mL) salt
¼ tsp. (1 mL) freshly ground pepper

Slice the cored (but unpeeled) tomatoes. Place in a serving dish, sprinkling each row with the green onions or chives.

Measure the remaining ingredients in a jar. Cover and shake until well mixed. Pour over the tomatoes. Do not mix. Cover and refrigerate 1 – 12 hours.

To serve, drain off dressing and arrange tomatoes on a bed of shredded lettuce. Keep the dressing refrigerated, in a covered jar, as it can be used a second time. *Serves 4 – 5.*

Fresh Tomato Mousse

Serve in a nest of watercress or shredded lettuce — a light luncheon dish. Or serve for dinner with cold or hot poached salmon.

6 – 8 medium tomatoes, peeled
3 tbsp. (50 mL) butter
1 tbsp. (15 mL) sugar
½ tsp. (2 mL) basil
2 tbsp. (30 mL) butter
2 tbsp. (30 mL) flour
1 cup (250 mL) milk

1 envelope unflavored gelatine
2 tbsp. (30 mL) cold water
1 cup (250 mL) whipping cream

Pour boiling water over the tomatoes, let stand a few minutes, then peel. In a saucepan melt the first measure of butter, and add the tomatoes cut in four, the sugar and basil. Simmer 15 minutes over low heat, stirring often, Make a white sauce with the remaining butter, the flour and the milk.

Salt and pepper to taste. Add the tomatoes, and mix well. Then pass through a fine sieve or in a food processor. Taste again for seasoning. Whip the cream and fold in the tomato mixture. Pour into a single mold or into individual ones. Cover and refrigerate 12 hours before serving. *Serves 6.*

Tomato-Eggplant Scallop

A few minutes of preparation and you can refrigerate this, even overnight, until you're ready to pop it into the oven. It's a meal in itself, or a side dish if you wish.

1 small eggplant
4 medium tomatoes
1 small onion, grated
1 tbsp. (15 mL) chopped parsley
1 tsp. (5 mL) sugar
½ tsp. (2 mL) basil
4 soda crackers, crushed
3 tbsp. (50 mL) grated cheese of your choice

Peel the eggplant and cut into ½ in. (1.25 cm) cubes. Dice unpeeled tomatoes and stir into eggplant with a fork. Salt and pepper to taste, then stir in onion, seasonings and cracker crumbs. Place in a generously buttered 1-quart (1 L) baking dish, sprinkle with cheese, and bake in a 375°F. (190°C) oven until brown and bubbly, about 1 hour. *Serves 4.*

West Coast Tomatoes

Once, at a memorable barbecue party in Vancouver, I was served superb huge, thick tomato slices topped with lemon tartar sauce. I now use this recipe all year round, it is so good.

6 – 8 medium tomatoes
1 lemon
1 cup (250 mL) mayonnaise (homemade, if possible)

¼ cup (60 mL) minced green onions
¼ cup (60 mL) minced green olives
¼ cup (60 mL) minced parsley
1 tbsp. (15 mL) sugar
Chives and tarragon, to taste (optional)

Peel the lemon and remove all white parts and seeds; then cut up pulp as finely as possible (use a very sharp knife to prevent crushing the fruit) and add it to the mayonnaise along with the onions, olives, and parsley, and stir well.

Wash tomatoes, slice thickly, and set out on a flat dish. Sprinkle with sugar, top with sauce, sprinkle with chives and tarragon, and refrigerate. *Serves 6 – 8.*

Garden Fresh Zucchini

Although zucchini belongs to the *Brassica* (cabbage) family, it is very mild. So much so, in fact, that unless you can gather it fresh, and cook it steamed or panned, artistry is needed to make it appealing to persons who have never tasted it before. It is a favorite of Italians, and fresh zucchini can often be found at Italian markets. Flavor it with basil, oregano or rosemary, or eat it cold with a vinegar and oil dressing — or in a salad, mixed with endives.

Simmered Beets

This is my special way to serve beets with all types of casseroles, and it is especially good with fish. Rub fingers with a piece of lemon to remove beet stains.

4 – 6 medium beets
½ tsp. (2 mL) salt
1 tsp. (5 mL) brown sugar or honey
Grated rind of 1 lemon
Juice of ½ a lemon
¼ tsp. (1 mL) anise or caraway seeds
Minced parsley to taste

Peel and grate the raw beets (if you have a food processor, use the fine shred blade). Place in heavy metal saucepan. Sprinkle with salt, sugar or honey and lemon rind. Stir well and let stand 20 – 30 minutes. Then place, covered, over low heat 25 – 30 minutes, stirring once. Add lemon juice and seeds. Cook another 5 minutes. Add parsley, stir, and serve. *Serves 6.*

Sunshine Beets

Beets and oranges are the best of friends; they help each other's color and flavor. Diced canned beets are very tasty prepared this way.

Grated rind of ½ an orange
½ cup (125 mL) fresh orange juice
2 tbsp. (30 mL) lemon juice
¼ cup (60 mL) sugar
1 tbsp. (15 mL) cornstarch
½ tsp. (2 mL) salt
2 tbsp. (30 mL) butter or margarine
3 – 4 cups (500 – 750 mL) diced cooked beets

Heat rind and orange and lemon juice together in a saucepan over low heat. Mix sugar with cornstarch and salt, then add all at once to the orange juice mixture. Stir quickly until thickened and clear, then add butter and beets. Simmer 15 – 20 minutes over low heat. *Serves 4 – 6.*

The French Artichoke

The French or globe artichoke is easy to understand and recognize if we remember that it's a distant regal relative of the ordinary thistle. It's a sort of budding flower head, of which the edible parts are the fleshy base of each leaf and the thick bottom or heart, considered to be the choice bite.

Artichokes are in season from October to June. They can be quite large, medium or small. Size is immaterial as far as quality is concerned, so it is a matter of personal preference. I like the medium or small ones. When buying artichokes make sure they feel heavy in your hand in proportion to their size. The leaves should be clinging tightly into a compact head and the stem should be firm. When the leaves are open and the stem rubbery or brown-stained, it means the artichoke is growing old.

Allow half a large, one medium or two small artichokes for each serving, depending on the manner of preparation.

Because eating an artichoke is somewhat complicated, requiring time and attention for its full enjoyment, I like to serve them as a separate course, usually as a first course or immediately after the meat course.

To eat an artichoke, pull off the leaves one at a time. Hold the tip of the leaf with your fingers and dip the fleshy base into the butter or sauce. Then nibble off the tender fleshy part or scrape off the flesh with your teeth. The remainder of the leaf is discarded.

Eventually you come to the heart, which is covered with the "choke," a prickly, feathery bit. Remove it with a knife or sharp-edged spoon. When this is done, you've got the heart, the best part of the artichoke. Cut it into pieces, dip a piece into the sauce and enjoy it to the fullest.

Cooking Globe Artichokes

Break off the stem; then, using a heavy, sharp knife, cut about 1 in. (2.5 cm) off the base and break off the small leaves at the base.

Lay the artichoke on its side and slice ¾ in. (1.875 cm) off the top. Trim the points off the rest of the leaves with a pair of scissors.

Wash under cold running water, and rub bottom of artichoke and tip of each leaf with a piece of lemon to prevent discoloration.

Have ready a large saucepan almost full of lightly salted boiling water. (Don't use aluminum or iron, because it turns the artichoke a grayish color.) Make sure the pan is large enough to accommodate all the artichokes comfortably. Lower them into the boiling water and bring water back to a full rolling boil as quickly as possible. Because the artichokes tend to float (and it's necessary to keep them below the water line so they'll retain their color), the tops should now be covered with a cloth to hold them down. Boil slowly uncovered 35–45 minutes, or until a leaf will pull out easily.

Lift artichokes out of the saucepan with a slotted spoon and drain upside down on a plate. Serve hot or warm with melted butter; melted butter and lemon juice; or Hollandaise sauce. Serve cold with vinaigrette sauce; mayonnaise; or oil and lemon juice.

Pumpkin

A single memorable dinner changed my opinion about pumpkin. I no longer think of it, as most do — and as I used to — only in connection with Halloween, jack o'lanterns, corn roasts, and pies.

Pumpkin brings to my mind the sophisticated opening of a dinner arranged by an Oriental friend in Vancouver. When we sat down for the soup course, a beautiful large white plate was carried in. It bore a high, black iron holder, resembling an austere crown, which was topped by a glistening, hollowed-out, deep orange pumpkin filled with a clear fresh oyster consommé that had been cooked right in the pumpkin, absorbing its flavor and sweetness. The garnish was tiny floating flowers, delicately shaped from Chinese black mushrooms.

My friend told me that in the East, the pumpkin is a symbol of health and prosperity. This made me recall with pleasure the dreams of my youth about the pumpkin being changed into a golden carriage, and being sure it could happen when you were grown up. But later in life I remember my delight when looking at the autumn garden, after an early frost, and seeing it had turned cornstalks from green to a straw color and the great globes of orange gold shone among the corn. It certainly was a symbol of health and prosperity. To me, it has always been one of peaceful happiness — from my very young days I have loved autumn more than any of the other seasons.

Alas, many of the very good autumn dishes prepared with pumpkin are almost forgotten. If you have never tasted a cold pumpkin pudding topped with thick sour cream and sprinkled with finely shaved maple sugar — try it now and make up for the loss.

When we say cooked pumpkin, we usually think of pie, and forget it can be turned (just like the golden carriage) into soups, puddings, cakes, and pancakes, to name but a few dishes that this adaptable vegetable can enhance.

In France, for instance, they make *Potage au Potiron*, a delicate cream of pumpkin soup. From India comes a very interesting curried pumpkin, served as a meal; the Turks have their **Ara Strambouli**, a delicious and unusual pumpkin dessert.

But putting first things first, we should make our own pumpkin purée, one that keeps all year round and can be turned into so many exciting dishes.

Pumpkin Purée (Strained Pumpkin)

This basic recipe can be transformed into pies, pancakes, puddings, and whatever you like to make with a cup or two of strained pumpkin to begin with. (To freeze it, simply cook, chill, package, and freeze. It will keep 10 – 12 months.)

Take one large pumpkin, wash, remove seeds, cut into sections, and pare the skin off. Cut the pumpkin into cubes and place in a steamer (it's the same as a double boiler, only the bottom of the top part is perforated); or use a large sieve or colander set in a saucepan. Either way, place over boiling water and steam until tender, about 30 minutes. Put through a strainer or food mill, or purée in a blender.

The same procedure can be followed without puréeing the pumpkin, but don't freeze pumpkin cubes; they will not be satisfactory. To keep cubes, can them by the hot pack method, pressure sterilized at 10 pounds; 55 minutes per pint (500 mL). (Yield varies according to type of pumpkin used.)

Toasted Pumpkin Seeds

Even the seeds get into the act. Toast your supply in the time of plenty just before the frost touches the colorful autumn leaves. They will keep for 1 year stored in the freezer, or a few months in a cool place in sealed jars.

Remove the fibres from the seeds of a large pumpkin and place seeds in a saucepan. Top with cold water, add 1 tsp. (5 mL) of salt, cover, and simmer 2 hours. Drain and spread on paper towelling 4 – 8 hours to dry. When completely dried, place on a baking sheet, sprinkle with a few spoonfuls of vegetable oil — just enough to make seeds slightly oily when rubbed together with your hands.

Set in a 350°F. (180°C) oven 20 – 35 minutes, or until a nutty brown color, stirring a few times with a fork. When done, spread on brown paper, salt to taste, and let cool. Eat, as is, immediately — or store for future use. And if you then want crisper seeds, warm them up in a 350°F. (180°C) oven 15 minutes. *Yield:* 2 – 4 cups.

Eggplant and Onion Casserole

This is a simple version of the Persian "Iman's Delight." Delicious served hot, and just as good cold. (Perfect served cold as an appetizer with a barbecue feast.) Do not worry about what seems to be a lot of big pieces of garlic on top of it all. You will barely taste it. It melts into everything the moment you serve it.

1 medium eggplant
2 large onions
3 large tomatoes
½ tsp. (2 mL) sugar
½ cup (125 mL) chopped fresh parsley
Salt and pepper to taste
2 tbsp. (30 mL) vegetable or olive oil
2 coarsely chopped cloves of garlic
¼ cup (60 mL) cold water
Juice of ½ a lemon

Wash eggplant, and cut off flowered top and stem end. Peel and slice ½ in. (1.25 cm) thick. Slice the onions the same thickness as eggplant. Slice unpeeled tomatoes. Chop parsley. Mix the crushed and chopped garlic with the oil.

Arrange eggplant slices in the bottom of a medium-sized stainless steel or copper saucepan. Top with onions, and then with the tomatoes. Sprinkle with the sugar, salt and pepper. Cover with the parsley. Mix the oil with the garlic and pour over all. Add the cold water, and bring to boil. Cover, lower the heat, and simmer 30 – 35 minutes.

If you are not ready to serve it immediately, just turn off the heat and let stand. When ready, uncover, bring to a boil, and boil until liquid is almost completely reduced — only the oil remains. Then sprinkle with the lemon juice and serve. *Serves* 4 – 5.

Cauliflower Casserole

I have a weakness for vegetable casseroles, cooked in layers and never stirred. This one and the **Eggplant and Onion Casserole** are my favorites. To me, they make a whole meal, served with good toasted homemade bread.

1 medium head of cauliflower
2 tsp. (10 mL) salt
3 slices bacon
2 cups (500 mL) soft bread crumbs
¼ – ½ tsp. (1 – 2 mL) dill seeds
2 large or 3 medium tomatoes, sliced
Pinch of pepper

Cut cleaned cauliflower into flowerets. Place in a saucepan with 1 tsp. (5 mL) of the salt. Pour boiling water on top and boil, uncovered 10 – 12 minutes, or until almost tender.

Fry bacon until crisp, and drain on paper. Place in a bowl the bread crumbs, dill seeds, crumbled bacon and 3 tbsp. (50 mL) bacon fat.

Make layers in a casserole in the following order: sliced tomato, salt and pepper to taste, cauliflower, bread crumbs. Repeat if necessary, until all ingredients are used, leaving bread crumbs as the top layer. Bake in a preheated 400°F. (200°C) oven 30 – 40 minutes, or until top is golden brown. *Serves* 4 – 5.

New Potatoes à La Menthe

It is really a delight, more in July than in autumn, to pick the first little potatoes just after they have flowered. In July there is lots of fresh mint and, as the old Chinese saying goes, "What grows under the same moon should be eaten together." It is so true. Try it!

Scrub as many freshly-dug small potatoes as you need. Do not peel — the more peel that stays on the better.

Line the top of a steamer thickly with sprigs of fresh mint. Bring water to boil under the steamer. Place potatoes over the mint. Do not salt. Cover and steam 20 – 30 minutes, depending on the size and quantity of potatoes. Do not overcook. When ready, place potatoes in a hot serving dish. Dot with fresh mint butter made by mixing 2 tbsp. (30 mL) of butter with an equal quantity of fresh mint chopped fine. Salt the potatoes. Stir and serve.

Dilly Mashed Potatoes

Have you ever tasted potatoes mashed with cottage cheese and flavored with fresh or dried dill? Try them with pork chops, roast chicken, or simply with a green salad for a light, nourishing meal.

4 cups (1 L) hot mashed potatoes
1 cup (250 mL) any cottage cheese
3 tbsp. (50 mL) butter
2 green onions, finely chopped
½ tsp. (2 mL) dry dill or
1 tbsp. (15 mL) fresh dill
½ cup (125 mL) grated Parmesan or Cheddar cheese

Beat the potatoes with the cottage cheese, butter, green onions and dill. Salt and pepper to taste, sprinkle with cheese, and serve immediately — or put in a 1 quart (1 L) casserole, and bake uncovered in a 350°F. (180°C) oven 20 minutes. Sprinkle the grated cheese on top after 15 minutes. *Serves 4.*

Understanding the Mushroom

This is written for people with a passion for mushrooms, and in the hope that the non-passionate will join us in the appreciation of a delicious vegetable that can be everyday fare as well as the epitome of party elegance.

If you have any past prejudices about mushrooms, forget them — and try again, following these rules:

1. Mushrooms should be very fresh. When fresh, they are a smooth white or brown color, quite firm and not fully open.

2. Brown mushrooms have a stronger flavor than white. Both are delicious and the choice is a matter of personal taste.

3. Mushrooms come in different sizes: large, medium and the button variety — used for garnishes and in hors-d'oeuvres.

4. Mushrooms are usually sold in ½ lb. (250 g) boxes or loose, by the pound or kilo. In boxes they are mixed as to size. It's usually best to buy large mushrooms for stuffing or button mushrooms for garnish by the pound at stores that specialize in fresh produce.

5. Fresh mushrooms should never be allowed to stand in water. Never wash them in hot or warm water — always rinse quickly in cold water.

6. Some recipes call for peeled mushrooms. Peel large ones umbrella-wise from the edges to the center. Peel buttons like an apple — in a spiral, with a small sharp knife. But don't peel them unless the recipe says to.

7. To prepare mushrooms for cooking, neatly trim off the tips of the stalks and lightly scrape the stalks. If the stalks must be removed, break them off; don't cut them.

8. To clean unpeeled mushrooms, rub with an absorbent paper towel. If they are very sandy, wash them in the following manner. Throw them in a large bowl of cold water and rub them lightly and quickly with your hands for 30 seconds. Remove immediately and dry on absorbent paper. If left in the water they will lose their flavor and become limp. Cool them as soon as they're dry.

9. Never peel or prepare mushrooms beforehand, only just as they are going to be cooked.

10. Never throw away mushroom peelings and stalks. When chopped, they add a delicious flavor to most soups and sauces.

11. Mushrooms are too often overcooked. They become limp, watery and tasteless. They should be cooked over a high heat, quickly, just enough to warm them through. They cook in 30 seconds to 2 minutes, depending on size. They should be stirred constantly when cooking in butter or fat. Prolonged cooking toughens mushrooms.

Dried Mushrooms: In most major cities dried mushrooms can be bought in specialty or Oriental food shops. They come in a variety of beautiful shapes, colors and sizes. Their flavor is quite special, each one different. To experiment with dried mushrooms, add a few to your next casserole or mushroom sauce. They have a way of bringing out the delicate flavor of fresh mushrooms.

Before using dried mushrooms, wash them thoroughly under cold running water, then soak them 1 – 3 hours in hot water. Next, chop them fine and use. The soaking water should be used as part of the liquid called for in the recipe, or save it for soups, sauces or marinades.

Canned mushrooms, whole or in pieces, have a slightly different flavor than their fresh or dried counterparts. They are perfect to use in cream sauces, casseroles or stews. Always use or save their liquid for other dishes. Fresh, dried, or canned, mushrooms add a subtle, elegant touch to any dish or meal. So, use them!

Mother's Cabbage Gratiné

When I was growing up, whenever there was roast beef for dinner, there was also this cabbage, which has remained a treasured recipe. The secret of its success is a well-preheated oven.

4 cups (1000 mL) finely chopped cabbage
¼ cup (60 mL) butter
½ cup (125 mL) flour
3 cups (750 mL) milk
1 tsp. (5 mL) salt
½ tsp. (2 mL) pepper
¼ cup (60 mL) fine dry breadcrumbs
2 tbsp. (30 mL) melted butter

Place the minced raw cabbage in a buttered 2 quart (2 L) baking dish. Make a white sauce with the butter, flour and milk. You will have a fairly thick sauce. Add salt and pepper, and pour over the cabbage and mix the two together.

Mix the fine breadcrumbs with the melted butter and sprinkle on top of cabbage. Place in a preheated 400°F. (200°C) oven for about 20 minutes or until top is light brown and sauce is bubbling all around.

Serve as soon as ready — as it does not wait. To be perfect, the cabbage must be hot and crunchy, never soft and watery. *Serves 6.*

Old-Fashioned Creamed Celery

Years ago, a creamed celery dish was a must with roasted veal, egg dishes of all types, and poached fish. Try it sometime — you may be tempted to bring back the fashion!

2 cups (500 mL) diced celery
½ cup (125 mL) chopped celery leaves
½ tsp. (2 mL) salt
½ cup (125 mL) celery water
2 tbsp. (30 mL) butter
2 tbsp. (30 mL) flour
3 green onions, chopped fine or
  2 tbsp. (30 mL) chopped fresh chives
½ cup (125 mL) milk or light cream
1 bay leaf
Salt and pepper to taste

Place the diced celery and leaves in a saucepan. Add the salt and pour 2 cups (500 mL) boiling water on top. Bring to a fast rolling boil, and boil 10 minutes. Drain, reserving ½ cup (125 mL).

Melt the butter, and stir in the flour and green onions or chives. Mix well and add the reserved water and the light cream or milk, salt and pepper, and stir over medium heat until creamy. Add the celery. Mix well. Taste for seasoning and serve.

To Make a Casserole: Proceed in the same way, placing the celery in a buttered casserole. Pour the sauce on top and sprinkle top with ½ cup (125 mL) grated mild Cheddar. Place in preheated 350°F. (180°C) oven until top is browned. *Serves 4.*

The Onion: "The Rose of the Roots"

"The Rose of Roots," as Robert Louis Stevenson named the onion, can be cooked in many ways, made into many unusual dishes, apart from being used as an interesting flavoring in so many dishes. A root that is a must in any kitchen.

The onion has been a great traveller. It came a long, long way from Syria to Egypt . . . and kept going all over the world, for it is a universally used vegetable. Its name comes from the Latin *Unio* — meaning unity and many things in one. If it has many layers, it also has many qualities, and the price is fair enough that it may be included even in the low budget. It has medicinal properties of real value and is, believe it or not, a general stimulant to digestion. It contains Vitamin C, protein, minerals and nitrogen. It is the volatile oil in the onions, rich in sulphur, which gives them their pungent smell and taste. Boiling removes the oily content more than any other method of cooking. But it is a chemical property known as a "lachrymator," which is the agent that causes tears when peeling onions.

There are several members of the onion family which we use in cooking. While the most-used domestic onions are usually available all year long, some of the others, such as Spanish onions, appear only seasonally. Most onions are sold dried or "cured," but green onions, leeks and chives are sold fresh.

Here are the most familiar types of onions which are known to us:

Yellow Onions: Globe-shaped, sometimes called cooking onions. These vary in size from small to large, but we usually find medium-sized onions on the market; these are pungent. They are good for chopping, boiling, and making soup.

Spanish Onions: These have brown or yellow skins; they are mild. Excellent for slicing; good for deep-frying and stir-frying.

White Onions: Small in size, sometimes called silver-skins. These are fairly mild. Use whole to boil, or in stews and casseroles.

Red Onions: The large ones are mild, even sweet, and are used for salads, often referred to as Italian sweet onions. The medium-sized onions are strong and are used for frying as well as in stews and hash. (Referred to as the Quebec strong onions, they are becoming more and more difficult to find.)

Green Onions, or Scallions: Very young onions, pulled before the bulbous base has been formed. Both the green and white parts can and should be used.

Trim and wash green onions, then wrap in absorbent cloth and refrigerate; these are perishable. They are used chiefly for flavoring, garnish or salad, but they can be served as a vegetable as well. Cook them as you would cook asparagus. They are delicious served on toast with a butter sauce.

Chives: Well known to most, they are a gentle summer delight.

The French Shallot: A small dry onion, pinkish in color and always expensive. A mixture of onion and garlic, it gives an interesting flavor and should be used as an herb more than in quantity like onions.

Because of the oil and sugar an onion contains, there are about 125 calories in a medium-sized onion. Nevertheless, calorie-counters should give them a place in their reducing diet. For instance, steam or boil a "diet" onion, and dress with fresh lemon juice, chopped parsley, mint or thyme.

Half a large onion equals 1 cup (250 mL) chopped onion. Two medium-sized yellow or red onions make 1 cup (250 mL) chopped.

To Make Onion Juice: Cut a slice from the root or bottom end of an onion large enough to hold comfortably in the hand, and twist on a grater or on a fruit juicer, the same as you would an orange. Do not add the onion juice to the dish before you are ready to serve as it does not retain its flavor.

To flavor a casserole that does not include onions, rub the sides and bottom with a freshly-cut piece before pouring the ingredients in the dish; the flavor will be very delicate.

When necessary to store a cut onion, store in a glass container that has a glass or a plastic lid. A metal lid will retain the odor.

Allow 1 lb. (500 g) or 4–6 onions for 4 people, if the dish is part of a dinner course. As a main dish, allow 3 medium-sized onions per person.

Peel onions from the root toward the top. A thin slice removed from the root will permit you to release the first and second layers of skin very easily.

Choose small or medium-sized onions to boil whole. Larger ones are better sliced if they are to be boiled before creaming.

To save time in peeling and cutting large onions, slice them before peeling them. The outer skin ring will slip off easily and you will save time and tears.

When boiling or steaming a whole onion make a cross-cut in the top of each one; this will prevent the centers from coming out, as the moisture swells the onion during cooking.

When boiling onions whole or sliced, always add 1 tsp. (5 mL) of lemon juice or white vinegar to help preserve their whiteness. They turn dark when overcooked, or if there is not enough water in the pan.

Start boiling old winter onions in cold water, new ones in boiling water. Onions will be cooked in 25 – 45 minutes, depending on their size.

When some of the dinner is baking in a 350 – 375°F. (180 – 190°C) oven, place peeled onions in glass or earthenware baking dish, and barely cover with boiling water. Cover and bake 20 – 40 minutes, depending on size of onions. One of my favorite methods.

Another interesting way is to bake the onions in the oven the same as potatoes. Doe not peel. Place in pan and bake 40 – 60 minutes in a 375 – 400°F. (190 – 200°C) oven. To remove peel when done, cut through skin from top to bottom, then pull off skin. These can replace boiled onions in my recipes, and they are superb in flavor.

To season boiled onions, remember that onions and freshly ground pepper are compatible. They also like nutmeg, paprika and mustard, whole cloves, dill and savory.

After peeling all these onions, if you wish to remove odor from your hands, rinse under cold water, rub hard with salt, celery tops or lemon, then wash with soap and cold water.

How to Fry Onions

For onions to be evenly browned and crisp, peel the onions, chop, dice or slice. Heat 1 tbsp. (15 mL) butter and 1 tbsp. (15 mL) oil for 6 – 8 onions. Place in the hot oil, add 1 tbsp. (15 mL) cold water and ½ tsp. (2 mL) sugar.

Start browning over high heat, stirring quite frequently. When the onions are browning, continue cooking over medium heat until well browned. Salt and pepper to taste, and serve. Serves 4

How to Melt Onions, the French Way

To use as a garnish or to add to a sauce.

12 medium onions
¼ cup (60 mL) butter or margarine
1 tsp. (5 mL) salt
Pinch of pepper
½ tsp. (2 mL) sugar

Peel and slice the onion ¼ in. (0.5 cm) thick.

Melt the butter in a frying pan. Add the sliced onions and the remaining ingredients. Cover, and simmer slowly, stirring only occasionally, 25 – 30 minutes. To brown the onions slightly, do not cover the saucepan. Slow cooking improves their flavor. *Serves 6.*

French-Fried Onions

These can be cooked, cooled on absorbent paper, then packaged and frozen. They will keep 3 – 4 months. To reheat, place frozen onions on a baking sheet, one next to the other. Set in a 400°F. (200°C) oven until hot and crisp, about 5 – 8 minutes.

2 large white onions
1 egg white, lightly beaten
1/3 (80 mL) cup milk
½ cup (125 mL) fine breadcrumbs

Slice onions ¼ in. (0.5 cm) thick, then peel. Break up into rings. Beat the egg white lightly and blend with the milk. Soak each onion ring in this mixture and then in the fine breadcrumbs.

Place a few at a time in a deep fat frying basket and immerse in hot fat — 375°F. (195°C). Fry until well browned. Drain on absorbent paper and serve at once. *Serves 4 – 6.*

Creamed Onions

An old standby, always a favorite. For a special dish surround them with a crown of fresh or frozen bright green peas.

8 – 10 medium onions
2 cloves per onion
1 tbsp. (15 mL) butter
Pinch of thyme
1 bay leaf
Salt and pepper to taste
Breadcrumbs to taste
Grated cheese to taste

The Sauce:

2 tbsp. (30 mL) butter
2 tbsp. (30 mL) flour
1½ cups (350 mL) liquid (onion cooking water and milk to complete, if necessary)

Stud each onion with 2 cloves. Place in a saucepan. Cover with boiling water. Add the butter, thyme, bay leaf, salt and pepper. Bring back to boil, then simmer (do not let it boil) uncovered for 40 – 50 minutes. Remove onions from liquid and boil water over high heat until reduced by half.

Prepare a medium white sauce with the butter, flour and onion cooking water.

Pour the sauce over the drained onions. Sprinkle with breadcrumbs and grated cheese. Brown in a 450°F. (230°C) oven for 15 – 20 minutes and serve. *Serves 6.*

Onion Delicious

In the Spring, I add a pound or two of cooked fresh green peas to the onions when adding the cream. For a complete vegetable meal, also add 6 – 8 new cooked potatoes.

18 – 20 medium-small white onions
2 tbsp. (30 mL) sugar
¼ cup (60 mL) butter or margarine
¼ cup (60 mL) heavy cream
Salt and freshly-ground pepper to taste

Peel the onions, and place in a saucepan. Pour enough boiling water on top to cover, and salt to taste. Cover and simmer over medium heat for 20 – 25 minutes. Drain.

In a heavy metal frying pan, place the sugar and butter, stir until both are melted. Add the onions and stir around over medium heat until onions are shiny and glazed. Just before serving, add the cream. Simmer until quite hot, season to taste and serve. *Serves 4.*

Onions Madeira

These are excellent with game, pork or beef.

1½ lb. (750 g) small or medium white onions
¼ cup (60 mL) honey
¼ cup (60 mL) butter
1 bay leaf
Pinch of powdered cloves
¼ cup (125 mL) dry Madeira wine
2 tbsp. (30 mL) currants
¼ cup (125 mL) toasted slivered almonds (optional)

Peel the onions. Melt the butter in a frying pan, add the honey and stir until syrupy. Add the onions and cook over medium heat, shaking pan frequently until they are glazed here and there, and evenly browned. Very easy to do, if heat is not kept too high. It should take about 30 – 40 minutes. Place the onions in a shallow baking dish. Add the bay leaf and cloves. Salt and pepper to taste. Pour in the Madeira and the currants. Çover tightly — a foil paper will do.

Bake in a preheated 350°F. (180°C) oven 25 to 30 minutes. If any juice remains in the dish, it can be added to the meat gravy that will be served with the onions. *Serves 6.*

Onion Gravy

An old-fashioned recipe that should be kept alive. Our grandmothers, through their necessary sense of economy, discovered the value of onion skins for color and flavour. Double the recipe, and keep on hand in the refrigerator, or freeze to garnish, complement or warm up many foods.

Skin of 3 – 4 large red or deep yellow onioins
1 small onion, chopped fine
3 tbsp. (50 mL) vegetable oil
2 cups (250 mL) consommé
2 tbsp. (30 mL) margarine or bacon fat
¼ cup (125 mL) flour

Place the onion skins in the hot oil, stir over medium heat until the oil takes on red or deep yellow colour from the skins. Remove pieces of skin from oil, add the chopped onion, stir until lightly browned. Place the margarine or bacon fat in a heavy metal fying pan over medium heat. When melted, add the flour and cook, stirring constantly, until the mixture turns golden yellow. This is called a Basic Roux. Add to the onions. Stir and add the consommé. Stir until creamy and smooth. Season to taste. Strain. Reheat if necessary. *Yield:* about 2 cups (500 mL).

Uncooked Onion Summer Relish

Tasty and colourful. Keep refrigerated in a glass dish or jar. Will keep 6 – 8 days. Cucumber can be replaced by 1 cup (250 mL) of slivered celery.

3 – 4 medium onions, thinly sliced
1 green pepper, thinly sliced
1 tomato, peeled and thinly sliced

1 cucumber, peeled and thinly sliced
3 tsp. (50 mL) sugar
Juice of 1 lemon
½ cup (125 mL) cider or red wine vinegar
2–4 tbsp. (30–60 mL) vegetable oil

Combine all ingredients and refrigerate until ready to serve. *Serves 4–6.*

The Leeks

Leeks belong to the lily family, and can be considered a kind of onion. They are delicate in flavour. Sometimes they are difficult to find and they are nearly always expensive. In France, where they are easily available, they are known as "the poor man's asparagus." In Wales, they not only eat them, but they use them as their emblem as well.

Leeks have long flat green leaves, closely folded together. The bottom, or bulb, is white in colour, but it is only a little fatter than the leaves, in contrast to the more familiar onions which develop a much larger-sized bulb.

To Prepare: First, cut off the root ends and about 2 in. (5 cm) of green tops. Then peel off the first leaves, from top to bottom. Soak the trimmed leeks in cold water to loosen the soil. Leeks are very gritty so they must be carefully and thoroughly cleaned. After a brief soaking, run water into the tops down through the leaves opening them as you do to let the water go down as deep as possible. If they are to be sliced, make 2 lengthwise cuts in the green part so you can open the tightly folded leaves and wash them.

To Cook: Leeks can be cooked and served in much the same way as celery and asparagus. They can be blanched whole for 20 minutes, then freshened, cooled and served as a salad with **French Lemon dressing.**

Leeks and Tomato Sauce

A sauce when served over noodles or other pasta of your choice. A casserole when poured over diced cooked chicken or minced roast beef, topped with croutons and baked 15–20 minutes, or simply served as a sauce with fish or chicken.

4–6 leeks
3 tbsp. (50 mL) vegetable oil
1 large onion, minced
½ cup (125 mL) grated raw carrots
1 cup (250 mL) fresh tomatoes, diced

1 tsp. (5 mL) sugar
½ tsp. (2 mL) salt
½ tsp. (2 mL) basil
Pepper to taste

Clean the leeks and cut them in 1 in. (2.5 cm) lengths, both the green and white parts. Heat the oil, brown the onion in it, over high heat, add the carrots, tomatoes, sugar, salt, pepper and basil. Stir well and simmer 5 minutes. Add the leeks and simmer covered for 20 minutes or until the leeks are tender and the sauce slightly thickened. *Yield:* 3 cups (750 mL).

Braised Leeks

Served as an elegant spring vegetable in the best Paris restaurants. In Canada, delicate young leeks are at their best in late July.

6 young leeks
4 tbsp. (60 mL) butter
½ tsp. (2 mL) sugar
½ tsp. (2 mL) salt
Pinch of pepper
Juice of 1 lemon

Clean the leeks. Leave them whole, but cut them all the same length. Lie them flat in a frying pan. Pour boiling water on top. Cover and boil 10 minutes. Drain the water. Put back in the frying pan.

Heat the butter until nutty brown and pour over the leeks. Sprinkle with salt, pepper and sugar. Cook, uncovered for 20 minutes over medium heat, turning once. To serve, pour the lemon juice on top. *Serves 4 – 5.*

Chives

These are the tiny bulbs of another hardy member of the *Allium* family. I have grown mine for years and cannot conceive of being without my row of fresh chives. I know Spring is with us when the fresh spindly leaves come up and there are enough to cut so I can make a spring chive omelet for my husband's breakfast. It is my way of knowing that Spring "is with us to stay."

Chives are the mildest type of onion and are often considered a mild natural antibiotic. They also stimulate the appetite and strengthen the stomach — Victorian thinking maybe, but rather amusing to think it is true.

My own philosophy about breakfast is moderation, simplicity, quiet elegance, and respect for the tastes and early morning personalities of others.

Chives Mayonnaise

Chives and mayonnaise are perfect companions. I like to use this one with chilled shrimp or lobster meat or cold poached salmon steak.

1 large clove garlic
1 cup mayonnaise
3 tbsp. (50 mL) chopped fresh chives
1 tbsp. (15 mL) chopped fresh parsley
1 tbsp. (15 mL) chopped pimiento
Salt and pepper to taste

Remove a slice from the unpeeled clove of garlic. Rub the inside of a bowl with cut side, pressing hard on garlic. Discard. Combine the remaining ingredients in the bowl and mix throughly. Pour into a container of your choice. Cover and keep refrigerated. *Yield:* 1¼ cups (300 mL).

Garlic

Another member of the *Allium* family, perhaps the most misunderstood, in spite of the fact it has been with us since the early Greeks. If you like it, why not try growing it; it is rather attractive with its tall, flat leaves of graying green and its delicate flowers which form a lovely round, white head. I can never resist cutting a few to mix with red roses or in a large bowl of multi-colored nasturtium flowers. It is amusing to realize that garlic is fully appreciated or disdained in just about equal measure. I am convinced that to learn how to appreciate it is only a matter of proportion. Think of garlic as a delicate but pungent herb, use more or less of it (regardless of what a recipe may ask for) following what your taste demands — and not what the recipe suggests.

For a mild flavor, add the unpeeled cloves of garlic to the sauce or other dish. Prick it with a wooden pick; it will be easy to remove. Another way is to crush the unpeeled clove of garlic with a heavy knife. Do not remove the peel if you wish a mild garlic flavor. When adding it whole to a roast or a sauce, remove the peel and chop.

This is one of many pleasurable moments cooking with my daughter Monique. I call her "Chop-Chop" because she does the fine chopping so well, something I have little patience for.

Garlic Vinegar

I always like to keep some garlic vinegar on hand — one type made with cider vinegar, one with red or white wine. Superb, used on summer salads or winter cabbage salad. A spoonful added to a beef or lamb stew, just before serving, is very intriguing, or use to flavor a gravy or add a bit to scrambled eggs. The more you use it, the more you will enjoy it.

6 cloves garlic
1 pt. (500 mL) cider vinegar or red or white wine vinegar
1 tsp. (5 mL) sugar
½ tsp. (2 mL) salt

Crush the unpeeled garlic with the blade of a heavy knife. Add to the cider or wine vinegar with the sugar and salt. Shake well. Cork. Let stand 2 – 6 weeks, depending on how strong you like it. Then strain through a fine sieve. Put back in bottle. Will keep same as vinegar. *Yield:* 1 pint (500 mL).

Variations: Make "garlic oil" proceeding the same as for vinegar. Simply replace the cider vinegar or wine vinegar by pure olive oil. Use this on salad dressing; or in a marinating mixture.

The French Shallots

The glorious *Allium* of the French Cuisine. In France, whether you're a chef or a housewife, the *shallot* is counted among "the musts" in one's kitchen. It is of the onion family. What makes it distinctive is its ideal blend of mild onion and mild garlic flavor and aroma — just one shallot can give a lot of flavor to whatever food it is used with.

They are somewhat like a small onion of light brown or pinkish color, with variated layers of color, from white to pink, when peeled. They are somewhat costly, but little is needed to do a lot of flavoring, and they keep well in a cool place (not refrigerated).

For me they are a must in my salad dressing or sprinkled on barbecued or broiled chicken or steak, or mixed with the almonds in Sole Amandine, and of course to pour over my favorite potato salad.

To replace French shallots when they are not available, you can use this *petit truc de cuisine* that a well-known French chef taught me. Replace 1 shallot with 1 small mild onion chopped fine and mixed with ⅛ tsp. (0.5 mL) crushed garlic.

12. *Cakes, Pies, Cookies and Candies*

Sour Cream Lemon Cake

This cake will keep fresh in a cool place for 3 weeks, wrapped in foil.

1 cup (250 mL) margarine
2 cups (500 mL) fine granulated sugar
6 eggs
Grated rind of 2 lemons
4 cups (1000 mL) all-purpose flour
2 tsp. (10 mL) each baking soda and powder
½ tsp. (2 mL) salt
2 cups (500 mL) commercial sour cream
1½ – 2 cups (400 – 500 mL) chocolate chips
1 cup (250 mL) chopped walnuts (optional)
Topping

Prepare two 9 × 13 in. (22.5 × 32.5 cm) pans or two 10-in. (25 cm) tube pans or three 9 × 5 in. (22.5 × 12.5 cm) loaf pans.

Cream the margarine at high speed in an electric mixer until light. Gradually add sugar, and beat until creamy and light. Add eggs one at a time, beating well after each addition. Add lemon rind; stop mixer.

Sift flour with soda, baking powder and salt. Add all at once to creamed mixture, pour sour cream on top. Mix with a spatula, just enough to cover the flour, then mix at high speed for 2 minutes. Add chocolate chips and walnuts, beat 1 minute at high speed.

Divide batter into pans, and bake in a 350°F. (180°C) oven 40 – 60 minutes, depending on size of pans used. Test for doneness, then let cool on a cake rack 10 minutes.

Unmold on to waxed paper and baste while hot with *Syrup Topping:* bring to a boil over low heat 1 cup (250 mL) of sugar, the juice of 1 fresh lemon and 4 tbsp. (60 mL) of fresh orange juice or orange liqueur. *Serves 20 – 30.*

Maple Cloud Cake

This light feathery cake has a delicate flavor and a delectable icing. The cake, by itself, will freeze beautifully.

¾ cup (200 mL) maple syrup
4 eggs, separated
½ tsp. (2 mL) vanilla
1 cup (250 mL) sifted all-purpose flour
1 tsp. (2 mL) baking powder
⅛ tsp. (0.5 mL) ground coriander (optional)
¼ tsp. (1 mL) salt
Icing:
1¼ cups (325 mL) maple syrup
2 egg whites

Boil the ¾ cup (200 mL) maple syrup exactly 2 minutes. Beat the 4 egg whites until stiff and set aside. Beat the 4 egg yolks and vanilla until light, then gradually mix in boiled syrup.

Fold egg yolk mixture gently into egg whites. Sift remaining dry ingredients together 3 times and fold into egg mixture. Pour batter into an ungreased 9 or 10 in. (22.5 or 25 cm) tube pan. Bake at 325°F. (160°C) for 50 minutes, or until done. When cake is cooked, invert pan on a cake rack and let cool for 1 hour. To unmold, pass a knife around the edges and ease cake out of the pan.

To make icing, boil maple syrup until it forms a firm ball when tested in ice water — 328°F. (160°C) on candy thermometer. Beat egg whites until stiff, then add hot syrup on top. beating constantly with an electric beater. If you use a hand rotary beater, pour in a little syrup, beat, pour more and beat again, until all the syrup is used. Continue beating until frosting stands in peaks, or until it cools. Spread on top and sides of cake. *Yield:* 1 cake.

Blue Ribbon Jelly Roll

My husband's favorite cake is a French Mocha Cake, but mine is this old-fashioned jelly roll, especially when I have good tart homemade jelly to fill it, my favorite jelly being a black currant one I make with 2 wild rose petals in each jar. I always use my electric mixer to make this cake, but an electric hand beater will also do.

4 egg yolks
½ cup (125 mL) sugar
½ tsp. (2 mL) vanilla

4 egg whites
1/3 cup (80 mL) sugar
¾ cup (200 mL) all-purpose flour
1 tsp. (5 mL) baking powder
½ tsp. (2 mL) salt
1/3 cup (80 mL) icing sugar

Preheat the oven to 375°F. (190°C). Butter (do not use other fat) a jelly roll pan 15 × 10 × 2 in. (37.5 × 25 × 5 cm).

Place the egg yolks in the mixer bowl and beat at high speed until thick and foamy, and a pale lemon color. Then gradually beat in the first ½ cup (125 mL) sugar and the vanilla.

Beat the egg whites until they reach the soft peak stage, then start to add the other ½ cup (125 mL) sugar, about 2 tbsp. (30 mL) at a time. Gently fold the beaten whites into the yolks using a spatula.

Sift together the flour, baking powder and salt. Fold into the egg mixture until thoroughly blended.

Spread in prepared pan and bake 18 – 20 minutes or until cake springs back when pressed lightly with finger and has a pale golden color.

Sprinkle a cloth with the icing sugar. Loosen edges of cake with small spatula and invert on sugared towel. Then using towel to help roll the cake, let stand on cake rack until cooled. Unroll, spread with jam or jelly of your choice. Lift to a plate, sprinkle generously with icing sugar. *Yield:* 1 jelly roll.

Note: I still have my mother's jelly roll plate, which is a long, narrow dish, in blue Limoges porcelain, decorated with pink roses and gold scroll work, with the knife and serving plates to match. I am told that it is not easy, but still possible, to find these. If you like table elegance, this dish, filled with a perfect jelly roll, and served with black Chinese tea flavored with a white lily or rose, is certainly something to remember.

Tom Collins Torte

I have a few cakes I keep making as the years go by. This is one of them:

5 eggs
1 cup (250 mL) rum
1 cup (250 mL) very fine breadcrumbs
1 cup (250 mL) walnuts, finely chopped
½ tsp. (2 mL) cinnamon
½ tsp. (2 mL) ground cardamom

Grated rind of 1 lemon
1 tsp. (5 mL) baking powder
2 tbsp. (30 mL) sugar
1 cup (250 mL) boiling water
¼ cup (60 mL) dry gin
Whipped cream to taste

Separate the eggs. Beat the whites until stiff. With the same beater, beat the yolks, add the sugar, and beat again until lemon-colored. Add the next 6 ingredients, and stir until well mixed. Fold in the beaten egg whites.

Butter two round 8 in. (20 cm) cake molds, and divide batter evenly into each.

Bake in a preheated 350°F. (180°C) oven, about 25 minutes, or until golden brown. Unmold on foil.

Prepare "Collins" topping by mixing the remaining ingredients, stirring over medium heat until sugar is dissolved. Pour ½ cup (125 mL) of this mixture over each "torte." When cold, put tortes together one over the other. Wrap and keep refrigerated until ready to serve.

To serve, top with sweetened sliced strawberries and whipped cream. (In the winter I use only the cream.) *Yield:* two 8 in. (20 cm) layers.

Boiled Raisin Cake

Often referred to as Pioneers' Boiled Cake, this is a delicious, low-cost type of fruit cake with excellent keeping qualities.

1 cup (250 mL) dark brown sugar
½ cup (125 mL) pure lard
1 cup (250 mL) seedless raisins
1 cup (250 mL) hot water
1 tsp. (5 mL) soda
1 tbsp. (15 mL) water
1 – 2 eggs, beaten
½ tsp. (2 mL) salt
1 tsp. (5 mL) baking powder
1½ cups (400 mL) all-purpose flour
2 tsp. (10 mL) allspice
1 tsp. (5 mL) cloves
1 tsp. (5 mL) cinnamon

Bring the sugar, lard, raisins and hot water to a boil while stirring, then boil over medium heat 5 minutes. Pour into a bowl and let cool.

Stir soda into 1 tbsp. (15 mL) of water. Add to raisin mixture with egg (2 eggs will give a richer cake), salt, baking powder, and mix well. Add flour sifted with spices, beating until well mixed.

Bake in a well greased 9 × 5 in. (22.5 × 12.5 cm) loaf pan at 325°F. (160°C) for 1 hour, or until well done. Let cool 10 minutes, then unmold on a cake rack. When cold, keep wrapped in foil in a cool place. *Yield:* 1 cake.

Monique's Blender Banana Cake

This takes 10 minutes to prepare, 5 minutes to blend, and 35 minutes to cook two tasty, light 9 in. (22.5 cm) single layer cakes. They keep well, and freeze *very* well.

2½ cups (625 mL) flour
1¼ tsp. (6 mL) baking powder
1¼ tsp. (6 mL) baking soda
½ tsp. (2 mL) salt
½ cup (125 mL) walnuts
3 ripe bananas or 1½ cups (400 mL) sliced
3 eggs
2/3 cups (160 mL) soft butter
2/3 cup (160 mL) sour milk or buttermilk
1 2/3 cups (410 mL) sugar
1 tsp. (5 mL) vanilla

Place the first 4 ingredients in a mixing bowl.

Place walnuts in blender, cover and blend 2 seconds. Add to flour. Add remaining ingredients to the blender, cover and blend 20–30 seconds, or until smooth.

Pour over the dry ingredients and stir until well mixed. Divide batter into two 9 in. (22.5 cm) round layer pans, buttered.

Bake in a 350°F. (180°C) oven 30–35 minutes, and unmold to cool on cake rack. *Yield:* 2 single-layer cakes.

Gingerbread Mix

The late Nellie Lyle Pattinson was far ahead of her time. In her well-known *Canadian Cook Book*, first published in 1923, Miss Pattinson gives a recipe for Gingerbread Spice Mix, which I have found extremely useful, and have adapted to make my own formula.

9 cups (2.5 L) sifted all-purpose flour
2 cups (500 mL) sugar
2 tbsp. (30 mL) baking powder
2 tsp. (15 mL) baking soda
2 tsp. (10 mL) salt
4 tbsp. (60 mL) ginger
2 tbsp. (30 mL) cinnamon
1 cup (250 mL) very cold shortening
½ cup (125 mL) very cold bacon fat

Thoroughly mix the flour, sugar, baking powder, soda, salt, ginger and cinnamon, then sift 2 or 3 times. Grate the shortening over the dry ingredients on a medium grater. Cut in the bacon fat.

When the mix is ready, pour into a quart sealer (spoon lightly and do not pack) and keep in a cool place. I usually double the recipe and keep a supply in my freezer.

To Make the Gingerbread: Mix 1 beaten egg with ¾ cup (200 mL) of molasses and 3 cups (750 mL) of the gingerbread mix. Stir in ¾ cup (200 mL) of boiling water. Bake in a greased 8 × 10 in. (26 cm × 20 cm) pan at 325°F. (160°C) for 35–40 minutes. *Yield:* 1 gingerbread cake.

Sensational Cake

Even after ten years, I still receive a few dozen letters asking for this recipe every pre-Christmas season. The recipe hails from the U.S.A., but I have never found the creator.

¾ cup (200 mL) flour
¾ cup (200 mL) sugar
½ tsp. (2 mL) baking powder
½ tsp. (2 mL) salt
3 cups (750 mL) shelled Brazil nuts
2 packages (454 g each) pitted dates
1 cup (500 mL) well-drained maraschino cherries
3 eggs, well beaten
1 tsp. (5 mL) vanilla

Preheat oven to 300°F. (150°C). Grease, then line with waxed paper, a 9 × 5 × 3 in. (22 × 12 × 7 cm) loaf pan.

Stir thoroughly together the flour, sugar, baking powder and salt. In a large bowl place the nuts, dates and cherries. Pour flour on top. Mix with hands until nuts and fruits are well coated with the flour mixture. Add the vanilla to the beaten eggs and pour on top of floured fruits. Mix well, with hands, as it is easier than with a spoon.

Spread evenly in prepared pan. Bake in preheated oven 1¾ hours or until done. Test with a straw. Cool 15 minutes in pan set on wire rack. Unmold, peel off paper. Cool completely on rack. Wrap in transparent paper, then in foil. Will keep 3 months in refrigerator, 6 months in freezer.

Note: Use about 2 lb. (1000 g) unshelled or 1 lb. (500 g) shelled Brazil nuts.

Super Pastry

A fast way to make a light puff pastry. My daughter who gave me the recipe uses it to make her own Napoleons — the problem is there never seems to be enough to make everyone happy. A great advantage is that the pastry will keep 2 weeks refrigerated. Even at the cost of butter and sour cream, it is more economical than buying your own pastry.

1 cup (250 mL) butter
1½ cups (400 mL) sifted all-purpose flour
½ cup (125 mL) commercial sour cream

Cut the butter into the flour with two knives or a pastry blender until completely mixed, or with a granular appearance. Stir in the sour cream with a fork until thoroughly blended. Divide dough into four equal portions. Wrap each tightly, refrigerate at least 8 – 12 hours before using.

To bake, preheat oven to 350°F. (180°C). Roll one portion of dough on a well floured board into a 12 X 6 in. (30 X 15 cm) rectangle. Place on ungreased cooky sheet. Bake 15 – 18 minutes or until pastry is puffed and golden brown. Repeat with other three portions.

When the pastry is cooked, transfer carefully to wire racks. Cool completely.

To Make Napoleons: Trim sides carefully with a sharp knife, so all layers are the same size. I use a sheet of paper, cut it the size I need [12 X 6 in.] (30 X 15 cm), and place pastry on top to trim it. You will soon learn to make them almost perfect. (Keep trimmings, sprinkle on a bit of jam, top with whipped cream or sour cream and serve as an extra dessert.)

Place 1 layer of the trimmed pastry, puffed side up, on separate wire rack — to be decorated for the top of the Napoleon. Place on layer, puffy side up on service platter. Spread with cold **Crème Patissière**, and repeat with second and third layers.

Decorate the reserved layer as follows, and place over the 3 others:

¼ cup (60 mL) chocolate chips
1 tsp. (5 mL) shortening
1 cup (250 mL) sifted icing sugar
1 tbsp. (15 mL) corn syrup
1 tbsp. (15 mL) water
½ tsp. (2 mL) vanilla

Melt in double boiler the chocolate chips and shortening. Stir to blend.

Combine in saucepan the icing sugar, corn syrup, water and vanilla. Cook over low heat, stirring most of the time just until frosting is smooth and shiny and coats the back of a wooden spoon. Beware of overcooking, or frosting will become too hard. Remove from heat. Pour gently over top pastry layer set on rack. Spread evenly with a long metal spatula.

Pour chocolate mixture into pastry bag with a small writing tip. Pipe lengthwise strips 1 in. (2.5 cm) apart over frosting. With a wooden or metal pick, make chevron markings, also 1 in. (2.5 cm) apart — pull pick gently left to right, then right to left. When icing has set, gently place this top over the others. Chill 1 hour before serving. It will make 6 pastries when cut.

Refrigerator Pie Dough

Keep this handy in the refrigerator, wrapped in foil, and take it out one hour before rolling. Light and flaky, and it browns beautifully. Will keep one month.

5 cups (1.25 L) all-purpose flour
½ tsp. (2 mL) baking powder
1 tsp. (5 mL) salt
¼ cup (60 mL) brown sugar
1 lb. (500 mL) pure lard
1 egg
2 tbsp. (30 mL) vinegar
Cold water

Sift the flour with baking powder, salt and brown sugar. Cut in lard with 2 knives until the size of peas.

Beat egg in a measuring cup, add vinegar and enough cold water to make ¾ cup (200 mL). Pour over pastry, blend until it forms a ball, then knead a few seconds.

Wrap dough and refrigerate. *Yield:* 4 double crusts, or 5 bottom crusts and 5 lattice tops.

Super Lemon Pie

One of my favorite pies. Through the years I have tried many recipes, but none were ever better than this one.

- 1 baked 9 in. (22.5 cm) pastry shell
- 1½ cups (400 mL) sugar
- ¼ cup (60 mL) cornstarch
- 1 tsp. (10 mL) salt
- ½ cup (125 mL) cold water
- ½ cup (125 mL) fresh lemon juice
- 3 egg yolks, well beaten
- 2 tbsp. (30 mL) butter
- 1½ cups (400 mL) boiling water
- 1 tsp. (5 mL) grated lemon rind

In a saucepan, mix sugar, cornstarch and salt. With a whisk, beating all the time, add the cold water, lemon juice and egg yolks. When very smooth, add the butter and the boiling water. Stir well, then over medium heat, gradually bring mixture to boil, stirring constantly. When mixture starts to bubble thickly, lower the heat and simmer 1 minute. Remove from heat. Add lemon rind. Mix well and pour filling into cold cooked lemon pastry shell. Let cool, which will cause a thin film to form, while preparing the meringue. This will prevent sweating of the meringue while baking.

Meringue:

- 3 egg whites
- ¼ tsp. (1 mL) cream of tartar
- 6 tbsp. (100 mL) sugar

Beat the egg whites at medium speed until frothy, then add cream of tartar. Beat at high speed until whites have lost their foamy appearance; reduce speed to medium, and start adding the sugar, 1 tbsp. (15 mL) at a time, beating with each addition. Then to high speed and beat until whites are fairly stiff but still glossy. Place in mounds around edge of pie. Then with a spatula, push meringue gently around inner edge of pie. Bake in a preheated 350°F. (180°C) oven, 12 – 15 minutes or until golden brown. Cool on a wire rack, away from drafts. It takes at least 2 hours to cool. *Yield:* 1 9 in. (22.5 cm) pie.

My Favorite Apple Pie

- 1 9 in. (22.5 cm) unbaked pie shell, and pastry top
- 5 cups (1.25 L) peeled and sliced apples

½ cup (125 mL) brown sugar
1 tsp. (5 mL) ground cardamom
Grated rind of ½ a lemon
1 tsp. (5 mL) vanilla extract
2 tbsp. (30 mL) cubed butter

Stir together in a bowl the apple slices, brown sugar, ground cardamom, lemon rind, and vanilla extract. Stir gently. Pour into unbaked pie crust. Spread the cubed butter on top, and top with crust. Bake in a preheated 425°F. (220°C) oven for 35 – 45 minutes, or until golden brown. *Yield:* 1 9-in. (22.5 cm) pie.

Rhubarb Pie

This summer perennial uses almond flavoring — an old-fashioned trick that does wonders for rhubarb pie.

4 cups (1 L) rhubarb, cut in ½ in. (1.25 cm) pieces
Pastry for single-crust, 9 in. (22.5 cm) pie, with lattice top
2 eggs
2/3 cup (160 mL) sugar
2 tbsp. (30 mL) flour
Juice of ½ a lemon
Pinch of salt
¼ tsp. (1 mL) almond extract
2 tsp. (10 mL) sugar

Place the rhubarb in a well-buttered 9 in. (22.5 cm) pie plate lined with pastry. Beat eggs lightly, then stir in the first measure of sugar, the flour, lemon juice, salt and extract, and pour over rhubarb.

Weave pastry strips in a diamond pattern over top and sprinkle with the 2 tsp. (10 mL) of sugar. Bake in a 450°F. (230°C) oven 15 minutes, then reduce heat to 350°F. (180°C), and bake until crust is browned — about 25 – 35 minutes. *Serves 6.*

Chicago Raspberry Pie

I cut this recipe out of the Chicago *Tribune* in 1949, and faithfully pull it from the file every year when the fresh berry season comes around. It is an elegant and scrumptious dessert.

2 tsp. (10 mL) unflavored gelatine
2 tbsp. (30 mL) cold water
½ cup (125 mL) sugar
⅛ tsp. (0.5 mL) salt
⅓ cup (80 mL) water
2 egg whites, beaten stiff
1 tbsp. (15 mL) lemon juice
1 cup (250 mL) whipping cream
1 9-in. (22.5 cm) baked pie shell, cooled
3 – 4 cups (750 – 1000 mL) raspberries
⅓ cup (80 mL) sugar
4 tsp. (60 mL) cornstarch
Whole berries for garnish

Pour the gelatine over the cold water, and let stand 5 minutes. Stir the ½ cup (125 mL) of sugar, salt and ⅓ cup (80 mL) of water in a saucepan until sugar is dissolved, then cook to soft-ball stage — 235 – 240°F. (113 – 116°C) on a candy thermometer.

Pour hot syrup in a fine stream over beaten egg whites, beating constantly — this is very easy with an electric mixer. Add lemon juice and continue beating until thick.

Dissolve gelatine over hot water until clear. Pour slowly into beaten egg whites, beat 1 minute, and refrigerate until cool. Whip cream, fold into mixture and pour into cool shell. Refrigerate 4 – 5 hours.

Mix together the raspberries (you can purée them by pressing them through a sieve if you like, to remove the seeds, although it is not necessary), the ⅓ cup (80 mL) sugar, and the cornstarch, and cook over medium heat, stirring constantly until thick and clear. Let cool and spread in center. Garnish around edges with fresh berries or whipped cream, then refrigerate until ready to serve. *Serves 6 – 8.*

My Mother's Pumpkin Pie

The only difference between my mother's pie and any pumpkin pie is the browning and drying of the pumpkin before mixing with other ingredients; but believe me, it makes all the difference between an everyday pie and superb dessert.

1½ cups (400 mL) strained pumpkin, browned
3 tbsp. (50 mL) all-purpose flour
1 cup (250 mL) light brown sugar
2 cups (500 mL) milk

1 cup (250 mL) heavy cream
1 tsp. (5 mL) cinnamon
½ tsp. (2 mL) ginger
½ tsp. (2 mL) nutmeg
2 eggs, well beaten
Pie dough for two 8 in. (20 cm) pie plates
2 tbsp. (30 mL) sugar
Pinch of ginger or cardamom

To brown the pumpkin, measure 2 cups (500 mL) of strained (or canned) pumpkin. Butter generously the bottom of a large cast-iron frying pan. Put in the pumpkin and cook over medium heat, stirring most of the time, and turning it over occasionally so all parts dry properly. Keep this up until it is reduced to 1½ cups (400 mL). It will be slightly brown and the natural sweetness of the pumpkin will be greatly enhanced.

Place the browned pumpkin in a bowl, sprinkle with 2 tbsp. (30 mL) flour, add the brown sugar, and stir until thoroughly mixed. Scald the milk, and add to it the cream, cinnamon, ginger and nutmeg. Pour over the pumpkin mixture. Mix and add the eggs. Beat together until well mixed. Line a pie plate with dough, well built up around the edges.

Mix together the 2 tbsp. (30 mL) sugar, the remaining tbsp. (15 mL) flour and the pinch of ginger or cardomon. Sprinkle over with tips of fingers. This prevents sogginess in the bottom of the pie. Fill the shell three-quarters full with the pumpkin mixture. Place strips of foil paper around the edge of the pie to keep it from browning too fast.

Bake 15 minutes in a preheated 450°F. (250°C) oven. Reduce heat to 325°F. (160°C) and bake 30 minutes more. Mother knew the pumpkin pie was cooked when the mixture shook just in the middle as it was moved back and forth. Serve this pie hot or cold with wedges of Canadian Cheddar. *Serves 6.*

Molasses Pie

Sometimes called *Tarte à la Farlouche* or *Tarte à la Pichoune*. Whatever the name, the recipe remains the same, and it is another one that is almost forgotten.

½ cup (125 mL) flour
1 cup (250 mL) molasses
1 cup (250 mL) water
½ cup (125 mL) raisins
1 tsp. (5 mL) butter
¼ tsp. (1 mL) almond extract

Stir together in a saucepan, the flour, molasses and water, then cook over medium-low heat, stirring all the time, until creamy and smooth. The cream is ready when it becomes somewhat transparent. Add the raisins, butter and almond extract. Stir well. Cover and cool.

Pour into an 8 in. (20 cm) pie plate lined with a baked and cooled crust. Cover lightly with wax paper. Serve cold as is or with whipped cream or ice cream. *Serves* 6.

Monique's Summer Forgotten Pie

She so named this fabulous dessert because she mixes and cooks her meringue after the evening dinner. When the cooking period is over, turn off heat of oven — and "forget" the pie in the oven until the next morning, a method consistent with producing a crunchy meringue that is never gummy in the middle. In the summer, the filling is all the variety of fresh fruits, topped with lemon sauce; in the winter, it is superb with balls of ice cream topped with a maple sauce or simply filled with a cooked maple or lemon pie filling.

4 egg whites, or enough for ½ cup (125 mL)
¼ tsp. (1 mL) salt
1 tsp. (5 mL) white vinegar
1 cup (250 mL) sugar

Topping:

4 egg yolks
2/3 cup (160 mL) sugar
1/3 cup (80 mL) fresh lemon juice
2 tsp. (10 mL) grated lemon rind
Sugar to taste (for fruit).

Beat egg whites until fluffy. Add salt and vinegar and continue beating until whites start to form a peak. Add the 1 cup (250 mL) sugar, 1 tbsp. (15 mL) at a time, beating at least one minute between each of the first 6 tbsp. (90 mL); then the rest of the sugar can be added quickly, but beat well at each addition.

Generously butter an 8 in. (20 cm) pie plate. Fill with the beaten whites, hollowing out the center lightly with a spoon to form a sort of nest.

Bake in a preheated 250°F. (120°C) oven, about 1½ hours or until a light golden color. Leave overnight in the oven or let cool in oven for 2 hours, then keep on cake rack until ready to serve.

To Make the Lemon Sauce Topping: beat the egg yolks until thick and lemon-colored. While beating, gradually add the sugar, 1 tbsp. (15 mL) at a time. Then add the lemon juice and rind, stirring constantly; cook over low heat, until creamy and smooth, about 5 – 8 minutes. Do not let mixture boil. Cool, cover, then refrigerate.

To serve, slip meringue onto a large glass plate, fill with any sweetened berries or sliced fresh fruit and pour lemon sauce on top. If you're not counting calories, top with a fluff of whipped cream. *Serves 6.*

Sugar Pie

Every summer, requests pour in for this sugary yet creamy pie. People travel, eat it in restaurants, then look for the recipe, which is almost as old as Canada. The following is made the way *grand-mère* taught me, though there are all kinds of recipes.

Pastry of your choice for single-crust pie
½ tsp. (2 mL) baking soda
¼ tsp. (1 mL) vanilla
1½ cups (400 mL) maple syrup
1 cup (250 mL) all-purpose flour
1 cup (250 mL) dark brown sugar
Pinch of nutmeg
⅓ cup (80 mL) butter

Line a 9 in. (22.5 cm) pie plate with pastry. Stir soda and vanilla into syrup and pour into pastry.

Blend remaining ingredients with your fingertips until mixture is crumbly, then spread over syrup. Place a piece of foil under pan, because this pie often bubbles over while cooking. Bake at 350°F. (180°C) for 30 minutes, and let cool — it is best cold. *Serves 6 – 8.*

Five Rules for Perfect Shortbread:

1. Always use first-quality (sweet or unsalted) butter at room temperature;
2. Use rice flour; difficult to find — easier at health food shops;
3. Sift *at least 3 times* the flour, cornstarch and rice flour;
4. Bake "gently." Do not try to bake them until dark brown — or just even brown. They should have a pale beige color;
5. Let them "ripen," well covered, in a plastic box for at least 6 days.

If you can do all this, shortbread success is yours. If you wish, you can cut the recipe in half. But remember, they will keep 4 months, well covered in a cool place. (Do not refrigerate.)

Christmas Shortbread

In the early Sixties, we had a contest on T.V. for the best traditional or family shortbread. I tested them all — over 75 entries. Out of these we chose three as winners.

Mr. A. was the first. At that time it was not unusual to have men participate in what was thought to be a "women's business." The three winners had to come and make them with me live on T.V. Every year I still make all three recipes, but my favorite remains Mr. A's entry.

Mr. A., Quebec

1 cup (250 mL) butter
2 cups (500 mL) sifted pastry flour
1/3 cup (80 mL) fruit sugar
1/3 cup (80 mL) rice flour

Use one ungreased baking sheet. Preheat oven to 325°F. (160°C). Baking time: 30 minutes.

Beat butter in a large bowl with a wooden spoon until it is very creamy. Add sifted pastry flour and beat well.

Combine fruit sugar and rice flour. Add to butter mixture and blend all the ingredients together thoroughly. Cover bowl and place mixture in the refrigerator for 1 hour.

Using palms of hands, pat dough out to ¼-in. (0.625 cm) thickness. Cut with a 2 in. (5 cm) round cookie cutter. Place on ungreased baking sheet. Prick each shortbread several times with a fork. *Yield:* twenty-eight 2 in. (5 cm) round shortbread.

Carrot Oatmeal Cookies

Very old-fashioned, big, soft, spicy cookies, they were loved by the children and mother said, "They are very good keepers!" Surely more nourishing than commercial cookies.

1 cup (250 mL) firmly packed light brown sugar
½ cup (125 mL) soft shortening
2 eggs

1/3 cup (80 mL) milk
1 cup (250 mL) grated raw carrots
1½ cups (400 mL) all-purpose flour
1 tsp. (5 mL) baking powder
½ tsp. (2 mL) soda
½ tsp. (2 mL) salt
½ tsp. each (2 mL) cinnamon and nutmeg
2 cups (500 mL) oatmeal
1 cup (250 mL) seedless raisins

Cream the sugar, shortening and eggs until light and creamy. Add milk and carrots, and stir until well mixed. Sift together flour, baking powder, soda, salt, cinnamon and nutmeg. Add remaining ingredients and stir until raisins are well coated with flour mixture.

Mix with creamed mixture. This is a fairly stiff batter. Drop by spoonfuls onto a greased cookie sheet and bake at 350°F. (180°C) about 15 minutes, or until brown all over. *Yield:* 4 dozen.

Pumpkin Cookies

In my youth, pumpkin cookies were regularly given away to children on Halloween. They are large and soft and will keep 9–10 weeks in a freezer.

½ cup (125 mL) lard or bacon fat
1¼ cups (325 mL) dark brown sugar
2 eggs
1 tsp. (5 mL) vanilla
1½ cups (400 mL) **Pumpkin Purée**
2½ cups (625 mL) all-purpose flour
4 tsp. (20 mL) baking powder
½ tsp. (2 mL) salt
½ tsp. (2 mL) cinnamon
½ tsp. (2 mL) nutmeg
1 cup (250 mL) chopped nuts
1 cup (250 mL) seedless raisins

Cream the lard with sugar, then add eggs, vanilla and beat until creamy and light. Add purée and mix thoroughly.

Sift flour, baking powder, salt and spices together, add to creamed mixture, then stir in nuts and raisins. Drop by large teaspoonfuls (5-6 mL) onto a greased baking sheet. Bake in a 375°F. (190°C) oven 15 minutes or until lightly browned. Yield: 4-5 dozen.

Monique's Christmas All-Year-Round Squares

Christmas, because they are made with canned mincemeat that she keeps handy. Very nice with hot tea or a glass of port wine or brandy.

- ¾ cup (200 mL) margarine
- 1 cup (250 mL) brown sugar
- 1½ cups (400 mL) flour
- ½ tsp. (2 mL) baking soda
- 1 tsp. (5 mL) salt
- 1 cup (250 mL) rolled oatmeal
- 1 – 1½ cups (250 – 400 mL) mincemeat
- 1 cup (250 mL) grated unpeeled apples

Beat together the first 6 ingredients. Spread half of mixture in a well greased 13 X 9 in. (32.5 cm X 22.5 cm) baking pan. Press with hands until the bottom is all covered.

Mix the mincemeat and apples, spread on top of mixture. Sprinkle the remaining dry mixture on top of mincemeat. Gently spread and press on top.

Bake in a preheated 400°F. (200°C) oven 25 – 30 minutes, or until light golden color. Cut into squares while warm. *Serves* 9 – 12.

Monique's Scotch Crunchies

Soft the first day, crunchy the next, they keep for days and are always a pleasure to serve, as well as to eat.

- ½ cup (125 mL) butter or margarine
- 1 cup (250 mL) brown sugar
- 2 cups (500 mL) rolled oats, any type
- ¼ tsp. (1 mL) salt
- 1 tsp. (5 mL) baking powder

Melt the butter in a frying pan, add the brown sugar and stir until sugar has softened into a sauce. Add the oats and salt. Mix well. Spread as evenly as possible in an 8 X 8 in. (20 X 20 cm) well-buttered dish. Bake in a preheated 350°F. (180°C) oven, 20 – 25 minutes, or until golden in color. Cool 20 – 30 minutes, and cut into bars or squares. Keep in a covered plastic box. *Yield:* 12 – 16 squares.

Coconut Pink Candy

I just love the belief from the Middle Ages that the birds began to mate on St. Valentine's Day, though I am sure they had never met up with the *Canadian* February.

But even in such a grim month, the traditions go on. When I was a young girl at school, we made special sweets as gifts for everyone we liked, male and female. This custom may be passé, but the desire to eat sweets is still strongly embedded in all of us. Too much, *hélas!*

This is one of the sweets I used to make as a child, and I was offered the same candy on a recent trip to the West, but it was white and named Ranch Candy. By either name, it is a delightful, old-fashioned Valentine.

3 cups (750 mL) sugar
1 cup (250 mL) light cream
3 tbsp. (50 mL) corn syrup
2 tbsp. (30 mL) butter
½ tsp. (2 mL) almond extract
1 tsp. (5 mL) vanilla
1/8 – ¼ tsp. (0.5 – 1 mL) pink vegetable coloring
1 cup (250 mL) coconut

Put sugar, cream and corn syrup into a large saucepan and stir over low heat until sugar is all dissolved.

Clean sides of pan with a small piece of damp cloth wrapped around fork tines, or with a wet pastry brush. Then cover pan and cook 3 minutes to steam down any sugar crystals still sticking.

Uncover and cook over medium heat, stirring occasionally, until candy forms a soft ball in cold water; on a candy thermometer, 234 – 240°F. (112 – 115°C). Remove from heat and set pan on cake rack. Add butter, but don't stir.

Let cool until bottom of pan feels lukewarm to your hand. Add remaining ingredients, then beat until mixture just begins to lose its gloss and will hold its shape. Make sure it has a good pink color.

Pour quickly into a buttered 8 × 8 in. (20 × 20 cm) cake pan. Mark squares quickly with a sharp knife, or use a heart-shaped cutter. Let cool an hour or so, break into squares or hearts and serve. *Yield:* 12 – 14 pieces.

Lake St. John Sucre à la Crème

A beautiful maple fudge, unusual because of the flour and baking powder which are part of the ingredients. Whenever possible, use a candy thermometer to be sure of cooking stage. The finished product should be thick, creamy and sort of "fondant." The recipe was given to me about 23 years ago by a charming old lady born in the Lake St. John district of Quebec. She valued it "as a family heirloom." For many years, I have enjoyed her heirloom recipe.

2 cups (1 L) maple syrup
1 cup (250 mL) brown sugar
1 cup (250 mL) white sugar
2 tbsp. (30 mL) flour
2 tsp. (10 mL) baking powder
2 cups (500 mL) light cream
Pinch of salt
1 tbsp. (15 mL) butter
2 tsp. (10 mL) vanilla or maple extract
Walnuts to taste

Place all the ingredients except the butter and vanilla in a large saucepan. Bring to boil, over medium heat, stirring constantly. The syrup will swell quite a bit at the beginning of the cooking, but it will soon go down. Then let simmer over medium-low heat until it reaches 234 – 240°F. (112 – 115°C), or soft-ball on the candy thermometer (or when a bit in very cold water forms a soft ball).

Remove pan from heat. Add the butter and vanilla, but do not stir. Let it cool until tepid. Then, add nuts to taste and stir until mixture is pale and creamy. I use my electric hand beater, as it is a long process by hand. Pour into a buttered pan, cover and cool. *Yield:* 2 lb. (1 kg).

Walnut Brittle

What's unusual about this brittle — in which you can use peanuts instead of walnuts if you like — is its molasses content, old fashioned but nice.

1 – 1½ cups (250 – 400 mL) whole walnuts or
   salted peanuts
3 cups (750 mL) light brown sugar
2 cups (500 mL) molasses
½ cup (125 mL) butter or margarine
1 tbsp. (15 mL) cider vinegar

Generously butter an 8 × 8 in. (20 cm × 20 cm) pan. Sprinkle nuts evenly in the bottom.

Place remaining ingredients in a saucepan and boil over moderate heat until a brittle ball is formed in cold water; on candy thermometer,

260–265°F. (121–130°C). Immediately pour over nuts as evenly as possible and do not scrape saucepan. Let cool on a rack and break into pieces to serve. *Yield:* 16–18 pieces.

Heart-Shaped Meringues

4 egg whites
Pinch of salt
½ tsp. (2 mL) cream of tartar
1 cup (250 mL) fine granulated sugar
½ tsp. (2 mL) vanilla or almond extract

Beat egg whites with salt and cream of tartar to a soft foam with a whisk or a non-electric hand beater (electric mixers beat too fast and prevent a certain amount of air from getting into the egg whites). Sprinkle 1 tsp. (5 mL) of the sugar on top of eggs and beat well until completely incorporated. Continue adding sugar, 1 tbsp. (15 mL) at a time, beating hard each time. When all the sugar has been added, beat in the extract of your choice and continue to beat until the mass holds its shape.

Cover cookie sheet with freezer paper (waxed on one side). Shape meringues into little hearts or circles, leaving ½ in. (2.5 cm) between shaped meringues.

Bake in a preheated 300°F. (150°C) oven until the meringues reach a delicate pale golden color. Depending on size, it may take 20–60 minutes.

13. *Desserts*

I have no guilt complex about desserts. I satisfy my sensuous delight in making, creating and serving a perfect dessert. I cheat on my pleasure and fool myself by serving them "miniature," in half portions, glamorously set in fluted champagne glasses — of course only half full. Or in small dainty ramekins, or porcelain demi-tasses, which are more often used for dessert nowadays than for coffee. And always decorated, for that generous look, while keeping the "culprit" a miniature.

Desserts cannot be ignored, since they are the fitting climax to a luncheon or dinner. No one can explain why, but they do give one a sense of luxury, of well-being and of relaxation. As they finish the meal, they must be a conversation piece and be followed by an equally perfect cup of coffee or tea.

I assure you that you do not have to be a professional chef or a great expert to make a delightful dessert. I have long known that the surest guarantee of perfection is to keep in tune with the seasons. No fresh strawberry dessert in January, but serve apples, citrus fruits, richer desserts or flambee creations which are seasonal. But serve strawberries in June, raspberries in August, peaches in September – and all the hot or cold souffles, and the cool pies that are the very essence of summer. An attractive basket filled with assorted fruits is an all-year-round dessert that should be used very often. Present your desserts with glamour, let them harmonize quietly but beautifully with the surroundings, and with the color and texture of the main course. For example: don't serve a white dessert following a chicken in white sauce.

Will you enjoy desserts or desert them? I leave it to you to decide, but I shall try to win you over with the following suggestion: when I give 6 portions, you may read 9 – 12 portions — of course, they are miniatures.

Strawberry Time

One of the early joys of summer is the ripe, fresh, perfectly-shaped versatile strawberry. The first ones of the season should be served in all their deep red beauty, set in a mound on an attractive white plate, with a crystal bowl of fruit sugar, a jug of rich cream, a bottle of orange liqueur, and I always add to the table a tiny Victorian silver and cut-glass container of rosewater. The vial comes with a tiny silver spoon that holds a few drops of rosewater, but this is enough to bring all kinds of beautiful romantic feelings around you — and with strawberries the marriage is perfect. Let each one partake of the offering to their taste and desire.

Strawberries flow in great quantities from the market to our table for such a short period that we are forced to make the best of them by serving them in all kinds of attractive ways, bringing the gracious short season to a close with a strawberry jam-making session.

Think of beautiful desserts. Or very simple desserts. Or deep, pink fruit compotes. Or elegant French tarts. Strawberries are perfect for all of these. There are dozens of ways to serve them, but here are some of my favorites:

Fill a small silver or cut-glass with peeled and finely-grated fresh ginger, a big bowl with cleaned, lightly-sweetened strawberries and a bowl of sour cream. Place these on a tray, with a silver shaker of fine fruit sugar. Then flavor the strawberries according to your taste.

On a tray, make a mound of icing sugar, sprinkle with pink sugar and surround with a thick circle of unsweetened whipped cream. Around this, place a crown of big unhulled berries. Dip each berry in the sugar, and roll it in the cream.

Whip up a cup of cream with a cup of sliced strawberries and five or six rose petals. Sweeten to taste and heap on wedges of sponge cake.

Fill a dish with fresh sliced strawberries, sweeten to taste with fruit sugar, and add a small spoonful of rosewater. Serve with a rich, cold custard sauce.

Make alternate layers of sliced strawberries, brown sugar and sour cream in a glass bowl, then refrigerate for five hours before serving.

Strawberry – Rhubarb Cobbler

What an affinity there is between strawberries and rhubarb; this superb pudding would not be nearly as good made with just strawberries or rhubarb alone.

1 cup (250 mL) sugar
1 cup (250 mL) apple juice
2 cups (500 mL) diced rhubarb
2 cups (500 mL) sliced strawberries
1 tsp. (5 mL) vanilla
1 cup (250 mL) all-purpose flour
2 tbsp. (30 mL) sugar

1½ tsp. (7 mL) baking powder
½ tsp. (2 mL) mace
¼ cup (60 mL) butter
¼ cup (60 mL) milk or cream
Sugar and nutmeg
Soft butter

Bring the sugar and apple juice to a boil, and stir until sugar is dissolved. Remove from heat, add the rhubarb, strawberries and vanilla. Mix well and pour into a pudding dish.

To prepare the batter, sift together the flour, sugar, baking powder and mace. Cut in the butter and add the milk or cream.

Stir quickly to blend, and drop by spoonfuls over the fruit. Sprinkle top with sugar and a dash of nutmeg, and brush with soft butter. Bake at 450°F. (230°C) for 20 – 25 minutes. *Serves 6.*

Strawberry Clouds

Any type of small baked meringue can be used to make this beautiful dessert. Use a clear glass bowl to reveal the contrasting ingredients.

4 cups (1 L) strawberries
4 tbsp. (60 mL) icing sugar
8 – 10 small baked meringues
1 cup (250 mL) whipping cream
2 tbsp. (30 mL) icing sugar
Vanilla or rosewater to taste

Clean the strawberries and slice half of them. Sweeten each lot with 2 tbsp. (30 mL) of the icing sugar.

Cover the bottom of a bowl with the meringue and sprinkle the sliced berries on top. Cover with the whipped cream sweetened with the 2 tbsp. (30 mL) of icing sugar and flavored to taste. (You can make as many layers of this as you have ingredients for.) Place the whole strawberries, "points up," on top of the cream and refrigerate 1 – 2 hours before serving. *Serves 6.*

Rhubarb Sauce over Strawberries

I have a thing about "fruits on fruits." The combinations are always successful and the idea lets you create many a new sweet. To try your hand at it, first think in terms of color, then flavor, and finally texture. As an example, a soft rhubarb sauce over juicy medium strawberries gives a pleasant texture. For color, you have pink on pink and for flavor you have "late fresh spring," since they are both in season at the same time.

2 cups (500 mL) rhubarb
2/3 cup (160 mL) sugar
1 tbsp. (15 mL) cornstarch
Grated rind of ½ a lemon
¼ tsp. (1 mL) ground cardamom or cinnamon
½ cup (125 mL) cold water
Juice of ½ a lemon
4 cups (1 L) whole strawberries
2 tbsp. (30 mL) Sabre or an orange liqueur (optional)

Clean and cut rhubarb into ¼ in. (1.25 cm) pieces, then measure.

Place in a saucepan the next 4 ingredients well mixed together. Add the cold water, stir well and cook over low heat, stirring until all the sugar is dissolved and sauce is transparent. Add the rhubarb, then cook about 5 minutes over medium heat, or until rhubarb is cooked. Add the lemon juice. Stir well. Place the strawberries in a clear glass compote dish, pour liqueur on top, and stir gently with a rubber spatula.

Pour the hot rhubarb over the strawberries. Cover and refrigerate 6 – 12 hours before serving. *Serves 6.*

Fresh Strawberry Sauce for Ice Cream

When in a rush for a quick dessert, and you have ice cream, strawberries and a blender, try this one.

1 quart (1 L) basket cleaned strawberries
1 cup (250 mL) fresh orange juice
Grated rind of ½ an orange
¼ cup (60 mL) fine granulated sugar
2 – 3 tbsp. (30 – 50 mL) orange liqueur or Vodka

Place in glass jar of blender, or in a food processor, all the ingredients, except the liqueur. Cover and blend 40 – 50 seconds. Pour into a jug. Add the liqueur of your choice. Serve over fresh fruits or ice cream or sponge cake, or use to replace a simple syrup in a drink of your choice. *Yield:* 2 cups (500 mL).

Victorian Summer Pudding

We seldom find a recipe for this well-known family favorite so popular in the early 1900s. It can be made all through the summer, replacing the strawberries with raspberries or fresh red currants. Thick, cold, fresh cream was served with the summer pudding, but it is also delicious just served plain.

- 2 cups (500 mL) strawberries, sliced
- ½ cup (125 mL) red currant jelly
- ½ cup (125 mL) sugar
- 6 slices white bread, crust removed
- Soft butter

In a saucepan, place the strawberries, red currant jelly and sugar. Do not add any water. Cook over low heat 3 – 5 minutes, stirring and crushing the berries. When the jelly and sugar are melted, cool the red, juicy syrup. Line a round pudding bowl with buttered bread slices cut to line the dish completely, bottom and sides. Place the fruit over the bread, reserving a few spoonfuls of the juice. Cover the fruit with another layer of buttered bread. Pour the reserved juice on top. Set a plate on the top layer and, on the plate, place a weight. Refrigerate overnight, unmold and serve as is, or with cream or ice cream. *Serves 4.*

Dip for Strawberries

Another one of my quick favorite summer desserts. Fill small liqueur glass with dip. Set on a green leaf, in an attractive white or pale pink plate, surrounded with fresh strawberries. Wash them, but do not remove the stems which can be used as handles to dip the strawberries into the cream.

- 1 quart (1 L) basket strawberries
- 1 cup (250 mL) commercial sour cream
- 1 tsp. (5 mL) each fresh lemon juice and grated peel
- ½ cup (125 mL) icing sugar

Drain washed strawberries in colander. Refrigerate until ready to use. Beat remaining ingredients until well mixed. Refrigerate until ready to use. *Serves 4.*

Victorian Strawberries

A summer dessert that graced many of our grandmothers' dinner tables. Mother served it in a scooped-out pineapple with its top used as a cover.

- 1 fresh pineapple
- 4 tbsp. (60 mL) brandy or Madeira
- 4 cups (1 L) fresh strawberries

Sugar to taste
1 cup (250 mL) apricot jelly
1 cup (250 mL) whipping cream

Peel the pineapple and cut across into ½ in. (1.25 cm) slices. Cut the four center slices in half and marinate them at room temperature in 2 tbsp. (30 mL) of the brandy or Madeira.

Dice remaining pineapple. Wash and hull strawberries, setting best 10 or 12 aside; halve the remainder, and combine with diced pineapple. Sweeten to taste, cover and refrigerate for a few hours. Heat apricot jelly (without boiling), add remaining brandy or Madeira, and refrigerate.

Mound the diced fruits in the center of a round glass dish. Surround with the pineapple slices, rounded side out, and pour on most of apricot mixture. Whip the cream, sweeten to taste, and place over mounded fruits. Garnish with reserved whole strawberries, pouring a spoonful of the apricot mixture over each. Then refrigerate until ready to serve. *Serves 6 – 8.*

Strawberry Rhubarb Compote

I would need many superlatives to describe this early summer delight. Serve it in a glass dish with a bowl of whipped, sour, or ice cream.

½ cup (125 mL) fresh orange juice
¾ cup (200 mL) sugar
2 lb. (1 kg) rhubarb, in 2-in. (5 cm) pieces
1 pint (500 mL) fresh strawberries or
  1 15 oz. (425 g) pkg. frozen strawberries.

Bring the orange juice and sugar to a boil, then stir until sugar is dissolved. Add rhubarb, simmer over low heat 5 minutes and remove from heat.

Stir in fresh (cleaned and halved) or frozen strawberries (the hot mixture will thaw them); then refrigerate. *Serves 4.*

Apples

They're apples in English, *Apfels* in German; *appils* in Norwegian; and *eppels* in Dutch — and in any language, they're delicious.

For some reason, apples are a favorite subject for sayings and proverbs all over the world, while other fruits are never mentioned: "The apple grows so bright and high, and ends its days in apple pie." "An apple a day keeps the doctor away." And *Année venteuse, année pommeuse* (Lots of wind, lots of apples). And Charles Lamb wrote: "Coleridge holds that a man cannot have a pure mind who refuses apple dumplings. I am not certain but he is right."

Let's talk about our Canadian apples. As a country, we are particularly rich in apples — we have wonderful varieties like McIntosh, Delicious, Northern Spy, Greening and Winesap — so much so that most people would call the apple *the* Canadian fruit.

The origin of the word "apple" is surrounded in mystery, although it is found in many forms, and is common to most European tongues, just as the fruit itself is common to most countries. In Canada, apples have been eaten and enjoyed for generations.

Most of us have nostalgic memories of apple orchards in their full, flowering, beauty, followed by the lovely pinks, reds and greens of the trees laden with fruit. I'll never forget the perfume they have on a warm morning after a night of rain. One of my favorite childhood memories is climbing into what was called the apple loft, on a cold winter's day just to inhale that same gorgeous perfume that reminded me so much of perfect autumn mornings I spent in the orchard.

Canadian Apples

Red Delicious: Superb dessert apples that are available from October through June, these aren't too good for cooking.

Greening: An excellent cooking apple, this variety is available from October through April.

Northern Spy: Excellent for cooking and good for eating, you'll find these available from October through May.

Cortland: Good for cooking and eating, and best for salads, these are available from October through February.

McIntosh: Good for apple sauce, as well as eating, these are sold from September to June.

Radiant with color, crisp fresh apples will brighten a bowlful of fresh winter fruits, give cool freshness to a piece of cheese, quench a thirst and ease the hunger pangs of dieters. They'll also be the main ingredient in something as unusual as a European soup served hot or cold. The countless varieties differ widely in appearance, texture, flavor and suitability, so it's important to buy them by name, following the guide shown above.

If the apples are firm when you buy them, they can stand at room temperature until they reach the ripeness you like, but should then be refrigerated. While apples like to be cold, they don't freeze well. Ideally they should be returned to room temperature before being eaten. Check stored apples occasionally, as a bad one will soon spoil the others.

Valuable in low-cholesterol and low-salt diets because they're high in Vitamins A and C and low in sodium, the bulk in apples satisfy hunger while their natural sugar provides quick energy — all on 60 calories each. In the winter, try eating two or three apples daily; you might find you have fewer colds, fewer headaches and less nervous tension.

Homemade Applesauce

Quick, easy, and very tasty. As this is a basic recipe, you can make a cup (250 mL) or a gallon (4 L) with the same directions. Will keep 3 weeks refrigerated, 10–12 months frozen.

2 cups (500 mL) unpeeled apples, thickly sliced
½ cup (125 mL) water
White or brown sugar, or honey to taste
1 tbsp. (15 mL) fresh lemon juice

Wash apples. Do not core, nor peel. Cut into thick slices, about 5 slices per apple. Place water in enamel cast-iron pan. Place apple slices on top. Cover and bring to boil over medium heat, stir well, cover again, and cook 5–8 minutes, or until apples break up when stirred.

Place about ¼ cup (60 mL) white or brown sugar, or honey in the bottom of a bowl, large enough to take the quantity of cooked apples. Place on top a food mill or a strainer, and pour in the cooked apples. Add the lemon juice and strain over the sugar (the heat of the apples is sufficient to melt the sugar). Discard the apple peels collected in the top of a sieve. Stir the applesauce with the sugar, taste, and add more sugar according to your taste.

To vary the quantity, simply multiply the ingredients according to your needs. *Yield:* about 2 cups (500 mL).

Monique's April Fool Applesauce

In early spring our storage apples are not too exciting. My daughter makes a homemade applesauce, or uses the canned type, and presents it this way, with a dash and a smile — and it *is* good.

Place a thick layer of applesauce in a glass dish and sprinkle generously with grated *unsweetened chocolate*. Top with a thin layer of applesauce and cover with lightly sweetened whipped cream, and sprinkle cream with more grated chocolate. Refrigerate an hour or so before serving.

Marzipan Baked Apples

A superb dessert. For years, I have made these as a special Christmas treat. It's always a success.

4 baking apples
½ cup (125 mL) marzipan
1 – 2 tbsp. (15 – 30 mL) rum
2 tbsp. (30 mL) currants
Soft butter
1 cup (250 mL) dry white wine
4 tbsp. (60 mL) apricot jam

I like to use big Roman Beauty apples for this dessert, but any good-sized apple will do. Core and pare apples one third of the way down, but do not cut through the bottom of apple when removing core.

Using a fork, mash marzipan with enough rum to make it soft. Add currants to paste, place a dot of butter in the core of the apple, then stuff with the marzipan mixture. Top with additional dots of butter.

Set apples in a deep baking dish. Place apples close enough together to keep them from toppling over, but make sure they are not too crowded. Pour in enough wine to come about one third of the way up the sides of the apples. Bake in a preheated 350°F (180°C) oven, 25 – 30 minutes, or until apples are tender. To test for doneness, pierce apples with skewer. They will become light golden brown on top. Baste twice with the wine while baking.

When done, remove apples to a dish. Pour remaining wine in pan into a saucepan, add the apricot jam, boil gently together until a thick syrup is formed — it will take just a few minutes. Stir most of the time. Spoon the hot apricot glaze over each apple. Let set in a cool place, but do not refrigerate. *Serves 4.*

Molded Apple Charlotte

Another superb dessert (rich and fattening, yes!) made with 4 simple ingredients — bread, butter, brown sugar and apples — and usually no one can tell how it was made. In my home we sometimes used to mix apples with pears. Hailing from the Victorian table, this dessert was served with a custard sauce, but I feel it can be served without today.

5 slices raisin or white bread
½ cup (125 mL) butter
¾ cup (200 mL) brown sugar
¼ cup (60 mL) white sugar
2 tbsp. (30 mL) rum

1 tsp. (5 mL) vanilla
3 cups (750 mL) apple slices

Do not remove crust from bread. Butter generously one side of each slice. Place in heavy metal frying pan, buttered side down, over medium heat. Cook until browned, turn and brown unbuttered side. As they are ready, use to place around a *Moule à charlotte* or an 8 in. (20 cm) round casserole. (A French charlotte mold is 6½ × 5 × 3 in. (16 × 10 × 5 cm) with handles on both sides; some are larger, but for the above quantity this is the best size.) The last slice of bread is used to line the bottom of the mold.

Place the remaining butter in the frying pan, add the sugar and brown sugar, and stir until bubbly. Next add the slices of apples, stir until mixed, then the rum and vanilla. Keep on simmering until the apple slices are softened, but not falling in a purée — it will take about 15 minutes on medium heat.

Pour the whole thing in the bread-lined mold. If any bread remains uncovered on top, simply bend down to form a sort of cover or edge on the apples. Let it cool 1 hour before serving. Do not refrigerate. *Serves 4 – 5.*

Scottish Apples

Mother served it the Scottish way — hot, in a ceramic bowl, with a decanter of whiskey. In the summer, she served it cold with a pitcher of cold water or plain lemonade.

4 apples, unpeeled and grated
2 tbsp. (30 mL) honey
Juice of ½ lemon
1 cup (250 mL) toasted rolled oats

To toast oats, spread in shallow cake pan, place in 350°F. (180°C) oven until golden brown and crisp. Mix together with apples, honey and lemon, and serve. *Serves 4.*

C.P. Stuffed Pears

In the Forties, these were a specialty of the Canadian Pacific Railway's dining cars. They were popular with everyone.

Fruits, fruits-on-fruits, cakes without icing, beautifully flavored butter cookies, whipped cream and chocolate. Oh, how I love desserts!

4 pears
¼ cup (60 mL) raisins (muscat, when possible)
2 tbsp. (30 mL) walnuts, finely chopped
2 tbsp. (30 mL) maple sugar or brown sugar
1 tbsp. (15 mL) lemon juice
2 tbsp. (30 mL) water
½ cup (125 mL) maple or corn syrup

Peel and core the pears at the blossom end, leaving stems intact, easy to do with a small coffee spoon or an apple corer.

Mix raisins, walnuts, sugar and lemon juice. Stuff an equal amount into each pear. Place standing up in a deep baking dish. Add the water and pour the syrup over the pears. Cover. Bake in a 350°F. (180°C) oven for 1 hour. When done, uncover, sprinkle each pear lightly with white sugar and place under direct heat for a few minutes or until nicely browned. Serve hot or cold, with cream. *Serves 4.*

The Marvelous Peach

Next to the simple joy of biting into a whole ripe peach, I like to taste peaches that have been marinated a few hours in honey and brandy, then served with cold sour cream or yogurt — ¼ cup (60 mL) of honey and 2 – 3 tbsp. (30 – 50 mL) of brandy are about right for 2 cups (500 mL) of peeled, sliced peaches. But this is only one way of serving this gorgeous, versatile fruit.

There's peaches-and-cream, of course, but how about sliced peaches sweetened with maple syrup or brown sugar mixed with a few drops of almond extract? Or broiled peaches, if you want a hot dessert. Arrange peeled halves cut side up in a baking dish, dot with butter, sprinkle with brown sugar and, if you wish, a bit of brandy. Broil 3 in. (7.5 cm) from heat until sugar melts and peaches blister here and there.

Freezing: After you've served peaches as often as you can during their short season freeze some for the winter. Peel and slice, halve or quarter them and keep in cold water with fresh lemon juice added to prevent discoloration. Prepare a medium syrup by boiling 3 cups (750 mL) of sugar and 4 cups (1 L) of cold water for 5 minutes. Add ½ tsp. (2 mL) of ascorbic acid (purchased at drugstore) or 1 tbsp. (15 mL) of fresh lemon juice. (This amount of syrup will do for 6-9 peaches.)

Teapots and coffeemakers fascinate me. Here you see a few of my favorites, but I dare not say how many I have. Serving the right tea with the right food is just as important as serving the right wine. I always grind my coffee beans just before I make my coffee.

Almost fill frozen food containers with the well-drained peaches. Pour some syrup on top, leaving a 1½-in. headspace (3.75 cm). Crumple up a square of wax paper and place on top to keep peaches submerged. Cover, label, and freeze at 32°F (0°C). To use, thaw out at room temperature for 3 – 4 hours, or overnight in refrigerator; they'll keep 6 – 8 months in perfect condition.

Poached Peaches

Poach them with their peel on. They will have a very attractive rosy flush and will retain much of their delicate flavor; besides, the peel is very easy to remove once the peaches are cooked. In poaching peaches and apples, a vanilla bean or 4 – 6 slices of orange or lemon peel are a must. Do not discard the vanilla bean, wipe with paper and bury in a container of sugar. Not only will you have vanilla sugar to use on your fresh fruits *nature*, but you will also be able to use the vanilla beans over and over again, until the perfume is gone.

- 6 – 8 ripe peaches
- 1 cup (250 mL) sugar
- ½ cup (125 mL) honey
- 1 vanilla bean *or* 4 – 6 slices of orange *or* lemon peel
- 3 cups (750 mL) water

In a large low saucepan (a *sauteuse*) bring to boil the sugar, honey, vanilla bean or orange or lemon peel, and the water. Then simmer over low heat 10 minutes. Place the unpeeled peaches in the hot syrup, cover and simmer 15 – 20 minutes, or until peaches are tender. Once or twice gently stir them around in the syrup. When ready, remove the peaches to serving dish. Remove skin by pulling on it. Strain syrup over fruits. Cover, let stand refrigerated for 24 hours before serving.

The syrup can be drained into a jar, covered and refrigerated. Use as long as you have enough to poach, not only peaches but also all other fresh fruits.

To Poach Apples: Proceed the same as for poached peaches, but peel and core the apples. Depending on the type and size of the apples, cooking time will vary quite a bit. Just keep them simmering, this time without a cover. To prevent discoloration, rub peeled apples with half a cut lemon.

Orange Sauce over Sliced Oranges

I use this sauce with other fruits or over ice cream or sponge cake or poured hot over cold custard.

1 cup (250 mL) orange marmalade
1/3 cup (80 mL) orange-flavored liqueur
3 tbsp. (50 mL) dry sherry
6 – 8 oranges, peeled and sliced

Place the marmalade, liqueur and sherry in a small saucepan. Simmer, stirring often, until bubbling all around. Pour over orange slices, already placed in a serving bowl. Do not mix. Cover and refrigerate 24 hours before serving. *Serves* 6.

Stewed Plums

Use any type of plums, whole or halved, for this dessert. If the plums are not freestone, it's easier to cook them whole and then remove the pits.

1 cup (250 mL) sugar
1 cup (250 mL) apple juice, water or red wine
2-in. (5 cm) cinnamon stick
2 lb. (1 kg) pitted plums

Make a syrup of the sugar and apple juice, water or red wine by boiling them together for 10 minutes. Add the cinnamon stick. Place the plums, one next to the other, in the syrup, then cover and simmer over very low heat 20 – 25 minutes.

When cooked, gently place the fruit in a glass dish and pour the syrup on top. Cool, then refrigerate until ready to serve. *Serves* 4 – 5.

Potted Prunes

I like prunes as long as they are not cooked. They will be very intriguing soaked each time in a different tea. Use rose, strawberry, or mint tea. Go to a good tea house, you will be surprised at the vast world of teas you will discover. My friend Dinah has one of the most interesting tea shops in Toronto, called *Dinah's Cupboard*. Go and talk to her, she will take you on a trip through a garden of tea delights.

Prunes, any type
Boiling tea
2 – 3 tbsp. (30 – 50 mL) honey
Juice of ½ – 1 lemon

Wash prunes and place in a jam jar. Add the honey and lemon, and pour the boiling tea on top. Stir to mix. Cover pot. Leave a few hours at room temperature, then keep refrigerated.

To vary, omit lemon, and add a few cloves or a star anise, or a blade of mace or stick of cinnamon.

Red Wine Cherry Compote

Particularly nice made with the large B.C. black Bing cherries. This will keep 2 weeks refrigerated in a covered glass jar. Eat it plain or spoon it over sponge cake or ice cream.

1 lb. (500 g) Bing cherries
½ cup (125 mL) light brown sugar
½ cup (125 mL) Canadian red wine or fresh orange juice
3 tbsp. (50 mL) brandy or maraschino juice

Pit the cherries directly into a dish and drain off any excess juice into a saucepan. Add it to the sugar, wine or orange juice, and boil over medium heat until it becomes a thick syrup. Pour over cold cherries and let it cool. Stir, add brandy or juice, and stir again. Let stand 1 hour at room temperature, and refrigerate. *Serves 4.*

Vancouver Cherry Betty

This was created by the owner of a Vancouver restaurant specializing in broiled chicken and excellent desserts. This one is served either warm with rich cream or hot with pink hard sauce.

2 cups (500 mL) soft breadcrumbs
2 tbsp. (30 mL) melted butter
2 cups (500 mL) pitted cherries, halved
¼ cup (60 mL) sugar
Grated peel and juice of ½ a lemon
½ cup (125 mL) hot water

Mix the crumbs with the butter and place about one-third of the mixture in a buttered 8 × 8 in. (20 cm × 20 cm) casserole. Sprinkle with half the cherries, and some of the sugar, lemon peel and juice. Repeat layers, ending with crumbs. Carefully pour water in at side of dish, cover and bake in a 400°F. (200°C) oven about 30 minutes. Uncover and bake just long enough to brown the top here and there. *Serves 4.*

Stewed Rhubarb

The secret here is to add the sugar after the rhubarb has been quickly cooked.

2 cups (500 mL) rhubarb, in 1 in. (2.5 cm) pieces
1 slice unpeeled lemon
¼ cup (60 mL) each honey and sugar

Place the rhubarb and lemon slice in an ovenproof glass, enamelled, or stainless steel saucepan, add ¼ cup (60 mL) of cold water and cover. Cook over medium heat 5-8 minutes, stirring once or twice. Remove from heat, add honey and sugar, and stir until melted. Remove lemon slice, pour mixture into a dish, cover and refrigerate. *Serves 2.*

Baked Rhubarb

Baked rhubarb retains its shape better than stewed rhubarb; and though the cooking period is longer, it does make for a more elegant appearance.

2 cups (500 mL) rhubarb, cut in 2 in. (5 cm) pieces
½ cup (125 mL) honey or sugar
Grated peel of ½ an orange or lemon

Make a layer with some of the rhubarb in the bottom of a 1 quart (1 L) ovenproof glass or earthenware dish, then distribute remaining ingredients and rest of rhubarb on top. Sprinkle with 2 tbsp. (30 mL) of cold water, cover and let stand 3 hours at room temperature.

Bake uncovered in a 300°F. (150°C) oven 45 – 60 minutes, or until tender. *Serves 4.*

Cupidon Jelly

There was a time in life, not so far away, when the celebration of Valentine's Day was a feast full of happiness and smiles. One of the desserts we often saw on the dinner table was this Red Wine Jelly, or Cupidon Jelly as we called it. Of course, it was made in a heart shape. To remind one that love has its ups and downs, the transparent red heart was set on a bed of frosty eggnog. The frosty part was made with egg yolks; and the egg whites we used to make the dainty **Heart-Shaped Meringues** to serve with Cupidon Jelly. Be an old-fashioned Valentine, and make this for someone.

1 envelope unflavored gelatine
¼ cup (60 mL) apple or cranberry juice
½ cup (125 mL) boiling apple or cranberry juice
¼ tsp. (1 mL) salt
½ cup (125 mL) sugar
1 cup (250 mL) dry red wine
1 tbsp. (15 mL) fresh lemon juice

Sprinkle the gelatine over the first measure of juice, and let stand 5 minutes. Then pour into the rapidly boiling juice. Remove from heat and stir until gelatine is melted. Pour into a well-oiled (sweet almond oil is the best and can be purchased at the drugstore) heart-shaped mold, or into 6 small molds. Refrigerate overnight. *Serves 6.*

Molded Fruit Gelatine

Nowadays, molded gelatines are usually thought of as "jello." Once you learn to make your own gelatine, you will keep on experimenting and enjoying all you make.

1 envelope unflavored gelatine
¼ cup (60 mL) cold water
1¾ cups (425 mL) hot juice of your choice
¼ – ½ cup (60 – 125 mL) sugar

Sprinkle gelatine over the cold water, and let stand 5 minutes.

Heat the juice, add the gelatine and stir well until dissolved. Add the sugar, and stir until melted. Pour into a dish or mold. Cool, then refrigerate until set. *Serves 4.*

Note: For a hot juice, you can use apple juice, grape juice, cranberry juice or strained juice of frozen raspberries or strawberries (it will be a bit thicker); or any of the frozen juices, using only the water needed to make up the required amount; red or white wine; or fresh orange juice. (Honey can replace part of the sugar.)

Lemon Fruit Gelatine

I love this one in the summer, poured over a cup or two of sweetened fresh raspberries, strawberries, blueberries or sliced peaches, and then chilled. In the winter, I use melon, thinly-sliced apples or pears.

1 envelope unflavored gelatine
¼ cup (60 mL) fresh orange juice or cold water
1½ cups (400 mL) boiling water
½ cup (125 mL) sugar or honey
3 tbsp. (50 mL) fresh lemon juice

Soak gelatine 5 minutes in the orange juice or cold water. Add the boiling water and honey or sugar. Stir over low heat until sugar is dissolved. Add the fresh lemon juice. Mix well. Pour into a mold or over 1 – 1½ cups (250 – 400 mL) fresh fruits. Refrigerate a few hours or until set. *Serves 4.*

Molded Concord Grapes

I just love the dark Concord grapes that turn to a deep purple when cooked. I have used this recipe as a mold surrounded by a white cloud of whipped cream, and as a sauce over ice cream, cake, yogurt, and rice pudding.

As we can buy them in our markets in the autumn only — and not for very long — we should make a quantity of sauce. The sauce from these grapes, which usually come from Ontario, can be frozen and used later.

5 cups (1.25 L) Concord blue grapes
½ cup (125 mL) sugar
3 tbsp. (50 mL) cornstarch
⅛ tsp. (0.5 mL) salt
2 tbsp. (30 mL) fresh lemon juice

Wash and remove grapes from stems. Measure the *full* 5 cups. Slip skins from grapes, place pulp in saucepan. Reserve skins. Bring pulp to a boil, reduce heat and simmer 5 minutes. Press through sieve or food mill to remove seeds. Combine pulp with skins. Add remaining ingredients mixed together. Place over medium heat, and bring to boil, stirring constantly until sauce is thick and clear. Use as a sauce, hot or cold. To mold, proceed as above, but increase the cornstarch to ¼ cup (60 mL). *Yield:* 5 cups (1.25 L).

Variations: Add 4 tbsp. (60 mL) brandy to sauce, when cooked. Replace fresh lemon juice with an equal amount of fresh orange juice. Add the grated rind of ½ an orange.

My Anise Syrup for Fruit Salad

This syrup can replace the sugar on any combination of fruits, for an unusual and tasty dessert.

¾ cup (200 mL) water
½ cup (125 mL) sugar
2 tbsp. (30 mL) lime or lemon juice
½ tsp. (2 mL) anise seed, crushed
Pinch of salt

Combine all the ingredients in a saucepan, and mix well. Slowly bring to a boil, and boil 2 minutes. Cover and cool 30 minutes, then refrigerate. To use, strain the desired amount of syrup over your choice of fruits. I love to serve it topped with fresh mint leaves. This syrup will keep for months, refrigerated. *Yield:* 1¼ cups (330 mL).

Eaton's Fruit Salad Dressing

In the Thirties, we used to lunch in the dining room of Eaton's main department store in Montreal. The great favorite was their fruit salad, with the blushing pink dressing elegantly poured over the beautifully arranged *fresh fruit*. We had not reached the "canned everything" days.

1/3 cup (80 mL) soft cream cheese
1/3 cup (80 mL) fresh orange juice
1 tbsp. (15 mL) fresh lemon or lime juice
1 tbsp. (15 mL) honey
Pinch of salt
1 cup (250 mL) fresh strawberries

Keep cheese a few hours at room temperature to soften it. Mash with a fork and grandually add the orange juice, then the lemon or lime juice, honey and salt. Mix thoroughly. Crush the strawberries and beat into the cheese dressing.

I now use my food processor for this. First I mash the strawberries, then I add all other ingredients and switch machine on and off for 1 minute. Keep refrigerated. *Yield:* 1½ cups.

Sherbet: Summery Cool Comfort

A sherbet is made by freezing a water ice (fruit juice, water and sugar) to a mush, adding gelatine or beaten egg whites, then completing the freezing. They are sweet and savory. Their added attraction is that there is no need to worry about too many calories. Ice cream, for instance, is often by-passed because of its rich cream content; so, if you have a "cold sweet tooth," do try sherbets.

Lemon Sherbet

For an elegant dinner make the sherbet in lemon shells, served on large fresh green leaves. In the summer, I surround them with colorful nasturtiums. Let each guest drizzle some orange liqueur of his choice on top of the sherbet. The lemon shells are a choice for special presentations, otherwise freeze as any other sherbet.

How to Prepare the Lemon Shells: Eight lemon shells will be needed for the amount of sherbet the recipe will make. Cut a thin slice from the sides of 8 large lemons. Scrape out pulp and juice with a spoon, over a bowl. Press the juice from the lemon pulp through a fine sieve, and set aside.

1 cup (250 mL) sugar
2 tbsp. (30 mL) unflavored gelatine
2 cups (500 mL) milk
½ cup (125 mL) light cream or milk
Pinch of salt
Grated rind of 1 lemon
¾ cup (200 mL) fresh lemon juice
2 egg whites

Combine in a saucepan the sugar, gelatine, milk and cream. Then stir over low heat for 5 – 10 minutes or until gelatine is melted. Add salt. Set aside to cool. Measure reserved lemon juice and add more if needed to make ¾ cup (200 mL). When milk is cooled, stir in the lemon juice and pour into one large or two smaller freezing trays. Freeze until mushy all around the edges.

Turn into a bowl, add the egg whites and beat together until light and fluffy. (I use my mixer or electric hand beater.) Freeze again, this time until firm enough to heap into the lemon shells. Wrap each one in foil or place one next to the other in a large plastic box with a good cover. Freeze at least 12 hours, and serve. *Serves 10.*

Cantaloupe Sherbet

This is a refreshing first course or a pleasant summer dessert.

4 cups (1 L) peeled and seeded cantaloupes
Juice of 1 lemon or lime
⅓ cup (80 mL) honey
½ tsp. (2 mL) dry unflavored gelatine
¼ cup (60 mL) cold white wine or water
Orange liqueur

Dice the cantaloupes and mash through a sieve, or purée in a blender to make 3½ – 4 cups of pure. Add juice and honey, stir until well mixed. Soak gelatine 5 minutes in wine or water, then melt over hot water until clear. Stir into cantaloupe, and pour this mixture into an ice-cube tray and freeze — this sherbet should not be too hard, so remove from freezer about 30 minutes before serving. Serve in small parfait glasses, topped with fresh mint. Let each one add liqueur to taste. *Serves 6 – 8.*

Homemade Refrigerator Ice Cream

The recipe for this creamy, smooth, old-fashioned crank-style ice cream was sent to me a few years back by the Ontario Department of Agriculture and Food. It has none of the work of the old-fashioned type because it is made in the refrigerator freezer. I have made it ever since and even added my own variations.

1 8 oz. (227 g) package cream cheese, softened
2/3 cup (160 mL) sugar
2 tsp. (10 mL) vanilla, *or* coffee or maple extract
1 cup (250 mL) heavy cream
1 cup (250 mL) light cream

Beat together until creamy the cheese, sugar and vanilla. Slowly add the cream, mixing thoroughly. (I like to use my electric beater to mix this.) Then freeze in a mold of your choice, covered, in the refrigerator freezer until partially frozen to a soft mush 1 – 3 hours, depending on your refrigerator.

Break up mixture in a bowl and beat until smooth. Work fast so mixture does not melt completely. Return to mold or tray. Cover and freeze until firm. *Yield:* 4 cups (1 L).

Variations:

Banana: Add 2 mashed bananas to cheese and sugar, and replace vanilla with 1 tbsp. (15 mL) rum.

Coffee: Add 3 tbsp. (50 mL) instant coffee, to sugar and ½ tsp. (2 mL) coffee extract.

Orange: Add the grated rind of 1 orange to the sugar and replace ½ cup (125 mL) light cream by ½ cup (125 mL) orange juice.

Strawberry: Mash 1½ cups (375 mL) strawberries with 3 tbsp. (15 mL) sugar, 1 tbsp. (15 mL) orange liqueur of your choice (optional). Add to cream cheese-sugar mixture.

Rum and Raisin Ice Cream

An elegant dessert. Freeze in a fancy mold, unmold to serve. I like to serve mine with a bowl of hot buttered rum. Each guest puts a spoonful or so over their ice cream.

5 egg yolks
½ cup (125 mL) brown sugar, well packed
Pinch of salt
2 cups (500 mL) *warm* milk
1 cup (250 mL) golden seedless raisins
2 cups (500 mL) heavy cream
3 tbsp. (50 mL) rum

Beat egg yolks until thick and yellow. Add sugar and salt, and beat again for 5 minutes. (Use electric mixer.) Add hot milk and raisins. Cook in top of double boiler, stirring until mixture thickens, being careful not to let it boil.

Pour into a bowl, cover and refrigerate until cold. Add cream and rum. Pour into mold or ice cream container or ice cube trays and freeze. Stir 3 – 4 times in the first 3 hours to prevent crystals from forming. *Yield:* 1½ quarts. (1½ L).

Pumpkin Ice Cream

This is a South American specialty that I serve with toasted slivered almonds sprinkled over each portion.

1 cup (250 mL) **Pumpkin Purée**
½ cup (125 mL) packed brown sugar
¼ tsp. (1 mL) pumpkin spices
¼ tsp. (1 mL) salt
1 tsp. (5 mL) grated orange peel
3 tbsp. (50 mL) sherry or rum
1 cup (250 mL) whipping cream

Combine all ingredients except cream in a bowl and stir until sugar is dissolved. Whip cream until stiff and fold in; then turn mixture into an ice cube tray, and freeze until firm. When firm, cover with foil until ready to serve to prevent change of texture. *Yield:* 4 cups (1 L).

Maple Ice Cream

As I did in my youth, I still make this perfect ice cream in my very old ice cream freezer — it belonged to my grandmother. Now you can get easy-to-work electric types. One thing is important to remember for your ice cream freezer to operate efficiently, whether it's electric or hand-turned. Make alternate layers of 4 cups (1 L) of crushed ice and ⅓ cup (80 mL) coarse or rock salt or kosher salt — *never* use fine table salt. Add 1 cup (250 mL) cold water after packing the salt and ice, to start the ice melting and prevent grainy ice cream.

4 cups (1 L) maple syrup
1½ cups (480 mL) water
¼ cup (60 mL) flour
4 eggs, separated
¼ tsp. (1 mL) salt
4 cups (1 L) heavy cream
2 tsp. (10 mL) maple extract
2 tsp. (10 mL) fresh lemon juice

Heat maple syrup to just below the boiling point. Gradually blend the water and flour into a smooth paste. Add to boiling syrup and whisk until syrup loses its milky appearance and thickens. Beat the yolks with the salt and the maple extract. Pour a cup of hot syrup over the eggs, beat until well mixed, add to the remaining syrup, and beat again. Then remove from heat and beat in the cream and the lemon juice. Cover and refrigerate until cold.

Pour the cold mixture into the can of the ice cream freezer, which is already filled with the ice and salt. Cover, making sure the can is only three-quarters full, then turn until the mixture is partly frozen; it should take 15 – 20 minutes. When ready, open carefully. Beat the egg whites until stiff and add to mixture with a spoon. Do not attempt to mix completely, only what you can do with ease. Cover again, checking the ice — and continue to stir and freeze until cranking becomes difficult and the motor sort of slows down. Remove the dasher. (You are even allowed to lick its goodness!) Replace cover, cork the hole in some way. I use a wine-bottle cork, wittled down to size. Let stand to ripen 1 – 2 hours. Remove water and pack again with 4 parts crushed ice, 1 part salt; or place ice cream in container and leave in freezer until ready to serve. *Yield:* 5 – 6 cups (1.25 – 1.44 L) of ice cream.

Frosted Eggnog

5 egg yolks
½ cup (125 mL) sugar
2 cups (500 mL) dry sherry
2 cups (500 mL) whipping cream
Nutmeg to taste

With a hand beater, beat the egg yolks until foamy and lemon-colored. Gradually add the sugar, 1 tbsp. (15 mL) at a time, beating well at each addition. Then gradually add the wine, 2 – 3 tbsp. (30 – 50 mL) at a time, beating constantly.

Whip the cream and fold carefully into the sherry mixture. Pour into freezer trays or molds, then cover with heavy duty foil paper and freeze 1 – 3 days. Take eggnog out of freezer about 30 minutes before serving. *Serves 6 – 8.*

Cold Lemon Soufflé

I sometimes turn this one into a frozen soufflé by placing it in my freezer overnight.

1 tbsp. (15 mL) unflavored gelatine
¼ cup (60 mL) cold water
3 egg yolks
1 cup (250 mL) sugar
⅓ cup (80 mL) fresh lemon juice
Grated peel of 1 lemon
2 cups (500 mL) heavy cream
3 egg whites

Soak the gelatine in a bowl of cold water for 10 minutes. Place the container in a bowl of hot water, and simmer until the gelatine is clear. Beat the egg yolks until they're pale and lemon-colored; then gradually add the sugar and beat until very light and sort of creamy.

Add the lemon juice and peel, and mix well. Pour in the melted gelatine gradually while beating, then refrigerate the mixture until it has the texture of egg whites.

Whip the cream, beat the egg whites until they're stiff, and fold each into the lemon mixture. Pour into individual molds, or a ¾-qt. (750 mL) soufflé dish without a collar. *Serves 4.*

Country Pudding Mix and Pie Filling

What a time and money saver — and so much better than commercially-prepared puddings. I always have on the pantry shelf a container of caramel pudding, one of chocolate and a plain one to make as I please. They will keep for months in a cool place, or refrigerated.

Basic Pudding Mix:

2½ cups (625 mL) instant dry milk
1½ cups (525 mL) sugar (or a little less)
1 cup (250 mL) flour
¼ cup (60 mL) cornstarch
1 tsp. (5 mL) salt

Place all the ingredients together, then sift 3 times. This is important, if you wish to have a smooth pudding like the prepared type. Store in a covered plastic container, in a cool place. *Yield:* 5 cups (2.5 L).

For Caramel Pudding: Proceed the same as above, replacing the white sugar with brown sugar. Very nice flavored with maple extract or rum.

For Chocolate Pudding: Proceed the same as for the Basic Pudding Mix, adding ¾ cup (200 mL) cocoa to the dry mix before sifting 3 times. Nice flavored with rum or vanilla, orange rind or a bit of cinnamon.

La Crema

Do not let the simple ingredients in this dessert deceive you into thinking it is just a milk pudding. It is a delicate, flavorful, creamy dessert — and always enjoyed. It was given to me in 1956 by Olympia Marketos, a Greek lady who is quite an epicure.

½ cup (125 mL) sugar
4 tbsp. (60 mL) cornstarch
4 egg yolks
3 cups (750 mL) hot milk
Grated rind of 1 orange
1 tsp. (5 mL) vanilla
Cinnamon to taste

Mix together the sugar and cornstarch, and add the egg yolks one by one, beating well at each addition. Continue beating until light and smooth. (For this I use my food processor or electric hand beater.)

Gradually add the hot milk, mixing well. Add the grated orange rind. Cook over very low heat, stirring often until mixture is thick and creamy. Stir in the vanilla. Pour into glass dish. Cover, refrigerate until cold, and sprinkle with cinnamon or pink sugar to taste. In the summer, I top the cold *Crema* with cold, sweetened strawberries or raspberries. *Serves 6.*

Crème Pâtissière

Use for pastry or to fill cream puffs, éclairs, sponge cake, or jelly rolls. Will keep 2 weeks refrigerated in a covered glass jar.

1½ cups (400 mL) milk
½ cup (125 mL) sugar
4 egg yolks
¼ cup (60 mL) flour
½ tsp. (2 mL) vanilla
2 tbsp. (30 mL) brandy or rum

Scald the milk. Beat together in a bowl the sugar and egg yolks until light and pale. Add the flour, and mix just enough to blend. Add the scalded milk gradually, stirring until well mixed.

Cook over low heat, stirring most of the time, until the cream reaches the boiling point. Make sure you stir bottom and sides of saucepan. Then remove from heat, add the vanilla, brandy or rum. If any lumps appear, pass through a sieve, as this type of cream must be absolutely smooth. Pour into jar, cover, cool, then refrigerate. *Yield:* 3 cups (750 mL).

Scented Geranium Coeur de Crème

Our grandmothers used the rose-scented geranium to flavor foods as often as we now use vanilla. Very early, I learned to enjoy this flower, and keep one potted all year round to add to pleasurable eating. This is my grandmother's recipe, the only difference being that the cream she used was thicker and richer than the cream we have today — and she made her own cream cheese.

Served with strawberries, raspberries, even wild blackberries, it is a superb summer treat. In winter it is good served with a decanter of brandy.

1 cup (250 mL) whipping cream
4 tbsp. (60 mL) fine fruit sugar
2 rose geranium leaves
4 oz. (120 g) cream cheese, at room temperature.

Place in a saucepan the cream, sugar and geranium leaves. Cook over very low heat until sugar melts, stirring often. Do not let it boil. Cook thoroughly. Cream the cheese gradually, add the cooled cream, and remove the leaves. Beat until light and foamy. Pour into a cut-glass dish. Cover and refrigerate 12 – 24 hours. To serve, garnish top with a few fresh leaves of geranium. *Serves* 6.

French Petits Pots de Chocolat

My husband's favorite dessert. Usually served with small almond paste macaroons. When made in the *petits pots*, they will keep 5 – 6 days, covered, in the refrigerator.

4 oz. (114 g) semi-sweet chocolate
½ cup (125 mL) sugar

¼ cup (60 mL) water
4 egg yolks
2 tbsp. (30 mL) Brandy
4 egg whites, beaten stiff

Melt the chocolate over hot (not boiling) water. Place in small saucepan, the sugar and water; boil uncovered, stirring a few times until syrupy, about 10 minutes; then pour this hot syrup into the melted chocolate, while stirring briskly with a wire whisk. Add the egg yolks, one at a time, beating vigorously after each addition, over the hot water.

Remove from heat and stir in the brandy. Fold in the beaten egg whites. Pour into the *petits pots*, individual custard dishes or coffee demi-tasses, cover and refrigerate at least 12 hours. *Serves 6 – 8.*

Chocolate Rum Bavarian Cream

Serve in a cut-glass dish, topped with a thick layer of crushed almond macaroons; and add to the table a bottle of coffee liqueur to be used by everyone to his taste. That is the authentic way to serve a Rum Bavarian.

½ cup (125 mL) hot milk or cream
4 oz. (110 g) semi-sweet chocolate
½ cup (125 mL) sugar
⅛ tsp. (0.5 mL) salt
1 envelope unflavored gelatine
¼ cup (60 mL) rum
4 beaten egg yolks
4 stiffly beaten egg whites
½ cup (125 mL) heavy cream

Heat the milk over hot water in top of double boiler. Add the chocolate and stir often until the chocolate is melted and the mixture is smooth. Add the sugar and salt and stir until sugar is melted.

Pour the gelatine over the rum, and let stand 5 minutes. Add this to the egg yolks, mix well, and pour over the chocolate while stirring, and cook until creamy, stirring often. Cool in refrigerator until it just begins to set. Then fold into the beaten egg whites and the stiffly whipped cream. Pour into a dish. Cover and refrigerate until set. *Serves 6.*

Quebec Pudding au Sucre

In the spring, I make this pudding with soft maple sugar; in the winter, with dark brown sugar. The pudding is on top, and on the bottom is a clear delicious syrup to be poured over the pudding when served.

4 cups (1 L) bread cubes
½ cup (125 mL) butter
1 tsp. (5 mL) cinnamon
Grated peel of ½ an orange or a lemon
1 cup (250 mL) maple or brown sugar
3 tbsp. (50 mL) apple juice or water
2 eggs, lightly beaten
2 cups (500 mL) milk, scalded

Melt the butter in a saucepan until it is a nutty brown color. Place the bread in a bowl, pour the melted butter on top, and add the cinnamon, sugar and orange or lemon rind. Mix together thoroughly.

Place the brown or maple sugar and apple juice or water in the bottom of a well-buttered pudding dish. Pour the bread mixture on top. Beat the eggs and hot milk together and pour over the bread, but do not mix. Place the dish in a pan of hot water and bake 40 – 45 minutes in a 350°F. (180°C) oven. Serve hot or warm, plain or with cream or ice cream. *Serves 6.*

Maple Bread Pudding

This is a real "homebody" recipe, but don't think it is dull. It's quick to prepare and the delicate maple flavor is a change from the usual bread pudding.

3 slices brown or white bread
2 tbsp. (30 mL) soft margarine
3 eggs
½ cup (125 mL) maple syrup
¼ tsp. (1 mL) ginger or nutmeg
⅛ tsp. (0.5 mL) salt
2½ cups (625 mL) milk

Spread margarine on both sides of each slice of bread — do not remove crust. Cut each in 4 and place in a generously-buttered 1½ qt. (1½ L) baking dish.

Beat eaggs until frothy; beat syrup, spices and salt into eggs; then stir in milk, and pour over bread. Let stand 20 minutes; then, with a fork, gently push down any bread that has stayed on the surface.

Set baking dish in a pan of hot water, cover and bake at 325°F. (160°C) for 1 hour, or until done. Serve as is, or with cream or ice cream. *Serves 4.*

Caramel Bread Pudding

I am not overly fond of very many bread puddings, but this one I enjoy anytime. The recipe was given to my mother by our Scottish cheeseman. Of course, there were no actual measurements or cooking directions of any kind. Whenever maple sugar is available, by all means use it instead of brown sugar — it was in the original recipe.

1 cup (250 mL) brown sugar
1 tsp. (5 mL) cinnamon or nutmeg
2 tbsp. (30 mL) butter, diced
2 eggs, lightly beaten
2 cups (500 mL) milk
1½ cups (400 mL) dry bread, diced
Pinch of salt
1 tsp. (5 mL) vanilla *or*
1 tbsp. (15 mL) rum

Place the brown sugar in the bottom of a round 8 in. (20 cm) baking dish. Sprinkle the sugar with cinnamon *or* nutmeg. Top with the diced butter.

Heat the milk. Beat the eggs in a bowl. Add the diced bread and hot milk. Stir until well mixed. Add the salt and vanilla, and pour the whole on the brown sugar, but do not stir.

Place dish in a pan of water. Bake in a preheated 350°F. (180°C) oven, about 35 – 45 minutes, or until top is browned. Serve hot or cold. It will fall as it cools, but that is as it should be. *Serves 4.*

Queen of Puddings

In French Quebec, we used to call it *Delices de la Reine*. It was a well-known pudding of the Victorian era. Of course, it is a bread pudding, but made as directed in the original recipe, it is delicious and delicate, with a beautiful flavor. The fresh citrus sauce is its crowning glory.

2 egg yolks
3 tbsp. (50 mL) soft butter
2/3 cup (160 mL) sugar
1 cup (250 mL) fresh white breadcrumbs (2 slices)
¼ tsp. (1 mL) salt
1¾ cups (475 mL) light cream or milk
1 tsp. (5 mL) vanilla
Juice and grated rind of ½ a lemon
2 egg whites, beaten stiff

With an electric beater, beat together the egg yolks, soft butter and sugar, until the mixture is almost white and very light. Add the breadcrumbs, salt and cream or milk. Mix well and simmer over low heat, stirring most of the time, until mixture has the texture of a light custard — this is the secret of a light pudding. Beat the egg whites until stiff, but not hard. At that moment, remove from heat and add the vanilla, lemon juice and rind, and beat briskly for 1 minute. Then carefully fold in the beaten egg whites. Pour gently into an attractive baking dish. (Mother always used an oval dish of English porcelain with birds and flowers by Minton. How I loved that dish.)

Place the dish in a pan of hot water. Bake about 35 minutes in a preheated 325°F. (160°C) oven or until a knife will come out clean and the top is golden brown. Serve with cream or an orange or lemon sauce. *Serves 4 – 6.*

Carrot Custard

This will prove to you that there is more to carrots than crunch. In the old days, we used to have an abundance of root vegetables (carrots, turnips, and beets) in the winter because we could keep them in the "root cellar." So women thought of all kinds of ways to use them, and baking was one of them. This carrot custard is delicate, with an attractive color and was a great favorite.

4 eggs
½ cup (125 mL) honey
¼ tsp. (1 mL) salt
3 cups (750 mL) hot milk
¾ cup (200 mL) finely grated carrots
2 tbsp. (30 mL) dry sherry
Grated rind of 1 orange
Nutmeg or cinnamon to taste

Beat together the eggs, honey and salt until frothy and light. Stir in the hot milk, carrots, sherry and grated rind of the orange. Mix well and pour into individual custard cups. Sprinkle with freshly grated nutmeg or cinnamon to taste.

Set cups in baking pan, add enough hot water to come halfway up the cups. Bake in a preheated 325°F. (160°C) oven, 40 – 50 minutes, or until custard is set. *Yield:* 6 custard cups.

Pumpkin Custard

A blender greatly improves the texture of this tasty golden custard; but if you don't have one, simply beat vigorously with a rotary beater.

1½ cups (375 mL) hot milk
¼ tsp. (1 mL) nutmeg
Pinch of ground cloves
¼ tsp. (1 mL) cinnamon
⅔ cup (160 mL) **Pumpkin Purée**
2 eggs
6 large marshmallows

With a rotary beater, or in a blender, mix all ingredients except eggs and marshmallows until thoroughly combined. Add eggs and beat just enough to blend. Pour into 6 buttered 4-oz. (125 mL) custard cups, and top each with a marshmallow. Place cups in a pan of hot water, bake in a 350°F. (180°C) oven 30 minutes, then refrigerate until needed. *Serves 6.*

Turkish Ara Strambouli

A delectable Turkish pumpkin dessert. My friend Simone from Egypt taught me how to make it. Serve it hot or at room temperature but not refrigerated. It can be warmed up covered with wax paper.

I just love this dessert whether hot, warm or cold. Eat as is, or serve with cream or ice cream. Nobody can ever guess what it is. One thing you cannot do is to refrigerate it.

Cut pumpkin into half-moons. Fry over medium heat until tender, in margarine. [About 15 – 20 half-moons and ½ cup (125 mL) margarine.]

Place a layer in a shallow dish. Sprinkle each layer generously with some of the following mixture:

1 cup (250 mL) chopped nuts
1 cup (250 mL) sugar
1 cup (250 mL) currants

Sprinkle each layer with just enough lemon juice to wet the sugar (the juice of approximately ½ a lemon for each row). To taste, pour over ¼ cup (60 mL) of rum.

Bake in a 350°F. (180°C) oven until lightly browned on top, here and there, about 30 minutes. Serve hot or warm or at room temperature. *Serves 4 – 6.*

Maple Syrup

Maple syrup is spring itself. The "brown sweetness" as people used to refer to maple syrup in the old days, has a way of giving charm and flavor to any food — pour a golden trickle on your morning cereal or yogurt; enjoy it on grapefruit halves, especially if they are warm, use to candy your sweet potatoes or ham; or simply heat it up with chopped walnuts to pour over ice cream for a hot maple sundae. Make a super spectacular maple soufflé. When the strawberry season is with us, sweeten them with maple syrup and top with rich cream. Try a homemade maple mousse or maple ice cream; you will keep on making it, it is so pure, and so tasty. Not too often, but at least once with the new syrup, make *Sucre à la crème,* the old-fashioned way . . . and on and on. A maple dessert is always loved by all.

Mary's Maple Soufflé

My dear friend Mary Baillie gave me this recipe years ago. Whoever ate it wanted to know the "how-to." It is a spectacular piece. What's more, it is a soufflé that takes 1 hour to cook, so you can easily time it to be ready when you are.

1 cup (250 mL) maple syrup
4 egg whites
½ cup (125 mL) icing sugar
2 tsp. (10 mL) baking powder

Sauce:

½ cup (125 mL) maple syrup
3 tbsp. (50 mL) brandy
1 tbsp. (15 mL) butter

Boil the cup of syrup until reduced to ¾ cup (200 mL). Cool. Beat the egg whites until stiff, but not dry. Add the icing sugar sifted with the baking powder. Then fold the cooled syrup carefully. Bake in a preheated 300°F. (150°C) oven in an 8-in. (20 cm) soufflé dish. Place the dish in a pan of hot water. Bake 1 hour. Serve as soon as ready, with the sauce prepared by heating together the sauce ingredients. Let each guest help himself. *Serves 4 – 5.*

Maple Mousse

The quality and thickness of the maple syrup is very important in this dessert. If you are not too sure, measure 1½ cups (400 mL) of syrup and boil down to 1 cup (250 mL). Cool, and then use. If you have *petits pots* for dessert, by all means use them for this mousse.

4 egg yolks beaten
1 cup (250 mL) maple syrup
1 tsp. (5 mL) vanilla extract
2 cups (500 mL) heavy cream
¼ – ½ cup (60 – 125 mL) chopped walnuts

Mix the well-beaten yolks with the maple syrup and beat over boiling water until the mixture coats the spoon and looks like a custard. Cool, then add the vanilla, and fold in the stiffly-whipped cream. Pour into individual molds or *petits pots*. Sprinkle chopped walnuts on top. Cover and refrigerate 24 hours before serving. Or serve as a frozen mousse, by setting dish in freezer 4 – 6 hours. When frozen, you can use a mold as it can be unmolded after 12 hours. *Serves* 6.

Maple Cream

2 cups (500 mL) hot milk
3 tbsp. (50 mL) cornstarch
¼ cup (60 mL) cold milk
¾ cup (200 mL) maple syrup
2 tbsp. (30 mL) butter

Heat the milk. Dilute cornstarch in the ¼ cup (60 mL) cold milk, and add to hot milk. Cook, stirring constantly, until mixture is thick and smooth. Cook another few minutes over low heat, then remove from heat.

Place maple syrup and butter in a heavy frying pan and cook until syrup becomes very thick and bubbly. It must caramelize without burning. Add to the cream. Stir over low heat until mixture is very smooth. Pour into a mold. Cool. Unmold to serve and garnish with whipped cream. *Serves 4.*

14. *Breakfasts, Brunches and Lunches*

Breakfast

Food and cooking have not escaped the tumultuous changes that have become so common to our daily life, so why not make some changes of your own at breakfast. For the sake of your health and energy, use breakfast-time to try whole wheat, buckwheat, barley, old-fashioned oatmeal, brown or raw sugar, sea salt, brewer's yeast, coconut or wheatgerm. Learn to use them and discover what a delicious breakfast can be produced with a minimum of effort.

My husband Bernard and I breakfast early — quite early — because we both enjoy the quietness of the surroundings, the way our two big dogs and four cats sit around and listen to us talking and enjoying our food.

For me, breakfast is black coffee, one slice of crisp toast spread with a bit of cheese — how I love cheese — and a bit of one of my latest summer jams. In the summer, fresh fruits replace the jam. A few times a year I will have crisp, maple-smoked bacon, and eggs, and fried potatoes, finishing with a small spoonful of my favorite marmalade.

But for my husband it is another story. He thinks in terms of "he-man" breakfasts. Bacon, eggs, broiled tomatoes or lamb kidneys or sausages, and hashed browns or hot cereal with honey . . . and on and on. To me early in the morning there is nothing like the very manly smell of bacon cooking and sizzling — especially when it is sliced paper-thin and comes to the table properly cooked — crisp, but not dry.

For many people, breakfast is not so much a meal as it is a habit, a mood, a coffee on the run — eyes on the financial section while the mouth is swallowing something or other. Some people will not start the day without orange juice; for others grapefruit is a must. For some the most important ingredient is scrambled eggs, and for still others only "sunny-side up" is acceptable.

When I talk with my friends about breakfast, the comment I hear most often is that it is nearly impossible to get a good meal on the table each morning — especially on time — without becoming thoroughly depressed about the whole business. Keep in mind that some breakfast dishes provide an atmosphere that is just right for leisurely mornings, while others fit days when everyone is rushing about at a dizzy pace, getting ready for school or work.

My own philosophy about breakfast is summed up in a few words: moderation, simplicity, quiet elegance and respect for the tastes and early morning personalities of others. This is the way I avoid that muddled morning mood: When I'm getting into bed at night, I plan what I will serve the following morning, in which room I will serve it, and what I will wear. When I get out of bed the next morning, I know exactly what I am going to put on, and what and where we'll eat. And believe me, when you only have one eye open it's a relief not to have to start thinking about things like that!

The first thing I do, once I make it to the kitchen, is run water — fresh and cold — for the coffee. Then I grind the coffee beans, using the right grind for the coffeemaker I intend to use (it's usually a filter coffeepot). To this day I haven't decided which pleases me more — the tantalizingly fragrant smell of the freshly ground coffee *or* the actual taste of that first cup.

When I serve cold cereal, first I place it in dishes and then pour milk and cream into pitchers. Next, I assemble fruit, eggs, butter, bacon or anything else I'm going to serve.

By this time the water is boiling. I make the coffee and warm a teapot for my husband, who drinks tea in the morning. Then I set the table the way I have decided the night before. I always try to make my breakfast table look as fresh and colorful as possible because I think we need this refreshing feeling more in the morning than we do at any other time of day. Next I prepare the bacon and eggs, or cook whatever else is needed for that particular meal.

Here are some of my hints for a tasty breakfast. All you have to do is use your own imagination on some of your favorite dishes. As long as you have the desire to make someone — even yourself — happy, you will start the day on a positive note — and chances are you will remain positive all day.

Pan-fried Bacon: Place bacon slices in a cold frying pan. Cook very slowly over medium heat, turning only once. Drain fat before you turn slices.

Broiled Bacon: Place bacon slices on a wire rack. Broil 3 in. (8 cm) from the heat source, without turning. Cook 3 – 4 minutes. (This is the best method for bringing out the full flavor of the meat.)

After cooking by either of these methods, drain bacon on paper towels and keep hot in a warmer or a 250°F. (120°C) oven. At the same time, warm the plates. Many breakfasts are spoiled simply because they are served on cold plates.

The Versatility of Eggs

Fried Eggs: To obtain the best results when frying eggs, use a small, heavy metal frying pan, the best being the enameled cast-iron type.

Two heats are used in frying an egg. Over high heat, melt the fat you prefer: butter, bacon fat, olive or vegetable oil — about 1 tsp. (5 mL) for 2 eggs. When the fat has reached the smoking point, without being too brown, of course, the eggs are added and the heat goes off. The heat in the pan is sufficient to cook the eggs. It may take 2–3 minutes.

The safest way to add eggs to the pan without breaking the yolks is to crack them, one at a time, into a saucer and lower the saucer almost on top of the hot fat. Tip the saucer sideways with the edge touching the bottom of the pan, allowing the egg to slip in slowly. When all the eggs have been added, cook gently over low heat, if you have more than 2 eggs.

To cook a completely fat-free egg, break the eggs in a cold, ungreased Teflon frying pan, cover, and cook over low heat 3–5 minutes. Serve immediately.

If you like your eggs "over" or "sunny-side down," proceed as for plain fried eggs; but just before they are done to your taste, turn each egg over swiftly with a well-oiled spatula; then cook on the remaining side for 30 seconds or to your taste.

Scrambled Eggs: Lots of practice is required to learn how to make perfect scrambled eggs, which should be both soft and creamy. This is the one method of cooking eggs that is done badly most consistently, and there seem to be no half way or in-between — they are either cooked to perfection or absolutely dreadful.

To proceed, break the eggs — usually two per person — into a bowl. Season to taste and beat with a fork or wire whisk until whites and yolks are well mixed. If you use a rotary beater, you will overbeat them and affect the creaminess of the finished product.

Use 1 tbsp. (15 mL) butter in your pan for each 2–3 eggs. This is twice the amount used for an omelet. Why so much? Because here the butter is not used solely to keep eggs from sticking to the pan, but also as necessary liquid, which must be incorporated into the eggs as they cook to give them a rich texture and flavor.

Always scramble eggs gently over low heat; for when the heat is too high, all the eggs' natural juices are forced out of them, making the finished product dry and unpleasant.

Now for the actual cooking. Place the frying pan over medium heat, melt the butter, and then pour in the whisked eggs. Let them set for a few seconds, then stir with a fork, making no attempt to retain any kind of shape. The constant stirring of the eggs is the secret to making them creamy. The easiest way is to lift the cooked eggs from underneath so that the uncooked eggs on top can flow to the bottom of the pan. Cook them, stirring constantly, until they are almost set but still appear a bit shiny and underdone. At this point, remove from heat. Add 1 tsp. (5 mL) cold 10 percent cream or milk for each 4 eggs, and stir fast for a second. This is to stop the cooking, which would otherwise continue for several minutes because of the internal heat retained by the eggs. Without this last step, the eggs will be overcooked and dry. Turn them on to a warmed plate and serve.

Poached Eggs: For successful poaching, eggs must be absolutely fresh. Use a deep saucepan, fill it with salted water, add ½ tsp. (2 mL) vinegar, and bring to a simmer. Break eggs into a saucer and add to saucepan as you would eggs for frying. Cover the saucepan and cook over very low heat for 3 – 5 minutes. When done, remove them from water with a slotted spoon.

For softer eggs, grease a deep frying pan with butter or margarine. Add 2 in. (5 cm) salted water, ½ tsp. (2 mL) vinegar, and bring to the simmering point, but do not boil. Add eggs, cover pan, and turn off heat, but do not remove pan from heat source. Let the pan stand for 3 – 7 minutes, depending on how well-cooked you want your eggs to be. Remove eggs from water with a slotted spoon, then serve.

Any number of eggs may be cooked in this manner; but when learning, it is better to cook them one at a time.

Farmer's Breakfast

This is still a popular morning dish on many Quebec farms. Although it makes a fine hearty breakfast for a hungry man, I would recommend it also for lunch or a light supper.

4 slices bacon
3 boiled potatoes, cubed
1 small onion, chopped
½ tsp. (2 mL) salt
Dash of pepper
½ cup (125 mL) grated Cheddar, mild or strong
5 eggs

Cut bacon in small pieces. Fry over low heat until slightly brown and crisp. Add potatoes, onions, salt and pepper. Cook, stirring often, until potatoes are somewhat brown. Sprinkle cheese over potatoes. Break eggs into pan over the cheese. Cook over low heat, stirring constantly, until the eggs are set and scrambled, and serve. *Serves 4 – 6.*

Misty Morning Breakfast

I was brought up on this delicious breakfast which was always served in October and November — that is why we named it "Misty Morning." When October rolled around, we always looked forward to this special breakfast, which hailed originally from the Scottish settlers of the Quebec Eastern Townships. I assure you it is worth trying.

6 – 8 slices bacon
2 potatoes, peeled
1 large apple, unpeeled

Fry bacon until crisp. Remove from frying pan. Slice potatoes as thinly as possible, and apple in medium-thick slices. Add both to bacon fat. Cook over medium heat, stirring occasionally until potatoes slices are tender and apple slices are soft. It takes about 15 minutes. Add salt and pepper to taste. Serve on hot plate, top with bacon. *Serves 4.*

Brunch

Sunday Brunch

I like a Sunday brunch, especially when it is long on good eating and short on work and cleaning up. Not possible, you say? Yes it is, I say— if you go at it the lazy way by preparing most of it the night before.

During the week, breakfast is usually a gulp and a goodbye — but Sundays are different; they offer the luxury of eating what you wish, when you wish and where you wish.

What to serve? For starters, a long, cool drink — strong, if you are so inclined. But I think fruit is much more special — beautiful fresh strawberries topped with fresh orange juice sweetened with a dash of orange liqueur, and there are so many more delicious fruit combinations. A wedge of papaya topped with green lime to squeeze on top. Beautiful, big, fat raspberries *nature* to nibble on one by one. Just think, and one fruit in season will come to your mind.

The following are just a few suggestions for a sparkling start to a Sunday brunch. I leave my fruit overnight at room temperature to bring out the full flavor, though you may prefer to refrigerate it.

Fresh strawberries, sweetened to taste and marinated in fresh orange juice, look lovely served in crystal cups, as do peeled oranges, in slices or sections, topped with chopped pecans or walnuts and a dash of sherry.

Angostura bitters can be used for more than cocktails. Halve a grapefruit, remove seeds, loosen sections, sprinkle each half with 1 heaping tsp.

(5 mL) of maple or brown sugar and about 10 drops of bitters. Cover and let stand overnight, or you can wait and prepare it only 10 minutes before serving.

Apples and oranges are also a nice overnight-stand combination. For 6 people, peel 4 oranges and slice thinly. Peel and core 3 apples and slice thinly. Place fruit in alternate layers in a glass dish, sprinkling each layer with sugar. [I use a total of ½ cup (125 mL) in all, but you may want more.] Sprinkle with the juice of ½ a lime or lemon, cover, and let stand.

If you want something exotic and spectacular, serve hot brandied citrus. For 4 people, carefully peel and section 1 large grapefruit and 2 oranges the night before. Arrange layers alternately in a shallow buttered dish and squeeze the juice of 2 oranges on top. Mix 3 tbsp. (50 mL) of brown sugar with ½ tsp. (2 mL) of mace or nutmeg and sprinkle on top. Dot with 2 tbsp. (30 mL) of butter, then pour 2 – 4 tbsp. (30 – 60 mL) of brandy on top.

When ready to serve, bake 25 minutes at 325°F. (160°C). This can also be served cold; omit the butter, cover and leave overnight at room temperature. The sugar will melt and form a syrup.

Then there are always moons of cantaloupe, with the juice of ½ a lime squeezed on top of each. Sweeten them with fruit sugar if you like.

And finally, a delicious combination is to thaw the contents of 1 package of frozen strawberries, pass them through a sieve or blender, and use as a syrup over fresh raspberries.

Then comes the important part — the coffee. Make lots of it, so there's enough for seconds and thirds. Please, not instant coffee; that is for the "gulp and run day;" serve a good black, freshly ground, filtered coffee.

Eggs are still a favorite at brunch time. In the warm weather you can make much of your brunch near the pool, on the patio or in the garden. If you have an electrical outlet around, use your electric frying pan, your barbecue, or your microwave.

Asparagus Quiche

A culinary showpiece and delectable to the taste, this quiche is a change from the type served much too often. Complete the brunch with a green salad, a basket of fresh fruits and freshly-brewed coffee — and maybe a glass of *liqueur frappée* to sip with the fruits.

9-in. (22.5 cm) pastry shell, unbaked
2 lb. (2 kg) fresh asparagus
2 cups (500 mL) light cream
1/3 cup (80 mL) grated Parmesan cheese
1/3 cup (80 mL) grated Swiss cheese

4 eggs
Salt and pepper to taste

Bake the pastry shell exactly 8 minutes at 400°F. (200°C). Boil and drain asparagus as instructed in "Vegetables" chapter, then cut off top 2 in. (5 cm) of each spear (reserve remainder to dice for salads).

Thoroughly mix cream with rest of ingredients and pour into pastry shell. Bake at 350°F. (180°C) for 30 minutes, or until custard is almost set. Remove from oven and place asparagus tips upright in quiche. Bake a further 5 – 8 minutes, or until firm, and serve immediately. *Serves 6.*

Buttermilk Pancakes and Their Garnishes

A nice way to finish off a brunch. I usually cook them in my electric frying pan or let each guest do them as they need them, and offer a choice of 2 or 3 toppings.

Lots of coffee and pancakes with a good choice of garnishes can also make a nice brunch at much lower cost than a brunch that includes meat.

1 cup (250 mL) all-purpose flour
1 tsp. (5 mL) salt
1 tsp. (5 mL) baking soda
1 egg
1 cup plus 2 tbsp. (280 mL) buttermilk
2 tbsp. (30 mL) butter

Stir the flour, salt and soda together in a bowl. Drop in unbeaten egg, and add the buttermilk and butter. Stir only until all flour is moistened (though you'll see a lump here and there), then let stand 5 minutes. The batter will look thick, spongy and puffy.

Drop by tablespoonfuls (15 mL) on to a hot greased pan, spreading batter a bit with the back of a spoon. Cook on one side until bubbles appear, turning before the bubbles break and become dry-looking. Brown a few seconds on other side.' *Yield:* 16 – 18 3 in. (7.5 cm) pancakes.

Pancake Garnishes: The more of these you have on the table, the more elaborate the spread. Your guests will enjoy choosing their favorite.

Honey Butter Whip: Beat at high speed in a mixer ¼ cup (60 mL) of honey, 2 tbsp. (30 mL) of orange juice, 1 egg white and a pinch of salt. When thick, stir in 2 tbsp. (30 mL) of melted butter and 2 tsp. (5 mL) of grated orange peel.

Orange Maple Butter: Whip ½ cup (125 mL) of soft butter or margarine with 2 tsp. (10 mL) of grated orange peel and ¼ cup (60 mL) of grated maple or brown sugar.

Bacon Chutney Butter: Fry 6 – 8 slices of bacon and drain on absorbent paper. Crumble and stir with ¼ cup (60 mL of soft butter and 2 tbsp. (30 mL) of chopped chutney.

Blueberry Pancakes: Clean 1 basket of fresh blueberries, and stir with 3 tbsp. (30 mL) of brown sugar and ½ tsp. (2 mL) of cinnamon. Pour a large spoonful on each pancake just after it's been poured into the hot pan. Serve with blueberry side down.

Devilled Sausages: In a cold frying pan, place 2 tsp. (10 mL) of Dijon mustard, 1 tbsp. (15 mL) of butter and ½ lb. (250 g) of sausages, sliced. Stir over medium heat until sausages are lightly browned and well coated with butter and mustard. Remove to a dish and place a few slices on each pancake, as for the blueberry garnish.

Monique's Sandwich 1867

My daughter created this one for her T.V. program in Canada's Centennial Year. You may wonder about the combination, but once you've tasted it, you'll stay with it. Makes a terrific brunch.

First, you make buckwheat pancakes. She buys the ready mix. I like to make my own — in the blender, nothing to it!

Blender Buckwheat Pancakes

Make the pancakes when you are ready. Warm up in a stack of 6 covered, in the oven. Or place 3 on a paper towel, cover with paper, and warm up 40 seconds in the Microwave oven.

To freeze. Stack 12 per package, with a square of wax paper between each. Wrap package. When you need 1 or 4, they are easily separated by pulling up on the paper that separates each crêpe.

1½ cups (400 mL) buckwheat flour
3 tsp. (15 L) baking powder
½ tsp. (2 mL) baking soda
½ cup (125 mL) whole wheat flour

2 cups (500 mL) buttermilk or sour milk *or*
2 cups water
½ cup (125 mL) instant powdered milk
1 tsp. (5 mL) vinegar
2 tbsp. (30 mL) molasses
1 egg
3 tbsp. (50 mL) soft butter or bacon fat
1 tbsp. (15 mL) brown sugar

Place in a bowl the first four ingredients. Place in the blender glass jar the remaining ingredients. Cover and blend 1 minute at high speed.

Pour over dry ingredients. Mix well and cook like any pancake. *Yield:* 10-15 pancakes.

To Make the Sandwich: Place sausages on a broiler tray, set under broiler 3 in. (8 cm) from source of heat, and broil about 4 minutes turning once.

Spread each hot pancake with ketchup or chili sauce to taste, place a hot sausage on top and roll pancake around sausage. You may also enjoy them with the pancake cold and the sausage hot.

Steak Vitesse

Thin club steaks at their supreme best. The secret is to have all the ingredients ready nearby, and hot plates and a good *thick cast-iron frying pan.*

Set your steak on a large toasted slice of crusty bread to catch its sizzling juices. Serve with broiled tomatoes — and if you want to go all the way, hash-browned potatoes.

4 club steaks, ½ in. (1.25 cm) thick
2 tbsp. (30 mL) butter
1 small garlic clove, finely chopped
Juice of 1 lemon or lime
1 tbsp. (15 mL) Worcestershire sauce

Have the steaks at room temperature. Melt butter and add garlic. When hot, turn heat as high as you can and quickly dip steaks, on both sides, in the butter. Then cook fast, 3 minutes per side, lowering heat if necessary.

When ready, push steak aside and throw remaining ingredients into pan. Quickly swish steak around in gravy, and serve immediately, letting guests salt and pepper to taste. *Serves 4.*

Lunch

Monique's Bean Pot Pork Chops

Easy – easy, she says. To enjoy when the weather is below zero, or the boys are "lambing" through the night — "a dish that sticks to a man's ribs," as the old-timers used to say. I admit Monique takes her usual short cuts, but I can tell you that by the time the dish is cooked, nobody knows she has used canned beans.

2 19 oz. (540 mL) cans or jars of beans with molasses
  or tomato sauce
5 – 8 *thin* pork chops
Salt and pepper to taste
Prepared mustard
1 tsp. (5 mL) brown sugar per chop
1 tsp. (5 mL) ketchup per chop
Thick slices of onion
Unpeeled lemon slices

Empty the beans into a casserole or bean pot — the easiest to use is a 9 × 13 × 2 in. (22.5 × 32.5 × 5 cm) dish.

Salt and pepper each chop. Place on top of beans. Sprinkle each chop with the brown sugar, top with the ketchup. On each chop place a slice of onion, then cover with a slice of lemon. Hold in place with a wooden pick.

Cover and bake in a 300°F. (150°C) oven 1½ hours. Uncover during the last 15 minutes of cooking. Serve with cucumber pickles and hot crusty bread. *Serves 6.*

Bernard's Favorite Sandwich

For a healthful, low-cost lunch, serve this with cole slaw or a green salad.

6 slices bacon
½ lb. (250 mL) chicken livers
1 tsp. (5 mL) lemon juice
¼ tsp. (60 mL) marjoram or tarragon
Salt and pepper to taste
¼ cup (60 mL) soft butter
8 slices bread

Fry the bacon until crisp, remove it from the pan and add chicken livers to bacon fat. Cook 10–15 minutes over medium heat, turning often. Pour contents of pan over cooked bacon and let cool.

With a fork, mash liver finely and crumble bacon. Add lemon juice and seasonings, and mix well. Add butter, and blend and spread over 4 slices of bread; cover with remainder. *Serves 4.*

Some of My Favorite Instant Lunches

Good on Saturday when Dad is helping around the house. No time to cook as the household seems to be at his beck and call. When I presented this assortment of my favorite instant lunches on T.V. in 1954, to my amazement it drew the most mail of the year. In a sense, things have changed little through all these years, since almost everyone is looking for something for lunch that is "quick, easy and good."

Marta's Favorite

Place in a pan 2 tbsp. (30 mL) butter, 2 tsp. (10 mL) good prepared mustard (Dijon type when available.) Cut 1 lb. (500 g) frankfurters in 1 in. (2.5 cm) lengths. Add to the butter-mustard mixture. Stir to blend, and cover. Cook over low heat 10–15 minutes. Serve in a nest of instant mashed potatoes. *Serves 4.*

Creamy Mashed Potatoes

Prepare instant mashed potatoes (enough for 4–6 portions) according to instructions on box, reducing the liquid by ¼ cup (75 mL). As soon as they are ready, add a few spoonfuls of commercial sour cream, minced parsley or chives, or fried onion to taste. Beat well and shape in a nest on a hot platter. Serve with sausages or thin slices of ham.

Tasty Cole Slaw

Chop cabbage fine. Place in a bowl. Cut a small onion on top. Sprinkle with fresh dill or dill seeds, and freshly ground pepper and salt to taste. Squeeze the juice of a lemon on top. Add vegetable oil to taste. Toss and refrigerate 1 hour before serving.

Saturday Bacon and Corn Fondue

Monique serves this cold with a salad or ghivetch or her summer relish. She also serves it hot, with baked ham or pork chops.

8 thin slices bread, buttered
1 19 oz. (540 mL) can creamed corn
3 green onions, chopped
½ tsp. (2 mL) sage or oregano
3 eggs
½ tsp. (2 mL) dry mustard
Salt and pepper to taste
2½ cups (525 mL) milk
6 – 10 slices bacon

In a buttered casserole, make alternate layers of the bread and creamed corn. Sprinkle each row with a bit of sage or oregano and the green onions, mixed together. Beat the eggs with the mustard, salt, pepper and milk, and pour over bread and corn. Lay slices of bacon on top.

Bake 1 hour in a 325°F. (165°C) preheated oven, or until puffed and golden brown. *Serves 4 – 6.*

Monique's Sandwich Champion

A surprising mixture which is unusually good, Monique uses it often when there is leftover cold roast of beef or pork or veal.

8 slices of rye bread or wholewheat bread
Butter or margarine
½ cup (125 mL) commercial sour cream
2 tsp. (10 mL) dry onion soup mix
2 tsp. (10 mL) drained prepared horseradish
Freshly ground pepper to taste
Slices of cooked cold meat (for 4 sandwiches)
Lettuce

Butter the bread. Mix together the sour cream, onion soup mixture, horseradish and pepper. Spread 1 tsp. (5 mL) of this mixture on each slice of bread. On 4 of the slices, place the meat and lettuce to taste. Cover with the remaining slices of bread. *Serves 4.*

Cottage Cheese Pie

Bake this just before serving and eat it hot, or bake it the day before and serve it cold. Either way it's one of my favorite lunches when served with a bouquet of watercress on top, or a bowl of minced chives and parsley for sprinkling over it.

5 eggs
2 cups (500 mL) cottage cheese
1 tsp. (5 mL) salt
¼ tsp. (1 mL) pepper
¼ cup (60 mL) finely minced parsley

Beat the eggs, add cottage cheese and stir until throughly mixed. Add remaining ingredients and stir until mixture turns slightly green. Pour into an oiled 8 in. (20 cm) pie plate, 1 qt. (1 L) casserole or 6 ramekins, and bake in a 350°F. (180°C) oven — 40 – 60 minutes for a large pie, 30 minutes for ramekins, or until slightly puffed, brown and firm to the touch. *Serves 6.*

Broiler Fines-Herbes

Ever since discovering it years ago, while studying at the Paris Cordon Bleu, I've enjoyed making this dish. It can be prepared a few hours before serving and kept covered in a warm place. Reheat when ready to serve.

½ lb. (250 g) chicken wings
½ cup (125 mL) butter
3 chicken breasts, halved
Peel of ½ a lemon, thinly pared
Juice of 1 lemon
1 tbsp. (15 mL) chopped parsley
½ tsp. (2 mL) each thyme and mint
3 tbsp. (50 mL) flour
1 tsp. (5 mL) sugar
¼ tsp. (1 mL) paprika

Place the chicken wings in a saucepan with a pinch of salt and 1½ cups (400 mL) of water. Cover, and simmer 1 hour to make a broth and strain (save the chicken meat for another meal).

Put 4 tbsp. (60 mL) of the butter in a heated frying pan. When foamy, add chicken breasts, skin side down, lemon peel, juice, and salt and pepper to taste. Cover at once, and simmer over low heat 30 minutes, or until breasts are tender (do not overcook). Strain juice from pan and let breasts cool a bit.

Remove bones and place breasts close together in an attractive, shallow baking dish. Rinse frying pan, add 1½ cups (400 mL) of the wing broth, plus the parsley, thyme and mint; cream 3 tbsp. (50 mL) of the butter with the flour, add to the sauce and beat with a whisk or spoon over low heat until smooth and creamy. Taste for seasoning and set aside, covered to prevent a skin from forming.

Just before serving, sprinkle sugar, then paprika over chicken. Melt remaining butter, spoon over chicken, and place in a 500°F. (260°C) oven just long enough for the surface to become brown and crisp. Heat sauce and pour around chicken.

15. *Special Occasions*

Monique's Easter Brunch

At Easter, my daughter entertains the family with a brunch that is always enjoyable. Last year we had her very good compote of rhubarb and fresh pineapple; **Scrambled Eggs Suprême,** which she does to perfection, garnished with broiled bacon and Noirmouton sausages; big fat hot popovers; cheese, **Sour Cream Hot Biscuits** and **Potatoes Macaire.** Fragrant, steaming-hot Chinese tea and a mixture of Black Arabian and Brown Mocha Java Coffee, freshly ground and brewed, make it a very special meal.

Easter Compote

This should be made with winter rhubarb, which is sweet and retains its pink color when cooked. Will keep 4 – 5 days refrigerated, so it can be made ahead of time.

- 2 bunches pink winter rhubarb
- 1 small pineapple
- 1 cup (250 mL) sugar

Clean the rhubarb by cutting off the leaves and end pieces, then dice remainder coarsely. Place in a saucepan with the water, and bring to a boil, while stirring. Boil 1 minute, then remove from heat.

Peel and grate the pineapple, and place in a bowl with the sugar. Stir well and add the hot rhubarb, continuing to stir until sugar is melted. Cover and refrigerate until ready to serve. *Serves 6.*

Scrambled Eggs Suprême

The addition of light cream and a dash of curry makes these eggs quite special. One hour before the brunch, have ingredients all ready to stir in the bowl, and the frying pan ready on the stove with the butter. Then the work is fast.

6 eggs, lightly beaten
2/3 cup (160 mL) light cream
½ tsp. (2 mL) curry powder
Salt and pepper to taste
1 tbsp. (15 mL) butter
3 tbsp. (50 mL) finely minced parsley or chives

Beat the eggs in a bowl with a fork — never use a hand beater. Add the cream, curry powder, salt and pepper. Stir again. Melt the butter in a large heavy frying pan — enamelled cast-iron is the best.

Pour in the eggs, let stand over medium heat without touching. The eggs will soon form a light custard; then with a fork, lift the cooked edges, letting some of the uncooked eggs get under and push the cooked part toward the middle (long to write, but quick to do). Repeat until the eggs start to look cooked, then remove pan from heat. The heat retained in the pan is sufficient to finish cooking the eggs. When they stay too long over the heat, they start drying up.

Pour parsley or chives on top. Serve as soon as ready. *Serves 6.*

Fat Cat Popovers

This is the name Monique gave her popovers, and *that* they are. Easy to mix and bake and a spectacle when brought to the table. She uses individual ramekins and gives one to each guest.

Popovers are at their best when all ingredients are at room temperature. So have everything ready. Then 2 minutes to mix and pour into molds, and 30 minutes to cook all by themselves without watching, and that's all there is to produce these "Fat Cats."

1 cup (250 mL) milk
2 eggs
½ tsp. (2 mL) salt
1 cup (250 mL) flour

Pour the milk into a bowl, and break the eggs on top. Add the salt, and measure the flour. Cover the bowl with a plate and let stand until ready to bake. When ready, pour the flour over the milk and stir with a spoon until *all the flour is moistened.*

Grease 6 – 8 custard cups (Monique also uses her ovenproof teacups, which are very nice too). Divide the batter into cups only half full. Place cups on baking sheet. Place in *cold* oven. Then set the oven to 400°F. (200°C) and bake 30 minutes. Let the timer do the thinking for you. *Yield:* 7 – 8 popovers.

Note from Monique: Don't peek while the "Fat Cats" bake.

Sour Cream Hot Biscuits

Make the day before. Warm up 5 minutes in the oven, when popovers are taken out. (Turn off the heat.) Or place in a basket lined with a cloth that covers all the biscuits, and heat 1 minute in a microwave oven before serving.

2 cups (500 mL) flour
3 tsp. (15 mL) baking powder
1 tsp. (5 mL) salt
½ tsp. (2 mL) baking soda
1 tsp. (5 mL) sugar
3 tbsp. (50 mL) shortening or margarine
1 cup (250 mL) commercial sour cream

Sift the first 5 ingredients together in a bowl. Cut in the shortening or margarine. Add the sour cream all at once. Blend lightly and knead 5 – 6 times. Roll ½ in. (1.25 cm) thick, cut into rounds, and place on ungreased baking sheet.

Bake in preheated 400°F. (200°C) oven about 15 – 20 minutes, or until golden brown. *Yield:* 8 – 12 biscuits.

Potatoes Macaire

The Swiss call these *roesti* potatoes. For the brunch, cook the potatoes early in the morning, or the night before, but do not refrigerate. Start to cook before putting the bacon under the broiler and making the scrambled eggs.

6 – 8 medium potatoes
2 tbsp. (30 mL) bacon fat or vegetable oil
Salt and pepper to taste
Green onions

Boil or steam the well-scrubbed, unpeeled potatoes. Beware of overcooking. The potatoes must be a little firm. Drain and cool. Peel and grate on medium-sized grater.

Melt the fat in a medium-sized frying pan (use cast-iron or enamelled cast-iron). Add the grated potatoes and press then into a flat cake. Brown over medium heat, lower the heat, and brown another ten minutes. Pass a knife around edges and invert on round serving platter. Top with finely chopped green onions. *Serves* 6.

Victoria Day Brunch

In Victorian days everything was splendor or misery. For those who had money — from the middle-class tradesman to the wealthy — to eat well, or at least heartily, was almost a duty. But for the most part, they were gluttons rather than gourmets, and the quantity they could consume at a sitting is awe-inspiring.

A woman of fame in that period was Mrs. A. B. Marshall. She owned and conducted a school of cookery situated in London, at 30 and 32 Mortimer Street West, which made her the very first woman to run a cooking school for non-professionals, and ladies, either in England or on the Continent. (All kinds of products bore her name, from leaf gelatine to a stove and an ice box.) She started her school around 1888, and published her second cook book, called *Mrs. Marshall's Larger Cookery Book of Extra Recipes, in 1891.* I am happy to say that I am the proud owner of an edition dated 1894 and signed by Mrs. Marshall.

Here are some comments on her work:

The Queen: "Go and see for yourself at this school what properly managed cookery is like," and "Mrs. A. B. Marshall must be doing a grand work for pupils seem literally to come through her school by thousands."

The *Daily Chronicle:* "Something like a revolution, or at all events a great change for the better is unostentatiously but gradually accomplished among ladies and their cooks in cooking, by the work carried on by Mrs. A. B. Marshall. Mrs. Marshall's genius in the art of cooking is a matter of notoriety."

This is all very exciting to me and I am sorry I was not around to enjoy it. The world of food always has been — and never ceases to be — exciting. Many of Mrs. Marshall's pupils were from Canada and the U.S.A. — hard to believe, but true. At the time, she was very "in."

In Victorian days, the pleasures of the table were enjoyed to the fullest and no one thought it unbecoming to show their sensuous satisfaction of a good meal.

Their late buffet breakfasts were served with the utmost elegance and bounty. So many dishes were presented that nowadays we can make a choice of two or three of them to compose one of our brunches.

I once served this buffet, to celebrate Victoria Day with some English friends and guests from Surrey.

Bacon Ragoût Omelet

This superb omelet was folded in a roll, and placed on the silver warmer, surrounded with a creamy mushroom sauce.

6 – 8 slices bacon
1 cup (250 mL) sliced fresh mushrooms
2 tbsp. (30 mL) butter
½ tsp. (2 mL) paprika
Salt to taste
2 green onions, chopped fine
1 tbsp. (15 mL) chopped parsley
3 tbsp. (45 mL) dry sherry
1 tbsp. (15 mL) flour
6-egg omelet

Dice the bacon and cook over high heat, stirring often, until crisp and brown. Drain off the fat, and set bacon aside on absorbent paper.

In the same pan, melt the butter, add the mushrooms, paprika, salt and green onions. Stir 2 minutes, over high heat. Add the flour, parsley, sherry and reserved bacon bits. Stir over medium heat, until well mixed, about 2 – 3 minutes.

Make the omelet, fill with the bacon *ragoût*, fold and set on warm plate. Garnish with a mushroom sauce of your choice or minced parsley or chives to taste. *Serves 6 – 8.*

Curried Eggs à la Poonah

A superb dish of eggs stuffed with rich cream and topped with a very interesting curried sauce. The same sauce can be used to make fish or seafood curry. The words "curried" and "poonah" were synonymous with elegance in the Victorian era.

6 – 8 hard-cooked eggs
½ tsp. (2 mL) curry powder
1 green onion, chopped fine
½ cup (125 mL) whipping cream
Salt and pepper to taste

Sauce:

2 tbsp. (25 mL) butter
2 medium onions, thinly sliced
1 small apple, thinly sliced
2 fresh tomatoes, peeled and diced
A good pinch thyme
1 bay leaf
2 tbsp. (25 mL) instant tapioca

1 tbsp. (15 mL) curry powder
1 tbsp. (15 mL) mango chutney
Juice of 1 lemon
2 cups (500 mL) chicken bouillon or consommé
1 cup (250 mL) milk
¼ cup (60 mL) whipping cream

Cut the eggs in half, and take out the yolks. To the yolks, add the curry powder, green onions and the cream, whipped until stiff. Blend thoroughly and use to fill the whites. Place in the middle of an 8 in. (20 cm) round or oval casserole.

To make the sauce, place in a saucepan the butter, onions, apple slices, tomatoes, mushrooms, thyme and bay leaf. Stir over high heat until it starts to brown lightly in the bottom, then add the minute tapioca, curry powder, chutney, lemon juice, chicken bouillon or consommé and milk. Bring to a boil, while stirring; then simmer over low heat, uncovered, about 30 – 40 minutes, or until slightly reduced in quantity. Add the cream. When hot, pour over the eggs. *Serves 6 – 8.*

Mrs. Marshall's Grilled Kidneys à la Neslé

Skewers of breaded lamb kidneys, broiled and served with a most unusual garnish and a very interesting sauce.

4 – 6 lamb kidneys
Salt and paprika to taste
2 green onions, chopped very fine
4 – 5 slices bacon
1/3 cup (80 mL) melted butter
1 cup (250 mL) fine dry breadcrumbs
2 tbsp. (30 mL) white wine or vermouth
2 tbsp. (25 mL) dry sherry
1 tbsp. (15 mL) chutney
1 tsp. (5 mL) French Dijon-type mustard
1 unpeeled lemon, thinly sliced
8 – 12 fresh oysters (optional)

Split the kidneys in half. Remove the white core (easy with a pair of scissors). Place cut side up on a table and sprinkle with salt and paprika to taste, then with the green onions. Top each piece with a piece of bacon long enough to completely wrap around kidney. Pass a small skewer through the half kidney and bacon. (A bamboo skewer was suggested by Mrs. Marshall.) Repeat for each half. Then dip each one in the melted butter, then in the fine breadcrumbs, and place on the broiler rack. To serve, broil 2 in. (5 cm) away from the source of heat until bacon is crisp, about 5 minutes; turn and broil 2 minutes.

In the meantime, heat together the white wine or vermouth, the sherry, chutney and French mustard. When liquid is hot, add the oysters to it. Cover and simmer over low heat for 3 – 4 minutes. Place each oyster on a thin slice of lemon. Set around a hot platter, and place the kidneys in the middle. Pour the juice from the broiling pan into the sherry mixture. When hot, pour over the kidneys. *Serves* 6.

Capitaine à la Campagne

In Victorian days it was a mark of *savoir-faire* to use the French name for a dish. Mrs. Marshall's recipe for the "Capitaine" usually started with, "Take any piece of cold game." We are not, or cannot be, so casual — game has become rare. But if you happen to have it, do not hesitate to use it.

Left-over roasted chicken or game of your choice *or*
1 or 2 uncooked chicken breasts (enough to serve 4 – 6)
2 tbsp. (30 mL) flour
3 tbsp. (45 mL) butter
2 tsp. (10 mL) curry powder
A good pinch of salt and pepper
½ tsp. (2 mL) paprika
3 tomatoes, peeled, seeded and diced
1 cup (250 mL) tomato sauce, of your choice
4 onions, thinly sliced
1 cup (250 mL) croûtons
¼ cup (60 mL) minced parsley

Slice the leftover chicken or game in pieces as even in size as possible. When using uncooked chicken breasts, bone, remove skin, and cut in small individual pieces. Dip each piece of cooked or raw chicken in flour. Melt the butter, add the curry powder, salt, pepper, and paprika. Stir over medium heat until blended in the butter, then add the pieces of cooked chicken, game, or uncooked chicken breasts, and brown on each side over low heat. Add the tomato and tomato sauce. Bring slowly to boil. (Simmer 15 minutes when using uncooked chicken breasts.) Remove to a hot platter. Fry the onions in the saucepan with a few spoonfuls of vegetable oil. When browned, remove with a slotted spoon and place on top of the chicken. Brown the croûtons in a 300°F. (150°C) oven, and place on dish to form a border. Sprinkle the middle with the parsley. *Serves* 4 – 6.

Cheese Petits-Pots

These are so named because they were baked and served in French *petits pots*, dainty little containers with a cover. They were served hot or cold, and they're good either way. An interesting entrée.

2 cups (500 mL) grated Swiss cheese (about ½ lb. or 250 g)
6 eggs
3 cups (750 mL) light or heavy cream
¼ tsp. (1 mL) cayenne or basil
¼ tsp. (1 mL) salt
¼ tsp. (1 mL) nutmeg

Beat the eggs with a whisk, adding the cream gradually, and season with the cayenne or basil, salt and nutmeg. Add 1 cup (250 mL) of the grated cheese and pour into 8 *petits pots* or use small custard cups. Place in a shallow pan with hot water, covering ⅓ of the height of the cups. Bake in a preheated 350°F. (180°C) oven until set, about 30 minutes. Just before serving, sprinkle the rest of the cheese over each dish. *Serves 8.*

Hot Breakfast Cakes

Very much like our own baking powder biscuits. In Victorian England, these were made with rendered bacon fat or lard, sour milk, and baking powder — known the world over as "Cowan's Baking Powder — the Magic in Baking"!

2 cups (500 mL) all-purpose flour
1 tsp. (5 mL) salt
1 tsp. (5 mL) baking powder
½ tsp. (2 mL) baking soda
4 tbsp. (60 mL) lard
¾ cup (200 mL) sour milk or buttermilk

Sift together the flour, salt, baking powder and soda. Cut in the lard until you have a mealy mixture. Add enough of the sour milk or buttermilk to mix into a rather soft dough. Turn on a lightly floured board and knead gently for 5 – 6 turns. Beware of over-mixing and over-kneading. Roll or pat gently to about a ¾ in. (1.75 cm) thickness. Cut into rounds with a 2-in. (5 cm) cutter and place on a greased baking sheet. Bake at 425°F. (225°C) 15 – 18 minutes, or until golden brown *Yield:* 2 dozen cakes.

Brentford Marmalade Rolls

Another hot bread, filled with marmalade. The fashion was to eat them with thin slivers of hot crisp bacon. For me they are a treat and have been for many years.

2 cups (500 mL) all-purpose flour
1 tbsp. (15 mL) baking powder
1 tsp. (5 mL) salt
¼ cup (60 mL) unsalted butter
½ – ¾ cup (125 – 200 mL) milk
Seville orange marmalade

Sift together the flour, baking powder and salt, and work the butter into the flour mixture, with two knives or a pastry blender until mixture resembles coarse oatmeal.

Stir in enough milk to make a soft dough. Turn on to a lightly floured board and knead 5 – 6 times. Roll or pat dough to a ¼ in. (cm) thickness. Cut with a 2 in. (5 cm) cutter and place on ungreased baking sheet. Make a depression in the middle, with a thimble (I use my thumb). Fill with marmalade. Bake in a preheated 450°F. (230°C) oven, 10 – 12 minutes, or until golden brown. *Yield:* 2 dozen rolls.

French Apple Marmalade

Eaten with hot biscuits, a treat you will not forget. In Victorian days, Mrs. Marshall suggested serving it as a sauce with the *Capitaine* or the kidneys. It is also a very interesting dessert, served with a slice of sponge or pound cake.

4 – 5 (about 1 lb. or 500 g) apples
½ cup (125 mL) water
2 tbsp. (30 mL) butter
Grated rind of half a lemon
Small piece cinnamon bark
2 bay leaves
½ cup (125 mL) sugar
1 tsp. (5 mL) orange flower water
1 tbsp. (15 mL) apricot jam or jelly

Peel the apples and cut in thin slices. Place in a saucepan with the water, butter, grated lemon rind, cinnamon, bay leaves and sugar. Cook over medium heat, stirring often until the apples are soft, then add the remaining ingredients. Remove the cinnamon and bay leaves and beat with a wire whisk or a spoon until creamy and well blended. Keep refrigerated. Serve cold. *Yield:* ⅔ – ¾ cup (160 – 180 mL).

Our Christmas Feast

I love to prepare and celebrate my family Christmas at our Noirmouton farm, because still alive in my mind and heart is the rambling old-fashioned country house of my grandparents. It had a dining room large enough to sit 40 of us around the Christmas table. The huge black stove in the *basse cuisine* (summer kitchen) could bake 10 – 12 loaves of bread at a time, while on top simmered a dozen kinds of delicious foods.

Excitement and anticipation rose in the old house, as it filled with the aromas from that great stove, while outside, the country lay serene under its beautiful white cover, with its dark evergreens and its blue, blue sky. The excitement began to build up a month before Christmas when the best secret recipes handed down from mother to daughter were taken out. Long shopping lists were made and tasks assigned to all of us. When the great day arrived, the main part of the dinner was a saddle of lamb and a haunch of venison, marinated in quarts of red wine before roasting. This was served on a bed of puréed chestnuts. Many desserts were served and the meal came to an end with the traditional *pièce de résistance:* plum pudding.

I can still picture the old blue Canton china from England, the finest, largest, purest white damask covering the long table, cut glass, and the old silver shined to perfection. These are *Noëls* of long ago that I can never forget. On the farm this year, we shall be sitting down to just such a traditional meal.

Following the tradition, lamb is the meat I serve at Christmas. Like my grandparents, I like to roast a *baron of lamb*, a truly spectacular dish on the table that easily serves 20, even 30, when properly carved.

Noël Galantine

My maternal grandmother learned how to make this superb dish from a Naspakis Indian woman, and it has been a traditional family recipe for us ever since. They used deer instead of pork, first braised over thick layers of red coals; then they placed the cut-up meat in large pieces of bark, first dipping each piece of meat in cool brook water, then covering it and letting it cook during the night, slowly as the fire died out. Today, we use a loin or a boned shoulder of pork. Ask your butcher for the pork rind. We used to buy it attached to the meat, but now it is removed. I never find it too difficult to get when I ask ahead of time.

4 lb. (2 kg) loin of pork *or*
  4 – 5 lb. (2 – 2.5 kg) boned shoulder of pork
2 lb. (1 kg) pig's feet
Good size piece of pork rind

2 large onions, minced
1 tbsp. (15 mL) coarse salt
¼ tsp. (1 mL) ground cloves
1 tsp. (5 mL) summer savory
1 cup (250 mL) hot water

Use a large cast-iron pan, or enamel cast-iron Dutch oven type. First place the meat in the pan, fat side up; then place the pig's feet, cut in three, around the meat. If you have a pork rind, place on top of meat. Add the remaining ingredients except the hot water. Do not cover. Place in a preheated 325°F. (160°C) oven. Roast for 2½ hours, without covering, basting or stirring.

Then pour the cup of boiling water over the meat. Cover but do not stir, and cook another hour. By this time, the meat will be very well cooked.

Remove meat from juice. Remove bones and cut meat into coarse shreds with two forks. Cut the rind and the pig's feet into very small pieces.

Place all the meat in a mold of your choice.

Set the pan over direct heat. Add ½ cup (125 mL) strong black tea (my grandmother and mother always used green tea). Scrape bottom of pan to remove all crunchy pieces. Pour liquid through a fine strainer over the meat. Let it cool. Cover and refrigerate.

Remove meat from mold, and serve on a platter — very cold, with pickled onions, beets and small gherkins. And lots of homemade bread!
Serves 12 – 20.

Noirmouton Saddle of Lamb

A jovial Scottish friend of my father used to say that a roast saddle of lamb standing proudly on the Christmas table was "hospitality sitting with gladness." A perfect saddle is prepared with the uncut loins and shortened leg of a young lamb. (It may be wise to order it in advance from your butcher.)

1 saddle of lamb, 8 – 12 lb. (4 – 6 kg)
¼ cup (60 mL) vegetable or olive oil
1 tsp. (5 mL) dry mustard
1 tsp. (5 mL) salt
½ tsp. (2 mL) pepper, freshly ground
½ tsp. (2 mL) rosemary
½ tsp. (2 mL) basil
2 cups (500 mL) lamb bone stock
2 tbsp. (30 mL) butter
1 tsp. (5 mL) curry powder
2 tbsp. (30 mL) all-purpose flour

Stir together the oil, dry mustard, salt, pepper, rosemary and basil. Place the saddle of lamb in a dripping pan and spread mixture on top. Roast at 400°F. (200°C) 10 – 15 minutes per lb. (500 g).

When done a deep, golden brown, with a lovely fragrance, remove from pan, cover with wax paper and set aside in a warm place. (The saddle comes to its point of perfection after 20 minutes.) Add the lamb bone stock to the drippings and stir all the crusty bits from sides and bottom of pan into the stock. Make a ball of the butter, curry and flour. Add to boiling stock in the dripping pan and stir quickly over low heat until creamy and smooth.

In Scotland, the Christmas saddle of lamb is brought to the table on a large silver platter, surrounded by a blue flame — hot whisky or brandy can be poured on top and lit just before the meal is served. My grandfather followed this custom. *Serves 12 – 18.*

Note: Lamb bone stock: Ask your butcher to give you the saddle trimmings. Boil them with 4 cups (1 L) water, a stick of celery, a small onion halved, 1 bay leaf, and salt and pepper to taste. Cover and simmer for three hours, then strain. When prepared in advance, as it should be, refrigerate, remove hardened fat, and pour cold over the hot gravy.

Mashed Turnip Petits Pois

This combination will be liked even by those who never eat turnip. One condition is that the turnip must not be over-cooked.

1 large turnip
1 tsp. (5 mL) sugar
3 – 4 tbsp. (50 – 60 mL) butter
½ tsp. (2 mL) freshly ground pepper
Juice of 1 lemon
2 cups (500 mL) frozen green peas, cooked
Salt to taste

Don't peel the turnip until you're ready to cook it. Remove a thick layer of the peel, enough to eliminate the color line that is clearly seen between the turnip and the rind — this is where the bitterness is. Slice the turnip and scald with just enough boiling water to generously cover it. Then add the sugar.

Boil rapidly, uncovered, for 20 minutes. (Prolonged cooking darkens the color of the turnip and gives it a strong flavor.) Drain and wash, and add the butter, pepper and lemon juice. Beat well and fold in the cooked green peas, making sure they have been well drained. Salt to taste and serve. *Serves 8 – 10.*

Golden Fan Potatoes

Potatoes can be presented with an air of *haute-cuisine*. When not too many are needed, they can be placed around the saddle of lamb to brown. But for more servings, use a large frying pan as follows.

12 medium potatoes, peeled
Tray of ice cubes
Paprika
¼ cup (60 mL) butter

Cut through the top of each potato in thin slices, but keep it together by not slicing right to the bottom. Place in a bowl of cold water, cover with ice cubes and let stand 1 hour. Drain and dry in absorbent cloth. Roll in paprika until they're well coated and blushing pink.

Melt the butter in a large frying pan and cook the potatoes, uncovered, over low heat. Turn them often, until tender and golden brown, about 35 – 40 minutes. (The cut side of the potatoes will open up like a fan.) *Serves 8 – 10.*

Tourtière Tartlets

In my family, these are traditional — and they are truly Canadian. When cooked and frozen, they will keep for as long as 6 months; just reheat and serve. Any pastry of your choice can be used but this one is the best, almost as flaky as French puff pastry.

Pastry:

2 cups (500 mL) all-purpose, flour
1 tsp. (5 mL) salt
½ tsp. (2 mL) baking soda
Pinch of turmeric
¼ tsp. (1 mL) savory
½ cup (125 mL) pure lard
⅓ cup (80 mL) ice water
⅓ cup (80 mL) butter

Stir the flour, salt, baking soda, turmeric and savory together in a bowl. Cut in the lard, or mix with a pastry blender or two knives until the particles are about the size of peas. Add ice water by the tablespoon (15 mL), stirring with a fork or the tips of your fingers, until just enough has been added so that you can pat the dough lightly into a ball. (Since flour varies, you may not need all the water.) Handle the dough as little as possible at this stage.

Roll out the pastry, dot with the butter, and roll up toward you like a jelly roll, and roll out again in a flat sheet. Roll out again 2 – 3 times. Refrigerate a few hours before using.

Filling:

1 lb. (500 g) ground pork
2 medium potatoes, peeled and grated
1 small onion, chopped
1 garlic clove, minced
1 tsp. (5 mL) salt
½ tsp. (2 mL) savory
¼ tsp. (1 mL) ground cloves
½ cup (125 mL) water

Place all the ingredients in a saucepan. Bring to a boil, stirring to break the meat into small pieces. Cover and simmer for 30 minutes. Remove from heat and cool.

Roll chilled pastry, cut into small circles, and use to line small tartlet moulds, or individual pie plates. Fill generously with meat mixture. Top with another circle of pastry and pinch the edges together. Brush top with an egg beaten with 2 tbsp. (30 mL) water. Bake at 400°F. (200°C) until golden brown, and serve hot. *Serves 6 – 8.*

Plum Pudding

I have never tasted a plum pudding that measures up to this one. As a child, I loved to help mother prepare the ingredients. She always made me sing as grandmother had made her do. Years later I discovered singing was supposed to prevent nibbling, though it never did in my case.

Once my daughter and I served the pudding immediately after it emerged from the steamer. It was light-textured and delicious, although lighter in color and a shade less rich than the usual mellowed version. However, if you belong to the old school and prefer to make your pudding ahead of time, this one keeps well for six months and can be frozen for as long as a year.

Pudding:

2 cups (500 mL) currants
1 cup (250 mL) seeded muscat raisins
1 cup (250 mL) seedless golden raisins
1 cup (250 mL) mixed peels, finely chopped
¾ cup (200 mL) brandy

1 cup (250 mL) unblanched almonds, sliced lengthwise
1 cup (250 mL) finely grated carrots
¼ cup (60 mL) unsifted all-purpose flour
1 tbsp. (15 mL) allspice
2⅓ cups (580 mL) finely chopped beef suet
6 cups (1.5 L) fine soft bread crumbs (do not use crust)
8 large eggs, separated
1¼ cups (315 mL) well-packed brown sugar

Molds:

4 tbsp. (60 mL) soft butter
½ cup (125 mL) well-packed brown sugar
10–12 glacé red cherries
Cinnamon
10–12 thin strips candied citron

Combine currants, raisins, and mixed peels in a large bowl. Add brandy and toss ingredients lightly. Cover bowl and let mixture stand overnight.

Prepare pudding molds the following day before combining remaining ingredients. To do this, spread 2 tbsp. (30 mL) soft butter over the bottom and sides of each of two 7–8 cup (1.75–2 L) crockery molds or bowls. Evenly pat ¼ cup (60 mL) well-packed brown sugar over butter in each mold; decorate bottom of each one with 5–6 glacé cherries. Lightly sprinkle cinnamon over molds, then arrange 5–6 strips of citron, in a vertical position, around the sides of each mold. (To keep them in position, press citron strips to sides of molds.) Refrigerate molds until you are ready to use them.

Add almonds, carrot, flour, and allspice to fruit mixture; toss lightly but thoroughly. Add suet and bread crumbs and lightly toss again.

Beat egg whites at high speed (of electric mixer) until they are stiff but not dry, then reduce to medium speed, and add egg yolks, one at a time. As soon as yolks are blended into whites, gradually add 1¼ cups (315 mL) well-packed brown sugar. Stop beating as soon as sugar and eggs are blended.

Fold egg mixture into fruit mixture — a rubber scraper is good for this. Turn batter into prepared molds, dividing it equally between the two. Place a large square of heavy-duty aluminum foil over each mold; press down on sides of foil, shaping them to each mold. Secure foil in place with string. Place each mold in a steamer.

Steam puddings for 3 hours, adding more boiling water to steamers as required. Remove molds from steamers; and let stand on wire cake racks, without removing aluminum foil, until puddings are cold. Store in a cool, dry place for at least 3 weeks before using. This gives puddings a chance to ripen. Each one makes 8–10 servings.

To Prepare a Pudding for Serving: Steam it for 30–40 minutes, then unmold on to a heated platter with sides. Spoon ½ cup (125 mL) flaming brandy over pudding and serve with a hard or caramel sauce.

How to Flame a Pudding

There are many ways to flame a pudding. My favorite way is easy and reliable, and it can be done right at the table.

Set up a small silver tray with cubes of sugar, a little plate with a good-sized piece of butter and a long-handled jug of hot rum or brandy. (Less expensive "young" alcohol flames better than fine old types.) Place the pudding on a silver, or unbreakable glass, platter. Put a good-sized pat of butter on top of each pudding, stick into it 6–8 cubes of sugar, then pour the hot brandy or rum over it. Light it and, without delay, start basting by pouring the rum or brandy back on top of the pudding. Keep pressing the sugar gently with the back of the spoon and continue to baste until the flames die out naturally. The more you baste, the more it will flame.

It is important to have the hot pudding on a hot plate, because the hotter the platter, the longer the alcohol will keep warm — and the longer the flames will last.

My Grandmother's Caramel Sauce

In the early 1900s this was a very popular sauce, served with all types of steamed puddings and also to top light sponge cake or ice cream.

3 tbsp. (50 mL) all-purpose flour
½ cup (125 mL) brown sugar
Pinch of salt
1 cup (250 mL) cold water
2–3 tbsp. (30–50 mL) butter
1 tsp. (5 mL) vanilla
¼ tsp. (1 mL) almond extract

Place in a saucepan the flour, brown sugar and salt. Mix well and add the water. Cook over medium heat, stirring all the time, until the sugar is melted; then continue cooking until smooth and creamy. Remove from heat, add butter and almond extract. Serve hot. (Will keep refrigerated for 10–12 days.) *Yield:* 1½ cups.

Mrs. Fleury's Boiled Fruit Cake

We bought our farm in November 1956. On that Christmas, our neighbours, the Fleury's, sent us a Boiled Christmas Fruit Cake. We enjoyed it so much that one day Mrs. Fleury graciously gave me the recipe, and ever since it has become part of our Christmas table. Peter, their son, has been with us ever since we started raising sheep — feeding, shearing, and "lambing" — and he certainly still enjoys his mother's Christmas cake, just as I am sure you will. It is easy, quick and economical to make.

2½ cups (550 mL) cold water
2 cups (500 mL) currants
2 cups (500 mL) sugar
1 tsp. (5 mL) salt
1 tsp. (5 mL) allspice
2 unpeeled and finely diced apples
2 cups (500 mL) seedless raisins
2 cups (500 mL) white raisins
2 cups (500 mL) dates, coarsely chopped
1 tsp. (5 mL) each cloves, and cinnamon
½ cup (125 mL) chopped walnuts
1 lb. (500 g) mixed candied fruit peel
4 cups (1 L) all-purpose flour
2 tsp. (10 mL) baking powder

Mix together in a saucepan all the ingredients except the walnuts and mixed peels. Bring to a boil, then boil over medium heat 5 minutes. Cool. When cold, add the walnuts and mixed peels. Stir well. Add the flour and baking powder sifted together. Stir until well mixed.

Pour into a well-greased 10-in. (25 cm) bundt pan or two 8-in. (20 cm) square pans. Bake 2½ – 3 hours in a 250°F. (120°C) oven, or until well done. Cool on cake rack. *Yield:* one 8 – 9 lb. (16 – 18 kg) cake or two 4 lb. (8 kg) cakes.

Christmas Pastilles

These were much like the "Florentines" now sold at good pastry shops. In my youth, they were homemade or we had none, and for some reason they seem to be part of the Christmas table.

We had to make the candied orange peel as there was no commercial type tender and delicate enough, and they were also flavored with Grand Marnier.

Candied Orange Peel

1 cup (250 mL) water
2 cups (500 mL) sugar
Yellow peel of 3 oranges
2 tsp. (10 mL) Grand Marnier

Bring the water and sugar to a boil, stirring often. Cut the orange peel into thin strips (easy with sharp scissors). Add peel to syrup, stir and add the Grand Marnier. Then cook over medium low heat 10–15 minutes, or until strips are tender. Cool. Drain and chop peel into small pieces. Keep syrup in a covered jar, refrigerated. If any peel remains, it can be kept refrigerated in a separate jar. *Yield:* 2 cups (500 mL).

Pastilles

1½ cups (125 mL) sugar
1/3 cup (80 mL) heavy cream
1/3 cup (80 mL) honey
4 tbsp. (60 mL) butter
¼ cup (60 mL) candied orange peel
3 tbsp. (50 mL) flour
½ cup (125 mL) blanched almonds ground fine
8 ounces (227 g) semi-sweet chocolate
1 tbsp. (15 mL) Grand Marnier
1 tbsp. (15 mL) butter

In a heavy metal saucepan, place the sugar, cream, honey and butter. Stir over low heat, just long enough to dissolve the sugar. Then raise heat just a little and let the syrup boil, this time without stirring, until a soft ball forms when a bit is dropped in cold water at 235°F. (112°C) on a candy thermometer.

Cool slightly, then gently stir in the candied orange peel and the ground almonds. Butter one or two baking sheets, and on them drop small spoonfuls of the mixture, leaving about 2 in. (5 cm) between each spoonful, as they spread quite a bit while cooking. Bake in a preheated 400°F. (230°C) oven 6–10 minutes, checking them after 6 minutes, as they are delicate and have a tendency to burn. (Cooking them at a lower temperature makes them too hard. While the "pastilles" are still quite warm, remove from pan with a wide spatula and cool on wire cake rack.

Place the semi-sweet chocolate, Grand Marnier and butter in a bowl, and set bowl in a saucepan of warm water. Simmer until chocolate is melted. Stir well. Spread the smooth part (the bottom) of the "pastilles" with some chocolate mixture, place on rack and refrigerate until chocolate has set, about 10–15 minutes. *Yield:* about 1 lb. (500 g).

They are a lot of work but worth all of it.

Our Family Christmas Eggnog

Many families have their own Christmas eggnog. I have tried many, but never succeeded in equalling the one that follows. (We had Grand Marnier only at Christmas time, so it was a must to use it for our big Christmas dinner.)

6 egg yolks
1 cup (250 mL) maple syrup or fine granulated sugar
1 cup (250 mL) rum of your choice
1 cup (250 mL) Grand Marnier
Grated rind of 1 orange
½ cup (125 mL) brandy
6 cups (1.25 L) milk
1 vanilla bean
3 cups (750 mL) heavy cream
6 egg whites, beaten stiff

Beat the egg yolks and the maple syrup or sugar with an electric beater, until very creamy and light. Keep beating as you add the Grand Marnier, rum and brandy. Cover and chill 2 hours. Add the vanilla bean to the milk and let stand for the same time. When 2 hours is up, remove the vanilla bean from the milk, and slowly add the milk (while stirring) to the egg yolk mixture. Whip the cream and gently fold in until it is well-blended.

Then fold in the beaten egg whites. At this point, the eggnog can be covered and will stay perfect for 12–24 hours. Sprinkle a bit of freshly grated nutmeg over each serving.

Pour any leftover eggnog into a container, cover and freeze. Serve it as a frozen eggnog for dessert, or thaw out and serve as a drink. I usually have enough with this recipe to serve 20.

Frozen Coffee Soufflé

These used to be frozen by burying them on Christmas Eve in deep snow mixed with coarse salt. Serve them on a large, flat cut crystal platter.

4 egg yolks
¼ cup (60 mL) sugar
3 tbsp. (50 mL) expresso
2 squares (57 g) unsweetened chocolate

2 tbsp. (30 mL) water
2 tbsp. (30 mL) rum
1½ cups (400 mL) whipping cream
4 egg whites
¼ cup (60 mL) sugar

Beat the yolks with the first ¼ cup (60 mL) of sugar and the coffee, until mixture is thick and creamy. Melt the chocolate (when possible use squares of Swiss bittersweet chocolate) with the water over low heat. Add the rum and stir into the egg yolk mixture.

Whip the cream until stiff. Beat the egg whites into a meringue with the remaining sugar. Fold the whipped cream and meringue into the yolk mixture. Pour into individual *petits pots* or custard dishes, or into a large soufflé dish. Cover and freeze 4–6 hours until ready to serve.

To unmold: dip dish or dishes a few seconds in hot water, then invert on a serving platter. If you can take some extra richness, top with a hot chocolate sauce. *Serves 8 – 10.*

My Granddaughter's Wedding

My granddaughter Susan was my first grandchild to marry — on a beautiful April day last year. Ways of life differ so much from my time — it was to be a home wedding. And for sentimental *grand-maman* reasons, I felt it should be at my home. Susan and Kenneth made their guest list and told me there would be 125 people, and that the entire wedding — mass, communion and all — would be in the house, a far, far cry from my "church day" customs. At first, I felt a little ill at ease about the wedding ceremony right in my living room; but when the time came, watching their happiness and love, I suddenly felt it was right.

I asked, what about the music? My husband had a brilliant idea: he would ask three of his friends who play hunting horns to come, in their red habits and tall black boots. They played outside in front of a long window, where the bride and groom stood in the sunlight. The glittering horns, the happy couple, the tenderly touched *grand-maman*, Susan's *maman* and Daddy filled with emotions, all the guests smiling — it was a moment I am not able to forget.

Then came the food — *that* was easy. And it would be easy for anyone wanting to do a large wedding at home, as long as all of it can be prepared ahead of time, which is what I did. This is what we served:

Crevettes Matane in Vodka
Crisp Arabic Bread Triangles
Chicken Crêpes Suprême
Asparagus Vinaigrette
Fresh Strawberries in Raspberry Sauce
Home-Made Macaroons
Champagne for the bride and groom
Sparkling Portuguese Rosé
Mouton-Cadet '73
Wedding Cake

Crevettes Matane in Vodka

Crevettes Matane are small shrimps, about 1 in. (2.5 cm) long, already cooked and peeled. If they are not "Matane," which means they are caught near this Gaspé village in Quebec, use other types of shrimp, as long as they are the small type. Serve with baskets of the **Crisp Arabic Bread Triangles.** I usually use small spoons to place them on the bread. Easy to serve; easy to prepare. Can be done 3–4 days ahead, and kept in a covered bowl refrigerated.

10 lb. (5 kg) small shrimps
2 cups (500 mL) vodka
Grated rind of 3 lemons
1 cup (250 mL) chopped fresh parsley
3 tbs. (50 mL) curry powder
Salt and pepper to taste

Place shrimps in a large pan, add the remaining ingredients and toss for a few minutes with your hands. Taste for seasoning. Prepare 12–24 hours ahead of time. Cover slightly, and refrigerate.

To serve, set on large platter with dainty spoons stuck in the shrimps here and there. Let each guest help himself.

Crisp Arabic Bread Triangles

These can be made 8–10 days ahead of time, and kept in a tightly closed metal or plastic box.

24 pieces of round Arabic bread
1 lb. (500 g) soft butter
½ cup (125 mL) sesame seeds
1 tbsp. (15 mL) ground coriander

Carefully split the pieces of bread in half, then cut each half into 6 triangles. Beat the butter until very creamy, add the sesame seeds and ground coriander and stir until well mixed. Spread a bit of this butter on each triangle, and set them on baking sheets. Cook until crisp and lightly golden in a 350°F. (180°C) oven, about 5 – 8 minutes. Cool on cake racks before putting in boxes.

Chicken Crêpes Suprême

An excellent recipe to have, even if you don't make it for 125, as it can be divided into portions of your choice. You can freeze them, and if you also have crêpes in the freezer, you have an easily-prepared luncheon dish or a dinner entrée. (Note: For 30 crêpes, to serve 6 – 8, use a 4 – 5 lb. (2 – 2.5 kg) chicken and reduce the other ingredients accordingly.)

12 4 – 5 lb. (2 – 2.5 kg) chickens
12 – 16 quarts (12 – 16 L) water
6 unpeeled onions, cut in four
8 sticks of celery, with leaves, cut in four
10 carrots, scrubbed and cut in half
4 whole leeks, cleaned and thickly sliced
4 bay leaves
1 tsp. (5 mL) whole peppercorns
2 tbsp. (30 mL) coarse salt
1 tsp. (5 mL) thyme
1 tbsp. (15 mL) tarragon

I use a 20 quart (20 L) hotel-sized soup pot. (You may be able to borrow one.) If you don't have a pot that large, divide the recipe according to the size of the soup kettle you have on hand.

This part is the basic cooking: Place all the ingredients in the pot, and bring to a full rolling boil, then lower heat to keep it simmering. Cover and simmer until chicken is tender. At this point, beware of overcooking — the meat of the chicken must not fall apart, but retain a certain firmness. (The cooling time will vary according to the quantity you cook at one time.)

When the chicken is ready, remove pan from heat, cool, then place pan in cool place for 6 – 12 hours. Then remove the chicken from the bouillon.

If you need the soup kettle for another lot of chicken, transfer the already cooked chicken, while hot, into a container that will hold the quantity you will have. Cover and cool for the 6 – 12 hours as above. The next day, remove the cold chickens, one at a time, from the bouillon.

(1) Remove skin and discard, (2) remove meat from carcass, (3) dice meat and place white and brown meat in separate bowls, (4) put the bones in the bouillon, (5) cover the diced chicken with a wet cloth, and a piece of paper and refrigerate.

Bring the bouillon to a boil, and boil over high heat, until reduced by half. Cool and strain through a fine strainer. Measure and set in a cool place, until the fat hardens on top and remove. You are then ready to make the sauce.

To Make Sauce Suprême: Chop fine 2 large onions and 4 garlic cloves. Melt ½ cup (80 mL) butter, and add the onions and garlic; let them simmer over low heat about 20 minutes, stirring often. Do not brown.

Meanwhile, wash and slice thinly 2 – 3 onions, after the 20-minute cooking period is over. Stir over high heat, 5 minutes, add the reduced defatted bouillon, and boil together 5 minutes.

Cream together (use an electric mixer when available) 1 lb. (500 g) butter and 3 cups (750 mL) all-purpose flour; the mixture must be creamy and well blended. Add a ladleful of the mixture at a time to the boiling bouillon, and stir until it is blended in. Repeat until sauce has the desired thickness. Do not make it too heavy, as the chicken must be added and a light, creamy texture is best to serve with the crêpes. (The sauce can be made 2 days ahead of time when you can refrigerate it or just keep it in a cold place.)

Three to four hours before serving, warm up the sauce and beat it well to give it lightness. Add all the chicken and simmer over low heat until quite hot. At that point, stir with care so as not to break up the chicken. Taste for seasoning.

Basic Crêpe Batter

For tender crêpes, it is important that the batter stand at room temperature 2 – 3 hours before cooking, to allow the flour particles to expand in the liquid. If less time is available, keep it in a cool place 30 – 60 minutes. In a rush, of course, the batter can be cooked as soon as it is ready. For a large quantity, the batter can be prepared 12 – 24 hours ahead of time, and does not have to be refrigerated.

Ingredients:

For 500 Crêpes

51 eggs
34 cups (8.5 L) flour
17 cups (4.25 L) milk
17 cups (4.25 L) chicken bouillon
4¼ cups (1.25 L) melted butter
8½ tsp. (42 mL) dried tarragon
17 tbsp. (250 mL) minced parsley
17 tbsp. (250 mL) minced chives

For 30 Crêpes

3 eggs
2 cups (500 mL) flour
1 cup (250 mL) milk
1 cup (250 mL) chicken bouillon
¼ cup (60 mL) melted butter
½ tsp. (2 mL) dried tarragon
1 tbsp. (15 mL) minced parsley
1 tbsp. (15 mL) minced chives

Cooking Crêpes: Set the pan over medium heat until thoroughly hot, then add a few drops of vegetable oil or margarine. When the oil is evenly spread, pour in 2 tbsp. (30 mL) of batter and, quickly tipping the pan in a clockwise direction, coat the bottom with the batter. (This quantity is for a 6-in. (15 cm) pan — add about 1 tsp. (5 mL) more for each additional inch (2.5 cm). Cook over medium heat until the underside of the crêpe is a golden brown color. (Check by lifting the edges gently with a spatula). To turn crêpe, raise edge again with spatula, grasp with fingers, slip spatula under, and flip. Cook second side about 10 seconds, then place — first brown side down — on a cake rack. Continue cooking crêpes in this manner, using oil each time and stacking them as they are cooked, until you have enough. Leftover batter can be refrigerated in a covered glass jar 3 – 4 days.

Storing Crêpes: If crêpes are not to be served immediately, cover with a towel or inverted bowl. To keep a day or so, refrigerate wrapped in foil, or a polyethylene bag, with a square of wax paper between each crêpe. Wrapped in this manner, they can also be kept frozen 6 – 8 weeks.

To reheat cold or frozen crêpes, unwrap, and overlap them on a baking sheet which has been brushed with melted butter. Also brush crêpes well with melted butter to prevent drying during heating. Bake in a 400°F. (200°C) oven 3 – 4 minutes. They are now ready to be stuffed, or topped with special sauces, such as I did for the Chicken Suprême. I make 3 Crêpes Suprêmes for each guest. Take the crêpes out of the freezer 12 hours before using. To serve, stack crêpes on baking sheets and heat in a 350°F. (180°C) oven about 10 minutes (if each stack consists of 3 – 6 crêpes). Take a hot crêpe, and set it on a plate, pour ¼ cup (80 mL) of the hot sauce on top and roll (not difficult to do). Repeat with 2 more crêpes, and serve.

Note: I prepared some baking sheets ahead of time with the thawed-out crêpes; I covered them with foil, and left them on the kitchen counter. Preheat oven to 400°F. (200°C), and put in 2 pans; they should take 10 – 12 minutes to be piping hot. Put in 2 more pans when the first ones have been taken out. I had 6 baking sheets ready with crêpes and 1 person to replenish each one as they were served. We served the 125 guests in 35 minutes.

Asparagus Vinaigrette

Clean and cook 25 – 35 lb. (12.5 – 17.5 kg) fresh asparagus. Do not overcook — keep a bit firm. The day before the wedding, cover a large platter with a linen cloth (do not use paper), and place the asparagus on top. Prepare a good vinaigrette of your choice (see Salads chapter). Two hours before serving, place in nice, neat rows on platters, and pour spoonfuls of the sauce on top. This is served instead of a salad. So the guests could help themselves, we passed the dishes around.

Fresh Strawberries in Raspberry Sauce

These were a great success — and a pleasant change from the usual ice cream desserts we often have at weddings.

My granddaughter chose the raspberry sauce, because it was her mother's recipe, and I chose the fresh strawberries, the first ones of the season. No whipped cream was used.

You will need 24 – 30 quart (L) baskets of strawberries for 125 guests. Clean the berries, wash before removing stems and place in large bowls. Sweeten to taste (but not too sweet) with **Vanilla Sugar.** Add 3 tbsp. (50 mL) orange liqueur for each quart (L) basket of fruit. Mix with your hands, being careful not to break the berries. Cover and set aside in a cool place. Can be prepared and flavored a day ahead of time. To serve, place 2/3 – 1 cup berries in a small bowl, top with a few spoonfuls of raspberry sauce. (You will need 15 times the original recipe in order to serve 125.)

Raspberry Sauce

1 container frozen raspberries
½ cup (125 mL) red or black currant jelly
½ cup (125 mL) sugar
Juice of ½ a lemon
2 tbsp. cornstarch
2 tbsp. (30 mL) cold water

Place in saucepan the frozen berries, black currant jelly and sugar. Slowly bring to boil, stirring often. Then boil 3 minutes. Mix together the lemon juice, cornstarch and cold water. Add to raspberry mixture while stirring, then simmer until creamy and transparent, stirring often. Use as is, or strain to remove raspberry seeds. Keep same as the orange sauce. *Yield:* 2¼ cups (625 mL).

My Granddaughter's Wedding Cake

This is the same recipe I had used for her mother's wedding — it did not seem to have "aged" at all. A lot of work, but very rewarding. On the top of the cake I had 2 marble lovebirds and the cake was set on a large silver tray surrounded with sweetheart roses and blue velvet bows.

2 cups (500 mL) coarsely chopped walnuts or pecans
2/3 cup (160 mL) halved candied cherries, red or green
2 cups (500 mL) dark muscatel raisins
½ cup (125 mL) rum or brandy
4 cups (1 L) all-purpose flour
1½ tsp. (7 mL) baking powder
½ tsp. (2 mL) salt
1 tsp. (5 mL) nutmeg
½ tsp. (2 mL) ground cardamom
1½ cups (400 mL) unsalted butter
2 cups (500 mL) fruit sugar
1 tsp. (5 mL) vanilla extract
½ tsp. (2 mL) almond extract
7 eggs
¾ cup (200 mL) rum or brandy
Coatings and icing (see following instructions)

In a large bowl, combine the first 4 ingredients. Stir until well mixed. Cover and let stand at room temperature 12 hours (or 4 minutes in a mircrowave oven). Liquid will then be absorbed.

Prepare the molds. I use 2 square pans with detachable bottoms; one 7 × 7 × 3½ in. (17.5 × 17.5 × 8.75 cm), the other 6 × 6 × 3½ in. (15 × 15 × 8.75 cm) Each pan should be well buttered, then sprinkled lightly with some flour.

Sift together the next 5 ingredients, then cream the butter at high speed until foamy. Add sugar, 3 tbsp. (50 mL) at a time, beating 2–3 minutes between each addition. When half the sugar has been added, add vanilla and almond extracts. Preheat oven to 350°F. (180°C).

When all the sugar has been added, start adding the eggs one at a time, beating well after each addition. Then beat at medium speed 4 minutes. Gradually beat in the flour mixture until smooth and creamy; then pour mixture over the fruit. Mix with a large spoon.

Divide between prepared pans and place on the middle rack of the oven. Cook the smaller cake about 80 minutes. Cook the larger one about 2–2¼ hours. In both cases, test for doneness.

Cool cakes in pans set on wire rack for 20–30 minutes, then invert on rack. Soak 2 pieces of cheesecloth in the ¼ cup (60 mL) rum or brandy.

Place each cake in center of a piece of cloth and wrap. Then wrap the whole cake in foil. Let ripen for a week at room temperature. It will then keep 3 – 5 weeks refrigerated.

Marmalade Coating: Heat 1 cup (250 mL) of orange marmalade with 3 tbsp. (50 mL) brandy or Cointreau. When it comes to a boil, stir over heat 1 minute, then let it cool. Rub top and sides of each cake with this — it makes a sort of sweet glue that will hold the marzipan, and also prevent crumbs from spreading on cake or icing.

Marzipan Coating: Knead ½ lb. (250 g) marzipan (usually sold in 1 lb. (448 g) containers — the Danish marzipan is the best), until it is smooth and pliable, adding a small spoonful of water if it's too dry. Then roll into an 18 in. (45 cm) cylinder. Measure height and length of the 4 sides of each cake, then roll pieces to fit. All this is easily done with a ruler and a good knife. When one strip is ready, gently place on the cake. The marmalade coating will make it stick. Repeat operation for the tops of the cakes, rolling squares of marzipan to the proper size.

To Ice: Stack cake layers. With mixer, blend 1 cup (250 mL) shortening and 2 tbsp. (30 mL) rum or brandy. Gradually add 2 lb. (1 kg) sifted icing sugar. When well mixed, beat in the whites of 2 eggs at high speed. Continue to beat until thick and smooth. Add a bit more sugar, if necessary. Refrigerate for 1 hour, then ice the top and sides right over the marzipan, using a flat metal spatula. (Have a jug of hot water handy to rinse off your spatula as often as necessary.)

Now you have to use your taste and imagination. Fill a pastry bag with some more of the icing. Using the nozzle you prefer, make ripples around the top edges of each layer.

The cake can be made and iced (without the roses, of course) a month in advance, and placed on a tray in the freezer until the icing has hardened. Wrap it with plastic wrap, then with heavy duty foil, and put it back in the freezer.

Unwrap it when you take it out of the freezer. It will take 24 hours to thaw. *Yield:* 1 small square to each guest, 125 in all.

16. The Pantry Shelf

Freeze the Bounty

Remember when we had to wait until summer for fresh strawberries and until close to autumn for corn? We had lamb in late spring, pork in winter, and so on; as each season offered its bounty, we enjoyed it. Then we waited for the arrival of next year's season.

Today we almost take for granted the miracle of the modern science of freezing and the rewards it brings. Thousands enjoy all the benefits it has to offer and it is important to learn how to make the most of each season's offerings and how to use freezer space properly.

Here are some suggestions for serving the gourmet's pleasures — so you can serve perfect strawberries in January, for example, and have on hand the base for a quick soup or a casserole or perhaps a sandwich.

I will not discuss technical points, except to say a word about packaging. Remember that freezer wraps and containers should be air-tight, moisture- and vapor-proof; they will prevent transfer of flavor among foods and the development of "off" flavors — they will prevent the loss of moisture, so often responsible for toughness of vegetables and darkening of fruits.

Liquids expand when frozen. Always allow a ½ in. (1.25 cm) space at the top of cartons holding liquids, or food that has been packed in liquids.

Never freeze more food in a container than you expect to serve at one time. This is particularly important with cooked foods.

Remember that a freezer is not a magician, it does not improve food; its function is to preserve the quality and prevent it from spoiling.

Make Use of the Refrigerator Freezer

Not everyone can own one of those lovely big, separate freezers, but few of us even bother to utilize what almost every kitchen does possess — the small freezer in the refrigerator.

Those with small families or those who live alone have the constant problem of leftovers, yet too often their refrigerator freezer serves only as a storehouse for ice cubes, bread, and T.V. dinners. While there's no way it can be crammed with a month's food, it can certainly be used in a much better way than it usually is.

Buy a freezer thermometer (you'll see why under Freezer Equivalents below), and follow the general preparation and packaging instructions given for large freezers. Follow the "don'ts" as well — don't try to freeze lettuce, celery, cucumber, fresh tomatoes, mayonnaise, cooked egg whites, cream (except whipped), custard, cream pies or gelatine salads. Don't put potatoes into stews before freezing. Don't overcook the food; slightly undercook it. Don't fill containers of sauce or gravy to the top, leave 1-inch (2.5 cm) of head space. Don't, if at all possible, thaw uncooked meat and poultry at room temperature, and don't cook it straight from the freezer. Thaw it in the refrigerator section to prevent food from becoming soggy when thawed out.

There are additional hints for small freezers. Take up less room by packing carefully and by first removing the fat and bone from meats, then slicing it. Wrap foods in meal-size portions — the smaller the package, the more quickly the food thaws. Freeze only a small quantity at a time, so as not to raise the freezer's temperature, and hold the remainder in the refrigerator section. Since the calculation of storage time is important (see table), keep an inventory of each marked package, as well as the date it was put in.

You'll find that, even with its limited space, a little freezer can be a big help.

Freezer Equivalents

The storage times given for frozen foods, unless otherwise specified, usually mean the items should be held at the normal 0°C of large, separate freezers. This low a temperature is impossible in refrigerator freezers, which are, as a rule, only 10– 18°C. Use a freezer thermometer to determine what yours is, then calculate the safe storage time:

12 months' storage at 0°C (32°F) is equivalent to
5 months at 5°C or
2 months at 10°C or
1 month at 15°C or
1 week at 25°C

The mathematics may get a bit involved, since foods vary in their keeping properties at 0°C (for instance, meat keeps 8 months, cooked casseroles keep 3 months), but the time spent calculating will save you the loss of spoiled food and pay off in convenience.

A last, but very important, word of advice: label your packages clearly because, as the weeks go by, frozen foods have a way of getting to look more and more alike and your memory can play a lot of tricks on you.

Imagination and Shortcuts

Use your freezer to keep bread and baked goods handy. Toast can be made from popping a slice of frozen bread in the toaster. I usually keep sliced bread and a few French crusty loaves ready — sliced, then wrapped, to make French toast or plain toast; in either case they come out perfect without being defrosted.

Homemade doughnuts, frozen, then warmed up in a 300°F. (150°C) oven, are the "best."

When the nice silverskin onions or the large sweet red onions are plentiful and cheap on the market, it is time to "put by" for the winter. Simply peel and place in good plastic containers. Then freeze. When you need them, open the container and take out what is required. They do not stick together. To slice or chop, it is much easier to do so when they are still partly frozen. To boil, do not thaw out.

In Scotland, I learned how to have light, tasty, frozen pancakes available at all times in my freezer. Here is the trick. Cook your favorite pancake recipe. Let cool completely on wire rack, one next to the other; then place a thickness of waxed paper between each pancake. Wrap in foil and freeze. To serve, preheat oven to 425°F. (220°C). Remove waxed paper from as many pancakes as you wish to serve, and rewrap what is left. Bake 15 – 18 minutes on baking sheet. They taste just as if they were freshly made.

When fruits are plentiful in the summer and fall, freeze your favorite fresh fruit pie filling in the following manner. Line an 8 or 9 in. (20 – 22.5 cm) pie plate with heavy foil paper or a double thickness of light foil paper, making sure foil extends at least 6 in. (15 cm) over rim. Prepare your pie filling as usual. Pour into plate and bring foil over top, to cover loosely. Freeze until firm. Then remove wrapped filling from plate, label the contents and return to freezer until ready to use. It will keep for 6 – 8 months. To use, unwrap, place frozen mixture on a pastry-lined plate, dot with butter and cover as your recipe directs. Place in a preheated 425°F. (220°C) oven for 45 – 50 minutes or until crust is golden brown.

If you grow your own herbs — gather some when they're at their prime. The best time is after a soft rainfall when they will be freshly cleaned. Place small portions, whole or minced, as you prefer, in plastic bags. Label and freeze. To use when whole, cut with kitchen shears while crisply frozen. They taste just like fresh herbs and retain their full green color. If you do not grow herbs, what about freezing nice fresh green summer parsley?

Freezer Sandwiches

If you pack sandwiches for your lunch, simply make a week's supply at once, wrap in portions and keep together in a freezer bag. In the morning it takes but a minute to make your choice for the day. Packed frozen, they'll be not only completely thawed by noon, but nice and fresh instead of hot and soggy. Remember not to use lettuce, tomatoes, cucumbers or celery.

Use day-old bread rather than fresh for sandwiches to be frozen, and vary the bread. Spread the slices generously with soft butter, margarine, sour cream or cream cheese to keep the filling from soaking into the bread. Don't use mayonnaise or salad dressing as a spread, they make a soggy sandwich. But either of them can be blended into chopped fillings in small quantities.

Following are a few suggestions for fillings — you'll soon start creating your own.

Roast pork and mustard; peanut butter, marmalade and crisp bacon; chopped chicken, walnuts and olives; devilled ham, chopped pickles and mustard; chopped dates, walnuts, orange peel and cream cheese; sweet cheese or mild Cheddar and relish; canned salmon, lemon juice and cream cheese; lamb and mint jelly; thinly sliced roast beef and well-drained prepared horseradish.

Cucumber Purée

Cucumbers, like tomatoes, have a way of flooding the market — or the garden — all at once. They are not good frozen as a straight vegetable, but frozen in a purée they can be added to French dressing, or to a potato cream soup, or used as a sauce for cold meat when a little lemon juice and cloves or dill are added to it as is. (It also makes a beautiful aspic.)

12 cucumbers
2 tsp. (10 mL) salt
½ cup (125 mL) boiling water

Peel cucumbers as thinly as possible. Cut lengthwise, remove the seeds and slice thinly. Sprinkle with the salt. Place in a heavy metal saucepan, add the boiling water. Let come to a boil. Cook, uncovered, for 10 minutes. Pass through a food mill or a sieve. Package in half-pint containers and freeze. *Yield:* 1 pint (500 mL).

Leek Base for Vichyssoise

Do this in the autumn when fresh leeks are plentiful and low in cost. Then a gourmet soup can be prepared in 20 minutes, all year round.

12 medium leeks
4 large, mild onions
1½ cups (375 mL) butter

Remove top coarse leaves from leeks. Make a long split from the white part to the end of the green part. Wash carefully under running cold water, shaking off surplus water. Cut into thin slices, starting at the white base. Peel and slice the onions as thinly as possible. Melt the butter in a saucepan, add the leeks and onions, stir well for a few seconds. Cover and cook over very low heat for 25 minutes, stirring a few times. The mixture must soften completely, but must not brown. (It will reduce quite a bit in volume.) Divide by cupfuls into containers and freeze.

To make the soup: bring 3–4 cups (750–1000 mL) chicken consommé to a boil, add 1 cup (250 mL) of the frozen leek mixture. Simmer 20 minutes. Beat in 1 cup (250 mL) instant mashed potatoes, previously stirred with ½ cup (125 mL) cold milk. Simmer together for a few minutes. Add 1 cup (250 mL) cream. When the soup is creamy, taste for seasoning and serve as is. The soup can be strained when ready, and refrigerated until cold. *Yield:* 1 qt. (1 L).

Freezing Golden Glazed Carrots

When I "thin out" my first baby carrots in the garden, I usually glaze some to serve at my New Year's dinner, but any fresh carrots can be used.

1½ lb. (675 g) baby carrots or
  1½ lb. carrots, cut in strips
2 tbsp. (30 mL) all-purpose flour
¼ cup (60 mL) light brown, or maple, sugar
½ tsp. (2 mL) salt
¼ tsp. (1 mL) thyme
1 tbsp. (15 mL) cider vinegar
1 tbsp. (15 mL) fresh lemon juice
½ cup (125 mL) orange juice
Grated peel of 1 orange
2 tbsp. (30 mL) butter

Place the carrots in a saucepan. Pour boiling water over them and boil exactly 5 minutes. Drain thoroughly.

Blend together the flour, sugar, salt and thyme. Add vinegar, juices and orange peel. Bring to a boil, while stirring, and continue stirring until creamy. Add the butter and cook 5 minutes over very low heat. Line a casserole with foil, leaving enough around the edges to cover, put in the blanched carrots and pour the sauce over them. Freeze uncovered.

When frozen, cover completely with the foil. Remove package from casserole and put back in freezer. To serve, unwrap carrots, put back in same casserole. Bake, covered, in a 350°F. (180°C) oven about 40 minutes. Uncover for the last 15 minutes. *Yield:* 2 pints (1 litre).

Emergency Sandwich Filling

I always keep some of these fillings in my freezer, plus packages of different types of sliced breads. Lunch box, picnic or unexpected company can be quickly taken care of the easy way. (Each will make a filling for 5 – 6 sandwiches.)

Peanut Butter Favorite: cream together 1 cup (250 mL) peanut butter and ½ cup (125 mL) each of orange marmalade and honey. Add the grated peel of 1 orange. Freeze.

My Husband's Preference: cream ½ lb. (250 g) crisp, crumbled cooked bacon with 1 cup (250 mL) peanut butter. Blend in ½ cup (125 mL) relish. Freeze.

Sardine Brittany: empty into a bowl 1 can of small smoked sardines with their oil, add 2 – 3 hard-boiled eggs, finely chopped, the juice of ½ a lemon and ½ teaspoon (2 mL) curry powder. Blend thoroughly together. Freeze.

B.C. Special: empty a 1 lb. (500 g) can of salmon in a bowl (when possible use the red sockeye), remove the skin, but not the bone or the juice. Mash the fish and crush the bones with a fork. Then add the juice and grated peel of 1 lemon, ½ cup (125 mL) chutney, 1 tsp. (5 mL) curry powder, 3 green onions, finely chopped and ¼ cup (60 mL) fresh parsley, minced. Freeze.

To Freeze Asparagus

Buy and freeze asparagus when its price is lowest and enjoy it all through the year. As in freezing all vegetables, the best results are obtained when they're processed as soon as possible after harvesting.

Wash asparagus carefully to remove all grit and sand. Swish in lots of cold water; lift out, leaving sand in bottom of pan, and repeat until water is clear.

Snap off hard core, and separate slender and thick spears. Cut evenly — 3 in. (7.5 cm) spears are the best length to freeze. Freeze any bits left over to use as diced asparagus in soups or in a cream sauce.

Fill a large kettle with 5 quarts (4.75 L) of water, bring to a full rolling boil. Place asparagus — one type at a time — in a basket or strainer and dip into boiling water. Put lid on, keep over high heat, and start timing immediately — 2 minutes for 1 lb. (500 g) of diced asparagus; 3 minutes per lb. (500 g) of medium spears, 4 minutes for thick. (The water may not boil again during blanching, but make sure it reaches a full boil before you start on a second batch.)

Then the important step: immediately plunge asparagus, still in the basket or strainer, into ice-cold water. I use 2 trays of ice cubes for each 2 lb. (1 kg) of asparagus. (Or let cold water run over it constantly.) Dip for same length of time as you blanched; drain thoroughly, package and freeze. To use, simply plunge frozen asparagus into rapidly boiling water, boil 2 minutes; then drain. *Yield:* ½ pt. (250 mL) for each lb. (500 g) of asparagus.

Frozen Baked Apples

I use large Rome Beauty or Baldwin apples to make these. They make an easily-prepared "dessert with style."

Peel and core as many apples as you like (about 8 – 14, depending on size). Make a syrup of 1½ cups (400 mL) of sugar, 1 cup (250 mL) of water, 3 whole cloves, a 2 in. (5 cm) piece of cinnamon stick and 8 – 10 coriander seeds, and bring to a boil over medium heat. Dip each apple into the boiling syrup for 3 minutes, then lift carefully to a baking pan. In each apple cavity put a few raisins, 1 tsp. (2 mL) of brown sugar and 1 tbsp. (15 mL) of butter.

Bake in a 350°F. (180°C) oven for about 35 minutes, or until the apples are soft but not mushy, then set under the broiler for a few minutes to brown the tops. Let cool; place uncovered pan of apples in the freezer and leave until fruit is frozen solid. Then put them in containers, or wrap individually in foil; label and freeze.

To serve, remove required number of apples from container, or fold foil back from tops. Let apples thaw at room temperature about 1 hour and serve. If you prefer them hot, place frozen apples in a pan and heat in a 425°F. (220°C) oven for 30 minutes, or until soft. *Yield:* 8 – 14.

How to Freeze Peaches

They are a delicious summer treat, but the season never seems long enough. When they are at their best, choose the ideal type, preferably the freestone variety. I prefer the Ontario Madison or Veteran varieties — in that order. It is often difficult in Canada to buy fruits by their true name; we usually just ask for peaches or pears or apples. Yet we have very interesting varieties of peaches — the Madison usually can be found at the end of August.

I prefer to freeze peaches by the "dry sugar" method.

4 cups (1 L) peeled, sliced peaches
¼ tsp. (1 mL) powdered ascorbic acid
⅔ cup (160 mL) sugar

Measure 4 cups (1 L) of peeled, sliced peaches into a bowl. Stir in ¼ tsp. (1 mL) of powdered ascorbic acid (buy at drugstore) mixed with ¼ cup (60 mL) cold water. Add ⅔ cup (160 mL) of sugar and stir gently until the whole is well mixed. I like to use my hands or a rubber spatula. Let sugar dissolve for 3 to 4 minutes. Package in desired amounts, leaving a 1 inch (2.5 cm) head space. Crush a piece of wax paper, place on top of peaches so they will stay in moisture. Seal, label and freeze immediately. *Yield:* 2 pints (1 L).

Preserves

Forty years or so ago, a woman looked upon the shelves of her cold room with pride and satisfaction: she saw row upon row of sparkling glasses of jelly; deep, rich preserves surrounded by ruby raspberry syrup, and jars of pickles and relishes. All this was "put up" — as the expression went — with loving care.

Today, the cold room has vanished. The long hours we could give to such tasks are gone with the wind; and the big kitchens and the many hands in the household have long since disappeared.

But our inherent taste for the "sweet and sour" has never left us. Today, even the city cliff-dweller can quickly make small quantities of delicious relish, pickles and jam. And when you learn about pickles and relishes, you soon learn that nowhere in cuisine is there more freedom for imagination than there is in pickling and preserving.

Chutney

Chutney comes from the Hindi word *catni* which means to lick or taste. Our most common chutney was developed around 1860 by an English army officer, Major Grey, who wanted to make his troops' meals a little more exciting. Inspired by Indian chutney, fresh and cooked, he created his recipe using available ingredients such as mangoes, hot peppers and spices. The relish was prepared by the barrel and the Major's recipe soon became famous all over the world. His name is now used to describe some of the sauces and chutneys customarily served with curry.

Top-quality commercial chutneys are always expensive, but some can be made quite cheaply. They make an interesting accompaniment, not only for curry, but also for cold meats, new lamb or any bland meat dish — even for macaroni and cheese. May these chutneys provide you with at least one pleasant alternative to good old ketchup.

Indian Chutney

In India, chutney is a must — their collection is endless. Chutneys are excellent with barbecued meats and roast pork, as well as curried dishes. The cardamom and cumin can be replaced by 1 tsp. (5 mL) of curry powder.

2 large tomatoes, unpeeled
1 tbsp. (15 mL) brown sugar
1 large sweet green pepper, diced
1 large sweet red pepper, diced
1 onion, finely chopped
1 cup (250 mL) fresh lemon juice
Peel of 1 lemon, grated
½ tsp. (2 mL) ground cardamom
½ tsp. (2 mL) cumin seeds
½ cup (125 mL) parsley, minced

Dice the tomatoes and sprinkle them with the brown sugar. Add the sweet peppers (all green or all red peppers can be used) and the onion to the tomatoes. Stir gently to blend. Add the lemon peel, cardamom, cumin seeds and parsley to the lemon juice. Stir together for a few seconds and blend into the vegetable mixture.

Cover and leave at room temperature for 1 hour, stirring occasionally. Then refrigerate until well chilled — it should be served cold with hot food. *Yield:* four 6 oz. (180 mL) jars.

Peach-Tomato Chutney

A recipe to be used with the last fruits of the autumn harvest.

25 ripe tomatoes, peeled and sliced
12 peaches, peeled and sliced
4 diced green peppers
4 sliced onions
½ lb. (250 mL) raisins
1 cup (250 mL) chopped ginger in syrup
4 cups (1000 mL) brown sugar
1 tbsp. (15 mL) coarse salt

Mix all the ingredients in a heavy saucepan, then bring to a boil and simmer uncovered, stirring often, for about 3 hours or until the chutney is thick. Pour into sterilized jars and cover. *Yield:* 5 pints (2.25 L).

Pineapple Chutney

Colorful and mild, this is delightful with baked ham.

3 lb. (1.5 kg) pineapple
3 cups (750 mL) cider vinegar
3 cups (750 mL) sugar
1 tsp. (5 mL) crushed chili peppers
3 minced garlic cloves
2 tbsp. (30 mL) grated fresh ginger
1 tbsp. (15 mL) coarse salt
½ lb. (250 mL) raisins, any type
½ lb. (250 mL) blanched almonds, whole or chopped

Peel the pineapple and dice. In a heavy saucepan boil up a syrup of the vinegar and sugar. Add the pineapple and the remaining ingredients and mix well. Stirring often, simmer uncovered for 2 hours or until the mixture is quite thick. Pour into sterilized jars and cover. *Yield:* 4 pints (2 L).

Brandied Cherries

This world-famous delight is easy to prepare and, if stored in a cool, dark place, will keep 8 – 9 months in perfect condition.

2 lb. (1 kg) any sweet cherries
2 cups (500 mL) sugar
brandy

Don't pit or hull the cherries. Place in a large bowl, cover with ice water and let stand 30 – 40 minutes. Drain and remove stems — you can leave them on, but it makes them a bit harder to pack.

Dissolve sugar in 2 cups (500 mL) of water. Bring to a rolling boil and boil rapidly for 5 minutes, stirring occasionally and gently with a wooden spoon. Add cherries and bring again to a full boil. Remove from heat, wait until boiling stops and repeat boiling-for-5-minutes operation twice. Fill sterilized jars three-quarters full, put cover on loosely, and let stand until cool.

Fill each jar with brandy, stirring it in with a silver or stainless steel spoon, and seal. Turn upside down overnight, then store right side up in a cool, dark place for a least 3 months before using. *Yield:* about 4 pints. (2 L).

Candied Lemon Peel

Well worth the work. Not to be compared with commercial type. Orange and grapefruit peel can be prepared in the same manner.

Peel from 2 large lemons
Cold water
1 cup (250 mL) sugar
Sugar

Remove peel from lemons in quarters or eights, put in small saucepan, and cover with water. Cover pan and simmer until tender, about 10 minutes. Drain, reserving 1 cup of the cooking water.

Lay the lemon peel, yellow side down, on the table. Scrape away the inner white part of the peel with a paring knife and discard. Cut the yellow part of the peel into strips ⅛ inch wide.

Combine 1 cup of the cooking water with the 1 cup of sugar. Stir over low heat until the sugar dissolves. Boil rapidly, without stirring, until syrup forms a soft ball when a small amount is dropped into cold water: 234 – 240°F. (112 – 115°C) on a candy thermometer. Add the strips of lemon peel and simmer 10 minutes.

Lift strips of lemon peel out of the syrup with a slotted spoon and set them on a cake rack to drain.

Put about ¼ cup (80 mL) sugar in a small bag and add the strips of peel, a few at a time, shaking the bag until they are well coated with sugar. Put them back on the cake rack to cool and dry. Shake in sugar a second time and store in a cool dry place.

Vanilla Sugar

A delicately flavored sugar with a thousand uses. The vanilla is the dried bean of an orchid. Long, slim and dark brown, it imparts its permeating perfume to all it touches. Choose a container with a tight-fitting cover, attractive enough to use on the table.

2 vanilla beans
1 lb. (500 g) fine fruit sugar

Run the point of a knife along the beans, but don't split them open. Place in a jar tall enough so the beans can stand up. Pour sugar over beans until they are completely covered. Cover jar and store for 1 month before using. When half the sugar is used, replace with more sugar and shake well. This can be repeated as long as the vanilla gives off its perfume.

Sprinkle the sugar on sponge cake, fresh berries, grapefruit, fruit salad, toasted raisin bread, Danish pastry or baked custard. Use it to sweeten hot cocoa, hot buttered rum, baked apples, oranges, poached pears or peaches. Or use instead of plain sugar in chocolate, pound or chiffon cake.

Variations:

Add 6 broken bay leaves and grated peel of 2 oranges. Mix thoroughly, and pour into a glass jar. I always use this sugar with raw pears in a salad, or poached.

Add 6 to 8 finely chopped rose geranium leaves to the sugar. Mix thoroughly. Pour into glass jar. Cover. This one is super. Try it first on oranges or cantaloupes. Now create your own, it is fun.

Pickled Dill Carrots and Celery

These crunchy, tasty little sticks of uncooked carrots and celery can be served with cocktails, seafood or chicken salad. They are most elegant as a picnic vegetable.

4 cups (1000 mL) long, thin carrot sticks
4 cups (1000 mL) long, thin celery sticks
2 cups (500 mL) cider vinegar
4 cups (1000 L) water
1 cup (250 mL) sugar
½ cup (125 mL) chopped dill or
  2 tbsp. (30 mL) dill seeds
2 tbsp. (30 mL) mustard seeds
1 tbsp. (15 mL) salt
¼ tsp. (1 mL) Tabasco sauce

Cut the sticks of carrot and celery over a bowl of ice water. When done, drain them in a colander and pack together in glass jars.

Combine the remaining ingredients in a saucepan, stir until the sugar is dissolved and bring to a rolling boil. Pour hot mixture over the carrots and celery. Cover and keep refrigerated for 2–3 days before using. *Yield:* 3 quarts (3 L).

Pickled Mushrooms

Every year I make two to three dozen jars of pickled mushrooms which I keep in a cool room for up to a year. What a pleasure they are to serve as a change from pickles.

1 lb. (500 g) very fresh button mushrooms
1 medium onion, thinly sliced
1 tsp. (5 mL) salt
½ cup (125 mL) water
¾ cup (200 mL) cider or white wine vinegar
10 peppercorns
8 whole allspice
2 bay leaves

Using a covered stainless steel (not aluminum) or enamelled cast-iron saucepan, simmer 15 – 20 minutes over medium-low heat the whole mushrooms, together with the onion, salt and water. Add remaining ingredients, simmer 3 minutes, then let cool slightly. Divide mushrooms equally into small glass jars, cover with the warm liquid and seal tightly. Keep in a cool dark place or refrigerate. *Yield:* 4 cups (1 L).

Spiced Lemon Pickles

A colorful gift that's sublime with any curry or with strong cheddar cheese and port wine. With a favorite type of cheddar, it makes an ideal man's gift; add a bottle of old port, and you have a very special gift. For someone who likes to cook, add a bottle of curry powder to your gift basket, and *voilà.*

9 large lemons
2¼ cups (575 mL) sugar
⅛ tsp. (0.5 mL) salt
1 cup (250 mL) cider vinegar
1 cinnamon stick
½ tsp. (2 mL) whole allspice
1 small fresh ginger root
4 – 5 whole cloves

Wash and dry lemons; cut across into ¼-in. (0.625 cm) slices. Place sugar, salt, vinegar and ¼ cup (60 mL) of water in a saucepan, bring to a rapid boil. Add spices tied in a cheesecloth bag and the lemon slices; boil 1 minute.

Discard spice bag and pack lemon slices into hot sterilized jars. Cover with syrup and seal at once. *Yield:* 6 half-pint (250 mL) jars.

Yvette's Pickled Pumpkin

In 1967 we had 4 young housewives come on my T.V. show, each of them having been married less than 2 years. They were each invited to bring a jar of their own homemade pickles and the best would win the prize, a day at *Terre des Hommes* (Man and His World).

Yvette McKeow (French mother, Scottish father; had studied in Quebec, and lived in Nova Scotia) was the delightful winner. She told me she had learned from her husband to enjoy a spice-scented kitchen at pickling time.

I am sure you will enjoy Yvette's pickled pumpkin. I have made it every year since she taught me.

1 pint (500 mL) white or cider vinegar
4 lb. (2 kg) sugar
1 tsp. (5 mL) whole cloves
1 tbsp. (15 mL) cinnamon stick, broken
5 lb. (2.5 kg) pared pumpkin, in 1 in. (2.5 cm) pieces

Place the vinegar and sugar in a saucepan. Tie the whole cloves and the pieces of cinnamon stick in a piece of cotton and add to the vinegar.

Slowly bring the mixture to a boil, stirring continually, and boil for 5 minutes. Add the pumpkin and cook for another 10 – 15 minutes, or until the pumpkin is tender. Put the mixture into hot jars, cover with syrup, and seal. *Yield:* 5 pints (2.5 L).

Peach-Cantaloupe Marmalade

The recipe and a jar of this luscious marmalade were given to me by a Galt, Ontario, woman who grew beautiful cantaloupes.

3 oranges, halved and seeded
2 lemons, halved and seeded
4 cups (1000 mL) finely diced, peeled cantaloupe
4 cups (1000 mL) peeled, diced peaches
6 cups (1.5 L) sugar
6 – 8 maraschino cherries, halved (optional)

Put the oranges and lemons through a food chopper. Place cantaloupe and peaches in a large saucepan and simmer over medium heat 2 minutes. Add oranges and lemons and stir in sugar. Simmer over low heat, stirring often, until the sugar is melted. Then increase heat a little, stirring often so the mixture won't stick, until it "sheets," and forms a single drop from a spoon. (Beware of overcooking. This should remain a light, syrupy jam, not a thick, hard type.) Pour into hot, sterilized jars; drop a cherry into each one, and seal. *Yield:* six 8 oz. (250 mL) jars.

Tomato-Lemon Jam

An old-fashioned preserve that never loses its appeal; my grandmother used either red or yellow tomatoes for this.

5 lb. (2.5 kg) firm tomatoes, peeled
5 lb. (2.5 kg) sugar
3 unpeeled lemons, thinly sliced
1 tbsp. (15 mL) grated fresh ginger root

Chop peeled tomatoes coarsely and place in a saucepan in alternate layers with sugar and lemon slices. Add ginger and, stirring frequently, simmer slowly over medium-low heat until thick, about 45 – 50 minutes (it must have the consistency of jam). Pour into hot sterilized glasses, seal immediately, and store in a cool, dark place. *Yield:* four to five 6 oz. (180 mL) jars.

Emergency Jam

A good homemade jam to make anytime.

4 cups (1000 mL) canned purple plums, undrained
½ cup (125 mL) seedless raisins
1 cup (250 mL) sugar
1 orange, peeled and thinly sliced
1 tbsp. (15 mL) fresh lemon juice

Turn plums into a heavy enamelled cast-iron pan; break up and discard pits. Add raisins, sugar and orange slices. Bring to a boil over medium heat; then simmer over low heat until thick, 35 – 45 minutes. Add lemon juice and cook 2 minutes longer. Pour hot mixture into 2 sterilized pint (500 mL) jars and seal. Keep refrigerated. *Yield:* 2 pint (500 mL) jars.

Mother's Raspberry Jam

For me, this perfect raspberry jam has been failure-proof for 40 years. As soon as the ripe red raspberries appear on the market, I make a few glasses of this ruby-red jam, just as my mother did before me.

4 cups (1000 mL) fresh raspberries
1 tbsp. (15 mL) vinegar
4 cups (1 L) sugar

Place the berries in a sieve and quickly run them under cold water. (Raspberries absorb water easily, so too much will spoil the jam.) Remove the stems and measure the berries.

Divide the sugar equally into 3 pie plates and heat in a 275°F. (130°C) oven for 20 minutes.

Place the berries in a large saucepan with the vinegar. Bring to a boil over medium heat, without stirring, then boil for 5 minutes.

Add the hot sugar to the berries, one plate at a time. (Adding the sugar this way does not stop the boiling.) Boil over high heat for exactly 2 minutes. Pour into hot, sterilized glasses; wax and seal. *Yield:* four to five 6 oz. (180 mL) jelly glasses.

Spiced Carrot Jam

This is quite different from marmalade in texture and flavor, and is excellent with meats, especially ham and game.

4 cups (1000 mL) finely chopped raw carrots
3 cups (750 mL) sugar
Juice and grated peel of 2 lemons
½ tsp. (2 mL) each powdered cloves, allspice and cinnamon

Place all the ingredients in a saucepan. Slowly bring to a boil over medium-low heat, stirring constantly. Then, stirring frequently, cook over low heat 30 – 40 minutes, or until mixture is as thick as jam. Pour into hot sterilized jars and seal. *Yield:* four 6 oz. (180 mL) jelly glasses.

Pumpkin Jam

Pumpkin jam is unusual and tasty enough to warrant the use of two cups (250 mL) of gin. In the old days, it was made with sweet Dutch gin. I still think it best. Fresh ginger root is essential.

4 lb. (2 kg) pumpkin, diced
4 lb. (2 kg) sugar
Fresh ginger, grated
½ tsp. (2 mL) allspice
Peel of 3 lemons, grated
Juice of 3 lemons
1 cup (250 mL) sweet Dutch gin

Peel and clean the pumpkin, remove seeds, dice, and weigh. Place in a large dish in alternate layers with the sugar. Cover with a cloth and let stand two days in a cool place.

Place in a large saucepan with the ginger, allspice, lemon peel, and juice. Simmer over medium heat, stirring often, until the pumpkin is tender and transparent. Remove from the heat, cool slightly, and add the gin. Stir well. Pour into hot sterilized jars and seal. *Yield:* 6 – 8 quarts (3 – 4 L).

Plum-Mint Jelly

Perfect served with roast lamb or chicken, good on fruit salad, a treat with cottage cheese on the side, or cream poured on top — in other words, a must in your jam cupboard. The plum stones float to the top, so you can remove them after cooking if you wish.

3 lb. (1.5 kg) any type ripe plums
2 lb. (1 kg) sour apples
Sugar
1 cup (250 mL) fresh mint leaves

Boil the plums with 4 cups (1 L) of water until soft. Cut up apples without peeling or coring and boil with another 4 cups (1 L) of water until soft. Combine fruits and liquids thoroughly; then pour into a jelly bag over a bowl and let juice drip through.

Measure juice, bring to a fast rolling boil and add an equal amount of sugar. When it's dissolved, add mint tied in a cheesecloth bag hanging from handle of pan. Boil until jam passes "jelly test," then remove mint, pressing juice out against side of pan. Skim, remove stones if you wish, pour into sterilized glasses and seal. *Yield:* six to eight 6 oz. (180 mL) jelly glasses.

Mint Currant Jelly

This is a minute-style jelly.

2 tsp. (10 mL) chopped fresh mint leaves
½ tsp. (5 mL) grated orange rind
6-oz. (180 mL) jar any currant jelly

Remove currant jelly from jar, and place all ingredients in top of a double boiler. Stir gently until well blended. Pour jelly back into glass and cover. Refrigerate 24 hours. You can use the same method with any herb combined with any jam, jelly or honey. *Yield:* one 6 oz. (180 mL) jar.

Grapefruit-Wine Jelly

Superb with roast turkey or baked ham, very good with toasted muffins or crumpets, this gourmet's treat is made in ten minutes.

1 cup (250 mL) fresh grapefruit juice
3½ cups (875 mL) sugar
1 cup (250 mL) port wine
½ bottle liquid pectin

Combine in a saucepan the freshly squeezed and strained grapefruit juice and 3 cups (750 mL) of the sugar. Stir until sugar is well mixed; add the port wine and the remaining ½ cup (125 mL) of sugar, and stir again. Then set over low heat, stirring frequently until sugar is dissolved, about 8 minutes. Bring to a fast rolling boil. Remove from heat, stir in the liquid pectin. Mix well, pour into hot sterilized jars and seal. *Yield:* five 6 oz. (180 mL) jelly glasses.

Preserved Summer Pears

This method of preserving our very good summer pears makes them quite glamorous. They are equally good served plain as a dessert, on top of ice cream, sliced to fill a sponge cake, or with roast turkey or baked ham. When possible use freshly-made pineapple juice, made in a blender.

1 lb. (500 mL) pears
1 cup (250 mL) pineapple juice
½ cup (125 mL) water
1½ cups (400 mL) sugar
1 unpeeled lemon, sliced paper thin
8 thin slices fresh ginger

Wash and peel the pears. Cut them in half, remove the cores and keep the pear halves in cold water until ready to use.

In a saucepan, make a syrup with the pineapple juice, water and sugar. Bring the syrup to a full rolling boil and add the pears to the hot syrup one piece at a time, so that the syrup continues to boil. Cook until the pears are transparent and tender. (The syrup should then register 230°F. (110°C) on a candy thermometer). Remove from heat and let the pears stand at room temperature overnight in the syrup.

In the morning, bring the pear mixture again to a rapid boil, and pack the fruit only into 4 hot, sterilized jars. Continue to boil the syrup until it reaches 230°F. (110°C) on a candy thermometer. Then fill the jars to overflowing (to eliminate air bubbles) with the hot syrup. Add 2 slices of lemon and 2 slices of ginger to each jar and seal. (You may use paraffin if you wish. In that case, leave ½ in. (1.25 cm) air space.) Makes 4 pints (2 L).

Honey Jelly

A delicious, amber-colored jelly that can be made anytime during the year. I love this with bran muffins.

2½ cups (650 mL) clear honey
¾ cup (200 mL) strained fresh lemon juice
½ cup (125 mL) liquid pectin

Blend the honey and lemon juice in a large saucepan (it foams quite a bit when it cooks) and bring to a full rolling boil over medium heat, stirring constantly. Add pectin while stirring, bring again to a full boil and boil 1 minute. Remove from heat, skim and pour into 5 sterilized jelly glasses. Cover with paraffin while still hot. *Yield:* five 6 oz. (180 mL) jars.

Index